D1175698

An
E. M. Forster
Glossary

by

ALFRED BORRELLO

The Scarecrow Press, Inc.
Metuchen, N.J.   1972

Library of Congress Cataloging in Publication Data

Borrello, Alfred.
   An E. M. Forster glossary.

   1. Forster, Edward Morgan, 1879-1970--Dictionaries,
indexes, etc. I. Title.
PR6011.058Z635   823'.9'12   74-188548
ISBN 0-8108-0475-1

To

J.M.J.

and

Flora and Leonard Sarra

Richard, Christine, Lenora, Philip, Lucille

and

John Sarra

Table of Contents

Preface

"What? A glossary of a modern author? Absurd!"
But not really when that "modern" author is E. M. Forster
whose last major and largely original work, A Passage to
India, was published in 1924. It is not so absurd when one
considers that he was born in 1879 and grew up developing
his ideas and ideals in the smothering atmosphere of Victorian England. Nor is it absurd when one understands that he
shaped those ideas and ideals in terms of a noble and somewhat self-righteous reaction to Victorian hypocrisy and those
evils committed in the name of social and material progress.
Nor is it absurd when one realizes that he, like so many hu-
manitarians of his day and the recent past, had a firm belief
in a better tomorrow provided that the rules of fair play and
the code of a gentleman be applied universally. For those
of us sensitive to the intellectual, social, and emotional
traumas of the Sixties and to the promise of the Seventies for
still more devastating events, his concepts sound alluring yet
naive, simplistic, and vaguely antique. But more significantly, the context in which he set these concepts, ideals, and
themes is archaic, as much so as the Model T and the
British Raj.

Forster wrote in a world gleefully, even smugly, witnessing the death of Victorian prudery and aspirations. He
was an Edwardian certain of his beliefs, which generally were
negations of those the Victorians held sacred and dear. He
never quite made it beyond this point of reacting. Even as
late as 1936 ("Mrs. Grundy at the Parkers" in Abinger Harvest) he was still flogging the somewhat dead horse of prig-
gishness.

Even more antique than his anti-Victorianism, seen in
the light of the contemporary world that has achieved most
of the ends he championed, is the learning out of which he
wrote. Though he reacted as violently as his nature permitted to the ideals of the age into which he was born, he
was still blessed with the education which that age demanded
of its golden youth. In his day, members of his class were
expected to be literate. To be so meant to be actively con-

versant with the past, with the arts, with culture in general, and with matters of the spirit and the mind. In these days, when the democracy he loved has been falsely applied to the realms of the intellect (which would have revolted him, believing as he did in an aristocracy of the intellectual and the cultured), knowledge of the past, even scanty, has been relegated to the limbo of the irrelevant.

Consequently, his writing and his intent in that writing continue to suffer from a growing opacity. Hundreds of examples of passages that have already achieved obscurity may be offered to support the point. Let one suffice. Forster uses the word Ilissus as an ironic commentary in a passage in The Longest Journey (Chapter XX). It is the rare contemporary reader who will sense the subtle point he makes.

But a gloss of a writer who has achieved Forster's eminence serves a greater purpose than the dissolution of obscurities as important as that is. The unique value of this work is that it serves as a key to the scope and the depth of his mind. The scholar, the student, the interested reader who would know E.M. Forster--not through the cloud of bewildering commentary which has grown up about his works but as he really is--need only to consult this volume. Herein are his interests, his knowledge, his education, his reading, his aspirations, his friends and his friendships, his understanding of the world. All are here as he chose to reveal them in his writing.

It would be presumptuous at this point to suggest further uses of this glossary or to attempt a fuller explication of its place in the canon of Forster scholarship. That is for others to do. I should like, rather, to thank those who made this work possible. I must first thank Mr. Thomas Hurley whose conversations suggested not only the need for a volume such as this, but also for two other volumes on Forster, one of which, An E.M. Forster Dictionary, has already been published by The Scarecrow Press (1971), and the other, An Annotated Bibliography of Works About E.M. Forster, which is the process of completion. He must also be thanked for the difficult task of proofreading the manuscript.

Dr. Samuel Ceccherelli must also be thanked for supplying literal translations of the Latin Forster used. Despite the awkwardness of my requests for yet another translation and the impossible deadlines I set, he always produced the required text.

I want also to thank Rae Dalven, a translator of the Greek poet, Cavafy, whom Forster admired. We met by chance when we were asked to serve as judges of a literary contest at Columbia University. Taking a meal with him at the Butler Hall Restaurant, I discovered between appetizer and main course that my charming luncheon partner was the Rae Dalven. She answered all of my questions about Cavafy willingly and affably and gave me the sources of answers to other questions I had.

My pleasant experience with Dr. Dalven was duplicated again and again at the New York Public Library whose librarians always supplied the answer to some dilemma. The librarians at St. John's University also deserve special commendation. Though they had no idea I was writing a book such as this, their patience was infinite.

Lastly, I want to thank my family and friends who never tired nor questioned my using my work on this volume as an excuse for turning down familial and social engagements.

A. Borrello

Brooklyn, New York
August, 1971

Introduction

This is the second of three volumes of basic tools of reference for the scholar, student, and general reader interested in the works of E. M. Forster. The first of these volumes, already published, An E. M. Forster Dictionary, was created in the tradition of the Dickens and Faulkner dictionaries, but is more uniform and more inclusive. It contains summaries of all of Forster's work accompanied by full publication data. It also lists and describes all of his characters, key geographical locations, sites, hotels, etc. The third volume, An Annotated Bibliography of Works About E. M. Forster, now in preparation, will identify and summarize the books, pamphlets, and articles which constitute the corpus of critical and scholarly commentary on his writings.

This volume is an alphabetical listing of Forster's allusions drawn from the works the titles of which are listed in Appendix I. For obvious reasons, some works have been excluded, namely those signed and unsigned contributions to periodicals and newspapers which Forster's bibliographer, B. J. Kirkpatrick, has been unable to locate. Also excluded are those of his pieces not reprinted in his three collections of essays: Abinger Harvest, Pharos and Pharillon, and Two Cheers for Democracy. It should be noted, however, that these uncollected essays are slight in scope and importance.

The nature of the allusions contained herein are as disparate as Forster's interests. There are, of course, allusions to writers and writing in general. There are also allusions to historic personages, many of whom, though important in their own day, have been all but forgotten in our own time. Geographical locations have, in addition, been included. Surprisingly in this age which has shrunk the globe so, many are relatively obscure. There are allusions to art and artists, to music and musicians; to Greek, Roman, Norse, Indian, and Egyptian mythologies; to Roman Catholic and Mohammedan saints; to statues and paintings, antique and modern; and to historical events. All of these are elaborately cross-referenced.

The reader will also note that an attempt has been made to trace the originals of many of Forster's characters (e.g., Stuart Ansell, Mrs. Wilcox), as well as fictional sites (e.g., Howards End, Pensione Bertolini). Quotations and their sources are also listed, including literal translations of passages in foreign languages. In addition, short summaries are offered of the works to which Forster refers.

The source of each allusion has been identified with an abbreviation of the title of the work in which it appears (e.g, LJ, WAFT) and a key to these abbreviations follows this introduction. In each instance, only the first mention of the allusion has been cited in each work, hence, the reader will note a Roman numeral which follows the abbreviation of certain works. These numbers refer to the chapters in which the allusions appear (e.g., WAFT I, LJ VII). When an allusion in Alexandria is cited, the abbreviation, Alex, is followed by a Roman then an Arabic numeral (e.g., Alex I, 2). The Roman numeral refers to the part and the Arabic to the section of that part in which the allusion is to be found. An abbreviation of a title of one of Forster's collections of essays (AH, PP, Two Cheers) is followed by another abbreviation (the key to which also follows this introduction). The second abbreviation (e.g., AH-HOS) refers to the essay in the collection in which the reference occurs.

Long quotations from other authors have been, in the case of poetry, shortened to the first line followed by "etc.", to indicate that the quotation is extensive.

In every instance, an attempt has been made to offer succinct descriptions or definitions of allusions that by their very brevity make no pretension to definitiveness. They do however claim, and I believe the claim is generally justified, to acquaint the uninitiated with sufficient information to understand better the context in which the allusion appears.

An attempt has also been made to offer equally succinct summaries of works cited by Forster. This is generally a simple task when he alludes to novels, but is manifestly impossible when he refers to certain works of non-fiction which, because of their complexity (e.g., Darwin's Origin of the Species) or their length (e.g., the nine-volume English Local Government by Beatrice and Sidney Webb) elude simple summarization. In these instances, however, enough information has been given the reader to permit a general understanding of the contents. Often, Forster himself will supply summaries or indicate in some way the contents of these works as well as of novels, plays, and poetry. In these instances no summary is given.

As has been noted, this list is arranged alphabetically. The arrangement, however, is always in the manner in which Forster makes the allusion. Consequently, when he refers to a character in the novel of another author by his given name (e.g., Clara--Clara Middleton in The Egoist), the reader will discover the entry under the first name alone. The family name is, of course, supplied in the entry. When Forster offers a title rather than a first name (e.g., Lord, Lady, Mr., Mrs.), the title, for the purposes of alphabetizing, is considered the given name. Again, the full name, especially for historic personages, is given in the entry. Misspellings, alternate spellings, and errors have been retained; corrections and standard spellings are given in the entry. While it is comforting to note that even masters nod, no attempt has been made to find the origin of his errors, which may, of course, be ascribed to faulty proofreading.

Purists may fault the translations offered here for their lack of art. In every instance, only a literal translation has been given. The reader is asked to remember that the purpose of these translations is not art, but information.

While no claims to absolute completeness are made, the reader will discover that this volume's breadth is immense. I would welcome, nevertheless, any suggestions which would make it more nearly approach completeness in future editions.

Further, despite the exhaustive effort which has been made to eliminate errors from this work, it would be foolhardy to declare that it is free from fault. Should the reader encounter errors, I should be grateful to hear of them.

A List of Abbreviations Used

AH   Abinger Harvest
  Ab   "Abinger Pageant"
  Adrift   "Adrift in India"
  Ba   "Battersea Rise"
  Birth   "The Birth of an Empire"
  Capt   "Captain Edward Gibbon"
  Car   "Cardan"
  Chess   "Chess at Crakow"
  Cn   "Cnidus"
  Conso   "The Consolations of History"
  Doll   "The Doll House"
  Early   "The Early Novels of Virginia Woolf"
  Emp   "The Emperor Babur"
  For   "Forrest Reid"
  Game   "The Game of Life"
  Gem   "Gemistus Plato"
  Hap   "Happiness"
  Hickey   "Hickey's Last Party"
  HOS   "Howard Overing Sturgis"
  Hymn   "Hymn Before Action"
  Ibsen   "Ibsen the Romantic"
  It   "It is Different for Me"
  JA   "Jane Austen"
  Joseph   "Joseph Conrad: A Note"
  Lib   "Liberty in England"
  Mac   "Macolnia Shops"
  Marco   "Marco Polo"
  Me   "Me, Them and You"
  Mickey   "Mickey and Minnie"
  Mind   "The Mind of the Indian Native State"
  Mos   "The Mosque"
  Mr   "Mr. and Mrs. Abbey's Difficulties"
  Mrs   "Mrs. Hannah More"
  Mrs G   "Mrs. Grundy at the Parkers' "
  Muse   "For the Museum's Sake"
  My   "My Wood"
  My Own   "My Own Centenary"
  Note   "A Note on the Way"
  Notes   "Notes on the English Character"

AN E. M. FORSTER GLOSSARY

A

A.E. --(Aspects VII)--The pseudonym of George William Russell, 1867-1935. He was an Irish poet known especially for his verse which has a mystical quality. He was also a playwright (Deidre, 1902). Among his many volumes of poetry are The Divine Wisdom, 1904; The Renewal of Youth, 1911; Midsummer Eve, 1928; and Enchantment and Other Poems, 1930.

AARON--(PP-Eliza)--He is considered the traditional founder of the Hebrew priesthood. He was the first Jewish high priest, and the brother of Moses with whom, according to the Biblical Book of Exodus, he led the Israelites out of Egypt (c. 1200 B.C.). He was succeeded by his son, Eleazar; another son, Ithamar, was the ancestor of the prophet Eli.

ABBAS II--(AH-Will; Alex II, 7; Egypt)--Abbas Hilmi Pasha, 1874-1944. He was the Khedive of Egypt (1892-1914) and the son of Tewfik Pasha (q.v.). He cooperated with British officialdom in matters of justice, taxation, irrigation, reconquest of the Sudan, etc. (1900-1914). He was deposed, nevertheless, when the British established their protectorate over Egypt in 1914.

ABBEY, MRS--(AH-Mr)--Eleanor Jones Abbey, the wife of Richard Abbey, the guardian of the Keats children. Aileen Ward, in her biography of Keats (q.v.) (John Keats: The Making of a Poet, New York: 1963), calls her a "stupid and querulous woman." See also: Richard Abbey.

ABBEY, RICHARD--(AH-Mr)--The legal guardian of the four Keats children. He was a broker in tea and coffee and a landowner and churchwarden. He was a member of the Port of London Committee and of the Honourable Company of Girdlers; he was Steward of the City of London National Examinations, and twice was Master of the Honourable Company of Patten Makers. Aileen Ward, in her biography of Keats (John Keats: The Making of a Poet, New York: 1963), says "stout, conscientious, unimaginative, he was as old-fashioned in his dress as in his opinions." See also: Mrs. Abbey.

ABEL--(Collect Ta-Co-ord)--The second son of the Biblical Adam ["Genesis"], the first man. He was a shepherd whose sacrifice was pleasing to God and, as a consequence, was murdered by his brother, Cain, out of envy. See also: Cain.

ABERCROMBIE, SIR RALPH--(Alex I, Sect V)--[alternate spelling: Abercromby] 1734-1801. A British general born in Menstry, Scotland. He led an expeditionary force which conquered St. Lucia and Trinidad (1795-6) and commanded troops in the Mediterranean (1800); defeated the French at Alexandria (1801) and died of wounds there. He is credited with restoring discipline and efficiency to the British Army.

ABERDEEN TERRIERS--(HE XV)--A breed of terrier originally developed in Aberdeen, Scotland. The terrier receives its name because it was used to attack animals living in the earth (Fr. terre).

ABOUKIR [ABUKIR]--(Alex Sect V)--The name of a bay between the Rosetta mouth of the Nile and Alexandria, Egypt. It is also the name of a village (Abu Qir) about 13 miles NNE of Alexandria on Abukir Bay. It is the approximate site of Canopus (q.v.). The "Battle of the Nile" was fought in the Bay [Aug. 1-2, 1798] during the course of which Admiral Lord Nelson (q.v.) defeated the French fleet under Brueys; near the village, Napoleon (q.v.) defeated the Turks (1799) and Sir Ralph Abercrombie (q.v.) landed and defeated the French.

"ABOVE THE BATTLE"--(Two Cheers-Romain)--A pamphlet by Romain Rolland (q.v.) about World War I. It was translated and published in England (London: Allen and Unwin, 1916) and America (Chicago: Opencourt Pub. Co., 1916).

ABRAHAM--(AH-For the Muse; AH-Mosque; LJ VII)--Traditional Patriarch of the Jews ("Genesis" xi:26-xxv:10). He was the father of Isaac and of Ishmael and the grandfather of Jacob.

ABRAM--(LJ VII)--see: Abraham.

ABRUZZI--(Two Cheers-Whiff)--Abruzzi e Molise is a compartimento (province) of central Italy. It lies between the

Adriatic and the Apennines. In 1240 it was made a single
province by Frederick II, and was incorporated in the Kingdom of Italy as part of Naples in 1866.

ACHERON--(Collect Ta-Celest)--In classical mythology, the
river in the underworld around which hover the spirits of the
dead.

ACHILLES--(Collect Ta-Celest)--The hero of Homer's The
Illiad. He is represented as being brave and relentless, but
at the beginning of the poem, he refuses to fight the Trojans
because of a quarrel he has had with Agememnon, the leader
of the Greek forces. The Trojans seem to be winning and
Achilles sends Patroclus, his friend, into the battle. He is
killed and Achilles rushes in and kills Hector. Achilles, in
other poems, dies by an arrow in his heel, the only spot
upon his body through which he is vulnerable, hence: the
Achilles heel.

ACHILLES TATIUS--(PP-Bet)--A Greek rhetorician and the
author of a romance Leucippe and Cleitophon. He lived in
Alexandria in A. D. 200's. There he became a Christian
and a bishop.

ACKERLEY, J. R. --(GLD XI)--Joe Randolph Ackerley (1896-
1967) was the author of Hindoo Holiday; an Indian Journal
(London, 1932); and My Dog Tulip (London, 1956); and an
autobiography: My Father and Myself (London, 1965).

ACROPOLIS--(AH-Early)--[Gr. akros, "point, height"; polis,
"city."] An elevated citadel in Greek cities of the classical
period; the most famous is that of Athens upon which stands
the Parthenon.

ACTIUM--(Alex Sect I)--An ancient town and promentory in
Greece. It was the scene of the naval battle (434 B. C.)
preliminary to the Peloponnesian War. It was also the scene
of the naval victory of Octavius (later Augustus, the first
emperor of Rome, (q. v.)) over Antony (q. v.) and Cleopatra
VII (q. v.) in 31 B. C. By means of that victory, he became
sole master of Rome and its emperor.

ACTON, LORD--(Two Cheers-Two Books)--John Emerich
Dalberg-Acton, 1834-1902, first Baron Acton. He was Regius
professor of modern history, Cambridge (1895-1902) and the
leader of English liberal Roman Catholics who were hostile to
the dogma of papal infallibility. Edited and planned The

Cambridge Modern History.

ADAGIO--(MT)--[Italian: "slow."] In music, a slow moveme
originally of a string quartet.

ADAM BEDE--(Aspects VII)--A novel (1859) by George Eliot.
The central figure, Adam Bede, is in love with Hetty Sorrel,
an attractive but empty-headed girl, who is pursued by
Arthur Donnithorne, the son of the village squire. She encourages him, hoping to live in the manor. Adam surprises
them one day in the woods. Arthur is unaware that Adam is
in love with Hetty, but when he realizes the situation, he
gives Hetty up and leaves for a military career. Hetty
agrees to marry Adam, but as the day approaches, her preg-
nancy becomes more obvious. When the child is born, she
murders it. She is found guilty and condemned to death. At
the last moment, Arthur arrives with a reprieve and her
sentence is commuted to deportation from the village. Adam
later marries Dinah Morris, a lay preacher.

ADAMS, THE--(MT)--Four brothers who were architects, the
most important of whom was Robert (1728-1792), the architect to George III. With James and William, he built the
Adelphi section of London (1769-1771). The brothers also
introduced a style of furniture marked by wreaths, honey-
suckle and the fan ornament. The fourth brother was named
John.

ADAMS, HENRY--(LJ XIII)--Henry Brooks Adams, 1838-1918.
An American historian, he was born in Boston of the famous
Adams family which produced two presidents. He was as-
sistant professor of history at Harvard and editor of The
North American Review (1869-79) and the author of many
works, among the most important of which are Mont-Saint-
Michel and Chartres (1904) and The Education of Henry Adam
(1906).

ADAMS, PARSON--(Aspects IV)--Parson Abraham Adams. A
character in Joseph Andrews (1742) by Henry Fielding (q. v.).
He is an earthy man who loves to eat and drink and smoke.
He is absent minded and the tutor and friend of Joseph. He
protects Joseph and Fanny and finally marries them.

ADDISON, JOSEPH--(AH-Ron)--1672-1719. English essayist,
most known for his contributions to the Tatler and the Spectator which established and brought to perfection the essay as
a literary genre. Addison also produced a tragedy, Cato

(1713), which proved enormously popular. It depicted the
last of the Roman republicans, Cato, making a final, tragic
stand for liberty.

"ADELAIDA"--(RWV III)--The "Adelaide" cantata for tenor
solo and pianoforte, from a poem by Matthison with music
by Beethoven (q.v.), opus 46. Published in Vienna, February 1797, and dedicated to the poet.

ADELAIDE HOUSE--(Two Cheers-Lon)--A huge block of ship-
ping offices designed by Sir John J. Burnet (1924) and situated near London Bridge.

ADES, ALBERT--(AH-Salute)--1893-1921. An Alexandrian
(Egypt) author of Greek parentage most noted for his novel,
Le Livre de Goha le Simple (Goha the Fool) (1919) which he
wrote with Albert Josipovici (q.v.). He also wrote Les Inquiets (1921) and A Naked King (translated in 1924).

ADONAIS--(GLD VII)--The poetical name given by Shelley to
Keats in his elegy on the death of the latter (1821). The
name is probably an allusion to the mourning for Adonis (q.v.)

ADONIS--(Alex I, Sect I; Hill)--In classical myth a beautiful
youth beloved by Venus. He was killed by a wild boar while
hunting, hence his name has become associated with any
beautiful young man who dies while still young.

ADVENTURES OF A YOUNGER SON, THE--(Aspects I)--A
semi-autobiographical novel (1831) by E.J. Trelawny. It is
the story of a wild, Byronic character who deserts from the
navy and becomes a pirate.

AENEAS--(AH-Proust; LJ XII)--The hero of Virgil's epic,
The Aeneid (q.v.). He was the son of Anchises and Aphrodite (q.v.), the goddess of love. He fought against the
Greeks in the Trojan war and carried his father from the
flames of Troy. After wandering for many years, he founded
the colony the Romans claimed as their origin.

AENEID, THE--(AH-Salute; Nordic; Two Cheers-Cul)--The
epic poem by Virgil in 12 books. It details the wanderings
of its hero, Aeneas, after the fall of Troy and his subsequent
founding of the colony out of which Rome sprang. The stories
offered are not original with Virgil. The story of the wooden
horse and the sacking of Troy comes from Arctinus of Miletus;
the loves of Dido and Aeneas from Apollonius of Rhodes, etc.

AESCHYLUS--(Alex II, 4)--A Greek dramatist born 525 B. C.
in Eleusis, Attica.   According to tradition, he served in the
Persian wars and at Marathon, Artemisium, Salamis, and
Plataea.   In the annual competitions at Athens he won first
prize in tragedy 13 times (bet. 484-468 B. C.).   Of his many
plays (some 90) only seven survive: The Suppliants, The
Persians, Seven Against Thebes, Prometheus Bound, and the
Oresteian trilogy (Oresteia): Agamemnon, Choephori, and
Eumenides.

AESCULAPIUS--(Alex I, 1)--The Latin form of the Greek
Asklepios, god of medicine and of healing.   Legend has it
that he assumed the form of a serpent when he appeared at
Rome during a pestilence.   It is for this reason that the god
of health bears in his hand a serpent.

AFFABLE HAWK--(Tribute)--The pseudonym of Desmond
MacCarthy (q. v.) when he was working as a literary journalist.

AGAMEMNON--(Alex I, 1)--The legendary king of Mycenae.
He was the son of Atreus and the leader of the Greeks in
their battle against Troy to recover Helen.   He is also the
brother of Menelaos, the husband of Helen.

AGATA, SANTA--(Collect Ta-Siren)--Saint Agatha.   She was
an illustrious Sicilian virgin who was martyred at Catania,
Sicily (A. D. 251) for refusing the solicitations of a Roman
Senator.

AGATHOCLEA--(PP-Eph)--Sister of Agathocles (q. v.), prime
minister of Ptolemy IV (q. v.) and nurse of Ptolemy V (q. v.).
With her brother, she attempted to control Egypt by keeping
the knowledge of the death of Ptolemy IV from the people.

AGATHOCLES--(PP-Eph)--Prime minister of Ptolemy IV.
See: Agathoclea.

AGRA--(PI XV)--A city in India about 110 miles SE of Delhi.
It was captured by Baber (Babur) (q. v.), founder of the
Mogul Empire (1526).   The present city dates largely from
that time.   Nearby is the Taj Mahal (1631-45) created by
another Mogul emperor, Shah Jahan, as a tomb for his empress.

AHAB--(HE XVI)--The 7th king of Israel (875-853 B. C.).
During most of his reign his kingdom was at peace.   He

established friendly relations with his neighbors through marriages, especially with Jezebel, the daughter of the King of Sidon.   Jezebel's foreign religion (worship of Baal) aroused strong opposition in Israel especially from the prophet Elijah.   Ahab was killed in battle against Benhadad of Damascus.   He was succeeded by his sons Ahaziah and Jehoram.

AHAB--(Aspects VII; Two Cheers-Enchanted)--A character in Moby Dick (q. v.) by Herman Melville (q. v.).   He is the proud, defiant, and somewhat megalomaniacal captain of the whaler, "Pequod."   Before the novel opens, he loses his leg to a white whale.   He has a vowed to avenge himself on the beast.   He has a livid scar that begins under the hair on his head and which, it is rumored, continues the length of his body.   The scar suggests the spiritual flaw in the man.   His missing leg is replaced by one of whalebone.   He dies while doing battle with the whale.   The line of the harpoon twines itself about his neck and he is pulled out of the whaleboat.

AIROLO--(WAFT X)--A commune in the canton of Ticino in SE Switzerland.   It is located at the southern end of the St. Gotthard Tunnel in the valley of the Ticino river.

AJANTA--(Two Cheers-Duty)--A village in south-central India.   Nearby, in a ravine, are 30 caves, the earliest dating from 200 B. C. to A. D. 200 and the latest from the A. D. 600's.   They were excavated by Buddhists and comprise halls, dormitories, and temples with walls covered with fresco paintings.   The caves were rediscovered in 1817.

AJAX--(Alex I, 1)--The most famous hero of the Trojan war after Achilles, King of Salonis.   Ajax was a man of great physical stature, daring, and self-confidence.   When the armor of the dead Hector, the champion of Troy, was awarded to Ulysses instead of to himself, he turned mad and stabbed himself.

AKBAR--(AH-Mosque; Hill; PI XIV)--Jalal-ud-Din Muhammad, known as the Great Akbar, 1542-1605.   He was Emperor of Hindustan (1556-1605) and the third emperor of the Mogul dynasty.   He was born at Umarkot, Sind, while his father was in exile.   He won back the empire from the Hindus at Panipat (1556) and ruled under a regency until his majority. He was involved in many wars; invaded the Punjab (1566) and subjugated the Rajput kingdoms (1561-69) and other areas

of India until his kingdom comprised all of northern India.
He was a great organizer and administrator and introduced
many reforms in the conquered areas: abolished extortion,
developed trade, and tolerated the many varied religions.
His later years were clouded by the rebellion of his son,
Prince Selim, later to become Jahangir.

AKENATON--(Aspects VIII)--see: Ikhnaton.

À LA RECHERCHE DU TEMPS PERDU--see: Remembrance
of Things Past.

ALAIN--(Aspects III)--Pseudonym of Emile Auguste Chartier
(1868-1951), a French philosopher and essayist. The editor
of Livres-Propos, he was a professor at the Lycée Henri
IV. Among his many books are Les Propos d'Alain (1920);
Les Idées et les Âges (1927), Propos de Littérature (1933),
Les Dieux (1934), Mars où la Guerre Jugée les Saisons de
l'Esprit (1937).

ALAMAGIR--(PI VII)--Aurangzeb or Aurungzeb or Aurungzebe,
1618-1707. He was the 6th emperor of the Mogul dynasty
of emperors. He was the son of Shah Jahan, the builder of
the Taj Mahal (q. v.). He imprisoned his father in the Agra
fort and caused the death of his three brothers. Upon as-
cending the throne he assumed the title of Alamagir [i. e.,
conqueror of the world]. His wars with the Marathas
brought him into contact with the British at Madras, Surat,
and Calcutta. Rebellions weakened the Mogul power forcing
him to find shelter in Ahmadnagar (1706). He alienated
both Mohammedans and Hindus because of his bigotry.

ALARIC--(WAFT II)--He was a Gothic king (A. D. 370?-410)
born on an island at the mouth of the Danube. When
Theodosius was emperor of Rome, he commanded the Gothic
auxiliaries (394). Failing to receive high command in the
Roman Army, he was elected King of the Visigoths and invaded Greece (395-6) until checked by Stilicho. He was appointed governor in Illyricum by Emperor Arcadius as a
bribe. He built strong military forces and invaded and
ravaged Italy (400) until again stopped by Stilicho (402 or
403). He was bribed by the Emperor Honorius with appointment as prefect of western Illyricum. Nevertheless, he
again invaded Italy (408) and beseiged, captured, and plun-
dered Rome (August 24, 410).

ALASTOR--(GLD VII)--The evil genius of a house which
haunts and torments a family. Also the title of a poem by
Shelley (1815): "Alastor; or, The Spirit of Solitude." The
poet wanders over the Earth and admires the wonderful
works he cannot help seeing, but finds nothing which satisfies
his inquisitive mind nor anything in sympathy with himself.

ALBERT--(Two Cheers-English)--Albert Francis Charles
Augustus Emmanuel of Saxe-Coburg-Gotha, 1819-1861.
Prince Consort of Queen Victoria, who was his first cousin.
When he came to England as her husband he met with dis-
trust and prejudice. He was active in promoting science
and art and was a philanthropist. He died of typhoid fever.

ALBERTI--(AH-Gem)--Leon Battista Alberti, 1404-1472.
Italian architect, painter, organist, and writer. He designed
the church of Sant'Andrea at Mantua and the church of San
Francesco at Rimini, the facade of Santa Maria Novella at
Florence, and the Palazzo Strozzi in the same city. He is
said to have been one of the first to investigate scientifically
the laws of perspective.

ALBERTINE--(AH-Proust; Aspects VIII)--A character in
Proust's Remembrance of Things Past (q.v.). She is a
lesbian attracted to and by Marcel. Their affair takes many
turns over an extended period of time. When his grandmother dies, Marcel turns to her for comfort; although he
is unhappy with her, he is despondent without her. His im-
maturity drives her from him. Marcel, however, receives
a note from her after her death telling of her intention to
return to him.

ALCESTIS--(HE XI)--The daughter of Pelias in Greek myth.
She was sought for by Admetus, King of Pherae in Thessaly.
Pelias promised that Admetus should have her on one condition: that Admetus should come for her in a chariot drawn
by lions and wild boars. Apollo helped him perform the
task. The god tended the flocks of Admetus for nine years
when he was forced to serve a mortal for having slain the
Cyclops. Apollo prevailed upon the Fates to grant Admetus
deliverance from death if his father, mother, or wife would
die for him. Alcestis willingly dies for Admetus but was
brought back from the underworld by Hercules. Admetus's
story is the subject of one of Euripede's most famous plays,
Alcestis, and served as the subject of an opera (Gluck's
Alcestis).

ALEXANDER--see: Alexander the Great.

ALEXANDER THE GREAT--(AH-Consol; AH-Emp; AH-Troop;
Alex I, 1; Collect Ta-Eternal; MT; Two Cheers-Two Books)--
Alexander III, 356-323 B. C. He succeeded his father,
Philip II of Macedon (336 B. C.), conquered Thrace and
Illyria, destroyed Thebes, and gained ascendancy over all
of Greece (335 B. C.). He began an expedition to attack
Persia (334 B. C.) and won the battles of Granicus (334) and
Issus (333). He conquered Tyre and Gaza, occupied Egypt
and founded Alexandria (332), destroyed Persian power (331)
invaded eastern Persia (330-327) and northern India (326).
He defeated Porus on the Hydaspes (325-324) and withdrew
from India to Persia (325-324). He died of fever in Babylon.
He is said to have been buried in Alexandria. Legend says
his body still lies there.

ALEXANDER, BISHOP OF ALEXANDRIA--(PP-St. A)--fl.
A. D. 310. He was the "Patriarch of all the Preaching of St.
Mark" with a prestige challenged only by Rome. He was
also the patron of St. Athanasius (q. v.).

ALEXANDRA, QUEEN--(Two Cheers-Duke)--1844-1925. The
eldest daughter of Christian IX of Denmark. She was the
Queen consort of Edward VII of England whom she married
(1863) when he was the Prince of Wales.

ALEXIUS COMNENUS--(PP-Poetry)--Alexius I Comnenus,
1048-1118, was the Emperor of the Eastern Roman Empire
(1081-1118), and the nephew of the Emperor Isaac Comnenus.
He was a talented soldier and was raised by his troops to
supplant Nicephorus III. He defended the empire against
Scythians, Turks, Normans. His domains were invaded by
the first Crusade (1096-1099). His life (The Alexiad) was
written by his daughter Anna Comnena.

ALFRED, KING--(Two Cheers-William)--Called Alfred the
Great, 849-899. King of West Saxons. Helped his brother
Ethelred I against the Danish invasions and succeeded him
as king (871) and had several battles with the Danes. He
captured London (885 or 886) and was recognized as sovereign of all England. He forced the Danes to withdraw from
England (897) and consolidated his kingdom. He compiled
laws, brought many scholars into the country and was the
author of several translations from the Latin: Pastoral Care
by Gregory the Great, several histories of Orosius and Bede,
and Boethius's Consolation of Philosophy.

ALI, MOHAMMED--See: Mohammed Ali

ALICE, PRINCESS--(MT)--Alice Maude Mary 1843-1878.
Princess of Great Britain and Ireland.   Duchess of Saxony.
Grand Duchess of Hesse-Darmstadt.   Second daughter of
Queen Victoria (q. v.).

ALIEL-MEHALLI--(Alex II, 7)--A Mohammedan saint who
died in the 16th century.   His tomb and mosque (built in
1721) is one of the sights in Rosetta near Alexandria, Egypt.

ALINARI'S SHOP--(RWV IV)--A shop in Florence specializing
in reproductions of works of Italian art notably those on view
in the museums of Florence.   Address: Vittorio Alinari,
19r, Florence.   Tel. 23081.

ALISON, GENERAL--(Alex I, 5)--Archibald Alison, 1826-
1907.   An army officer in the Crimean War and in the
Sepoy Mutiny; he was second in command of the Ashanti expedition.   He led the Highland Brigade at Tell el-Kebir in
the Egyptian campaign.   He was made a general in 1887 and
is the author of An Army Organisation (1869).

ALLAH--(Collect Ta-Mr.)--Arabic: al, "the"; ilah, "God."
The Arabic name for the Supreme Being and the Mohammedan war cry as well as the first phrase of their confession
of faith (La Ilah Illa 'Illah--"There is no God, but Allah. ")

ALLAHABAD--(PI IX)--A city in India on the Ganges at its
junction with the Jumma River about 72 miles W of Benares
(q. v.).   It is an ancient holy city of India and a one-time
residence of the Mogul emperor, Akbar (q. v.) and finally
ceded to the British in 1801.   It was also the scene of a
serious outbreak in the Sepoy Mutiny.

ALIEN, CLIFFORD--(GLD XIV)--Lord Allen of Hurtwood
(created 1st Baron of Hurtwood in 1932), 1889-1939.   He was
educated at University College, Bristol and Peterhouse,
Cambridge University.   He was a member and executive of
the Fabian Society (1912) and was three times imprisoned
as a conscientious objector (1916-1917).   He was Chairman
and Treasurer of the Independent Labour Party (1922-1926)
and Director of the Daily Herald (1922-1926).   He married
Marjory Gill in 1921.

ALLEN AND UNWIN--(GLD-Intro)--British publishing firm:
George Allen and Unwin, Ltd.   Established by Thomas

Fisher Unwin in 1882 as T. Fisher Unwin. Unwin has been
credited with discovering Joseph Conrad.

ALLENBY, LORD--(AH-T.E.; Alex II, 4; Egypt)--Edmund
Henry Hynman (1st Viscount Allenby), 1861-1936. English
field marshal who served in Bechuanaland (1884-5), Zululand
(1888) and in cavalry operations in the Boer War. He commanded cavalry in France in WWI. As the Commander in
Chief of Egyptian Expeditionary Forces, he took Beersheba
and Gaza (1917) entered Jerusalem (Dec. 9, 1917) and won
a sweeping victory over the Turks at Megiddo (1918). He
was raised to the peerage as Viscount Allenby of Megiddo
and Felixstowe (1919). He was the High Commissioner for
Egypt (1919-25). Sir Archibald Wavell wrote his biography
(1940).

ALLIES--(Two Cheers-G&G)--The United States, England,
The U.S.S.R., France, and other countries allied to them
in World War II and opposed to the Axis countries (notably
Germany, Italy and Japan).

ALLIOTT, KENNETH--(Two Cheers-Outsider)--The author
of Poems (1938), compiler of The Penguin Book of Contemporary Verse (1918-60), and co-author of The Art of Graham
Greene (1963).

ALLMERS, THE--(AH-Ibsen)--Chief characters in Ibsen's
play, Little Eyolf (q.v.).

ALL QUIET ON THE WESTERN FRONT--(Two Cheers-What)
--A novel by Erich Maria Remarque (q.v.) first published
in 1929. It is essentially a realistic novel about the disen-
chantment of war told from the point of view of a young
German engaged in the battle on the western front, Paul
Baumer, who suffers the horrors of war. When the war
ends, Paul is discharged and returns home to find his
mother dying of cancer.

ALL SOULS PLACE--(GLD I)--All Souls Langham Place. A
street in London which connects Regent Street with Portland
Place and contains All Souls Church built by John Nash
(1822-24) who created its circular classical portico and
needle-like spire surrounded by its ring of free standing
columns to close the vista up Regent Street. The church
was badly damaged in the bombing during WWII and restored
in 1951.

ALL THAT WAS POSSIBLE--(AH-HOS)--A novel by Howard
Overing Sturgis (q.v.) published, 1895.   Forster gives an
adequate summary of its plot in his essay on Sturgis in
Abinger Harvest.

ALMA-TADEMA, SIR LAURENCE--(AH-Roger)--1836-1912.
A painter and naturalized British citizen, his highly popular
paintings of Greek and Roman life brought him financial success but no lasting fame.

ALTAR OF THE DEAD, THE--(AH-HOS)--A collection of
short stories by Henry James (1909).   Almost all of the
stories have touches of the supernatural.

ALVING, OSWALD--(AH-Ibsen)--The principal character in
Ghosts (1881), a play by Henrik Ibsen (q.v.).   He is a neu-
rotic and dissipated young man who becomes insane from
syphilis inherited from his worthless father.

ALYOSHA--(Aspects VII)--A character in The Brothers Karamazov (q.v.).

AMARYLLIS--(LJ X)--A rustic sweetheart.   The name comes
from a shepherdess in the pastorals of Theocritus and Virgil
(q.v.).   The character also appears in Spenser's Colin Clout's
Come Home Again.

AMBASSADORS, THE--(Aspects VIII)--A novel (1903) by
Henry James (q.v.).   It deals with several Americans and
their reactions to a European environment.   Chad, the son
of wealthy Mrs. Newsome, has become entangled with a
Parisian woman.   Mrs. Newsome sends her fiancé, Lambert
Strether, to Paris in an attempt to have her son return to
the business he has inherited.   Strether becomes enamored
of the city and, as a result, Mrs. Newsome sends more
"ambassadors."   These people find it impossible to love the
city and Strether feels that he must return to America; he
advises Chad, however, to remain.

AMELIA--(Aspects III)--A novel (1751) by Henry Fielding
(q.v.).   William Booth, a penniless young man, has run
away with Amelia against her mother's wishes.   Their poverty and his weaknesses involve them in a series of adventures until it is discovered that Amelia is an heiress.

AMMON--(Alex I, 1)--The Libyan Jupiter, the Greek form
of the name of the Egyptian god, Amun.   He is usually

represented with the head of a ram and a human body or as a human figure with two upright plumes springing from his head and holding a scepter and the symbol of life, the ankh (q. v.). He was identified with Zeus and his oracle, consulted by Alexander the Great (q. v.), was in the oasis of Jupiter Ammon.

AMMON, ST. --(Alex II)--A Christian martyr. His feast day is December 20 and is celebrated in conjunction with those of Zeno, Ptolemy, Ingenius, and Theophilius who were Roman soldiers. During the persecutions of Decius (q. v.) at Alexandria, they were standing about the tribunal of the governor who was trying and sentencing Christians. One of those being tried under torture gave way and showed signs of betraying his faith. The soldiers: Ammon, Zeno, Ptolemy, Ingenius, and Theophilius, an old soldier, could not control their distress and made signs to him to stand fast. When the judge inquired what they were doing, they burst into the ring and proclaimed themselves Christians. The governor and his associates were greatly intimidated by the cheerfulness with which the Christians greeted their own suffering.

AMMONIUS SACCAS--(Alex I, 3)--c. A.D. 175-250. Called Saccas (i.e., "sack-bearer") because of his early occupation. An Alexandrian philosopher, he founded Neo-Platonism and was the teacher of Plotinus, Longinus, Origen, et al. He is said to have attempted to harmonize the doctrines of Aristotle (q. v.) and Plato (q. v.).

AMOROSO--(Two Cheers-C)--[Ital., "lovingly."] A musical direction to play "tenderly."

AMR--(AH-Mosque; Alex I, 2)--Ibn Al-As (d. A.D. 664). The Arab conquerer of Egypt. He was born in Mecca, possibly c. A.D. 580. He belonged to the tribe of Quraish (Koreish) and was an opponent of Mohammed until his conversion (629). Soon after becoming a Moslem and going to Medina, he was given a series of military commands. In 633, the caliph Aby Bakr put him in charge of one of three forces invading Palestine. His initiative brought about the movements of Arab expansion from Palestine into Egypt and North Africa. His sortie into Egypt (639) opened the way to rapid conquest. Alexandria surrendered (642), followed by Tripoli (643). He founded the forerunner of Cairo (Fustat), but was removed from power and then reinstated and rewarded with the governorship of Egypt until his death in 664.

AMRITSAR MASSACRE--(AH-Notes)--Amritsar is a city in India of some 400,000 people. A park there (the Jallianwala Bagh) in 1919 was the scene of a political meeting. Government troops fired upon the participants killing several hundred people. The site of the massacre was declared a national monument after India's independence.

AMSET--(Alex II, 1)--One of the gods of the visceral organs in Egyptian mythology. After the body was embalmed, the visceral organs were gathered in a jar topped by a representation of Amset and placed in the tomb.

ANCIENT MARINER, THE--(AH-Troop; Two Cheers-Enchanted)--The central figure in the poem, "The Rime of the Ancient Mariner," by Samuel Taylor Coleridge (q.v.) (about 1796). The poem treats of a seaman, the Ancient Mariner, who is condemned to do penance for shooting an albatross. The story is told by the Mariner.

"AND WHAT BUT GENTLENESS UNTIRED," etc.--(Two Cheers-William)--ℓℓ. 129-140 from "A Southern Night," a poem by Matthew Arnold (q.v.).

ANGELICO, FRA--(Collect Ta-Eternal; RWV IV)--Fiesole, Giovanni da, original name: Guido di Pietro, 1387-1455. An Italian Dominican friar and painter of religious subjects. Among his most famous works are the frescoes at Orvieto. His paintings and frescoes in the Dominican monastery of San Marco in Florence, and the Chapel of St. Nicholas in the Vatican, recall that he had his origins in Sienese painting. Though thoroughly schooled in perspective and plastic modeling, in his piety he still belonged to the Middle Ages.

ANGEL'S WINGS--(Two Cheers-Edward)--A series of essays on art and its relation to life by Edward Carpenter (q.v.) (London, 1898). Forster notes that he "expresses in esthetic criticism his love for the individual and the beauty of nature."

"ANGELUS AD VIRGINEM/ etc.--(AH-AB)--A Medieval Latin hymn. The following is a literal translation: An angel for the Virgin/Crossing into the room/In awe of the Virgin/To ask for a touch of her hand,/Hail Queen of Virgins,/Lord of heaven and earth/Conceiving and bringing forth untainted,/ The deliverance of men/You collect them at the gate of heaven/Remedy our sin./Oh come Mother of God/Who has given peace/To the angels and to man/You have begotten

Christ, /The Son originated in you /As favorably inclined to
us /Exposing and removing sins /Present to help /A blessed
life to the end /After this exile.

ANGOULÊME, DUCHESSE D'--(MT)--Marie Thérèse Charlotte de Bourbon, 1778-1851. As a child she was imprisoned in the Temple during the French Revolution (q. v.) with
her parents, Louis XVI and Marie Antoinette. After their
execution she was known as the "Orphan of the Temple."
She remained an ardent royalist all of her life.

ANIMAL FARM--(Two Cheers-George)--A satirical work by
the English novelist, George Orwell (q. v.), depicting totali-
tarian dictatorship in a barnyard in which the pigs seize
control of the farm.

ANKH--(Alex I, 3)--The Egyptian hieroglyphic for life, prosperity. It is a tau cross with a loop at the top used as a
sacred emblem symbolizing life--also called the crux ansata.

ANKHOR--(Two Cheers-Duty)--Angkor. The ruined ancient
capital of the Khmers in Cambodia, Indochina. It was
founded before A. D. 100 and flourished for several centuries.
About one mile south of it is Angkor Wat ("temple") a building of three stories entirely covered by carvings. The city
and temple were abandoned in the 14th century after being
conquered by the Siamese and lay buried in the jungle until
discovered by the French in 1860.

ANNA KARENINA--A novel (1874-76) by the Rusian novelist,
Leo Tolstoy (q. v.). It treats, essentially, of the illicit love
of Anna, the wife of Aleksey Aleksandrovitch Karenin, a
minister of the government, and Count Vronsky. She bears
an illegitimate daughter by Vronsky. Both she and her
lover are persons of integrity and high character. The
pressures of society, nevertheless, begin to tell. Anna
finds the strain unbearable and throws herself beneath a
train. Her and Vronsky's story is reflected more happily
in that of Konstantin Levin and Kitty Oblonsky. Levin's
courtship, though a clumsy affair, wins Kitty who has been
jilted by Vronsky, and the two marry.

ANNE--(AH-JA)--see: Anne Elliot.

ANNE, QUEEN--(AH-BA; Aspects I; GLD I; MT)--1665-1714.
Queen of Great Britain and Ireland (1702-1714), of the house
of Stuart. She was the second daughter of James II and

Anne Hyde. She married Prince George of Denmark (1683).
After she ascended to the throne, she was dominated by the
duke and duchess of Marlborough until their Whig sympathies
alienated them from her. The most important act of her
reign was the union with Scotland (1707).

ANNIANUS, ST.--(Alex I, 2)--He was a Jewish shoemaker of
Alexandria reputed to have been converted to Christianity by
St. Mark (A.D. 45) and thereby Christianity was introduced
into Alexandria. He was martyred in A.D. 62 for protesting
against the worship of Serapis.

ANSELL--(LJI MT)--A character in Forster's novel, The
Longest Journey, whose name and much of his character
were taken from that of a childhood playmate, a garden boy
at Rookrest, Forster's childhood home.

ANTIGONE--(Nordic)--In Greek myth the daughter of Oedipus
by his mother Jocasta. She was famed for her heroic attachment to her father and her brothers. She accompanied
Oedipus after he blinded himself and, after his death, she
returned to Thebes to discover that her uncle Creon, now
the king, had forbidden the body of her brother to be buried.
She defied the order, buried the body and was herself buried
alive in a vault. There she killed herself. She is the heroine of Sophocles' (q.v.) play Antigone (q.v.) and Euripede's
(q.v.) Phoenissae.

ANTIGONE--(Aspects V; Collect Ta-Road; New Disorder;
Reading; Two Cheers-Art; Two Cheers-Book)--A play by the
Greek dramatist, Sophocles 495-406 B.C., (q.v.), which
treats of the legend of Antigone after her return to Thebes.
See: Antigone.

ANTIOCH--(AH-Cn)--An ancient city in Pisidia, Asia Minor.
Its ruins lie about 80 miles from Konya, Turkey. It was
visited by St. Paul.

ANTIQUARY, THE--(Aspects II; MT)--A novel by Sir Walter
Scott (1816) set in the period of George III and one of the
Waverly group. Forster gives a good description of its
plot in Chapter II of Aspects of the Novel.

ANTONGINI'S BOOK ON D'ANNUNZIO--(Two Cheers-Whiff)--
The book referred to by Forster is Tom Antongini's (q.v.)
D'Annunzio, London: William Heinemann, Ltd., 1938. It
was written from "thirty full years" of friendship and some

700 autographed letters from D'Annunzio to the author.
Antongini notes in the preface that D'Annunzio had dedicated
his Faville de Maglio (Sparks from the Hammer) to him who
"during so many years, has been for the companion with the
attentive and penetrating eyes."

ANTONGINI, TOM--(Two Cheers-Whiff)--First name:
Tommaso, b. 1877. The secretary and sometime publisher
of D'Annunzio (q. v.) who wrote several books on his employer:
Gli Allegri Filibusteri di D'Annunzio (Milan, 1951); D'Annunzio
Aneddotico (Milan, 1939); Un D'Annunzio Ignorato: Vicende e
Aspetti Insospettati del Poeta (Milan, 1961); Quarant'anni con
D'Annunzio (Milan, 1957); and Vita Segreta di Gabriele D'Annun-
zio (Milan, 1938), which was translated into English (London,
1938) as simply D'Annunzio. Antongini has also written novels
and other works unrelated to D'Annunzio.

ANTONINUS--(Alex II, 7)--A pagan "reactionary" who settled
in Canopus attempting to revive the worship of Serapis in his
temple there before its destruction (A. D. 389).

ANTONIO--(Reading)--The merchant of Venice of Shakespeare's play of the same name. He is rich and generous.
In his attempt to help his friend Bassanio, he borrows the
needed money from Shylock who asks a pound of his flesh if
the money is not returned on a certain date. Antonio is
saved from certain death, when he cannot repay the loan, by
Portia's cleverness in court.

ANTONIO--(GLD)--The treacherous brother of Prospero who
has usurped his place as the Duke of Milan. In the end of
the play (The Tempest by William Shakespeare), he is for-
given.

ANTONY--(Alex I, 1; PP-Philo; Two Cheers-Jul)--Marcus
Antonius, 83?-30 B. C. Through his mother, he was related
to Julius Caesar. He was an orator, triumvir, and soldier
who was with Caesar (q. v.) during his campaigns in Gaul.
After Caesar's death (44 B. C.), through his oratory, he influenced the Romans to drive out his assasins. He became
a rival of Octavius, Caesar's nephew and heir. He went to
Egypt to punish Cleopatra (q. v.) for taking arms against the
triumvirate (Antony, Octavius, and Lepidus) only to succumb
to her charms. In the division of the Roman world, he took
the East. Though married to Octavia, Octavius's sister, he
continued living with Cleopatra. He settled in Alexandria.
His rivalry with Octavius increased. With Cleopatra he was

defeated by Octavius in the battle of Actium (q.v.). He fled
back to Egypt where, deserted by his troops, he committed
suicide.

ANTONY, ST.--(Alex I, 2)--Surnamed: of the Desert,
c.A.D. 250-350. He is known as the first Christian monk.
He was born in middle Egypt and was an ascetic from the
age of 20. He withdrew to solitude on a height near the
Nile and emerged only to organize communities of anchorites
and, late in life, to attack Arianism (q.v.). Legends record
that he was subject to terrible temptations. He is regarded
as the founder of Christian monasticism.

ANUBIS--(Alex II, 3)--Also called: Anpu. He is the Egyptian god of embalming often identified with the Green Hermes,
conductor of souls. He is represented as a black jackal
with a bushy tail or as a blackish-skinned man with the head
of a jackal or a dog, which was the animal sacred to the
god. He presided over embalmings. He is the "fourth son
of Ra" and his daughter is Kebehut, the goddess of fresh-
ness. In later dynasties, he was made part of the family
of Osiris and it was said that Nephtys, left childless by her
husband Set, bore him adulterously to Osiris. Abandoned by
his mother at birth, he was found by his aunt, Isis. She
felt no rancor at her husband-brother's infidelity and brought
the child up. When he was fully grown, he accompanied his
father Osiris on his conquest of the world. When Osiris was
murdered, he helped Isis and Nephtys to bury him. It was
then that Anubis invented funeral rites and bound up the
mummy of Osiris to preserve him. He was known thereafter as "Lord of the Mummy Wrappings."

APENNINES--(HE X)--A mountain range in Central Italy which
extends the full length of the peninsula.

APHRODITE--(LJ XIX)--The Greek goddess of love, so
called because she sprang from the foam (aphros) of the sea.
In Roman myth she is known as Venus.

APHRODITE, CNIDIAN--(AH-Cn)--A statue of Aphrodite by
the great Greek sculptor, Praxiteles (q.v.), which stood in
her temple in Cnidus, Asia Minor. The statue is known
through a Roman copy now in the Vatican Museum.

APIS--(Alex I, 1)--The bull-god of Memphis sacred to
Osiris (q.v.) of whose soul it was supposed to be the image.
The sacred bull had to have spots on its forehead forming

a triangle and a half-moon on its breast. It was not permitted to live more than 25 years at which time it was
sacrificed and buried with great ceremony

APOLLO--(AH-Cn; AH-Me; AH-Two; Collect Ta-Other; GLD
XII; LJ X; PP-Clement)--In Greek myth, he was the son of
Zeus and Leto, one of the great gods of Olympus, typifying
the sun in its light and life-giving as well as its destructive
power. He is often identified with Helios, the sun-god.
Apollo was the god of music, poetry, and the healing arts
which he bestowed upon his son, Aesculapius (q. v.). He is
represented as the perfection of youthful manhood.

APOLLONIUS OF PERGA--(PP-Ph)--A Greek mathematician
of the 3rd century B. C. known especially for his treatise on
conic sections.

APOLLONIUS OF RHODES--(Alex I, 1)--Known also as:
Apollonius Rhodius, 260-188 B. C. A Greek poet author of
the epic Argonautica based on the legend of the Argonauts.

APOSTATE--(Two Cheers-Fo)--The autobiography of Forrest
Reid, London: Constable and Co., Ltd., 1926. Forster
calls it "a memorable spiritual biography."

APPASSIONATA--(Two Cheers-Not Listening)--The word is
Italian meaning "with intense feeling, passionately." It is
the title of Beethoven's (q. v.) Piano Sonata, Opus 57. The
composer did not give it this name; it is a later addition.

ARABI, AHMED--(AH-Wil; Alex I, 5; Egypt)--1841?-1911.
Founder of the Egyptian Nationalist Party. He was an
Egyptian revolutionist who was born in lower Egypt and
served 12 years as a conscript in the Egyptian army. After
dismissal on unproved charges, he became the leader of
discontented Nationalists and acquired great influence over
the Khedive Tewfik Pasha (q. v.). He became the undersec-
retary for war (1882) and was dismissed from the ministry
(1882) on the intervention of the British. He was defeated
at Tel-el-Kebir (Sept. 13, 1882) by General Wolsely, was
captured, tried and sentenced to death, later changed to life
imprisonment. He was sent to Ceylon, pardoned and returned to Egypt in 1901.

ARACOELI, THE CHURCH OF--(AH-Capt)--Santa Maria
d'Aracoeli (i. e. altar of Heaven). A Roman church originally built well before the A. D. 500 and rebuilt in the 13th

century. It stands at the top of a huge staircase on the
Capitoline hill and contains, among other works of art,
paintings by Pinturicchio.

ARARAT--(AH-Marco; AH-Vo)--An isolated mountain in
eastern Turkey upon which Noah's ark is said to have come
to rest after the flood described in the Bible.

ARCADIUS--(Alex II, 7)--A. D.- 377?-408. The first Emperor
of the Eastern Roman Empire (395-408 B. C.). He was born
in Spain, the son of the Roman Emperor Theodosious I at
whose death the empire was divided. He lived in luxury and
complete indifference to the affairs of the empire while the
government was administered by others. During his reign,
Alaric (q. v.) ruled the Balkan region (396-401). Gainas,
the Gothic general, seized and held Constantinople (400) but
was driven out in the same year. Patriarch Chrysostom was
persecuted by the Empress Eudoxia and exiled (404).

ARCADY--(LJ X)--Also known as Arcadia. It is a district
of the Peloponnesus which, according to Virgil, was the home
of pastoral simplicity and happiness.

ARDEN, ENOCH--(Two Cheers-Snow)--The central figure in
the poem of the same name by Alfred Lord Tennyson (q. v.)
first published in 1864. He is a fisherman who marries his
childhood sweetheart, Annie, and lives with her happily for
seven years. He is then injured and his prosperity dwindles.
He sells his boat to finance Annie as a trader in order to
support their three children. He sails on a merchantman,
is shipwrecked on a desert isle, and worries constantly about
his family. Years later, he returns to England only to find
Annie has remarried and has had another child. He does
not reveal his identity until he is on his deathbed.

"...ARE TWO LIONS LITTER'D IN ONE DAY, AND I THE
ELDER AND MORE TERRIBLE."--(Two Cheers-Jul)--This
line is from the play Julius Caesar, by William Shakespeare,
Act II, Sc. ii, ℓ. 46.

AREOPAGITICA--(Two Cheers-Ter)--Full title: Areopagitica:
A Speech of Mr. John Milton for the Liberty of Unlicensed
Printing to the Parliament of England (1644).

ARGHUN, ZULAN--(AH-Emp)--fl. 1288. Ruler of the Persian Empire.

ARGO--(AH-Mac)--The name of the ship captained by Jason
of Greek myth who went in search of the golden fleece.

ARGONAUTS--(AH-Mac)--The sailors of the ship, Argo (q. v.)
who sailed from Greece to Colchis in quest of the golden
fleece.

ARIANISM--(Alex I, 3; PP-Clement)--A doctrine taught by
Arius (d. A. D. 330), a Greek ecclesiastic in Alexandria.
See: Arius.

ARIEL--(GLD IV)--A character in Shakespeare's play, The
Tempest, (q. v.). He is a spirit imprisoned by Sycorax and
released by Prospero whom he serves faithfully. At the
conclusion of the play, he is released by Prospero.

ARISONE II--(Alex I, 1)--The sister and second wife of
Ptolemy II Philadelphus (q. v.), King of Egypt.

ARISONE III--(Alex I, 1)--fl. 3rd century B. C. Sister and
wife of Ptolemy IV Philopater (q. v.), King of Egypt.

ARISTARCHUS--(Alex I, 1)--220?-150 B. C. Greek grammarian originally from Samothrace but as librarian, chiefly
resident in Alexandria. He edited Homer (q. v.), Hesiod,
Pindar, Aeschylus (q. v.), Sophocles, and other Greek authors. He was the first to arrange The Iliad (q. v.) and
The Odyssey (q. v.) into 24 books.

ARISTARCHUS OF SAMOS--(Alex I, 1; PP-Ph)--A Greek
astronomer (3rd century B. C.) who maintained that the earth
rotates on its own axis and revolves about the sun. He developed the method of estimating the relative distance of the
sun and moon from the earth from the angle formed by them
at the observer's eye when the moon is at first or third
quarter.

ARISTOPHANES--(AH-Cn; Aspects I; GLD V; LJ IV; Two
Cheers-Raison)--448?-380? B. C. An Athenian playwright
who is regarded by many as the greatest writer of comedy
of all time. Of his 40 comedies which railed against certain trends and personalities of his day in Athens, only 11
are extant, among the more famous of which are The Clouds
(423), The Wasps (422), The Birds (414), Lysistrata (411),
and The Frogs (405).

ARISTOTLE--(AH-Gem; Alex I, 1; Aspects V; Hill; PP-Return; Two Cheers-Raison)--A Greek philosopher (384-322 B. C.). He studied under Plato (q. v.) and tutored Alexander the Great (q. v.). He also taught in Athens as head of the Peripatetic school. His treatises, in the main his lectures, cover many topics: logic, metaphysics, natural sciences, ethics, politics, rhetoric and poetics.

ARIUS--(Alex I, 2; PP-St. A)--A Greek churchman in Alexandria, d. A. D. 336. He taught the doctrine (Ariansism) that God is alone, unknowable, and separate from every created being, that Christ is a created being and not God in the fullest sense. He is, therefore, to be worshipped as a secondary deity. In the incarnation, the Logos assumed a body but not a human soul. Arianism was condemned as heretical in the general councils of Nicea (325) and Constantinople (381).

ARJUNA--(AH-Hymn)--In Indian mythology, one of the five sons of Pandu who launch a war against their hundred cousins, the Kurus. They are aided by the god, Krishna. One of the five, Arjuna, hesitates to take part in the war wondering why he should kill his kinsmen. Krishna, who has become his divine charioteer, reminds him that he belongs to a caste of warriors. He cannot go to heaven if he displays such cowardice; besides, death is only an appearance. The soul is eternal. These remarks induce Arjuna to ask Krishna certain questions. Their dialogue results in a long philosophical poem The Bhagavad-Gita about which Forster writes.

ARK--(AH-Marco; Hill)--The ship which Noah (in "Genesis") built to withstand the flood the Lord sent to destroy the wicked of the world.

ARMADA, THE--(AH-AB; AH-Consol)--The fleet assembled by Philip II of Spain for the conquest of England in 1588.

ARMADO--(AH-Consol)--Don Adriano de Armado. A character in William Shakespeare's play, Love's Labour's Lost. He is a boastful Spanish soldier who fancies himself a gallant courtier but who in reality is too poor to own a shirt. He embroiders his affair with Jaquenetta, a country girl, and almost convinces himself that it is his "grande amour," in the tradition of the old ballads.

ARMIDE--(RWV XV)--An opera by Gluck (1772) with a libretto by P. Quinault. It is based on Tasso's poem of the Crusades, Jerusalem Delivered.

ARMY AND NAVY STORES--(LJ XXIV)--A large department
store in London located at 105 Victoria Street, S. W. 1.

ARNE, THOMAS AUGUSTUS--(Two Cheers-Stratford)--An
English composer of music, 1710-1778. In addition to com-
posing the music for Bickerstaff's Judith which was performed during the Garrick Shakespeare Jubilee in the Autumn of
1769, he also composed the music for Fielding's (q. v.) Tom
Thumb and Milton's (q. v.) Comus among other works. He
is also the composer of "Rule Britannia. "

ARNO--(RWVI)--A river in Tuscany (Italy) which flows from
the Apennines through Florence.

ARNOLD, MATTHEW--(AH-Note; Hill; MT; Two Cheers-In;
Two Cheers-Raison; Two Cheers-William)--Poet and critic,
1822-1886.   Educated at Rugby where his father, Matthew
(q. v.) was headmaster, and at Winchester and Balliol College, Oxford, Arnold was appointed inspector of schools
(1851).   Two years before he had published his first volume
of poetry, The Strayed Reveller, which he withdrew from
circulation.   Some of the poems in the volume, however,
were included in Empedocles on Etna (1852).   He was appointed to the professorship of poetry at Oxford (1857).
From this point, he produced few poems.   His remaining
volumes of poetry are Poems (1853), Poems, 2nd Series
(1855) and New Poems (1867).   Forster has pointed him out
as the Victorian he most admires. [See: "William Arnold"
in Two Cheers for Democracy.]

ARNOLD, THOMAS--(Two Cheers-William)--1795-1842. Son
of an inland revenue officer in the isle of Wight, he was educated at Winchester and Oxford.   In 1828, he was appointed
headmaster of Rugby.   Through his position, he helped to
reform English education.   He was also interested in church
affairs and became a zealous reformer.   He became professor of modern history at Oxford in 1841 and left at his
death an unfinished History of Rome.

ARNOLD, WILLIAM--(Two Cheers-William)--The brother of
Matthew Arnold (q. v.).

ARROWSMITH--(AH-Sin)--A novel (1925) by Sinclair Lewis.
It is the story of a doctor, Martin Arrowsmith, and his
struggle to achieve a life dedicated to scientific research.

ARROWSMITH, THE SECOND MRS.--(AH-Sin)--Joyce Lanyon. When Martin Arrowsmith meets her, she is a wealthy widow. Their marriage fails when she finds him crude and unculti- vated. She discovers that it is impossible for her to under- stand his devotion to research.

ART OF CREATION, THE--(Two Cheers-Edward)--A work by Edward Carpenter (q.v.) (London, 1904). Forster notes that it expresses in philosophic speculation his love for the individual and the beauty of nature. The object of the vol- ume is to "show the speculative and the practical" sides of the art of creation.

ART OF LIFE, THE--(GLD X)--Forster claims that the volume was written by Osbert Burdett. He is probably in error with regard to the title. Burdett did write a volume called The Art of Living (London: Eyre and Spottiswoode, 1933). It is a series of essays one of which contains a sympathetic impression of Goldsworthy Lowes Dickinson at Cambridge.

ARTEMIS--(PP-Clement)--In Greek myth, the daughter of Zeus and Leto and the twin of Apollo (q.v.). She is the goddess of the moon and the protectress of women and is identified with the Roman Diana.

ARTHUR, KING--(Collect Ta-Other)--A shadowy British chieftain mentioned first by Nennius, a Breton monk of the 10th century. During the middle ages, he became the sym- bol of chivalry. He was the illegitimate son of Uther Pen- dragon and Igraine, the wife of the Duke of Cornwall. His wife was Guinevere who committed adultry with Sir Lancelot, one of the Knights of the Round Table. Arthur was mortally wounded in battle against Modred, his nephew, who was re- volting against him. He is said to be buried at Avalon.

ARUNDEL PRINTS--(LJ VII)--Reproductions in color of Old Master paintings issued by the Arundel Society (1849-1897) to its members.

ASCENSION OF ST. JOHN--(RWV II)--A group of frescoes by Giotto (q.v.) in the Peruzzi Chapel, Santa Croce, Florence.

ASCENT OF F.6, THE--(Two Cheers-Ascent)--A "tragedy in two acts" by W. H. Auden (q.v.) and Christopher Isherwood (q.v.), London: Faber and Faber, Ltd., 1936. Forster has erred in its title. It is The Ascent of F6. He gives a good

summary of the play in his essay, "The Ascent of F. 6" in
Two Cheers for Democracy.

ASCHAM, ROGER--(AH-Cardan)--English prose writer and
teacher (1515-1568) and tutor to Queen Elizabeth (q. v.) before she succeeded to the throne.   In his work, he urged
that sports be adopted in the curriculum of the schools. His
most famous work is The Schoolmaster (published 1570).

ASHTON, LADY--(Aspect II)--A character in Walter Scott's
(q. v.) The Bride of Lammermoor (1819).   The wife of Sir
William, she is proud, vindictive, and dominating, and so
hated the Ravenswood family that she stooped to any means
to deceive Lucy into believing her lover to be unfaithful.

ASIRGARH--(PI XXIII)--A strong fortress on the Tapti in
Khandesh (India) believed to be impregnable, but which was
taken several times once by Akbar (q. v.).   In 1803, the
British East India Company captured it.

ASKLEPIOS--See: Aesculapius.

ASOKA--(Two Cheers-Tol)--An Indian king of the Magahada
Dynasty (263-226 B. C.) who, by a miracle, was converted
to Buddhism and became its protector in much the same way
Constantine (q. v.) helped to foster Christianity.   Asoka is
called "the beloved of the gods. "

ASQUITH, MR. --(AH-Wil; Aspects VI)--Herbert Henry Asquith, 1st Earl of Oxford and Asquith, 1852-1928.   Educated
at Balliol College, Oxford, he became a Liberal member of
Parliament (1886-1918, 1920-24), Home Secretary (1892-95),
Chancellor of the Exchequer (1905-08), and Prime Minister
(1908-1916).

ASSIOUT--(Alex I, 3)--Also called Asyut.   A city on the left
bank of the Nile noted for its pottery, and ornamental wood
and ivory work.   It is the probable birthplace of Plotinus
(q. v.).

ASSOUAN--(PP-Ph)--Aswan.   The location of a dam in
Egypt.   It was a popular health resort with modern hotels.
There are ruins of a temple built by Ptolemy III Euergetes
(q. v.).

AT THE DOOR IN THE GATE--(AH-Reid)--A novel (1915) by
Forrest Reid (q. v.).

ATHANASIUS, ST.--(Alex I, 2; PP-Clement)--A.D. 293?-
373.   Called the Great, he is known as the father of the
Greek Church.   He was the life-long foe of Arianism (q.v.),
controversialist, and early student of theology.   He attended
the Council of Nicaea (q.v.), (325) as a deacon, and became
a Patriarch of Alexandria (328-373).   As such, he refused
the command of the emperor to reinstate Arius.   He was
tried by the Council of Tyre (325) and exiled to Germany,
but was allowed to return to Alexandria (337) only to be
exiled again by Constantius (q.v.).   He found asylum with
Pope Julius I and was vindicated by the Western Council at
Sadica.   He returned to Alexandria and worked in peace for
ten years.   He was exiled a third time during which time he
wrote many books.   He returned and was exiled and returned
to Alexandria two more times.   He finished his life in Alexandria.   Though it bears his name, The Athanasian Creed is
not his composition.

ATHENE--(AH-Mac)--In Greek myth the goddess of wisdom
and of the arts and sciences.   She was the patroness of
Athens and the owl is sacred to her.   Her Roman counterpart is Minerva.

ATHOL, DUKE OF--(MT)--Forster refers most probably to
Sir John James Hugh Henry Stewart-Murray (1840-1917) 7th
duke of Athol (Atholl or Athole).

AUDEN, W. H.--(Two Cheers-Ascent; Two Cheers-Enchanted;
Two Cheers-Indian; Two Cheers-Outsider; Two Cheers-Vir-
ginia)--Full name: Wystan Hugh Auden, (1907-).   An
American (though English born) poet educated at Oxford.
Frequent collaborator with Christopher Isherwood (q.v.).
His many volumes include Poems (1930), Another Time
(1940), The Double Man (1941).

AUGUSTINE, ST.--(Two Cheers-Augustine; Two Cheers-
Book)--A.D. 354-430.   Early Christian church father and
philosopher.   Originally a Manichaean (q.v.), he was converted to Christianity through the prayers of his mother, St.
Monica.   He became Bishop of Hippo (396-430), and exercised great influence on the Christian world through his
writings.   He fought against heresies.   His most famous
works are The City of God and his confessions.

AUGUSTUS--(AH-Mac; AH-Salute)--Original name before
adoption by Julius Caesar: Gaius Octavianus; after adoption:
Gaius Julius Caesar Octavianus, 63 B.C.-A.D. 14.   The

first Roman emperor (27 B. C. -A. D. 14). Son of Octavius
and Attia, the daughter of Julius Caesar's youngest sister,
Julia. He was carefully educated and adopted by his great
uncle as his son and heir. After Caesar's death, he and
Antony (q. v.) defeated Brutus and Cassius at Phillipi and
received Italy as the portion of his spoils. His sister, Octavia, married Antony. The rivalry with Antony was settled when Antony was defeated at the battle of Actium (31
B. C.). The senate conferred on him the title "Augustus"
(exalted, sacred) in 27 B. C. He inaugurated reforms and
beneficial laws, and made his stepson, Tiberius, his heir.
He extended the empire by conquering Spain, Pannonia, Dalmatia, and Gaul. His reign marked the golden age of literature. He married three times and met with domestic difficulties, especially with his daughter Julia whom he banished
for her excesses. He also suffered because he had no son
and because his nephew, grandsons, and favorite stepson,
Drusus, all died young.

AURANGZEBE--(AH-Mosque)--Aurungzeb or Aurungzebe,
1618-1707. He was the 6th emperor of Hindustan (1658-
1707) of the Mogul dynasty. He was the son of Shah Jahan
against whom he rebelled and usurped the throne. He kept
his father imprisoned at Agra fort and caused the death of
his three brothers. He assumed the title of Alamagir, (q. v.)
(i. e. , ruler of the world).

AUSTEN, CAROLINE--(AH-JA)--1805- . One of the nieces
of Jane Austen (q. v.) and the author of My Aunt, Jane Austen. London: Alton, 1952.

AUSTEN, JANE--(AH-JA; AH-Notes; Aspects I; GLD II; MT;
Two Cheers-English; Two Cheers-Fo; Two Cheers-In; Two
Cheers-Raison)--1775-1817. An English novelist noted for
her portraits, delicately satiric, of the country gentry of
her time. Her best known novel is Pride and Prejudice
(1813), though she is the author of five other novels: Sense
and Sensibility (1811); Mansfield Park (1814); Emma (1816);
Northanger Abbey, and Persuasion (1818).

AUSTERLITZ--(Collect Ta-Coord)--A town in Moravia,
Czechoslovakia which was the scene of a battle on December
2, 1805 between the French under Napoleon (q. v.) and those
allied against him (Russia and Austria) under Kutuzov. It
was a victory for the French, thus terminating the third coalition against France.

AUTOBIOGRAPHY--(AH-Capt)--By Edward Gibbon.   It was
pieced together by his friend, Lord Sheffield, from various
fragments and first published in 1796.

AXIS--(Two Cheers-Ter)--The coalition formed chiefly by
Germany, Italy, and Japan in World War II which fought
against the Allies (chiefly the U.S., Great Britain, France,
and Russia).

AZIZ--(GLD XIV; PI II)--A young, sensitive Moslem doctor
and one of the central figures in Forster's Passage to India.
His original is Syed Ross Masood (q.v.).

B

BABBITT--(AH-Sin)--The chief character in the novel Babbitt (1922) by Sinclair Lewis (q.v.).   He is a prosperous
real estate dealer in Zenith, a typical American city in the
midwest, and a product of modern America and its ideals:
success and the accumulation of material possessions.   He
begins to question these ideals when his best friend, Paul
Riesling, shoots his wife and is sent to prison.   Babbitt has
a love affair with a client and mixes with her Bohemian
friends.   He refuses to join the Good Citizen's League.   But
the pressures of public opinion are too much for him and
his brief revolt against convention collapses.   He returns to
his old life.

BABUR--(AH-Marco; PI XIV)--Baber or Babar (i.e., "Tiger").
The Mongol nickname of Zahir ud-Din Muhammed, 1483-1530.
The founder of the Mogul dynasty of India and emperor 1526-
1530.   He was a descendant of Tamerlane (q.v.) and Genghis
Khan (q.v.).   He succeeded (1495) to his father's kingdom
of Fergana (q.v.); conquered Samarkand (1497); lost both
kingdoms (1501); crossed Hindu Kush and besieged and captured Kabul (1504); attempted to conquer Samarkand but was
completely defeated by the Uzbeks (1514).   He made raids
into India (1519-1524) and led a small army across the Indus
(1525).   In 1526 he defeated a much larger army of Ibrahim
Lodi, Afghan sultan at Panipat.   He occupied Delhi and Agra
and established the Mogul Empire.   He defeated the Hindus
in a second great battle (1527) near Agra.   He extended his
power to the east and began to organize his new realm only
to die in 1530.

BABYLON--(PP-Ph)--An ancient city, now in ruins, on the Euphrates River about 55 miles S of Baghdad.

BACCHAE, THE--(GLD VIII)--A tragedy by the Greek playwright Euripedes (q.v.). It is, essentially, a study of religious intoxication and the excesses such intoxication lead to.   Bacchus (q.v.), who has returned from India to his home in Thebes, finds King Pentheus determined to abolish the wild rites of the Bacchantes whom his mother Agave leads.   Angered, Bacchus slyly encourages Pentheus in his plan.   Pentheus searches the forests for the revellers only to meet his mother who mistakes him for a wild beast.   She tears him to pieces and Bacchus is revenged.   The play has had many versions, the latest of which, Dionysus in '69, was performed in one of New York's off-Broadway theatres.

BACCHUS--See: Dionysus.

BACH--(AH-Word; GLD IX; Two Cheers-Raison; Two Cheers-Virginia)--Johann Sebastian Bach, 1685-1750.   A German composer of high repute during his day as an organist.   His reputation as a composer is largely posthumous, the result of a 19th-century revival of his music.   He was born at Eisenbach and studied under his brother.   He held the post of organist in various cities.   In 1723, he was appointed Cantor (music director) of St. Thomas's Church in which position he died after becoming blind.   He married twice and fathered 20 children, several of whom became composers.   He wrote nearly 300 church cantatas (e.g., "The St. John Passion," "The St. Matthew Passion"), and many other works.

BACON, FRANCIS--(LJ X; Reading)--1561-1626.   He was an English philosopher, writer and statesman appointed Lord Chancellor under James I.   He also conducted philosophic and scientific experiments and was violently opposed to reasoning from authority and argued for clarity of observation as the basis of knowledge.   The larger part of his writings are in Latin.   The Advancement of Learning (1605), Novum Organum (1620), New Atlantis (1624), are among his most important works.   He is, perhaps, better known for a series of essays published 1597, 1612, 1625.

BADEN-POWELL, LORD--(Two Cheers-Last)--Robert Stephenson Smyth, 1st Baron Baden-Powell of Gilwell (1857-1941). He was a soldier who commanded the Ashanti levies.   He held Mafeking through its 215-day siege by the Boers until relieved (1900). He was made a lieutenant general in 1908, inaugurated the boy scouts in the same year and, with his sister, the girl guides in 1910. He is the author of many works on military tactics.

BAEDEKER--(AH-Mac; Collect Ta-Eternal; RWV I; WAFT I)-- Karl Baedeker, 1801-1859. He was a German publisher of travelers' guidebooks popularly called "Baedekers." They are generally exhaustive listings of a regions' "sights" with appropriate bits of history and descriptions. He established a book business in Coblenz and his first guide was to Coblenz (1829). This modest beginning was followed by a veritable avalanche of guides to other European countries as well as the rest of the world.

BALDER--(Aspects VII; PI XXIV)--In Scandinavian myth he was the son of Odin and Frigg. He is the god of light and is the central figure in many myths the most important of which are connected with his death. He is said to have been murdered by his rival, Hödr, while fighting for the beautiful Nanna. Another story has it that Frigg bound all things by solemn oath not to harm her son, but omitted the mistletoe thinking it harmless; with an arrow made of mistletoe Loki, the god of evil, induced Hoth [Hödr], Balder's blind brother, to unwillingly shoot and kill Balder, not the first nor the last to meet death by that most fatal plant. His death was the prelude to the final overthrow of the gods.

BALDERSTONE, CALEB--(Aspects IV)--A character in The Bride of Lammermoor (q. v.) by Sir Walter Scott (q. v.), he is Edgar Ravenswood's devoted servant who liked to speak of the ancient glory of the Ravenswood clan. To support his master, he made foraging expeditions to the village to secure food.

BALDOVINETTI, ALESSO--(RWV V)--1425?1499. A Florentine artist who is especially known for his frescoes in the Church of Santa Tinità, Florence.

"BALLAD OF SIR PATRICK SPENS"--(Two Cheers-Anon)-- A Scotch ballad written on the exploits of a hero, Sir Patrick Spens, who was sent on a dangerous mission to Norway in the dead of winter. On the way home, his ship was wrecked and all were lost.

BALMORAL--(Two Cheers-Eng)--A castle in Scotland built by Prince Albert (q. v.), the consort of Queen Victoria (q. v.).

He chose to employ a Victorian-cum-Scottish Gothic style.
It still remains the royal residence in the summer, probably
without the miles of tartans with which it once was decorated
in Victoria's day.

BANKS, SIR JOSEPH--(Two Cheers-George)--1743-1820.   An
English naturalist who accompanied Cook's expedition around
the world (1768-71) in the ship, Endeavour, which he equipped
out of his own pocket.   He also visited the Hebrides and
Iceland.   He was president of the Royal Society (1778-1820)
and aided the settlement of New South Wales.   His library
and collections are now in the British Museum (q. v.).

BANKS, WILLIAM (MR. BANKS)--(Two Cheers-Virginia)--A
character in the novel To the Lighthouse by Virginia Woolf
(q. v.).   He is a botanist and the oldest friend of Prof.
Ramsey (q. v.).   He is an angry widower who first comes
to visit the Ramseys out of a sense of duty, but remains on,
enraptured with life.   He is the object of the affections of
Lady Briscoe.

BARCHESTER TOWERS--(AH-Salute)--A novel by Anthony
Trollope (q. v.), published 1857.   It is the second novel in
the Barsetshire series and a sequel to The Warden, the
first.   When the Archbishop dies, Archdeacon Grantly, his
son, hopes to succeed him, but a change in the government
blocks his hopes and Dr. Proudie receives the appointment.
Mrs. Proudie is a formidable lady who rules her husband
and through him his domain with a firm hand.   The Proudies
give a party which includes Canon Stanhope and his rather
eccentric children who have just returned from Italy.   The
Canon has returned seeking a match for his son, Bertie,
with the widowed daughter of Dr. Harding, Eleanor Bold.
She, however, prefers the Rev. Arabin.   Obediah Slope,
chaplain to the Archbishop and a protégé of Mrs. Proudie,
also has his eye on Eleanor while courting Canon Stanhope's
daughter.   Slope has been hoping to be appointed to the lu-
crative position once held by Dr. Harding at the Hospital.
When Mrs. Proudie hears of his courting, he is dismissed,
but Dr. Harding is not reinstated.   The position goes to the
Rev. Quiverful who has 14 children.

BARING, SIR EVELYN--See: Lord Cromer.

BARNES, WILLIAM--(Two Cheers-William B)--1801-1886.
An English poet, philologist, clergyman, and master of a
Dorchester boys' school.   He is most famous for his poetry

in the dialect of Dorsetshire. His poetry, according to
Giles Dugdale, his editor, still attracts the study of poets
for its "infinite metrical variety and verbal purity of his
verse." Barnes was also deeply interested in philology and
produced several studies in that area. His biography has
been written by his daughter, Lucy Baxter (1893) and Coventry Patmore (1893). The latest collection of his verse was
made by Giles Dugdale: Poems Grave and Gay (1949).

BARRETT, ELIZABETH--(Two Cheers-Snow)--1806-1861.
She was born Elizabeth Moulton. Barrett was the name assumed by her father when he succeeded to the estate in
Jamaica. She read Homer (q.v.) in Greek at the age of
eight and, during her lifetime wrote many poems. At the
age of 15 she was injured when thrown from her horse and
remained a semi-invalid almost to the time of her marriage
(1846) to Robert Browning (q.v.). Nevertheless, she always
remained delicate. The couple chose to settle in Florence
where she became passionately interested in the struggle of
the Florentines for freedom. As a result she produced Casa
Guidi Windows (1851). She also wrote, on a different subject, Aurora Leigh (1856), a "novel" in verse, and Sonnets
from the Portuguese (1850), perhaps her most famous work.

BARRIE, SIR JAMES MATTHEW--(AH-Ron)--1860-1937.
Scottish dramatist and novelist. He is known for the whimsy
and sentimentality of his work. Perhaps his best known
plays are Quality Street (q.v.), 1902; The Admirable Crich-
ton, 1902; and Peter Pan, 1904, which has had many reviv-
als, the most recent as a musical on the New York stage.
His best known novel, The Little Minister (1891), was
dramatized in 1897.

BARROW, ISAAC--(Two Cheers-In)--1630-1677. An English
mathematician and theologian. He was the first Lucasian
professor of mathematics at Cambridge (1663) and resigned
(1669) in favor of his pupil, Isaac Newton. He is the author
of Methods of Tangents, and controversial pieces including
the posthumous Pope's Supremacy, 1680.

ST. BARTHOLOMEW'S SMITHFIELD--(Two Cheers-Lon)--
The Church of St. Bartholomew the Great. It is the oldest
church (after the chapel in the Tower) in London. The present church consists, however, of little more than the choir
of the great priory-church founded in 1123 for the Augustinian Canons.

BARTON--(AH-JA)--Barton Park: the estate of Sir John
Middleton in Jane Austen's novel, Sense and Sensibility. The
house was "large and handsome."

BASILISCUS--(PP-Tim)--d. A. D. 478. Emperor of the
Eastern Roman Empire (476-477). He was the brother-in-
law of Emperor Leo I, and was sent (468) by Leo in com-
mand of an expedition to Carthage against Genseric, the
Vandal chieftan. He was defeated. He deposed the emperor
Zeno, Leo's successor, only to be deposed by him in 477.

BAST--(Alex II, 1)--Greek: "Bubastis." The cat-goddess of
Egyptian myth, the Diana (q. v.) of the Egyptians. She is
the sister of Horus and the daughter of Isis. Her sacred
animal is the cat.

BATES, MISS--(Aspects V)--Hetty Bates. A character in
Emma (q. v.), a novel by Jane Austen (q. v.). She is the
daughter of Mrs. Bates whose husband was formerly vicar
of Highbury. Hetty is "active," talkative and helpful. She
is the aunt of Jane Fairfax.

BATOUALA--(Aspects III)--The chief character in the novel,
Batouala (1921), by Réné Maian. He is a chief of many vil-
lages in French Equatorial Africa--jealous, violent, and
vengeful. He honors Bissibingui, a young warrior, until he
becomes aware of the young man's interest in his favorite
wife. He then plots to kill him. Under the guise of friendship, the two go out hunting. Batouala hurls his spear at
the young man, but misses his target and, in turn, is torn
by the claws of a panther. As he lies dying, Bissibingui,
and Batouala's favorite yield to each other and decide to
flee.

BATTERSEA BRIDGE--(HE XV)--Located at the end of the
embankment on the Thames in the Chelsea section of London.
The bridge, an ugly iron structure (1887-90) was constructed
by Bazalgette as a replacement for the picturesque wooden
bridge of 1772 which appears in paintings by Whistler, Turner and others.

BATTERSEA RISE--(AH-Ba; MT; Two Cheers-Henry)--The
house which once belonged to Forster's maternal family. It
was razed in the 20th century. For a good description see
his essay "Battersea Rise" in Abinger Harvest.

BATTLE OF WATERLOO--See: Waterloo, Battle of.

BAUDELAIRE, CHARLES--(Two Cheers-Enchanted)--1821-
1867.   French Romantic poet and one of the first Décadents.
He was also the individual responsible for the introduction
of the works of Edgar Allan Poe to Europe.   His life reflected the Décadent pattern of debauchery, perversity, pro-
found introspection, eccentricity of conduct, and violent and
extreme moods.   He also displayed a strong attraction to
the mysticism and ritual of Roman Catholicism.   He foreshadowed the Symbolists in his poetry.   His most famous
work is Les Fleurs du Mal (1851).

BEACONSFIELD, LORD--See: Disraeli.

BEARDSLEY, AUBREY VINCENT--(AH-Ron)--1872-1899. An
English artist of the "Mauve Decade" who is famous for his
drawings on essentially erotic subjects produced chiefly as
illustrations for The Yellow Book and other periodicals and
books of the 1890's.

BEATRICE--(AH-Marco; LJ IX; Two Cheers-Raison)--Bice
Portinari, 1266-1290.   The wife of Simone dei Bardi, a
Florentine nobleman.   Dante (q.v.) immortalized her (and
called her "Beatrice" to signify her beatitude) because of his
love for her, in two of his works: La Vita Nuova and La
Divina Commedia.

BEATRIX--(Aspects IV)--Beatrix Esmond.   A character in
the novel, Henry Esmond (1852) by Thackeray (q.v.).   She
is the beautiful daughter of the Castlewoods whom Henry
fancies he loves until he discovers her true nature.

BEAUCHAMP--(Aspects V)--Nevil Beauchamp.   A character
in the novel, Beauchamp's Career (1874-5) by George Meredith (q.v.).   He is a young man burning to reform the
world.   A naval officer, he decides to leave the navy and
run for Parliament as a Liberal.   He has fallen in love with
the sister of a French officer whom he has rescued.   She
rejects him, to marry a man her father has chosen for her.
After another abortive love affair, he marries the woman
who has nursed him through an illness.   He loses the election and dies by drowning while trying to rescue a child.

BEAUCHAMP'S CAREER--(Aspects V)--A novel (1874-1875)
by Meredith (q.v.).   See: Beauchamp.

BEAUMONT AND FLETCHER--(Two Cheers-Jul)--Francis
Beaumont, 1584-1616; and John Fletcher, 1579-1625. They
were Elizabethan dramatists and joint authors of many plays,
among the more popular of which are The Maid's Tragedy
(1611), Philaster (1611), and The Knight of the Burning Pes-
tle (1609). After Beaumont's death, Fletcher wrote several
other dramas, and is said to have collaborated with Shakespeare on Henry VIII.

BECKFORD, WILLIAM--(Aspects VI)--1760-1844. An English
novelist and art collector, his most famous work is Vathek,
1782, a Gothic novel which he wrote in French. He spent a
large part of his life in his magnificent home, "Fronthill,"
and expended large sums on its decoration. He is also the
author of travel sketches.

BED OF PROCUSTES--(Aspects VIII)--In Greek legend, Procustes was a bandit of Attica who was in possession of an
iron bed on which he placed all who fell into his hands. If
the individual were too short for the bed, he would have him
stretched to fit. If the captive were too long, his legs would
be chopped off to fit. Now, the phrase "to be stretched on
the bed of Procustes" has come to mean any individual who
must tailor his thinking, especially about humanity, to fit
pre-conceived notions.

BEELZEBUB--(GLD X)--From Hebrew: "lord [Baal] of the
flies [bub]" or "of filth [bul]." The Baal originally worshipped in Ekron and then in Palestine and adjacent countries.
To the Jews, he became the chief representative of the false
gods. In Matthew xii, 24, he is the "prince of devils."

BEERBOHM, MAX--(AH-Salute; AH-Ron; Aspects VI; Two
Cheers-Eng)--An English author, critic, and caricaturist
known for his satire and parody, perhaps Beerbohm's best
known works are Zuleika Dobson (1911), a satirical novel
about Oxford, and A Christmas Garland (1912), a group of
caricatures of personalities of the day.

BEETHOVEN--(AH-Our D; AH-Word; Collect Ta-Co-ord; GLD
V; RWV III; Two Cheers-Clouds; Two Cheers-Not Listening;
Two Cheers-Romain)--Ludwig van Beethoven, 1770-1827. A
German composer and a student of Haydn, he is most noted
for adding to the traditions of formality of the music of the
18th century the emotional qualities of Romanticism. He
wrote nine symphonies which are, perhaps, his best known
works. He had many love affairs, but never married. By

1801 he showed signs of the condition which grew quickly to total deafness. [See below.]

BEETHOVEN'S FIFTH SYMPHONY--(Aspects VIII; HE V; Two Cheers-C)--This symphony in C minor, Opus 67, was composed 1805-1807 and dedicated to Prince Lobkowitz and Count Rasumovsky; it was published in 1809.

BEETHOVEN'S NINTH SYMPHONY--(Two Cheers-Raison)--This symphony in D minor, Opus 125, has a choral last movement.   The text is Schiller's ode 'Adie Freude,' "Freude, schöner Gotterfünken."   It was dedicated to Frederick William III of Prussia, composed in 1817-1823 and published in 1826.

BEETHOVEN'S SEPTET--(Two Cheers-Raison)--The septet in E flat major, Opus 20, for clarinet, horn, bassoon, violin, viola, cello, and double bass was composed 1799-1800 and dedicated to Empress Maria Theresa.

BEETHOVEN'S SEVENTH SYMPHONY--(Two Cheers-Not Listening)--This symphony in A major, Opus 92 (1812) was dedicated to Count von Fries and published 21 December 1816.

"BEFORE, A JOY PROPOSED, BEHIND, A DREAM."--(AH-My Wood)--Line 12 of Sonnet 129 by William Shakespeare (q. v.).

BELFAST--(AH-Reid)--A seaport in Northern Ireland and one of the chief shipbuilding centers of the world.

BELINDA--(Aspects VI)--The "heroine" of the mock-heroic epic poem by Alexander Pope, The Rape of the Lock.

BELL, CLIVE--(AH-Proust)--1881-1964.   An English critic who married Vanessa Stephen, the sister of Virginia Woolf (q. v.).   He became one of the "Bloomsbury Group" of writers and artists which clustered about Virginia and her husband, Leonard Woolf (q. v.).   Bell wrote critical articles for The New Statesman and Nation.   He believed in the complete separation of art from life.   Like the Woolfs, he was a friend of E. M. Forster.   For a better understanding of Bell's place in the Bloomsbury Group see J. K. Johnstone's, The Bloomsbury Group, New York: The Noonday Press, 1954.

BELL, JULIAN--(GLD XIV)--Son of Clive Bell (q. v.).   He was a poet, the author of We Did Not Fight (1935) and Work

for the Winter (1936).   He was wounded fatally while driving
an ambulance for the Loyalists in the Spanish Civil War.

BELL AND LANCASTER--(MT)--Alexander Melville Bell
(1819-1905), father of Alexander Graham Bell and an authori-
ty·on phonetics; and Joseph Lancaster (1778-1838).   Educa-
tionalists whose conflicting theories were espoused by teachers in England in the 19th century.   The Lancasterian system of education (in part the use of older boys as monitors
to oversee and instruct) was widely adopted by nonconform-
ists in competition with Bell's system supported by the
Church of England.

BELLINI--(AS; WAFT VII)--A Venetian family of painters including: Iacopo (c. 1400-c. 1470), the founder, and father-in-
law of Mantegna.   One son, Gentile (1429?-1507) was the
official painter of the Venetian state.   He introduced oil
paints in Venetian murals.   The other son, Giovanni (1430?-
1516) was the leading painter of the Venetian school.   He
was the master of Giorgione, Titian, Palma Vecchio, et al.,
and is known chiefly for his altar pieces and Madonnas.

BELLOC, HILAIRE--(AH-Wil; Two Cheers-Ascent; Two
Cheers-Eng; Two Cheers-Jew)--Joseph Hillaire Pierre Belloc, 1870-1953.   An English writer, born in France, author
of biographies, histories, essays, fiction, light verse, etc.
He was a staunch Roman Catholic, and described his conversion in The Path to Rome (1902).   He wrote biographies
of Richelieu, Cardinal Wolsey, James II, Napoleon, and
Marie Antoinette, among others.   His father was a French
barrister; his mother was English.   His overt anti-Semitism
was one element which cut short a career in Parliament.

BELSON, PIERRE--(Alex I, 4)--1517-1564.   French natura-
list and mapmaker.   The author of L'Histoire Naturelle des
Étranges Poissons Marines and L'Histoire de la Nature des
Oyseaux.

BENARES--(AH-Adrift; Hill)--Former name for Varanasi, or
Banaras.   A city on the Ganges River 400 miles WNW of
Calcutta and one of India's most ancient and most holy cities.
It is sacred to Hindus as well as to Jains, Sikhs, and Budd-
hists.

BENES, EDUARD--(Nordic)--1884-1948.   A Czechoslovak
statesman and disciple of Jan Masaryk with whom he worked
in the Czech nationalist movement (1915-19) in Paris.   He

became foreign minister of the new state (1918-35), prime minister (1921-22), and lecturer in the University of Prague, 1922-38. He became President of Czechoslovakia, 1935, but resigned in 1938 when the Germans occupied the Sudatenland, and went into exile. He returned in March 1945, and was re-elected President in 1946. He died in 1948.

BENNET, MR. --(AH-JA)--A character in Pride and Prejudice, a novel by Jane Austen (q.v.). He is the father of the Bennet girls: a mildly eccentric and mildly sarcastic small landowner. He is rather indifferent to his family save for his daughter, Elizabeth, whom he admires.

BENNET, MRS. --(LJ IX)--A character in Pride and Prejudice, a novel by Jane Austen (q.v.). She is the wife of Mr. Bennet and, though fussy and overly concerned with matchmaking for her unmarried daughters, genuinely has the good of her children at heart. She has a strong desire to see them well-married.

BENNETT, ARNOLD--(AH-Early; AH-JA; AH-Sin; Aspects II; Two Cheers-English; Two Cheers-London)--1867-1931. Enoch Arnold Bennett. An English journalist turned novelist, playwright. He is perhaps best known for his novel, The Old Wives' Tale (1908), and the Clayhanger series of novels. He was an extremely prolific writer, and abandoned law for writing.

BENTHAM, JEREMY--(GLD X)--1748-1783. An English Utilitarian philosopher. His motto was "The greatest good for the greatest number." He tried to work out scientifically, on a quantitative scale, the values of pleasure and pain in terms of moral motivation.

BERENICE--(Aspects V)--A dramatic tragedy (1670) by Racine (q.v.), in which the Roman emperor Titus is in love with the queen of Palestine, Berenice, who is also loved by Antiochus, King of Commagene.

BERENICE II--(Alex I, 1)--The cousin and wife of Ptolemy III Eugenetes (q.v.). She is sometimes surnamed "of Cyrene." She vowed to sacrifice her hair to the gods if her husband returned home the conqueror of Asia. He did. She suspended her hair in the temple of Arisone at Zephyiun, but it was stolen the first night. Legend had it that it was wafted to heaven and became the comet now called Coma Berenices.

BERENSEN, BERNARD--(GLD XIV)--1865-1959. American
art critic and author. He was born in Lithuania, the son of
a poor Jewish family and took his A. B. (1887) from Harvard.
He traveled in Europe on a stipend supplied by Mrs. Stewart
Gardner of Boston for whom he helped to form the art collection now housed on the Fenway in her former mansion.
He married (1900) Mary Logan Smith Costelloe. He is recognized as one of the greatest connoisseurs of Italian Renaissance art, and is the author of many volumes among which
are Venetian Painters of the Renaissance (1894) and Essays
in Medieval Art (1930).

BERENSON, MARY--(GLD XIV)--See: Bernard Berenson.

BERESFORD, LORD CHARLES--(Alex I, 5)--Charles William
de la Poer, (created 1st Baron Beresford in 1916), 1846-
1919. A British naval officer, born in Ireland, he took part
in the bombardment of Alexandria (1882) and the Nile expedition (1884-85). He was a firm advocate of a large navy
during a long career in Parliament and was created a full-
admiral in 1906. He wrote a Life of Nelson and His Times
(1898-1905).

BERETON, CLARA--(AH-JA)--A character in Jane Austen's
(q. v.) fragmentary novel, Sanditon. She is talented, good-
looking, and not wholly trustworthy.

BERGSON, HENRI--(GLD XI)--1859-1941. A French philosopher born in Paris, he was appointed professor at the College de France (1900), and had a wide influence and popularity in the years before World War I. He was awarded
the Nobel Prize for literature, 1927. His system of philosophy dwells on the anti-rational and the mystical and favors
intuition over rational and scientific methods. He held that
change or movement is the source of all reality, that the
past and present are inseparable. These views serve as
the framework for Proust's (q. v.) Remembrance of Things
Past (q. v.). Bergson's most famous work is perhaps his
L'Evolution Creatrice (1907) generally translated as Creative
Evolution.

BERGSONIANISM--(GLD XI)--See: Henri Bergson.

BERKELEY--(GLD X)--There are several English clergymen
of that name, but Forster is most probably referring to
George Berkeley (1685-1753) who was born in Ireland and
was one of the most important members of the school of

philosophy called Idealism.   He held that objects do not
exist in reality, but only in the mind.   His chief works are
Principles of Human Knowledge (1710) and Essay Toward a
New Theory of Vision (1709).   Stewart Ansell and Rickie
discuss his theories in the opening section of Where Angels
Fear to Tread.

BERLIOZ--(Two Cheers-Romain)--Louis Hector Berlioz,
1803-1869.   A French composer of music, he is noted as a
pioneer of modern orchestration and a creator of program
music.   He has also written operas.   Some of his works
are Symphonie Fantastique, Romeo et Juliette, La Damnation
de Faust.

BERNARD--(GLD XIV; Two Cheers-Virginia)--A character in
Virginia Woolf's (q. v.) novel, The Waves (1931).   He is the
phrase-maker, the chronicler of the group of childhood
friends as they grope toward death.   All the characters in
the book see life through him.

BERSAGLIERI--(WAFT II)--From Ital. bersaglio, "a target":
literally "targeteers" or "marksmen."   Historically, the
selected light infantry of the Italian army, the group was
founded by Charles Albert in the old Kingdom of Sardinia
(Piedmont) under the inspiration of Alessandro Ferrere della
Marmora in 1836.   They played an important role in the
campaign of 1848-49.   By the time of the Crimean War, the
corps was increased to ten batallions, and in the subsequent
wars of the Risorgimento they distinguished themselves.
Great emphasis was placed on rigorous physical training and
by 1914 they were famous not only for their beautiful plumed
hats, but also as some of the most rapid marchers in the
world.   After WWI, they were converted into cyclist units,
and after WWII they were mechanized and their function became that of armored infantry.

BERTOLINI, THE--(RWV I)--The hotel in which Lucy Honeychurch and Charlotte Bartlett stay in Florence.   It is most
probably the present-day Hotel Berchielli also located on the
Arno (Lung'arno Acciaioli) and in a position to afford the
splendid view which the two women craved.

BERTRAM, JULIA--(Aspects IV)--A character in Mansfield
Park, a novel by Jane Austen (q.v.).   She is the younger
daughter of Sir Thomas and Lady Bertram.

BERTRAM, LADY--(Aspects IV; MT)--A character in Mansfield Park, a novel by Jane Austen (q. v.). She was born
Maria Ward of Huntingdon. She is a woman of very languid
feelings and a temper remarkably easy and indolent.

BERTRAM, MARIA--(Aspects IV)--A character in Mansfield
Park by Jane Austen (q. v.). She is the elder daughter of
Sir Thomas and Lady Bertram.

BERTRAM, SIR THOMAS--(AH-JA; Aspects IV)--A character
in Mansfield Park, he is a dignified baronet, the owner of
Mansfield Park. He is reserved, fundamentally kind and
just, but too remote from his children. He is angered by
Fanny Price's refusal to marry Henry Crawford.

BES--(AH-Our Div; Alex II, 1)--In Egyptian myth, he is
associated with birth; he is also a god of marriage and presided over the toilette of women. He appears as a robust,
bestial dwarf with a large head, huge eyes, and prominent
cheeks. He has a hairy chin and an enormous tongue hangs
from his wide-open mouth. Often, he wears a headdress of
feathers and a leopard skin, the tail of which falls behind
him. His image is often carved into the handles of women's
mirrors. He is also considered a protector against the evil
eye.

BESS, OUR GLORIOUS QUEEN--(AH-AB)--See: Elizabeth I.

BESSARION--(AH-Gem)--Johannes or Basilius Bessarion. He
was a 15th-century Roman Catholic prelate and Greek scholar, and the Archbishop of Nicaea (1437). He strove for the
union of the Greek and Roman Churches, and supported the
Roman Church in the Councils of Ferrara and Florence. He
was made a cardinal (1439), and Latin Patriarch of Constantinople (1463). He collected a large library of Greek works
and presented it to Venice where it formed the nucleus of
the Library of St. Mark.

BETJEMAN, JOHN--(Two Cheers-Outsider)--b. 1906. An
English poet whose work, while reflecting the contemporary
scene with perceptive wit, is cast in traditional forms. His
books of verse include: Mount Zion (1933), A Few Late
Chrysanthemums (1954) Collected Poems (1958). He has
also written an autobiography in verse, Summoned by Bells
(1960), and is credited with inspiring a revival of interest
and enthusiasm for Victorian architecture.

BETWEEN THE ACTS--(Two Cheers-Virginia)--The last
novel of Virginia Woolf (q. v.), published posthumously in
1941.   It takes place in a remote village in the heart of
England on one night and the next day in June, 1939.   It
treats of a performance of a pageant depicting the history of
England.

BEWICK--(Two Cheers-In)--Given name: Thomas, 1753-1828.
An Englishman who restored wood engraving to popularity.
He illustrated many books among which is The History of
English Birds, the volume most likely owned by Forster and
described by him in the essay.   Bewick also illustrated, with
his brother, Gay's Fables, and with his son, The Fables of
Aesop.

BHAGAVAD-GITA--(AH-Hymn; PI XVIII)--An Indian (Hindu)
philosophical poem consisting of a dialogue between Arjuna
(q. v.) and the god, Krishna (q. v.) concerning life, death,
and the soul.

BHILS--(PI XX)--A primitive tribal people of West Central
India who speak an austric language.

BHOPAL--(PI XXVII)--A former princely state of Central
India now a part of the Republic of India; also a city, 360
miles S of New Delhi.

BICKERSTAFFE, ISAAC--(Two Cheers-Stratford)--c. 1735-
c. 1812.   An Irish playwright and author of comedies.   He
was also a musical composer having produced comic operas
and oratorios among which is "Judith" mentioned in the essay by Forster.   The name was also popular as a pen name.
It was used by Jonathan Swift, Richard Steele, and Benjamin
West.

BIG BEN--(Two Cheers-Virginia)--The name given to the
largest bell in the clock tower at the Houses of Parliament,
London.   It was cast in 1856 and named after Sir Benjamin
Hall, then chief commissioner of works.

BIJAPUR--(PI XIV)--Bejapur.   A town in India SE of Bombay.   It was the capital (1489) of one of the five Mohammedan Kingdoms of the Deccan, and has numerous Mohammedan
ruins, large mosques and palaces, and other buildings in the
Islamic style.   It was conquered by Aurangzeb (q. v.) in 1686,
and taken by the British in 1818.

BILLINGSGATE--(LJ VII; Two Cheers-Lon)--Originally a
gate of the walled city of London (named after the Billings,
the royal race of the Varinians), it became the site of a
fish market whose stall-owners, often women, were famous
for their vulgar language.

BILLY BUDD--(Aspects VII)--A novel (1924) by Herman Melville (q. v.); for a good summary see Forster's Aspects of
the Novel, Chapter VII.

BIRDS, THE--(GLD V)--A comic play (414 B. C.) by Aristophanes (q. v.) which pokes uproarius fun at the political spec-
ulations rife among the Athenians during their campaign
against Sicily.

BIRKENHEAD--(AH-Voters)--Frederick Edwin Smith, 1st
Earl of Birkenhead, 1872-1930. An English conservative
politician and lawyer, he held a number of government posts
including that of attorney general, lord chancellor, and secretary of state for India.

BISMARCK--(GLD XIV)--Otto Eduard Leopold Prince von
Bismarck and duke of Lauenburg, 1815-1898. Known as the
"Iron Chancellor, " he was largely responsible for the establishment of the German Empire in 1871. He served as
its first chancellor.

BIRTH OF VENUS--(RWV IV)--A painting by Botticelli (q. v.)
probably completed after 1478. It was originally planned,
with the "Allegory of Spring" ("La Primavera") as a Neo-
Platonic allegory.

BISHOP, THE--(Two Cheers-Three)--A character in "The
Three Hermits" by Leo Tolstoy (q. v.). He is scandalized
to discover the ignorance of the three hermits.

BIZET--(Two Cheers-George)--Alexandre César Léopold
Bizet (called Georges), 1838-1875. A French composer of
operas and other musical compositions. He is best known
as the composer of the opera Carmen (1875).

BJØRNSON, BJØRNSTJERNE--(AH-Ibsen)--1832-1910. A
Norwegian playwright, poet, and novelist. His first major
play was Between the Battles (Mellem slagene) in 1857.
Beyond Our Power (1883) is considered his finest play.

"BLACKBIRDS SING AND I SEE NO END OF AGONY, THE"
--(Two Cheers-Outsider)--Line 3 of the poem, "Men Walk
Upright, " by Kenneth Alliott (q. v.), as reprinted in Poets of
the Present, edited by Geoffrey Grigson, p. 31-34.

BLACKPOOL--(Two Cheers-Does)--A famous seaside resort
near Liverpool, England.

BLACKFRIARS BRIDGE--(Two Cheers-London)--A bridge in
London which marks the end of the Victoria Embankment. It
leads across the Thames to Southwark.

BLAKE, WILLIAM--(AH-Our Div; GLD XIV; LJ VI; Two
Cheers-Edward; Two Cheers-En; Two Cheers-Eng; Two
Cheers-Lon; Two Cheers-They)--1757-1827. A poet and
water-colorist, from youth he was subject to visions of a
prophetic nature. He was apprenticed to James Basire, an
important engraver of the period, and studied at the Royal
Academy (q. v.). His finest artistic work is considered to
be his illustrations for the Book of Job, and Songs of Innocence (1789) and Songs of Experience (1794), are, perhaps,
his best known poetical works. His poetry is marked by a
simplicity which arises from an intensity of feeling and a
directness of purpose. His subjects often deal with the
pious.

BLANC, MONT--(AH-Vo)--The highest mountain (15, 781 ft.)
of the Alps, it has mystical significance for a number of
poets, among them Wordsworth (q. v.). Beneath it is the
Mont Blanc tunnel connecting Chamonix (q. v.), France with
Courmayeur, Italy. It is the longest vehicular tunnel in the
world (1970).

BLANCHARD, EDWARD--(Two Cheers-Madan)--The Edward
Blanchard that Forster refers to could be Edward Litt Laman
Blanchard, an Englishman, 1820-1889. He is the author of
many children's books and Christmas pantomimes (e. g.,
Beauty and the Beast, 1869, and The Children in the Wood,
1872), as well as a Description of the Watering Places of
England (n. d.).

BLANCHARD, EMILE--(Two Cheers-Madan)--Forster does
not distinguish between the two individuals who bear the
given name, Emile. There is Emile Blanchard (1819-1900)
a naturalist, and Emile Théophile Blanchard (1797-?) author
of a number of works on the properties of color.

BLANCHARD, FRANK NELSON--(Two Cheers-Madan)--Author of a number of volumes on snakes including A Key to the Snakes of the United States, Canada, and Lower California, New York, Macmillan, 1925.

BLANCHARD, LAMAN--(Two Cheers-Madan)--1804-1845.   An English journalist, poet, and essayist.   He is sometimes called Samuel.   Some of his works are Sketches from Life (1846), and an edition of George' Cruikshank's Omnibus (1842). His Poetical Works appeared in 1876.

BLANCHARD, PIERRE--(Two Cheers-Madan)--1772-1856. Author of a number of works on morality and religion including Cabinet des Enfants; ou Le Marchand de Joujoux Moraliste (1820).

BLANCHARD, SAMUEL--See: Laman Blanchard.

BLAND, HERBERT--(GLD X)--d. 1914.   With his wife, novelist Edith Nesbitt (1858-1924), he founded in England the Fabian Society (q. v.); he was also a writer on Socialist themes and a collaborator with his wife on the novel The Prophet's Mantle (1885).

BLEAK HOUSE--(Aspects IV)--A novel by Charles Dickens (q. v.), 1852.   It treats of the mysterious affairs surrounding Esther Hawdon (Esther Summerson), the illegitimate child of Lady Dedlock and Captain Hawdon.   Lady Dedlock believes that Esther is dead.   Esther, however, is the ward of Mr. Jarndyce and lives with him at Bleak House.   Lord Dedlock's lawyer learns of Lady Dedlock's secret and, when he is murdered, she is suspected.   She disappears and is later found dead.

BLOCH, ERNEST--(Nordic)--1880-1950.   Swiss born, but a naturalized American composer.   He came to the U. S. in 1916, but returned to Switzerland 1930-38.   He was a pupil of Knorr, in Frankfurt.   Much of Bloch's music has specific Jewish associations (e. g., "The Israel Symphony").   In 1923, he wrote a symphony and a piano quintet which introduced quarter tones, the musical innovation with which he is most associated.

BLOOM, LEOPOLD--(Aspects VI)--One of the principal characters in Ulysses by James Joyce (q. v.).   He is a Jewish advertising salesman who is, symbolically, the Ulysses of the title.   He yearns for a son.   His compelling

desire stems from the death of Rudy, his 11-year old child.
Bloom is cuckolded by his wife's business manager, and he
too is having an affair of his own.

BLOOM, MRS. MARION--(Aspects VI)--A principal character
in Ulysses by James Joyce (q.v.).   Marion Tweedy Bloom
(Molly) is the wife of Leopold Bloom (q.v.).   She was raised
on a military post in Gibralter.   She is a lush woman and a
second-rate concert singer who finds married life, her husband, and Dublin boring.   Her escape from dullness comes
through her affairs with men.   Her latest is with Blazes
Boylan.   Her thoughts and reverie make up the final section
of the novel.

BLOOM, MOLLY--See: Marion Bloom.

BLOOMSBURY--(AH-For the Muse; Collect Ta-Intro; Two
Cheers-Forrest; Two Cheers-Virginia)--A London district
north of New Oxford Street which consists chiefly of quiet
squares laid out in the 18th and 19th centuries.   The area
was once favored by successful merchants and professional
men.   It is now known for its small private hotels favored
by foreigners, chiefly American.   The district is the home
of the British Museum and the University of London.   In
the Twenties and Thirties of this century, a group of writers,
artists and critics gathered about Virginia and Leonard Woolf
(q.v.) who lived there and operated their press, The Hogarth
Press, from the district.   They were called the Bloomsbury
Group.

BLUCHER--(MT)--Gebhard Leberecht von Blucher, Prince
of Wahstatt, nicknamed Marschall Vorwärts ("Forwards"),
1742-1819.   He was a Prussian field marshall who served
in the war against Napoleon (q.v.) (1813).   He beseiged the
Emperor at La Rothière, and was defeated, but later (1814)
he defeated Napoleon at Laon and entered Paris.   He aided
Wellington (q.v.) at Waterloo (q.v.).   He gave his name to
a heavy boot he used on his campaigns.

BLUEBEARD--(HE XXVII)--The villain of a story ("La Barbe
Bleue") included in the collection by Charles Perrault first
printed in 1697 as Conte de Ma Mère L'Oye (Mother Goose's
Tales).   The story, however, has parallels in European,
African, and eastern folklore.   It concerns an individual who
has a blue beard and keeps the bodies of his former wives,
all of whom he has murdered, in a locked room.   The name,
Bluebeard, has become synonymous with a wife murderer.

BLUNT, WILFRED--(AH-Salute; AH-Wil)--1840-1922.   An
English poet and traveler.   After travels in the Near East
and India, he became an out-spoken enemy of imperialism
and a severe and articulate critic of the white man's exploi-
tation of native races.   He was also an active supporter of
Mohammedan and Egyptian nationalism as well as the friend
of nationalist groups in Ireland and India.   Among his many
works are Love Sonnets of Proteus (1880) and a novel in
verse (Griselda, 1892).   My Diaries (1919, 1920) were re-
viewed by Forster in his article in Two Cheers for Democracy, "Wilfred Blunt."

BO TREE OF GYA--(PI XII)--Bo Tree (Bodhi Tree) is the
name given by Buddhists of India and Ceylon to the pipal
(peepul) tree, or sacred fig.   It was beneath a tree of this
species that Buddha is traditionally to have attained enlighten
ment at Buddh Gaya (Gya) which is still the most important
site of Buddhist pilgrimage in India.

BÖCKLIN, ARNOLD--(HE IX)--He was a Swiss painter who
was best known for landscapes.   These were often executed
with grace and often contained figures from mythology.

BOEUF EN DAUBE--(Two Cheers-Virginia)--Forster notes,
in the essay, that the dish forms the center of the dinner of
union in To the Lighthouse by Virginia Woolf (q.v.), whom
he notes was an excellent cook.   The dish is essentially a
stew or casserole of beef with vegetables.   The marinade in
which the ingredients are placed is generally composed of
brandy or gin and vermouth rather than the traditional wine.
Herbs and garlic are also generally added to the marinade
and the beef and vegetables are allowed to steep in the
marinade for a number of hours before cooking.

BOER WAR--(AH-Wil; GLD XI; HE XVIII)--Official title:
The South African War or Anglo-Boer War.   The war was
fought between Great Britain and the two Boer Republics,
The South African Republic (Transvaal) and The Orange Free
State, from October 1899 to May 1902.   The conflict was
caused by Britain's determination to extend its influence
over southern Africa to prevent the encroachment of its
colonial rivals, France and Germany.   Paul Kruger, on the
other hand, the president of Transvaal, was determined to
maintain the political and economic independence of his
country.   Britain won the war and a crown colony was established in the Transvaal and Orange River Colony.   The
treaty of Vereeniging contained a provision for and a promise

of self-government which was granted to Transvaal, December 1906, and to The Orange River Colony, June 1907. Ultimately, the Union of South Africa was established in 1910.

BONAPARTE--(MT)--See: Napoleon.

BOOBY, LADY--(Aspects VI)--A character in the novel Pamela by Joseph Andrews. She is a noblewoman who is torn between her pride of class and her desire for her handsome young footman whom she tries to seduce. When he leaves her service, she retires to her estate and uses all of her influence to prevent his marriage to Fanny.

BOOK OF THE DEAD--(Two Cheers-They)--Ancient Egyptian collection of magical incantations designed to see the soul of the departed safely to the land of the dead. The collection was generally buried with the mumified body and consisted chiefly of answers to certain questions which would be asked by the proper god before the soul was permitted to pass.

BOOK OF GENESIS--(Two Cheers-Anon)--See: Genesis.

BOON--(Aspects VIII)--A novel (1915) by H. G. Wells (q.v.) in which Henry James is caricatured. Its full title gives a good idea of what it treats: Boon, The Mind of the Race, The Wild Asses of the Devil, and The Last Trump, Being a Selection from the Literary Remains of George Boon, Appropriate to the Times.

BOOTH, CHARLES--(Two Cheers-Webb)--1840-1916. An English shipowner, statistician, and social reformer. He was president of the Royal Statistical Society (1892-94).

BOREAS--(AH-Mac)--In Greek myth, the god of the north wind. He was the son of the Titan Astraeus, and of Eos (the morning). He lived in a cave of Mt. Haemus in Thrace. He was the father of Zetes and Calais who took part in the expedition of the Argonauts (q.v.). Their mother was the nymph Ortithyia.

BORGIA, RODRIGO--(WAFT V)--A member of an Italian family of Spanish origin and influential in the papacy and in Italy during the 15th and 16th centuries from the time of the election (1455) of Alfonso Borgia as Pope Calixtus III. Rodrigo was his nephew. He, in turn, became Pope Alexander VI (1492). He was, before his election, father of five children by Vannozza dei Cattanei, three of whom became infamous in their own right: Giovanni, Cesare and Lucrezia.

BORKMAN, JOHN GABRIEL--(AH-Ibsen)--See: John Gabriel
Borkman.

BORKMANS, THE--(AH-Ibsen)--See: John Gabriel Borkman.

BORROMEO, CARLO--(AH-Car)--1538-1584. Italian nobleman, churchman, and saint of the Roman Catholic Church.
He was created cardinal and archbishop of Milan (1560) and
was especially noted for his ecclesiastical reforms. He
founded the order of Oblates of Saint Ambrose (1578).

BORROW--(HE XIV)--George Borrow, 1803-1881. An English author of adventure and travel books based largely on
his personal experiences while touring Europe as a salesman
of Bibles and a correspondent for a newspaper. Perhaps his
best known works are Lavrengo (1851) and The Romany Rye
(1857).

BOSCH--(Two Cheers-Not)--Jerome Bosch (Hieronymus Bos),
1450?-1516. A Dutch painter best known for his paintings
of fantastic nightmares and of the tortures awaiting the sin-
ner in hell. He also painted religious subjects, allegories,
and genre pieces, all, however, marked or marred by his
penchant for the unnatural and distorted. His name comes
from his birthplace, Hertrogenbosch. His real name is
Hieronymus van Aken (Aeken).

BOSPHOROUS, THE--(Alex I, 2; PI XXXI)--The Bosporous
Thracius, commonly called the Bosporous (Bosphorous), is
the name given to the narrow strait between European Turkey and Asiatic Turkey. It connects the Sea of Marmara
with the Black Sea and is about 20 miles long and from one
to 2.75 miles wide.

BOSWELL--(Collect Ta-Other; MT; Two Cheers-Stratford)--
James Boswell, 1740-1795. A Scotsman best known for his
massive biography of Dr. Samuel Johnson (1791). It is
composed largely of remembered conversations, sayings,
and reported events and is considered one of the greatest
biographies. Boswell was held to be merely a reporter
but, with the appearance of his journals edited by Frederic
Pottle, his great gifts as a writer have been recognized.

BOTTICELLI--(HE XXVII)--Sandro Botticelli, 1444?-1510.
His original name was Alessandro di Mariano dei Filipepi.

He was an Italian painter born in Florence and the protégé of several Florentine families as well as of Lorenzo di Pierfrancesco de' Medici, cousin of Lorenzo de' Medici (q. v.). He helped to decorate the Sistine Chapel (q. v.), but is, perhaps, best known for his allegorical paintings "La Primavera" (Spring) and "The Birth of Venus."

BOULANGER--(AH-Wil)--Georges Ernest Jean Marie Boulanger, 1837-1891. He was a French general who served at the siege of Metz (1870) and a statesman holding several cabinet positions. He was an ardent Bonapartist and was relieved of his command (1887) for disobedience of orders. He was called the "Man on Horseback" because he often addressed the Parisian crowds from that position. The author of Boulangerism, dedicated to revenge the defeat of France by Germany in the Franco-Prussian War, he was accused of conspiracy against the government and fled into exile. He committed suicide while in exile on the Island of Jersey.

BOUNCER, MRS. --(GLD IV)--A character in Cox and Box (q. v.).

BOURGH, LADY CATHERINE--(AH-Ja)--A character in Pride and Prejudice (q. v.) by Jane Austen (q. v.). She is Darcy's aunt, haughty and domineering, and wants him to marry her daughter.

BOURNEMOUTH--(HE XIII)--A county borough, Hampshire, in SE England on the English Channel at the mouth of the Bourne, 28 miles WSW of the city of Southampton. It is a summer resort.

BOVARY, MADAME--(Aspects IV)--Emma Bovary, a character in the novel, Madame Bovary (1857) by Gustave Flaubert. She is a sentimental young lady whose dreams of romantic love are frustrated by marriage to her husband, Charles, whom she finds dull. She attempts to fulfill her dreams through extramarital affairs.

BOWEN, ELIZABETH--(Two Cheers-Eng)--An Anglo-Irish novelist who writes of the upper middle class. She has written many novels, among the most popular of which are The Heat of the Day (1949) and The Last September (1929). She has also written criticism: Collected Impressions (1950) and Why Do I Write? (1948).

BOX AND COX--(GLD IV)--A farce by J. M. Morton (1847).
It has three characters: Box, Cox, and the Landlady who
rents the same room to the two. One works by day and the
other by night. The play turns on her hopes that they will
never learn of the arrangement.

BOXERS--(GLD XIII)--A secret society formed in the closing
days of the Manchu dynasty in China (19th century) and dedicated to the annihilation of all foreigners. The society is
responsible for the Boxer Rebellion (1900) which was suppressed by a European alliance and which ultimately caused
the downfall of the dynasty. The Chinese name for the society translates as "righteous, harmonious fists." Its members were supposed to be invulnerable to bullets.

BRACKNELS, THE--(AH-Reid; Two Cheers-Fo)--Subtitled:
A Family Chronicle. This novel (1911) by Forrest Reid (q.
v.), Forster discusses in his essay, "Forrest Reid," in
Abinger Harvest.

BRADSHAW, SIR WILLIAM--(AH-Virginia)--A character in
the novel To the Lighthouse, by Virginia Woolf (q.v.). He
is a physician hungering for worldly position who, though he
devotes three-quarters of an hour to each patient, is an
apathetic doctor.

BRAHMIN--(Two Cheers-Ger)--A member of the highest
caste in Indian Hinduism, a worshipper of Brahma, and generally of the order of priests. The name was applied satiri-
cally to New England aristocrats.

BRAHMS, JOHANNES--(AH-Adrift; AH-Word; HE V; Two
Cheers-Romain)--1833-1897. A German composer known especially for the strength and sentiment of his music. In
some circles, he is regarded as the heir of Beethoven (q.v.);
in others, he is not so highly regarded. He has some four
symphonies to his credit as well as other music for orchestra.

BRAHM'S VIOLIN CONCERTO--(Two Cheers-Not Listening)--
The concerto in D major for violin and orchestra, Opus 83
(1878), dedicated to Joseph Joachim, and published in 1879.

BRAND--(AH-Ibsen)--A drama (1866) by Henrik Ibsen (q.v.).
The hero, Brand, is an idealistic peasant-priest in violent
revolt against the evil and the pettiness of conventional society.
He perishes in the ruin of his ice-church under an avalanche.

BRANDENBURG CONCERTOS--(Two Cheers-Does)--A series
of six concertos by Johann Sebastian Bach (q.v.) completed
on March 24, 1771.   They were dedicated to Christian Ludwig, Margrave of Brandenburg, hence their name.

BRANDENBURGERS IN BOHEMIA, THE--(Nordic)--An opera
(1862-63) by Smetana (q.v.), Braniboři v Čechaćh, first performed in The Czech Theatre in Prague, 5 January 1886.

BRANDES, GEORG MORRIS--(AH-Ibsen)--A Danish literary
critic who was the chief Scandinavian advocate of the non-
historicity of Jesus.   He introduced feminism into Denmark.

BRERA--(AS)--In Milan, a 17th-century palace which houses
The Pinacoteca di Brera, one of the finest collections in
Italy.   It is especially strong in paintings of the Lombard
and Venetian schools.

BRIDE OF LAMMERMOOR, THE--(Aspects II)--A novel
(1810) by Sir Walter Scott (q.v.), set in the days of William
III.   Lucy, the daughter of Sir William Ashton, lord-keeper
of Scotland, is in love with Edgar, master of the Ravenswood clan, arch-enemies of the Ashtons.   She is, however,
forced to marry Frank Hayston, laird of Bucklaw.   In a fit
of insanity, the bride attempts to kill the bridegroom and
dies in convulsions.   The novel served as the inspiration of
Lucia di Lammermoor, an opera, by Donizetti (q.v.).

BRIDGES, ROBERT--(GLD IX: Two Cheers-Challenge)--
Robert Seymour Bridges, 1844-1930.   An English poet and
laureate (1913) perhaps best known for his work in metrics,
he also wrote plays on classical subjects and was the author
of critical essays on Milton (q.v.) and Keats (q.v.).   He
edited several volumes including the poetry of his friend,
Gerard Manley Hopkins (q.v.).   Some of his works are
Prometheus, the Firegiver (1884), Eden (1891), an oratorio;
and The Test of Beauty (1929).

BRISCOE, LILY--(Two Cheers-Virginia)--A character in the
novel, To the Lighthouse by Virginia Woolf (q.v.).   She is
an artist and a friend of the Ramseys (q.v.) who is unsure
of herself and, as a result, withholds her love and affection
from others until she passes a summer with them.   She is
not a great artist.   Nevertheless, her talent is spurred by
her relationship with the Ramseys.

BRITISH MUSEUM, THE--(AH-Early; AH-Cn; GLD VII; LJ
XX)--Located in the Bloomsbury (q. v.) section of London between Tottenham Court Road and New Oxford Street, it com-
prises the national museum of archeology and ethnography
and the national library. It is the largest and richest collection of its kind in the world. The original buildings were
designed by Sir Robert Smirke and built 1823-52. Other ad-
ditions have been built since that period. The museum was
founded in 1753.

BRITTEN, BENJAMIN--(GLD; Two Cheers-George C)--Sir
Edward Benjamin Britten, 1913- . An English composer of
music and a pianist. As a pianist he is noted chiefly as the
accompanist to Peter Pears (q. v.). He is also noted as a
conductor. He was the chief creator of the Aldeburgh Festival and the English Opera Group, and was the pupil of Frank
Bridge and of Ireland. He has been influenced by Purcell,
Mahler, and Stravinsky. Perhaps his best known work is
the opera, Peter Grimes (q. v.). He has written other
operas (e. g., The Turn of the Screw), ballets, and concert
works.

BRONTË, CHARLOTTE--(GLD I)--1816-1855. An English
novelist, and the most famous and most prolific of the three
Brontë sisters (Emily [q. v.], Anne). She was also a poet.
Her first published work was poetry. She and her two sisters published a collection of their poems under male pen-
names. Her most famous and most important novel is Jane
Eyre (1847). She also wrote Shirley (1849), Villette (1853),
and a fragment, Emma (1860).

BRONTË, EMILY--(Aspects II; Two Cheers-Anon; Two
Cheers-Eng)--1818-1848. English novelist and the sister of
Anne and Charlotte (q. v.). She is most famous for her only
novel, Wuthering Heights (1848), which is wildly passionate.

BROOKE, RUPERT--(AH-Own; GLD XI)--1887-1915. An
English poet, he was the son of a master at Rugby. He
graduated from Cambridge and traveled in America and New
Zealand (1913-14), and held a commission in the Royal Naval
Division (1914) but was weakened by sunstrokes and attacked
by blood poisoning. He died and was buried at Skyros in the
Aegean. He is, perhaps, best known for his poems on war.
He is the author of Poems (1911), 1914 and Other Poems
(1915), and Letters from America (1916).

BROTHERS KARAMAZOV, THE--(AH-Jo; Aspects I)--A novel
(1879-80) by Fyodor (Feodor) Dostoevsky. It is the story of
three brothers, each representative of distinct types in the
Russian national character: the soldier (Dimitri), the intellectual (Ivan), and the religious mystic (Alyosha). Dimitri
quarrels violently with his father over money and over a
woman to whom they are both attracted. When the father is
found dead, suspicion falls on Dimitri. The murder was,
however, committed by a fourth son, the illegitimate Smer-
dyakov, who commits suicide. The novel is filled with passionate introspection.

BROWNE, SIR THOMAS--(AH-Adrift; AH-Car; Collect Ta-
Celest)--1605-1682. An English physician, scholar, and
writer famous for his learning and his style as a writer.
His most famous work is the Religio Medici (1643).

BROWNING, OSCAR--(GLD X; Two Cheers-Camb)--1837-
1923. An English writer of history and an educationalist.

BROWNING, ROBERT--(AH-Note; GLD VIII; Two Cheers-
Snow)--1812-1889. English poet and the husband of Elizabeth
Barrett (q.v.). His poetry is marked by its learning, its
psychological analysis of character, and, especially in its
later phases, by its obscurity. Even in his own day his
work was considered "difficult." Among his many works
are The Ring and the Book (1868-9), Dramatic Idylls (1879-
80); the poetic drama, Pippa Passes and many dramatic
monologues which have become known to every school boy
(e.g., "My Last Duchess," "Sordello").

BRUCH, MAX--(Nordic)--1838-1920. A German composer
and conductor (of the Liverpool Philharmonic, 1880-83). His
works include three violin concertos, three symphonies,
operas, and other works.

BRUNHILDE--(LJ IX; Nordic; Two Cheers-Post; Two Cheers-
What)--Brünnhilde. The daughter of the King of Issland (i.e.,
Isaland, in the Low Countries) in German myth. She was
beloved by Gunther, one of the two great chieftans in the
Nibelungleid. She was carried off by force. Gunther asked
Siegfried to help him. Siegfried solved the problem by
snatching from her the talisman which was her protector.
She never forgave him for this treachery.

BRÜNNHILDE--(Two Cheers-Raison)--See under Brunhilde.

BRUTUS--(Two Cheers-Jul; Two Cheers-What)--Subtitled:
Or the Fall of Tarquin (1820), a drama by John H. Payne
based on the banishment of Tarquin by Lucius Junius Brutus
(509 B. C.).

BRYAN, WILLIAM JENNINGS--(GLD XI)--1860-1925. An
American lawyer and three-time Democratic candidate for
President of the United States (1896, 1900, 1908). He was
the Secretary of State in Wilson's cabinet, but is, perhaps,
most known for his "Cross of Gold" speech against the gold
standard and his leadership of the movement for prohibition
of liquor. His most important case was that of a Southern
teacher, Scopes, who was brought to trial (1925) for teaching
Darwinism to his pupils.

BRYAXIS--(Alex I, 1)--A Greek sculptor of the 4th century
B. C. He was one of the four sculptors who collaborated on
the mausoleum at Halicarnassus.

BRYCE, LORD--(GLD XII)--James Vicount Bryce, 1838-
1922. A British jurist, diplomat, and historian, he was a
Regius professor of civil law at Oxford (1870-73) and under-
secretary for foreign affairs in Gladstone's cabinet (1886).
He also held other cabinet posts and was a member of the
Hague Tribunal in 1913. He is the author of The American
Commonwealth (1888), considered by many as the classical
work on American government.

BUCHAN, ELSPETH--(AH-Mrs)--Née Simpson, 1738-1791.
She was the founder of a Scottish fanatical religious sect,
the members of which were called Buchanites. Her followers
believed that she was the woman of "Revelations" (xii).

BUCKLAW, THE LAIRD OF--(Aspects II)--A character in
Sir Walter Scott's (q. v.) novel, The Bride of Lammermoor
(q. v.). He is Frank Hayston, the bridegroom of Lucy Ashton. Before succeeding to the wealth of Lady Girnington,
he had run through his own inheritance and entangled himself with Captain Craigengelt, an adventurer.

BUDD, BILLY--(Aspects VII)--The principal character of
Billy Budd, Foretopman (a manuscript discovered after the
author's death and not published until 1924) by Herman Melville (q. v.). He is 21, a member of the crew of merchantman, "Rights of Man, " and extremely handsome, cheerful,
and a stabilizing influence on the crew. He is popular with
all except John Claggart, whom he eventually kills, uninten-

tionally, in a fight. He is sentenced to be hanged and dies blessing the man who condemned him.

BUDDHA--(Collect Ta-Mr; PI XII)--Gautama Buddha, 563?-?483 B.C. His original name was Prince Siddharta and was called Sakyamuni (i.e., sage of the Sakyas). An Indian philosopher and the founder of Buddhism (q.v.), he was of noble birth but became weary of luxury and resolved on a renunciation of the material world of the nobility (c. 533); he left home and journeyed about Northern India. At Budh Gaya, he underwent a long fast and emancipation of spirit came to him under a Bo tree (q.v.) at Buddha Gaya, hence the name Buddha. He founded monasteries and spread his faith. He died not far from his birthplace.

BUDDHISM--(Alex I, 3; GLD VII)--A system of religion inaugurated by the Buddha (q.v.) in India in the 6th century B.C. In its belief, the world is a transient reflection of the deity. The soul is a "vital spark" of the deity. It will be bound to matter until its "wearer" has, by divine contemplation, so purged and purified it that it is fit to be absorbed into the divine essence. There are four sublime virtues of Buddhism: 1. The existence of pain; 2. the cause of pain, which is "birth-sin" (man has passed through many previous existences and all of the heaped-up sins accumulated in these existences constitute this "birth-sin"); 3. Nirvana (i.e., absorption into the divine essence), which ends pain; and 4. the "way," which leads to Nirvana (i.e., right faith, right judgment, right language, right purpose, right memory, and right meditation). The faith spread rapidly from India to Ceylon, Tibet, China and Japan.

BUDDHIST CAVES AT AJANTA--(Two Cheers-India)--See: Ajanta.

BUDGE, SIR WALLIS--(AH-For the Muse)--Sir Ernest Alfred Wallis Budge, 1857-1934. An English archaeologist and Hebrew and Assyrian scholar at Cambridge. He was also the keeper (1893-1924) of Assyrian and Egyptian antiquities at the British Museum (q.v.). He conducted digs in Mesopotamia, the Sudan, and Egypt.

BUFFON--(AH-Vo)--Georges Louis Leclerc (Comte de Buffon), 1707-1788. A French naturalist and the son of a wealthy lawyer, he studied law, but transferred his interest to science. While on a visit to England (1733), he translated Newton's Fluxions. He was admitted to the French Academy

and in 1739 appointed director of the Jardin du Roi. He
wrote an Histoire Naturelle (1749-67) in which he collected
all the known facts of natural science and discussed them in
lofty and eloquent language. He was made Comte de Buffon
by Louis XV.

BUNYON, JOHN--(Two Cheers-English)--1628-1688. An
English writer and a non-conformist lay preacher whose
writings were directly influenced by the Bible. The most
famous of his works is The Pilgrim's Progress (1678), an
allegory of the problems the good individual must face and
overcome on his way to his eternal home. His style is
simple and direct.

BUONAPARTE, PAULINE--(Collect Ta-Coord)--Maria Paulina
(originally Carlotta Buonaparte), 1780-1825. She was the
favorite sister of Napoleon (q. v.). Her first husband was
Charles Victor Emmanuel Leclerc, and her second, Prince
Camillo Borghese. Her semi-nude statue by Canova is to
be seen in the Museo Borghese, Rome.

BURDETT, OSBERT HENRY--(GLD X)--1885- . He is the
author of Art of Life (q. v.), as Forster titles the work. Its
title is actually Art of Living. It contains a sympathetic impression of Goldsworthy Lowes Dickinson (q. v.) as a lecturer
at Cambridge. Burdett is also the author of The Idea of
Coventry Patmore (1921), The Beardsley Period (1925) and
The Brownings (1928).

BURKE, EDMUND--(MT; Two Cheers-George)--1729-1797.
An English author and statesman best known for his defense
of the American colonies in Parliament and his orations in
favor of the Irish. He was an enemy of the French Revolution (q. v.). Perhaps his best known philosophical work is
A Philosophical Inquiry into the Origin of Our Ideas of the
Sublime and Beautiful (1756).

BURMESE DAYS--(Two Cheers-George)--A novel (1934) by
George Orwell (q. v.).

BURNE-JONES--(WAFT V)--Sir Edward Coley Burne-Jones,
1833-1898. An English painter and designer who was educated
at Oxford where he became acquainted with William Morris.
He began painting under the direction of Dante Gabriel Rossetti (1856) who, with Morris, founded the Pre-Raphaelite
movement (q. v.) in art. Burne-Jones was not well known
until he exhibited large oils (1877-78). Among his best

known paintings are "The Golden Stairs" (1880), and "King Cophetria and the Beggar Maid" (1884). He furnished the designs for the stained glass windows for Christ Church Cathedral, Oxford (1859) as well as for other churches.

BURNS, ROBERT--(AH-JA; Two Cheers-William)--1759-1796. A Scottish poet best known for his lyrics in Scottish dialect on various subjects but chiefly on love, and nature. Some of these are "To a Mouse," "Sweet Afton," "My Luv is Like a Red, Red Rose," and "Auld Lang Syne."

BUSCH, ADOLPH--(Nordic)--Georg Wilhelm Adolph Busch, 1891-1952. He was a German-born violinist who, in protest to the Nazi coup, and for his own safety, took Swiss nationality. He died in New York. He is well known as a soloist as well as the leader of the Busch String Quartet and as the partner of Rudolph Serkin, his son-in-law. He has also some musical compositions to his credit. He is the brother of Fritz Busch (q.v.).

BUSCH, FRITZ--(Nordic)--1890-1951. A German-born conductor who fled Nazi Germany and settled in Denmark. He is noted for his work as a conductor at Glyndebourne (England), and he died in London. He is the brother of Adolph Busch (q.v.).

BUSSY, DOROTHY--(Aspects IV)--Dorothy Bussy Strachey. The translator (into English) of Gide's Counterfeiters (q.v.) and other of Gide's work including If It Die, The Immoralist, Lafcadio's Adventures, etc.

"BUT NOW BEYOND QUESTION, THE SWANS SAIL ON TO-GETHER."--(Two Cheers-Outsider)--Line 14 from a poem, "The Swans," by E. J. Scovell on p. 186, Poetry of the Present, edited by Geoffrey Grigson (q.v.).

BUTCHER AND LANG'S ODYSSEY--(GLD X)--Samuel Henry Butcher (1850-1910) was a British classical scholar who collaborated with Andrew Lang (1844-1912), a Scottish scholar, poet, and writer, on a prose translation of the Odyssey (1979). It is still considered one of the best translations extant. Butcher is also the author of Aristotle's Theory of Poetry and Fine Art (1895). Lang, who was particularly interested in the history of the Stuarts, wrote The Mystery of Mary Stuart (1901) and John Knox and the Reformation (1905). He also proved that folklore is the foundation of literary

mythology (Custom and Myth, 1884), and is one of the
founders of the Society for Psychical Research.

BUTLER, SAMUEL--(AH-TS; AH-Vo; AH-Wil; Two Cheers-
Bk; Two Cheers-Eng; Two Cheers-Raison)--1835-1902.   An
English author and satirist perhaps best known for The Way
of All Flesh (1903) an autobiographical novel satirizing Victorian family life and, in particular, the Victorian father.
Butler was a sheep rancher who turned to art and exhibited
at the Royal Academy (q.v.).   Erewhon (1872), a Utopian
novel, and his first major work, was published anonymously.
He also studied music and developed the theory that the
author of The Odyssey was a woman of Trapani in Sicily.

BUTTERFLY--(Two Cheers-Raison)--The heroine of an opera
(Madame Butterfly) in Italian by Puccini (1904) which tells
the tale of a young Japanese girl, Butterfly, and her love
for an American naval lieutenant who deserts her.   She has
his child, and, when she learns that he has married an
American, she commits suicide.

BUTTON MOULDER, THE--(AH-Ibsen; Two Cheers-Mohammed)--A character in Peer Gynt (q.v.) (1867), by Henrik
Ibsen (q.v.).   He is an agent of God who awaits Peer's return to Norway to melt his soul with others which are
neither good enough to be given Heaven nor evil enough to
deserve Hell.

BY NILE AND TIGRIS--(AH-For the Muse)--By Wallis Budge
(q.v.).   Subtitled: "A Narrative of Journeys in Egypt and
Mesopotamia on Behalf of the British Museum Between the
Years 1886 and 1903" (1920).

BYRON--(GLD IV; LJ XXIX; Two Cheers-Whiff; WAFT I)--
George Noel Gordon, Lord Byron, 1788-1824.   An English
Romantic poet of international fame which flows, perhaps,
more from his colorful life than the quality of his poetry.
He created the "Byronic hero"--a sad, handsome, melancholy young man, haunted by some mysterious and perhaps
evil aspect of his past which he never explains.   He is
driven by this mysterious something through a life filled with
adventures as well as love affairs.   Byron's poetry, aside
from the presence of this hero, is marked by satire and a
free-flowing rhetorical verse.   Generally, his subjects are
exotic.   Some of his works are "Childe Harold" (1812, 16,
17), "The Prisoner of Chillon," and his masterpiece, incom-
plete at his death, Don Juan (1818).

BYRONIC HERO, THE--(Two Cheers-George)--See: Byron.

C

CADOVER--(LJ III)--The home of Rickie Elliot's Aunt Emily Failing. The original is Acton House, near Felton.

CAESAR, JULIUS--(GLD XIV; Two Cheers-Jul; Two Cheers-What)--Caius Julius Caesar, 100-44 B.C. He was a member of a leading Roman family who made himself ruler of the Roman world by defeating his chief rival, Pompey. He ruled supreme until his assasination by a group headed by Brutus and Cassius who hoped, by his death, to preserve the republic. His nephew, Octavius Caesar Augustus (q.v., under Augustus) succeeded him and founded the Empire of Rome. Caesar has appeared as a character in many works of literature, most notably in Julius Caesar (q.v.), by William Shakespeare (q.v.).

CAIN--(Collect Ta-Co-ord)--In the Bible, "Genesis," he is the son of Adam and Eve, and the murderer of his brother, Abel (q.v.), because of jealousy: Abel's sacrifice was accepted by the Lord, and his was not.

CAIUS--(Two Cheers-Cam)--[Pron. "keys."] A college of Cambridge University founded for men in 1348 and named after John Caius (1510-1573), its second founder, who enlarged it and endowed it. He was a Roman Catholic who suffered for his faith.

CALAS, JEAN--(AH-Vo)--1698-1762. A French Calvinist merchant of Toulouse who was convicted of murdering his son, (actually a suicide) to prevent him from becoming a Roman Catholic. He was condemned to be broken on the wheel.

CALIBAN--(GLD V; Two Cheers-Stratford)--A character in the play, The Tempest (q.v.), by William Shakespeare (q.v.). He is deformed and the son of a devil and a witch. The magic of Prospero, whose servant he is, keeps his violence in check. At the end of the play, he is given his freedom.

CALIGULA--(Alex I, 3)--Gaius Caesar, called Caligula (little boot), a name given to him by the Praetorian guard with whom he used to play as a child. He would dress in a miniature version of their uniform, including their boots. He was Roman Emperor (37-41) and the youngest son of Tiberius's nephew, Germanicus Caesar and Agrippina. He was probably born at Antium, the present Porto d'Anzio. He was declared heir to the throne by Tiberius and, for a time, ruled with moderation. He suffered a severe illness (c. A. D. 38) after which his reign was marked by wild cruelty and tyranny. He was undoubtedly insane (he made his horse a consul, demanded that a marble ship be made to float, etc.) and was murdered by members of the Praetorian guard.

CALLIMACHUS--(Alex I, 1)--3rd century B. C. He was a Greek scholar who, though born in Cyrene, was chief librarian of the library of Alexandria and head of a school there. Though he wrote some 800 works, almost nothing survives other than fragments.

CAMBRIDGE--(AH-Consol; AH-Early; Aspects I; Collect Ta-Intro; GLD II; LJ I; Two Cheers-Gibbon; Two Cheers-India; Two Cheers-John; Two Cheers-Virginia)--Founded in 1209 by scholars who migrated from Oxford following problems between the townspeople and members of the University.

CAMBRIDGE CIRCUS--(LJ XV)--Located in London's West End, it is at the crossing of Shaftsbury Avenue and Charing Cross Road.

CAMBRIDGE SHAKESPEARE--(Aspects I)--A nine-volume edition of Shakespeare's works and the most important 19th-century critical edition. It appeared in parts between 1863-1866 under the editorship of W. G. Clark, J. Glover, and W. A. Wright. A second edition (1891-3) was revised by Wright.

CAMDEN TOWN--(HE XXII)--A district in London in the borough of St. Pancras.

CAMPBELL, SIR MALCOLM--(Two Cheers-Last)--1885-1948. An English businessman and automobile racer. He was on the staff of Lloyds of London and served through World War I. For part of the war he was an airplane pilot. He began motor racing as a hobby in 1910 and subsequently established at Daytona Beach, Florida and Salt Lake City, Utah many world records for land speed. He is the author of several volumes among which are Speed (1931), and The Romance of Motor Racing (1936).

CAMPBELL, MRS. O. W.--(GLD XIV)--Mrs. Oliver Ward
Campbell. She is the author of Shelley and the Unromantics
(1924), Mary Kingsley: A Victorian in the Jungle (1957),
Thomas Love Peacock (1953), and others.

CANDIDE--(Two Cheers-Vo)--A philosophical tale (1758) by
Voltaire (q. v.). The story opens in Westphalia where the
hero, Candide, who, though earnest and simple, is very
happy. Cunégonde, the daughter of the Baron Thunder-ten-
Tronckh, has taught him the joys of love, and Pangloss, a
philosopher, has relentlessly taught him that this is the best
of all possible worlds, the doctrine of Leibnitz. The Baron
learns of Candide's interest in his daughter and throws him
out. Candide is pressed into the army and thus begins a long
series of adventures which take him to Portugal, South America, and Turkey. The book ends in Constantinople where
Candide is reunited with Cunégonde grown ugly, who has had
similarly wild adventures, and Pangloss, supposedly
hanged in Lisbon, who still ceaselessly philosophizes. The
three then settle down to "cultivate their own garden, " in
Candide's words.

CANOPUS--(Alex I, 1)--A seaport of ancient Egypt, situated
about 15 miles NE of Alexandria.

CANUTE--(AH-My W; Two Cheers-En)--The name of six
kings of Denmark, two of whom were also kings of England.
Forster is most probably referring to Canute II (994?-1035)
who is known as "the Great. " He became King of England
in 1016 and King of Denmark, 1018. Although the opening
years of his reign were marked by cruelty, through most of
his rule he was an able, just, and popular king. He was a
supporter and a defender of the Church. He defeated Norway and became its king (1028) and made a pilgrimage to
Rome (1026-27). He is the subject of many legends one of
which is alluded to when Forster notes "why should even the
world be the limit of possession?" in the essay, "My Wood. "

ČAPEK, KAREL--(Nordic; Two Cheers-What Would)--1890-
1938. A Czechoslovakian playwright best known for his play,
R. U. R. (1923) in which robots take over the world. Some
of his other plays are The Makropoulus Secret (1925), which
treats of the prolongation of life; Power and Glory (1938);
and The Mother (1939).

CARACCI--(Collect Ta-Eternal)--Also: Carracci. The
family name of a group of influential Italian artists of the

late 16th and early 17th century. The family originated in
Bologna and was founded by Agostino (1557?-1602) and Annibale (1560?-1609) who were brothers. It was continued by
Antonio (1583-1609), the son of Agostino; and Ludovico (1555-
1619), cousin of Agostino and Annibale. They founded the
school of painting known as Eclecticism, essentially a reaction to and a revolt against Mannerism. They established
the Accademia degli Incamminati in which the style was
taught.

CARDANO, GIRALAMA--(AH-Car)--1501-1516. Forster discusses the life of this extraordinary Italian in his essay
"Cardan" in Abinger Harvest. There is a more extended
biography in English by Henry Morley (1854), and it seems
highly likely that Forster took much of the information he
uses from Morley.

CARDUCCI--(Alex I, 1)--Giosuè Carducci, 1835-1907. Early
in his career, he used the pseudonym Enotrio Romano. He
was an Italian poet and professor of literary history at the
University of Bologna (1861-1904), and was awarded the
Nobel Prize for literature (1900). His poetry was staunchly
classical. Through it, he attempted to introduce classical
metrical schemes into modern poetry. He is considered the
national poet of modern Italy.

CARLTON HOUSE--(Two Cheers-London)--Formerly the residence of George IV (q. v.) when he was the Prince of Wales.
It was pulled down in 1826. Its name survives in Carlton
House Terrace, a group of buildings designed by John Nash
(1827-1832). They were once the homes of the aristocracy,
but are now occupied in the main by government departments.
The Terrace is located near Hyde Park (q. v.).

CARLYLE--(AH-Me; AH-Note; Collect Ta-Machine; GLD VII;
HE XVI; Nordic; Two Cheers-English; Two Cheers-Gibbon;
Two Cheers-Lon Lib; Two Cheers-What Would)--Thomas
Carlyle, 1795-1881. He was born in Scotland, though recognized as an important writer of the English Victorian period.
His writings are associated with the distrust of democracy
which they reflect and their attacks on hypocrisy and ma-
terialism. His work also displays an intense belief in the
individual especially in the form of a heroic, strong-willed
leader. His writings show the influence of German literature, most notably of Goethe and Schiller. One of his works
is A History of the French Revolution (1837). On Heroes,
Hero Worship, and the Heroic in History were originally

lectures (1840) published in 1841.

CARLYLE, MRS. --(Two Cheers-Mrs)--The wife of Thomas
Carlyle (q.v.), née Jane Baillie Welsh, 1801-1866. She was
a descendant of John Knox. At first, she wanted to marry
her teacher who could not because he was already engaged
to marry someone else. She began writing to Carlyle and
eventually married him in 1826. She suffered from his
temper and from his friendship with Lady Ashburton. Nevertheless, she established a comfortable home for him in
Chelsea (q.v.) where he could write in relative peace. The
home, No. 25 Cheyne Walk, is preserved as a museum and
kept much as it was when they occupied it. In 1858, Mrs.
Carlyle became an invalid and remained so until her death.

CARMEN--(Two Cheers-George)--An opera (1875) by Georges
Bizet (q.v.), based on a novel by Prosper Mérimée. It
treats of the affair of a gypsy, Carmen, and a young Spanish
officer, Don José, and her subsequent death at his hands
when he realizes that she has given her love to another.

CAROL, KING--(Two Cheers-Jew)--1893-1953. Carol II of
Rumania, the second king of Rumania. He contracted a
morganatic marriage only to be divorced and then marry
Princess Helen of Greece (1917) by whom he had Michael,
the third king of Rumania. In 1925, Carol renounced the
throne, deserted his wife, and lived in exile in Paris with
Mme. Magda Lupescu. In 1928, he divorced Princess Helen.
He returned to Rumania in 1930 and supplanted his son as
king. In his foreign policy, he tried to please Germany and
Russia, and attempted to become dictator. In 1940 he was
driven from the throne by the Germans. He fled to Spain,
thence to Cuba (1941) and, finally, to Mexico (1942).

CARPENTER, EDWARD--(GLD XIV; Two Cheers-Edward)--
1844-1929. An English writer who was educated at Cambridge. He was an Anglican minister (1869-74) but, becoming interested in Socialist movements, he renounced his
ministry, and began to lecture and to write on Socialism and
other subjects. Some of his works are Chants of Labor
(1888); Civilization: Its Causes and Cure (1889) (q.v.); and
The Art of Creation (1904) (q.v.).

CARTER, ANN--(GLD I)--The grandmother of Goldsworthy
Lowes Dickinson (q.v.). She was from Devonshire and
Forster describes her as "a woman of character."

CARTHAGE--(Alex I, 1)--An ancient city in North Africa
near Tunis. It was founded by Tyre in 814 B. C. and, from
the sixth century B. C., began conquests in Western Africa,
Sicily, and Sardinia. It developed a powerful navy and, as
a result, dominated the western Mediterranean. It began a
series of wars (The Punic Wars) with Rome (264 B. C.)
which were to end in its defeat at the hands of the Roman
general, Scipio the younger, in 146 B. C.

CASAUBON, DOROTHEA--(Two Cheers-Virginia)--A character in the novel Middlemarch (1871-72) by George Eliot.
Née Dorothea Brooke, she is a sensitive and well-bred
young woman who wants desperately to devote her life to a
cause. As a result, she marries Edward Casaubon, a
cleric and a dry, emotionless scholar. After his death, and
despite the provisions of his will, she marries her cousin,
Will Ladislaw, an artist.

CASAUBON, MR. --(Aspects VIII)--A character in the novel
Middlemarch (1871-72) by George Eliot. Full name: the
Rev. Edward Casaubon. He is the clergyman at Lowick,
near Middlemarch. Gloomy, unemotional, and without imagination, he is an unsuccessful scholar who marries Dorothea
Brooke. He destroys her life with him and is jealous of the
interest she shows in her cousin, Will Ladislaw.

CASCA--(Two Cheers-Jul)--Publius Servillius Casca, died
after 42 B. C. He was the first among the assassins of
Julius Caesar (q. v.) to strike him. He performs the same
act in the play, Julius Caesar (q. v.), by William Shakespeare
(q. v.).

CASSIUS--(Two Cheers-Jul; Two Cheers-What)--Gaius Cassius
Longinus. He was a Roman general and conspirator against
the life of Julius Caesar (q. v.). He distinguished himself in
the Parthian War (53 B. C.) and sided with Pompey against
Caesar. He also fought at Pharsalus (48 B. C.). He was
pardoned by Caesar; nevertheless, he was the leader in the
conspiracy against him (44 B. C.) and was one of the actual
assassins. Defeated at Philippi by Caesar's nephew and
heir, Octavius (q. v., under Augustus), he ordered his freedman to kill him (42 B. C.). His fictional counterpart in the
play Julius Caesar (q. v.) by William Shakespeare, plays
much the same role.

CASTE--(GLD V)--A comedy in three acts by Thomas William
Robertson, 1829-1871. It was first produced in London, at

the Wales, 6 April 1867.

CASTELFRANCO MADONNA--(Two Cheers-Not)--A painting
by the Venetian artist, Giorgione (Giorgio del Castelfranco,
1476-1510), which shows the influence of Giovanni Bellini
(q. v.).

CASTOR AND POLLUX--(Alex II, 1; Collect Ta-Point)--In
Roman myth, they are the twin sons of Jupitor and Leda.
Jupitor is said to have visited Leda in the form of a swan
and, as a result of the union, she produced two eggs from
one of which sprang Castor and Clytemnestra, and from the
other, Pollux and Helen. The two, Castor and Pollux, are
also known as the Dioscuri. They had many different adventures and, finally, were placed among the constellations.

CATHERINE, ST. --(HE XXII)--Forster's reference is not
entirely clear. There are several St. Catherines in the
church calendar--notably of Alexandria (q. v.), of Siena
(q. v.), of Genoa, of Ricci, and of Sweden. He is probably
referring to St. Catherine of Siena.

CATHERINE OF ALEXANDRIA, ST. --(Alex I, 2)--She is a
Christian virgin and martyr (c. A. D. 307) who was born in
Alexandria and, according to legend, was beheaded after her
persecutors failed to break her on a spiked wheel. She is
often pictured with a broken wheel.

CATHERINE OF SIENA, ST. --(Aspects VII)--1347-1380.
Born in Siena, she took vows as a nun over the objections
of her family. During her lifetime she was noted as a mystic. She was responsible for the return of Gregory XI to
Rome from Avignon, thus ending the "Babylonian Captivity"
(1377). She was also responsible for the recognition as
pope of Urban VI (1380). She is noted for her letters, and
the devotional works she has written.

CATHERINE WHEEL--(Aspects VII)--The sign of St. Catherine of Alexandria (q. v.) who is depicted holding it as well
as the palm of martyrdom.

CATILINE'S CONSPIRACY--(LJ VI)--Lucius Sergius Catilina
(64 B. C.) conspired with a large number of dissatisfied
young nobles to loot the Roman treasury and murder the
senators. Cicero (q. v.) who was the consul, was informed
of the plot and delivered his first oration against Catiline
(Nov. 8, 63 B. C.), whereupon the latter fled Rome. The

next day, Cicero delivered his second oration, and several
of the conspirators were arrested.   On Dec. 4, Cicero delivered his third oration which detailed the punishment which
should be meted out and, on Dec. 5, after his fourth oration,
the Senate passed sentence of death on the group.   Catiline
tried to escape into Gaul, was intercepted and died fighting
(62 B. C.).

CATULLUS, GAIUS VALERIUS--(LJ VI; Two Cheers-John)--
84?-54 B. C.   A Roman lyric poet born in Verona.   There
are over one hundred poems extant attributed to him.   Among
these, many are addressed to "Lesbia" who has been identified as Clodia, the notorious sister of Clodius and wife (63-
59 B. C.) of Quintus Metellus Celer.   Catullus's love for
"Lesbia" remained the great passion of his life.   He is regarded by many as one of the greatest lyric poets in the
literary history of Rome.

CAUDWELL, CHRISTOPHER--(Two Cheers-English)--The
pseudonym of Christopher St. John Sprigg (1907-1937), English writer and critic.

CAVAFY, C. P.--See: Kavaphēs, Konstantinos Petrou.

CAVALA--(Alex I, 5)--Kavalli.   A department and seaport
of Greece.   It was the birthplace of Mohammed Ali (q. v.),
founder of the royal house of Egypt which ended with King
Farouk.

CAVELL, EDITH--(Reading)--Edith Louisa Cavell, 1865-1915.
An English nurse who was shot by the Germans during World
War I (Oct. 12, 1915) for aiding Allied soldiers to escape.

CAVES AT ELEPHANTA, THE--(PI VII)--They are located on
a small island in the Bombay Harbor in India.   They are
entirely cut out of rock, therefore, more correctly called
excavations than buildings.   They were probably created
some one to twelve hundred years ago.   They contain temples which house colossal figures of Siva, Parvati, and other
Hindu deities.

CAWNPORE--(PI II)--[Alt. spelling: Cawnpur.]   A city in
India on the Ganges River some 245 miles SE of Delhi.   It
was garrisoned by British troops in 1778 and is known for
the massacre by Nana Sahib of British soldiers during the
Sepoy Mutiny, July 15, 1857.

CECIL, LORD ROBERT--(GLD XII)--Edgar Algernon Robert
Cecil, 1st Viscount Cecil of Chelwood, 1864-1958. A British
statesman who held several governmental posts including the
assistant secretariat for foreign affairs (1918). He is most
noted for his participation in drafting the covenant of the
League of Nations. He was in Stanley Baldwin's first and
second cabinets and was the president of the League of
Nations Union. He was awarded the Nobel Peace Prize in
1937.

CELIA--(Two Cheers-Two Bks)--Celia Coplestone. She is a
character in the play, The Cocktail Party, by T. S. Eliot
(q. v.). She is a sensitive young poetess who thinks that she
is in love with Edward Chamberlayne but is shocked when
she realizes what his true nature is. Julia and Alex take
her to a psychiatrist, and through him she finds her purpose
in life. She enters a religious order, goes to the East, and
is martyred.

CELLINI, BENVENUTO--(AH-Car)--1500-1571. A goldsmith,
sculptor, and by his own admission, a rake and an adventurer of incredible powers among which was a tremendous
attraction for the ladies and a remarkable ability at swords-
manship. He was a Florentine and pupil of Michelangelo
who, when banished from Florence, went to Rome and the
court of Pope Clement VII (1523). He also worked for
Francis I, the King of France (1540) and returned to Florence as protégé of Cosimo de' Medici (1545). His present
reputation as an artist rests on the small number of his
works which have survived, among which are a huge golden
salt cellar and the Perseus in Florence. What does survive
the depredations of time, however, is his autobiography
which records, in graphic detail, his adventures.

CERBERUS--(Alex I, 1; Collect Ta-Celest; Two Cheers-John)
--In Roman myth, he is the three-headed dog that guards the
entrance to the underworld. Hercules dragged the monster
to earth and then released him. Orpheus lulled him to sleep
with his lyre and the sybil who was the guide of Aeneas (The
Aeneid) through the inferno put him to sleep by throwing him
a cake seasoned with poppies and honey.

CERINTHUS--(Alex I, 3)--fl. A. D. 75? The founder of a
religious sect whose members were called Cerinthians. He
was probably from Syria.

CÉZANNE--(Aspects VI; Two Cheers-Does)--1839-1906.   A
French artist and one of the founders of the style called
post-impressionism (q. v.).   He was most at home with landscapes and still life painting, over which he labored inces-
santly to the point where many were never completed.
Nevertheless, there are few great museums which do not
possess at least one example of his work.   At first his pictures were not popular; now they are considered sound in-
vestments even by those whose appreciation and knowledge
of art are limited.

CHAD--(Aspects VIII)--Chadwick Newsome, a character in
the novel, The Ambassadors (q. v.) by Henry James.   He is
a wealthy young American whose education by Mme.
de Vionnet has unsuited him to take up his position as the
inheritor of a family business in the United States.   Because
of her guidance, he discovers that his proposed marriage to
Mamie Pocock is unthinkable.

CHALCEDON, COUNCIL OF--(Alex I, 2)--An ecumenical
council summoned by the emperor Marcian (Oct. 8-Nov. 1,
A. D. 451) for the purpose of ending the Monophysite (q. v.)
heresy.   It declared for the two natures of Christ.

CHALMERS, SIR GEORGE (PAUL)--(MT)--1836-1878.   A
Scottish portrait and landscape painter.

CHAMBERLAIN, AUSTEN--(GLD XI)--Sir Joseph Austen
Chamberlain, 1863-1933.   A British statesman and half-
brother of the far more famous Neville Chamberlain (q. v.).
He held various government posts including member of Parliament (1892), civil Lord of the Admiralty (1895-1900), Postmaster General (1902), and Chancellor of the Exchequer (1903-
1906).   He was also Secretary of State for India (1915-1917).
He was awarded the Nobel Peace Prize (1925), and helped
to facilitate Germany's entry into the League of Nations (q.
v.) in 1926.   He is the author of several volumes including
Peace in Our Time (1928).   These words were to be used
by his half-brother Neville (q. v.) when he returned to England from Munich with his agreement with Hitler.

CHAMBERLAIN, NEVILLE--(Two Cheers-Post)--Arthur Neville Chamberlain, 1869-1940.   He was a British statesman
perhaps best known for his agreement as prime minister
with Hitler at Munich which precipitated rather than retarded
the second world war.   As the leader of the Conservative
party, he stressed the need for the re-armament of Britain

and sought, through diplomacy, to draw Mussolini (q.v.)
away from Hitler (q.v.). At Munich, he agreed to the German partition of Czechoslovakia in an attempt to save the
peace. He pledged assistance to Poland (March 1939) and
to Rumania and Greece (April 1939). He declared war on
Germany (Sept. 3, 1939) after the German invasion of Poland.
He was attacked in Parliament for his failure to send sufficient military aid to Finland and he failed to receive a vote
of confidence for his government. He resigned as Prime
Minister and was succeeded by Winston Churchill (q.v.).

CHAMOUNIX--(WAFT I)--Chamonix. A valley in Haute-
Savoie, France, near the NW entrance to the new Mont Blanc
(q.v.) tunnel.

CHANDRAPORE--(PI I)--The scene of much of Forster's
Passage to India. Its original may very well be Chhatarpur,
which he visited a number of times. Chhatapur is in NE
central India.

CHAPLIN, CHARLIE--(AH-Our Div)--Charles Spencer Chaplin, 1889- . A motion picture actor who was born in London and began his career in the London music halls. He
came to the United States as part of a vaudeville act and
there made his debut in silent films (1914). He was not an
immediate success in the medium until he created the character of the Tramp with which he has become identified. He
organized his own film company in 1918 and produced films
which have become classics: The Kid, The Gold Rush, City
Lights, etc. His autobiography was published in 1964.

CHAPMAN, R. W.--(AH-JA)--Robert William Chapman,
1881- . He produced the "new" edition of Pride and Prejudice (q.v.), which Forster discusses as well as a critical
bibliography (1953) of Jane Austen (q.v.), a Samuel Johnson
bibliography (1939), and other works.

CHARING CROSS--(PI VIII)--It is the triangular open space
at the head of Whitehall on the south side of Trafalgar Square
in London. It receives its name from a cross set up in
1291 by Edward I as the last of the 13 crosses which marked
the stages in the funeral procession of Eleanor of Castile,
his queen. The cross was taken down in 1647 and is now
replaced by a statue of Charles I.

CHARLEMAGNE--(Collect Ta-Celest)--742-814. In English:
Charles the Great. The first emperor of the Holy Roman

Empire and, in the view of some historians, the savior of
western civilization. He was the son of Pepin the Short on
whose death he succeeded to the throne of the Kingdom of
Neustria (768). When his brother died, he became king of
all the Franks (771). He conquered Lombardy and became
its king (773). Pope Leo III on Christmas Day 800 crowned
him Holy Roman Emperor. The circle of porphyry upon
which he stood when he received the crown is still preserved
in St. Peter's Basilica. He founded schools and was a patron of art, literature, and science.

CHARLES--(Two Cheers-Fer)--The Charles who accompanied
Forster to Ferney is Charles Mauron (q. v.) to whom Forster
dedicated Aspects of the Novel. Forster also mentions
Mauron in his essay, "Not Looking at Pictures" published in
Two Cheers for Democracy. Wilfrid Stone in his study of
Forster, The Cave and the Mountain, calls Mauron "Blooms-
bury's Gallic representative." Mauron is the author of
several volumes on aesthetics and attempted a translation of
Forster's work into French.

CHARLES I--(AH-Liberty)--1600-1649. The second son of
James IV of Scotland, James IV becoming James I of Great
Britain upon the death of Elizabeth I (q. v.). Charles was a
sickly child who would not have succeeded to the throne were
it not for the death of his brother, Prince Henry. He was
tried as a tyrant by Parliament, and condemned to death,
the first monarch to be so tried in the history of England.
He was beheaded in 1649. His death marked the suspension
of kingly rule in England until the Restoration.

CHARLES II--(AH-AB; AH-Consol)--1630-1685. He became
the King of England in 1660 after the restoration. He was
the son of Charles I (q. v.) and is often called the "merry
monarch." His reign marked a reversal of the trend toward
Puritanism under the Protector, Cromwell. The theatres
were re-opened and many of the "vices" which were banished
during the Protectorate returned with greater vigor. The
king generally set the tone for the majority of them. He
married Catherine of Braganza but had no legitimate heirs.
He tried to secure toleration for Catholics and died profes-
sing his faith in Roman Catholicism.

CHARLES LAMB'S PORK--(Two Cheers-Virginia)--Forster
is referring to the essay by Charles Lamb, "A Dissertation
on Roast Pig, " one of the best known essays in his collection, Essays of Elia, 1820-1825.

CHARLOTTE, QUEEN--(MT)--1744-1818. The much ma-
ligned (by him) wife of George III of England. She was the
niece of the duke of Mecklenburg-Strelitz.

CHARLUS, BARON DE--(Aspects VIII; Two Cheers-Our)--
He is a character in the novel Remembrance of Things Past
(q. v.) by Marcel Proust (q. v.), and a homosexual who, because of that aberration, is fascinating yet repulsive to
Marcel who describes homosexuality in the volume Cities of
the Plain.

CHÂTELET, MME. ÉMILIE DU--(AH-Vo)--Gabrielle Emilie
le Tonnelier de Breteuil, Marquise du Châtelet, 1706-1749.
A French writer and the mistress of Voltaire (q. v.). She
is the author of Traité sur le Bonheur, Lettres, etc.

CHAUCER--(Aspects I; Reading; Two Cheers-John)--Geoffrey
Chaucer, 1340?-1400. An English poet. He was the son of
a vintner and was employed for ten years on governmental
missions which took him to various parts of Europe. There
he came into contact with the works of Boccaccio and Petrarch which influenced the direction in which his own work
was to go. He received pensions from John of Gaunt and
Edward III and served them in various capacities including
clerk of the works at royal palaces. He was buried in
Westminster Abbey because of his service to the state rather than for his poetry. Ironically, around his grave are
buried poets interred because of their work. The area has
become known as "The Poet's Corner." Chaucer's poetry
falls into three distinct phases: the French, when his poetry was created on French models (e. g., The Book of the
Duchess, 1369); the Italian, marked by the use of rhyme
royal, a seven-line stanza, (e. g., The House of Fame); and
the English, the period when he produced his greatest work,
The Canterbury Tales.

CHEKOV--(Aspects IV; Two Cheers-Raison)--Anton Pavlovich
Chekov [Chekhov, Tchekhov], 1860-1904. He was a Russian
playwright and a writer of fiction. He is best known for his
plays, but his short stories are among the finest produced
in the Russia of his time. He originally intended to pursue
medicine and after studying in Moscow, began a small and
unimportant practice. Most of his time was given over to
writing. Three of his best short stories are "A Boring
Story" (1889), "The Duel" (1891), and "Lady with Lapdog"
(1899). His most famous plays are The Sea Gull (1896),
Uncle Vanya (1899), The Three Sisters (1901), and The

Cherry Orchard (q. v., 1903). All four are beloved by repertory groups and barely a season goes by without a revival of one of them.

CHELMSFORD, LORD--(AH-Mind)--Frederick John Napier, (1st Viscount Chelmsford), 1868-1933. He was governor of Queensland, New South Wales, and Viceroy of India. While viceroy (1916-21) he helped to institute new reforms in British rule, although despite the degree to which they alleviated problems between the Indians and the British, Gandhi (q. v.) rejected them. After his service in India, Napier was appointed first lord of the admiralty (1924) and agent-general for New South Wales (1926-28).

CHELSEA--(AH-Early)--Once an independent village, it is now part of London. Once the home of such notables as Thomas More (q. v.), Thomas Carlye (q. v.) and Nell Gwyn and others of lesser stature and notoriety, it is now largely inhabited by artists and artistic types. The area is more or less bound by Sloane Square on the E and the Thames on the S.

CHELSEA EMBANKMENT--(HE XV)--An attractive esplanade along the Thames in London in the Chelsea district. It was laid out by Sir Joseph Bazalgette in 1874 and extends for over a mile from Chelsea Bridge to Battersea Bridge.

CHELTENHAM--(HE XIII)--A borough in Gloucestershire, England about 42 miles S of Birmingham. It is popular as a watering place with mineral springs.

CHERRY ORCHARD, THE--(Aspects V)--A play by Anton Chekov (q. v.) set in the Russia of the 1890's. Its central theme is the victory of industrialization over the old aristocratic order. Mme. Ranevsky, an aristocrat fallen on bad days, is beset by debts after her return to her estate from an extended stay in Paris. Lopakhin, a successful businessman, advises her to sell the estate of which a cherry orchard, now in bloom, is a prominent part. She refuses, but, in the end she is forced to sell. The final curtain falls on the sound of axes chopping down the trees.

CHERTSEY--(GLD IV)--An urban district, on the S bank of the Thames, in Surrey, England.

CHESTERTON--(Two Cheers-English)--Gilbert Keith Chesterton, 1874-1936. An English poet, critic, novelist, and

writer of short stories who was an avid and devout supporter
of the Roman Catholic Church. Heretics (1905), a volume of
essays, deals with a group of his contemporaries whom he
considered extremists. He was a conservative and tradition-
alist. Much of his work has found the oblivion that it, perhaps, deserves, but one of his characters seems to have a
more enduring life: Father Brown, an amateur detective.

CHEVALLEY, ABEL--(Aspects I)--1868-1934. Author of Le
Roman Anglais de Nôtre Temps (1921), translated by Ben
Ray Redman. He also edited the poems of Herbert Trench
and compiled a concise French dictionary (1934).

CHILDE HAROLD--(WAFT I)--Full title: Childe Harold's
Pilgrimage (1812), a long poem by Byron (q. v.) in Spenser-
ian stanzas. A legend long connected with it has it that
Byron was unknown before its publication and was famous
(some would have it "infamous") the day after. It centers
upon the pilgrim--the first of a long line of Byronic heroes
(q. v.)--who is seeking solace from the pain of unrequited
love by travel through exotic lands and equally exotic adventures.

CHINON--(AH-Vo)--A commune in France (Indre-et-Loire
Departement) and the birthplace of Rabelais.

CHIROL, SIR VALENTINE--(Hill)--Sir Ignatius Valentine
Chirol, 1852-1929. He was a British journalist who traveled
widely in the Near East, Persia, India, and Australia (1871-
1892) before those lands became fashionable or of easy and
safe access. For a time he was the Berlin correspondent
for the London Times and head of the foreign department.
He is the author of many volumes among which are The
Eastern Question (1896), The Middle Eastern Question (1903),
and The Egyptian Problem (1920).

CHITRA--(AH-Two)--A play (1913) by Tagore (q. v.). Forster gives an excellent summary of its plot in "Two Works
by Tagore" in Abinger Harvest.

CHOLMONDELEY, MARY--(AH-HOS)--[Pron. "Chumley"] d.
1925. She was an English novelist born in Shropshire who
wrote The Danvers Jewels (1887), published under the pen-
name of "Pax, " and Diana Tempest (1893), and The Lowest
Rung (1908).

CHOPIN--(Aspects VI; Two Cheers-Raison)--Frédéric François Chopin, 1810-1849. He is a composer associated with the Polish nationalistic movement though only his mother was Polish. His father was French and the young Chopin passed much of his productive life in France or, as some say, in the arms of George Sand (Mme. Dudevant) the French novelist, his mistress, who was perhaps best known for the masculine dress she affected and the cigars she smoked. He wrote almost exclusively for the piano, and vastly enriched and extended the literature for that instrument. He is most noted for his highly lyrical pieces including some 55 mazurkas, 13 polanaises, 25 preludes, and two piano concertos.

CHRISTOPHER, JOHN--(Two Cheers-Romain)--Jean-Christophe Krafft. He is the central figure in the novel by Romain Rolland (q.v.) which Forster calls John Christopher, but is, perhaps, better known in America by its French title, Jean Christophe. Krafft is a musical genius who is underrated by his contemporaries. He has many passing love affairs, and becomes involved in an abortive political movement. He dies alone in Paris recognized as the greatest composer of modern music. Long considered as a modern classic, as Forster mentions, the novel is now not considered so favorably.

CHRZANOWSKI, IGNACY--(Nordic)--1866-1940. Authority on Polish literature killed by the Nazis.

CHURCHILL, FRANK--(Aspects IV)--The son of Mr. Weston in Emma (q.v.), a novel by Jane Austen (q.v.). He is adopted by Mr. and Mrs. Churchill whose name he takes upon coming of age. He was a very good looking young man whose face reflected much of the spirit and liveliness that had been his father's best qualities.

CHURCHILL, LORD RANDOLPH--(AH-Wil)--Full name: Randolph Henry Spencer Churchill, 1849-1895. A British statesman and the third son of the 7th Duke of Marlborough. He was the father of Winston Churchill (q.v.) by Jennie Jerome of Brooklyn, New York. He was a "fierce" Tory, chancellor of the exchequer and leader of the House of Commons.

CHURCHILL, WINSTON--(AH-Voter's; Two Cheers-Eng; Two Cheers-George)--Sir Winston Leonard Spencer Churchill, 1874-1965. He was the eldest son of Lord Randolph Churchill (q.v.), and like his father was deeply interested in politics. He held various governmental positions but is best known for his war-time post of Prime Minister from May 10, 1940 until July 1945, perhaps the most heroic period in Britain's history. During his retirement, he returned to his writing and his painting.

CICERO--(AH-Mac)--Marcus Tullius Cicero, 106-43 B. C. He was a Roman philosopher, orator, and statesman born in Arpinum, Italy. As a boy he went to Rome to study law, oratory, philosophy, and literature. He held a number of government posts including consul (63 B. C.). He foiled the Cataline conspiracy (q. v.) through his brilliant oratory. Although he sided with Pompey against Julius Caesar (q. v.), Caesar pardoned him. Caesar's nephew, Octavius (q. v. under Augustus) was not so merciful when Cicero ran afoul of the second triumvirate (Antony, Octavius, Lepidus). Octavius ordered his death. There are some 57 of Cicero's orations extant as well as many letters and such works as De Oratore, De Republica, De Legibus.

CID, THE--(Two Cheers-Raison)--Rodrigo Diaz de Bilvar, 1040?-1099. He was a Spanish soldier who won the title Compeador (champion) in a battle fought between Sancho I (Castile) and Sancho IV (Navarre). He has become idealized as the perfect hero who won many battles under the Arabs. His deeds, much romanticized by time and desire, are recorded in Poema del Cid (c. 1140) and other works of that as well as other periods, including the play Le Cid (1636) by the French playwright, Corneille, and the opera, Le Cid (1885) by Jules Massenet.

CIRCE--(Aspects VI)--In Greek myth, she is a sorceress who lived in the island of Aeaea. Ulysses landed there, in an incident recorded in The Odyssey. She turned his companions into swine. He escaped her curse by using an herb given him by the god, Mercury.

"CIRCLES OF THE STORMY MOON, THE, etc. "--(AH-TS)-- From the poem "Sweeney Among the Nightingales, " by T. S. Eliot. The lines appear in the second stanza (ℓ. 5ff.). The poem has been reprinted in The Complete Poems and Plays, 1909-1950, New York: Harcourt Brace, 1950.

CITHAERON--(LJ XXXIII)--A mountain in Greece sacred to Dionysus and the Muses. It is located on the NW border of ancient Attica.

CITY OF GOD, THE--(Two Cheers-St. Augustine)--By St. Augustine (Latin title: De Civitate Dei). The title refers to the Church, the whole body of believers. It is the Kingdom of Christ in contradistinction to the City of Destruction.

CIVILISATION, ITS CAUSE AND CURE--(Two Cheers-Edward --By Edward Carpenter (q.v.), first published in London, 1889. It expresses in economic terms the author's love for the individual and for the beauty of nature. He held that civilization should properly be given an historical instead of ideal value and that man must achieve: 1) the realization of a new order of society in close touch with nature; 2) a science which will no longer be a mere thing of the brain but a part of actual life; and 3) a morality which will express the vital and organic unity of man with his fellows.

CLAGGART--(Aspects VII)--A character in Billy Budd, Foretopman, by Herman Melville (q.v.). He is the master-at-arms of the "Indomitable," who becomes envious of Billy Budd (q.v.), and provokes his own death when Billy hits him. Little is known of Claggart's life ashore.

CLAPHAM SECT--(MT)--The name given to a group of 19th-century evangelical Christians in England all of whom were Anglicans (except for the Unitarian, Sir William Smith) prominent from 1790 to 1830. The group was drawn together by Forster's forebear, Henry Thornton, a banker who in 1792 invited Wilberforce (q.v.) to share his home, Battersea Rise (q.v.), in Clapham. Most of those in the sect were members of Parliament and were nicknamed "the saints." Their greatest achievement was the abolition of slavery. They worked for, among other things, better prison conditions. They were chiefly conservative in outlook, but always ready to work with radicals and free-thinkers. The group had its own journal, The Christian Observer (1802-1816) edited by Zachary Macaulay (q.v.) and wielded a powerful influence over English society. Some of the group were Hannah More (q.v.), Thomas Babington, and John Venn.

CLAPHAMITES--(Two Cheers-Henry)--See: Clapham Sect.

CLARA--(Aspects V)--Clara Middleton. A character in the novel, The Egoist (1879), by George Meredith (q.v.). She is betrothed to Sir Willoughby but is, nevertheless, his severest critic. She is at first attracted by the force of his personality but she soon discovers that he is a manipulator of people. She tries to break her engagement, but he refuses. She is helped by his scholar-cousin, Vernon Whitford, whom she later marries.

CLARK, SIR KENNETH--(New Disorder; Two Cheers-Anon)--
Sir Kenneth Mackenzie Clark, now Lord Clark.   He is an
English connoisseur of art and the director of the National
Gallery, London.   He is also the author of several volumes
on art and the current television series, Civilisation (Fall,
1970), broadcast over educational television channels in the
United States.

CLARK, WILLIAM GEORGE--(Aspects I)--1821-1878.   An
English classical and Shakespearean scholar.   He was a
Fellow of Trinity College, Cambridge, and established the
Cambridge Journal of Philology (1868); he was the editor,
with John Glover and William Aldis Wright, librarians of
Trinity, of The Cambridge Shakespeare (nine volumes, 1863-
66); he also edited with William Aldis Wright, The Globe
Shakespeare (1864).   He is the author of Gazpacho (1853) and
Vacation Tourists (1861-64).   For more detailed biographical
information, see: the first chapter of Forster's Aspects of
the Novel.

CLAUDEL--(Aspects VII; Two Cheers-Anon; Two Cheers-
Gide; Two Cheers-Raison)--Paul Louis Charles Claudel, 1868-
1955.   He was a French diplomat, poet and dramatist, closely associated with the symbolic school.   He entered the diplomatic service in 1892 and held many foreign posts chief of
which was ambassador to Japan.   He is the author of many
works including the play L'Annonce Faîtes à Marie and a
lyrical drama with music by Milhaud, Christophe Colomb.

CLEMENT OF ALEXANDRIA--(Alex I, 2; PP-Clement)--Titus
Flavius Clemens.   150?-A.D. ?220.   A Greek theologian of
the early Christian Church who was probably born in Athens
and studied in Alexandria where he entered the Church.   He
was made the head of the catechetical school in Alexandria
(A.D. 190-203) which by his teaching and that of Origen (q.
v.) became one of the centers of learning.   He left Alexandria during the persecutions of Christians (c. 203).   He is
regarded as a founder of the Alexandrian school of theology.
His works include: Who is the Rich Man That Shall be
Saved?, The Tutor, Exhortation to the Greeks.

CLEOPATRA III--(Alex I, 2)--2nd century B.C.   The niece
and second wife of Ptolemy VIII of Egypt.   He was nicknamed
Physcon, ("fat paunch").

CLEOPATRA VI--(Alex I, 1)--Cleopatra VI Philopater (Try-
phaena). Sister and wife of Ptolemy XII Philopater Neos
Dionyson (he was nicknamed Auletes, "flute player"), 1st
century B.C. The mother of Cleopatra VII (q.v.), the Great.

CLEOPATRA VII--(AH-Salute; Alex I, 1; PP-Philo)--Called
"the Great," 68-30 B.C. The Cleopatra of legend. She was
the daughter of Ptolemy Auletes King of Egypt (d. 51 B.C.)
and appointed by him as his successor. She ruled jointly
with her younger brother, until dethroned by Pothinus. She
was restored to her throne by Julius Caesar (q.v.) who fell
under her spell and by whom she had a son. Later, she
was to exercise the same power over Mark Antony (q.v.)
with whom she had hoped to rule the world until his defeat
by Octavius (q.v. under Augustus) at which point she took
her own life. Though queen of Egypt, she was not an Egyptian but a Macedonian, descendant of Ptolemy, one of Alexander's (q.v.) generals who seized Egypt after his death.

CLIO--(Aspects VI)--In Greek myth, she is one of the nine
muses credited with the invention of historical and heroic
poetry.

CLISSOLD--(Aspects V)--The central figure in the novel by
H. G. Wells (q.v.), The World of William Clissold: A
Novel at a New Angle (1926) which discusses ad nauseum
his and his creator's philosophy of life in two volumes.

CLITOPHON AND LEUCIPPE--(Alex II, 1)--A novel by
Achilles Tatius (q.v.) set in Alexandria and translated from
the Greek by S. Gaselee in the Loeb Classical Library, Harvard, first printed, 1917. The title given is The Adventures
of Leucippe and Clitophon.

CLIVE--(AH-Our Div)--Robert Baron Clive of Plassey, 1725-
1774. He was a British militaryman and is credited with
founding the empire of British India. He went to Madras,
India, in 1743 as an employee of the East India Company.
His arrival was followed by a series of military adventures
which led to the East India Company's control of much of
India. In later life, he became addicted to opium and died
a suicide as a result of that addiction and the scandal which
arose from inquires made by Parliament into his method of
operating.

"CLOUD MESSENGER, THE"--(AH-Adrift)--A poem by
Kalidas (q.v.) [Kalides, Kalidasa]. There is an edition in

English: The Cloud Messenger; An Indian Love Lyric, trans. by Charles King (London, 1930). In all likelihood, this is the translation Forster read.

CLOUDS, THE--(LJ IV)--A comic play (423 B.C.) by Aristophanes (q.v.), the Greek playwright. An old man, overwhelmed by his debts, seeks out Socrates to teach him false logic in order that he may avoid having to pay his creditors. Socrates rejects him as too old and too dumb to teach. The old man sends his son in his place. Pheidippides, the son, learns quickly and so well that the creditors are routed. Pheidippides returns and beats his father noting that the new logic he has learned permits a son to beat his father. The old man, enraged, goes to burn down Socrates' "shop of logic."

CNIDUS--(AH-Cn)--An ancient city, now in ruins, on Cape Krio, SW Asia Minor. It was a Dorian city noted for its temples, statues, fine buildings, and its wealth.

COCKERALL, CHARLES ROBERT--(Two Cheers-Camb)-- 1788-1863. English architect and archaeologist who conducted excavations in the Levant. He was also professor of architecture to the Royal Academy (q.v.) of which he was a member. He designed chiefly along classical lines. Some of his buildings are at Oxford and Cambridge.

COCKNEY--(HE XVI; Two Cheers-Lon)--The name generally given to anyone born within the sound of Bow Bells, London. It is also applied to a type of pronunciation associated with Londoners of the lower classes. The origin of the word is obscure.

COCKTAIL PARTY, THE--(Two Cheers-Two Books)--A play by T. S. Eliot (q.v.) first presented in 1949. The Chamberlaynes are giving a cocktail party in their London flat and a number of people have been invited all of whom are in the need of help which is supplied, along with direction for their lives, by a psychiatrist whom Lavinia, the hostess, has been seeing.

COELEBS IN SEARCH OF A WIFE--(AH-Mrs)--By Hannah More (q.v.). Subtitled: "Comprehending observations on domestic habits and manners, religion and morals," it proved so popular that, by 1809 it was in its sixth edition.

"COELESTIS URBS HIERUSALEM..." etc.--(AH-Ab)--A Medieval Latin hymn. The following is a literal translation: Jerusalem the City of Heaven/Beautiful vision of peace/In which the upright live/With stones uplifted to a star/To the bride whom you surround with a ceremony/With thousands of angels./Grace owed to the obedient/Let it be forever to all in the highest/Father and Son united/And in the glorious Paraclete/To Whom with praise, power, and glory/Let eternity be with the world.

COLERIDGE, ERNEST HARTLEY--(GLD IV)--1846-1920. A grandson of the poet, Samuel Taylor Coleridge, he, too, was an author. He was the son of Coleridge's second son, Derwent, and a graduate of Oxford and secretary to England's chief justice. He edited the letters (1895) and the complete works (two vols., 1912) of his grandfather, also the works of Byron (1898-1903), and, among other works, the notebooks of his grandfather.

COLERIDGE, SAMUEL TAYLOR--(AH-Troop; Two Cheers-Anon; Two Cheers-Camb; Two Cheers-Eng; Two Cheers-Raison)--1772-1834. English poet and critic. Educated at Jesus College, Cambridge which he left for the dragoons only to be rescued by his brother from the life of a soldier for which he was not fit. Always interested in radical ideas, he wanted to put them into practice by joining Southey's adventure in establishing a utopia on the Susquehanna River in Pennsylvania. This, like his romantic fling in soldiering, was doomed to failure. He turned his attention to writing poetry which had been his enduring interest. His first volume of poems was published in 1796. That same year he began using opium which was to control him for the remainder of his life. He met Wordsworth and joined him in the production of a very important book of poetry, Lyrical Ballads (1798), which was to herald a new approach to poetry. Among other pieces, it included the poem for which he is most known, "The Rime of the Ancient Mariner." He went on to write "Kubla Khan," a fragment which gained fame perhaps as much for the manner in which it was composed than for its contents. Coleridge is also known as the father of modern Shakespearean criticism.

COLOSSEUM--(MT)--The name given to the great Flavian amphitheater in Rome which, interestingly enough, did not receive its name because of its size but rather because a colossal statue of Nero stood close by in the Via Sacra. The amphitheater was begun by Vespasian (A.D. 72) and

was used regularly for over 400 years.   Only two-thirds of
it remains since it has also served as a quarry for the
building of medieval and Renaissance Rome.

COMBINATION ACTS--(MT)--These were laws enacted between 1799 and 1824 in England in order to control the growth
of labor unions.   They were repealed in 1825.

COMMINES, PHILIPPE DE--(Two Cheers-In)--[Alt. spellings:
Comines, Commynes, Comynes] Sire d'Argenton, 1447?-
?1511.   He was a French chronicler successively in service
to Charles the Bold, Louis XI, and Charles VIII.   He was
also a member of the council of regency during the minority
of Charles VIII.   He was arrested and exiled for political
mis-adventures.   He then retired to private life and devoted his time to writing his Mémoires which are widely regarded as one of the classics of Medieval literature.

COMMON READER, THE--(Two Cheers-Virginia)--A collection of essays (1925) on various subjects, by Virginia Woolf
(q.v.).   There is a second series (London, 1932).

CONCORD, TEMPLE OF--(MT)--A temple on the Capitoline
hill in Rome now almost totally in ruins.   It was first
erected in 370 B.C. in celebration of the right won by the
plebs to furnish one of the consuls from its own rank--a major triumph for the common man of ancient Rome.   The temple was restored a number of times and its platform still
dominates the forum.   Its frieze and some architectural fragments are displayed in the Tabularium.   During the period
of the Roman Republic, the temple became a type of museum.
In it were deposited works of art captured during the many
wars fought and offerings made to Concordia, the goddess of
peace, the deity to whom it was dedicated.   The Senate often
met in it.

CONFESSIONS--(Two Cheers-Book)--Written by St. Augustine,
Bishop of Hippo (North Africa) c. A.D. 400.   Essentially it
is an autobiography of the saint detailing his religious experiences played out against a background of mortal conflict
and deep personal tragedy.   On another level it is a defense
of the Latin Church.

CONFESSIONS OF A MIDDLEAGED MAN, THE--(Collect Ta-
Point)--A book of essays written by Michael in which
he "paid melodious tribute to youth, but showed that ripe-
ness is all."

CONFUCIAS [sic]--(GLD XI)--The Latinized name of the
Chinese Kung Fu-tzu ("Philosopher Kung"), c. 551-479 B.C.
He was a philosopher of the state of Lu, now the province
of Shantung, and was once its minister of state, but gave up
his position to wander about and meditate upon the problem
of life. This meditation produced a philosophy, based on
moral principles, the family, social reform and the conduct
of the state, which controlled the thinking of the Chinese
empire throughout its history to the very doors of the 20th
century. He composed a number of maxims on these subjects which were intended to serve as a guide for daily life.
These were collected into a volume titled Analects.

CONRAD--(AH-Joseph; Aspects IV; Two Cheers-Ter)--Józef
Teodor Konrad Nalecz Korzeniowski (which he shortened to
Joseph Conrad), 1857-1924. Born to parents of the Polish
gentry in a region of the Ukraine once a part of Poland, he
became a naturalized British citizen. He was a seaman as
a young man but left (1894) to devote himself to writing.
Despite the fact that he wrote in a language not his own, he
is recognized as a modern master of English prose. Many
of his novels are written against a background of the sea
and deal with man in conflict with his conscience. Some of
his more prominent works are The Nigger of the "Narcissus"
(1897), Lord Jim (1900), Heart of Darkness (1902), Typhoon
(1902), and Nostromo (1904).

CONSTANCE--(Aspects II; Two Cheers-Virginia)--Constance
Baines is a central character in The Old Wives' Tale by
Arnold Bennett (q.v.). She is the older sister of Sophia
who dominates her. She is capable in all things except in
managing her son. As she grows older, she becomes obese
and is plagued with sciatica, rheumatism and Sophia.

CONSTANTINE I--(Alex I, 2)--Called the Great. Flavius
Valerius Aurelius Constantinus, A.D. 280?-337. Emperor
of Rome (306-337), he was the son of Constantine Chlorus
who had been proclaimed by Diocletian as his successor.
When Chlorus died at York, England, the troops declared
Constantine to be their emperor. There were five other
claimants to the throne and, when confronting the last of
these he is said to have had a vision of the cross of Christ
and a motto In Hoc Signo Vinces ("In this sign you will conquer"). He took the cross as his sign, won the battle and
became sole emperor. He gave freedom of worship to the
Christians and called the great Council of Nicaea out of

which came the Nicene Creed.   He moved his capital to
Byzantium (Constantinople, now Istanbul).

CONSTANTIUS I--(Alex I, 2; PP-St A)--Flavius Valerius
Constantius, surnamed Chlorus ("the pale"), A.D. c. 250-
306.   He was the son-in-law of Maximian and the father of
Constantine (q.v.) by Helen.   He was adopted as Caesar by
Maximian (292) and given the government of Gaul and, on
the abdication of Diocletian and Maximian, he became emperor of the West (305-306).   He died at York, England.

COOLIDGE--(GLD XI)--John Calvin Coolidge, 1872-1933.
The 30th president of the United States.   He was born in
Vermont and held several political offices including the
governorship of Massachusetts.   He gained national renown
as governor when he quelled the Boston police strike (1919).
He was elected vice-president and held the post until August
2, 1923 when, because of the death of Harding, he succeeded
to the presidency.   He was elected president in his own right
in 1924 and served a full term which ended with his oft-
quoted words: "I do not choose to run."

COPPERFIELD, DAVID--(Aspects IV)--The central figure in
the novel David Copperfield by Charles Dickens (q.v.).   He
was born after the death of his father and his troubles began when his mother re-married.   He is the object of tyranny and cruelty and his life is marked by mis-placed trusts
and mis-directed emotions.   It promises to take a turn for
the better, however, when he turns to a literary career and
embarks upon a second marriage.

CORDELIA--(Two Cheers-Stratford; WAFT IV)--A character
in King Lear, a play by William Shakespeare (q.v.).   She
is Lear's youngest daughter who, like him, is stubborn.
She refuses to flatter him to obtain a share in his kingdom
as do his other daughters.   As a result, she loses her law-
ful inheritance.   But when Lear is mistreated by the two
daughters to whom he gave his kingdom, she returns from
France to comfort him, only to die at her sister's instiga-
tion.   Her death precipitates the death of Lear whose misfortunes have driven him mad.

CORDOVA--(PI XXX)--A city in S Spain, about 70 miles
ENE of Seville, where there are Roman and Moorish remains.

CORELLI, MARIE--(HE V; LJ I)--The pen name of Mary
Mackay, 1855-1924. She was an enormously popular and
equally prolific English writer of romances whose reputation
is now more than tarnished. She is the author of such
novels as: The Romance of Two Worlds (1886), Holy Orders
(1908), and The Secret Power (1921).

CORIOLANUS--(MT)--He is the chief character in the play
Coriolanus by William Shakespeare (q. v.). A noble warrior
of the Roman Republic, he refuses to beg the favor of the
crowd by destroying his integrity. His mother, the dominating force in his life, however, persuades him to betray
those principles for the success she feels he deserves. He
follows her advice and, as a result, brings about his own
doom.

"CORIOLANUS OVERTURE"--(Two Cheers-Not Listening)--
An overture (Opus 62) by Ludwig van Beethoven (q. v.) composed in 1807 and published in 1808. Despite its title, it is
not based on Shakespeare's play but rather on a tragedy by
Heinrich Joseph von Collin.

CORNEILLE--(Two Cheers-Raison)--Pierre Corneille, 1606-
1684. A French dramatist of the early neo-classical period.
He wrote many tragedies dealing with problems of honor,
patriotism, duty and the conflicts their pursuit present to
right-thinking individuals. His Le Cid (q. v.) was produced
in 1637. Most of his plays rest heavily upon classical
themes and subjects (e. g., Cinna and Horace, both 1640),
and he wrote excellent comedy as well (e. g., Don Sanche
d'Aragon, 1649).

CORNELIA--(Two Cheers-Ascent)--A figure in the history of
Rome. She was the wife of Titus Semponius Gracchus and
the mother of Tiberus and Gaius, the two tribunes. For the
Romans, she symbolized many of the virtues they held sacred. As a result, a statue was erected in her honor.
There is a story that, when asked to display her jewels,
she presented her two sons.

COROT--(Two Cheers-Not)--Jean Baptiste Camile Corot,
1796-1875. He was a French painter and one of the founders of the Barbizon School of painting which was revolutionary in its insistence that painters bring their easels out of
doors. Members, like Corot, painted landscapes, generally
containing cows and often with classical figures all diffused
with a romantic light. He was popular among American col-

lectors of the late 19th century.

CORTINA D'AMPEZZO--(Collect Ta-Intro)--A village in N
Italy N of Belluno and a famous ski resort.

CORTONA--(WAFT I)--An ancient Etruscan city containing
the remains of walls, Roman baths, a temple, and a good
museum of Etruscan antiquities. It is located in the province of Arezzo (Tuscany), in central Italy.

COSSACKS--(Two Cheers-Three)--A warlike people who live
on the Russian steppes (plains), they were skilled horsemen
who were used by the Czars as special cavalry. They
proved themselves loyal on many occasions.

COUCHE SOCIALE--(LJ XV)--A French idiom: Social class.

COUNCIL OF FLORENCE--(AH-Gem)--More correctly known
as the Council of Basel-Ferrara-Florence, it was convened
by Pope Eugene IV in order that the breach between the
Eastern and Western Churches be healed. Twenty-five ses-
sions were held from July 1431 to May 4, 1437. These
meetings began in Basel, were transferred to Ferrara, and
in January 1439 to Florence. Union was confirmed with the
Greeks in Florence, July 6, 1439; Armenians, November 22;
and the Jacobites, February 4, 1442.

COUNCIL OF TRENT--(AH-Car)--It is considered by many
as the most important Western ecumenical council. It was
convened by Pope Paul III on May 22, 1542, at Trent for
the purpose of condemning the Protestant revolt and to move
for reforms within the Roman Church. Two other popes are
associated with the council: Julius III, the successor of
Paul, and Pius IV, who followed Julius. The council ended
in 1563 after passing decisions concerning the authority of
Scripture and Tradition, original sin, the seven Sacraments,
the Mass, and the cult of the saints. Many reforms were
also promulgated.

COUNTERFEITERS, THE--(Aspects IV)--A novel by André
Gide. See: Les Faux Monnayeurs.

COUNTESS--(Aspects IV)--A character in the novel Evan
Harrington by George Meredith. Her full name is Louisa,
the Countess de Saldar. She is Harrington's sister who has
married well and works to find an equally good partner for
her brother.

COUSIN KATE--(PI II)--A comedy (1910) in three acts by
Hubert Henry Davis (1869-1917). Hugh Walpole wrote an introduction to Davis' collected plays (London, 1921). Davis
was born at Woodley, Cheshire, England and was a journalist in San Francisco. He returned to England in 1901 and
mysteriously disappeared in 1917.

COVENT GARDEN--(HE V)--The principal home of grand
opera and ballet in England. The building seats about 2000
and is the third on its site. It was designed (1856-8) by
Edward M. Barry and its acoustics are considered excellent.
It receives its name from a corruption in pronunciation of
convent garden on which the first building was erected after
the Reformation.

COWLEY--(GLD IV)--Abraham Cowley, 1618-1667. An English poet of the metaphysical school, he was a royalist who
followed the queen, Catherine de Braganza, into exile and
corresponded for her in cipher with the king, Charles I (q.
v.). After the Restoration, he was rewarded for his fidelity
with a living near Chertsey. There, he devoted himself to
botany and experimental science. His works include elegies,
odes, and an epic on the life of David.

COWPER--(AH-HOS; AH-JA; MT; Reading)--William Cowper,
1731-1800. An English poet and member of the bar, his
life was marked by a tendency to mental imbalance. One of
his most successful works, The Task (1785) is in blank
verse. He also translated Homer. The last poem he wrote,
"The Castaway" (1798), was an attempt to establish a freer
approach to English poetry. He is considered by many as a
forerunner of English Romanticism.

C. P. S. --(Aspects VII)--Forster is referring to Charles Percy
Snow, 1905- . Now Lord Snow, he was born in Leicester,
England and educated at its university and then at Cambridge
where he held a fellowship in physics and later became tutor.
He is one of the world's primary exponents of the integra-
tion of the two cultures, science and humanities. Best
known of his writings, perhaps, is the roman fleuve, Strang-
ers and Brothers, which he has recently concluded with
Last Things (1970).

CRABBE--(AH-JA; Two Cheers-George C.; MT; Reading)--
George Crabbe, 1754-1832. An English poet. Forster has
given a good summary of his life in the essay "George

Crabbe" reprinted in Two Cheers for Democracy. Crabbe's
son, George, wrote a biography of his father.

CRAFT OF FICTION, THE--(Aspects IV)--A book of criticism by Percy Lubbock (1879-1965). He was an essayist,
critic and the editor of the New York edition of Henry
James's novels and of his letters. The Craft of Fiction was
published in 1928, a year before Forster's work on the novel. Many maintain that Lubbock's volume is the first to
treat fiction as an art. His approach to that art is essentially Jamesian. Like James, he is uncomfortable in the
presence of the loose, sprawling novel. His volume contains
no index and no chapter-titles.

CRANFORD--(Aspects I)--A work of fiction (1853) by Elizabeth Gaskell, less a novel than a collection of 16 inter-re-
lated sketches of early Victorian life. There is a narrator,
Mary Smith, who visits the tiny village of Cranford and
tells tales of the villagers, mostly the aged who live in
genteel poverty. The work is especially effective in pre-
senting the customs of the day.

CRAWFORD--(AH-JA)--Henry Crawford. A character in
Mansfield Park (1914) by Jane Austen (q.v.). He is a wealthy
young man who flirts with Maria Bertram (q.v.), but falls
in love with Fanny Price. She refuses him and he elopes
with Maria who has become Mrs. Rushworth. After several
months, they part.

CREON--(Nordic; Two Cheers-They)--In Greek legend, the
King of Thebes and brother of Jocasta, the mother-wife of
Oedipus. His story is told and retold in the Greek drama,
notably by Sophocles (q.v.) and Euripides (q.v.). He is
generally depicted as a manipulator and an astute politician
who uses every event as an advantage for himself.

CREWE, LORD--(AH-BA)--Robert Offley Ashburton Crewe-
Milnes (First Marquis of Crewe), 1858-1945. An English
statesman and diplomat, he was lord lieutenant of Ireland,
lord privy seal, ambassador to France, secretary of state
for war, among other positions.

CRITCHLOW, MR.--(Aspects II)--A character in the novel,
Old Wives' Tale (1908) by Arnold Bennett (q.v.). Charles
Critchlow is the legal adviser and close friend of the Baines
family.

CRITERION, THE--(Two Cheers-Two Bks)--A periodical founded (1922) and edited by T. S. Eliot (q.v.) until it ceased publication in 1939. It was devoted to the publication of critical essays and reviews.

CRIVELLI--(Two Cheers-Not; Two Cheers-Whiff)--Carlo Crivelli, fl. 1457-1493. A Venetian painter of rather worldy-looking madonnas, saints, etc. His "Annunciation" is in the National Gallery, London, and several paintings are in New York's Metropolitan Museum of Art.

CROESUS--(Collect Ta-Other)--The King of Lydia (Asia Minor) 560-546 B.C. His wealth was held to be so enormous that the saying, "rich as Croesus," has come to be applied to any extremely wealthy individual.

CROMER, LORD--(AH-Wil; Alex II, 5; Egypt)--Evelyn Baring (1st Earl of Cromer), 1841-1917. He was the British agent and consul general of the Egyptian government (1883). He helped to stabilize Egypt's economy and to check the spread of nationalism. He resigned the post in 1907 and wrote a number of books, including Modern Egypt (1908).

CROMWELL, OLIVER--(Two Cheers-United)--1599-1658. He became the Lord Protector of England after Charles I (q.v.) was beheaded. He was a successful soldier and a Puritain who, nevertheless, tolerated all religions during his tenure in office. He was to be succeeded by his son, Richard, but Richard was unable to continue in the post and, therefore, Charles II (q.v.) was returned to the throne.

CRUIKSHANK, GEORGE--(HE XVIII)--1792-1878. An English caricaturist and illustrator noted especially for his work with Dickens (Oliver Twist, Sketches by Boz). He also illustrated the works of other authors notably Ainsworth, and Lever.

CRYSTAL PALACE--(MT)--A glass and iron-framed building erected in 1851 in Hyde Park (q.v.), London for the Great Exhibition. It was almost entirely destroyed by fire in 1936.

CTESIPHON--(LJ XVI)--He was the Athenian citizen of the Fourth Century B.C. who was prosecuted by Aeschines for proposing that Demosthenes receive a crown for his distinguished services. His defense was conducted by Demosthenes.

CUMBERLAND, DUKE OF--(AH-Capt)--William Augustus (1721-1765), the third son of George II and Queen Caroline. He was trained in the Royal Navy and was given command of the British, Hanoverian, Austrian and Dutch forces and was soundly defeated by Marshal Saxe at Fontenay (1745). He was again defeated by Saxe in Flanders in 1747. He retired to private life in 1757.

CUMBERLAND, DUKE OF--(MT)--Ernest Augustus, 1771-1851. The son of George III and the first King of Hanover after the separation (1837) of the English and Hanoverian crowns at the accession of Victoria (q.v.) to the throne of England.

CUPID--(AH-Mac)--In Roman myth, the god of love in its passionate and fleshy aspect. He is identified closely with Eros in Greek myth, the son of Venus and Mercury, and is generally represented as a winged boy blindfolded and carrying a quiver of arrows and a bow.

CURLE, RICHARD--(Two Cheers-Snow)--1883- . The editor of the Julia Wedgewood-Robert Browning correspondence mentioned in Forster's essay. He was also the friend of Joseph Conrad (q.v.) and author of several books on his life.

CURZON, LORD--(AH-Me; GLD XII; PI VII)--George Nathaniel Curzon (1st Baron and 1st Marquis Curzon of Kedleston), 1859-1925. He was an English statesman who held many offices including that of Viceroy and Governor General of India (1899-1905). He also held the post of Secretary of State for foreign affairs, among others. He wrote several volumes, including: Lord Curzon in India (1906).

CURZON, ROBERT--(Alex II, 7)--1810-1873. The 14th Baron Zouche, he was the author of Monasteries of the Levant (Visits to Monasteries of the Levant) (q.v.). He was the son of Viscount Asheton and Baroness de la Zouche and was private secretary to Lord Stratford de Redcliffe at Constantinople. He was appointed (1843) as part of a joint commission to determine the boundaries between Turkey and Persia and the journey resulted in Armenia: A Year at Erzeroom. Ill health then forced his return to England.

CURZON STREET--(HE XXVI)--A street in Mayfair, London, named after Lord Curzon (q.v.). At No. 19 lived Lord Beaconsfield (Disraeli, q.v.), and No. 32 was the town house of the Marquis of Crewe.

CUST, MRS. HENRY--(GLD XIV)--Emmeline (Nina) Cust.
Author of many volumes including an edition of Queen Victoria's (q. v.) letters.

CYCLADES--(Collect Ta-Celest)--A group of islands (about
200) in the Aegean Sea between the Peloponnesus and the
Dodecanese. They were given their name in ancient times
because they form a circle around the island of Delos.

CYR, ST. --(Alex II, 7)--St. Quiricus, d. A. D. 304. The
infant son of St. Julietta. She was an aristocratic widow
martyred at Tarsus for her Christian faith. Before her
death, her son, St. Cyr, was killed because he had scratched
the face of the magistrate before whom she was arraigned.

CYRIAC OF ANCONA--(AH-For the Muse; Two Cheers-
Whiff)--Ciriaco de' Pizzi, 1391-c. 1449. He was an Italian
humanist and antiquarian who traveled in Egypt, Syria, the
Aegean Islands, and Greece collecting manuscripts, coins,
works of art, making copies of inscriptions and noting all
evidences of the ancient life of Greece still visible. The
material he gathered was of great value to later scholars.

CYRIL, PATRIARCH--(Alex I, 2)--St. Cyril of Alexandria,
A. D. 376-444. He was an early Roman Catholic churchman,
Archbishop of Alexandria (412), and is considered now a
doctor of the Church. He vigorously defended the Church
against the Novatians, Nestorians and presided at the Council
of Ephesus (413) at which Nestorius was condemned as a
heretic.

CYRUS, PATRIARCH MUKAUKAS--(Alex I, 2)--Appointed by
the Emperor Heraclius as Archbishop of Alexandria and
Imperial Viceroy (c. A. D. 631). Heraclius had hoped that
Cyrus would conciliate both the orthodox supporters of the
decisions of the Council of Chalcedon and the Copts through
the doctrine of monotheism. But Cyprus persecuted the
Copts. It is said that his tactics prepared the city for its
fall into the hands of the Islamic world.

                                    D

DACOIT--(Hill)--A member, in India and Burma, of a society or band dedicated to murder and robbery.

DAILY TELEGRAPH--(HE XIV)--The first daily newspaper to be issued for a penny. Founded in 1855, its highly color-ful style made it enjoy, for a time, the largest circulation of any English newspaper.

DALE, LAETITIA--(Aspects V)--A character in the novel, The Egoist (1879), by George Meredith (q. v.). For years she silently admires Sir Willoughby Patterne who is more interested in the pursuit of Clara Middleton (see: Clara) marriage to whom would flatter his ego. When Clara re-fuses to marry him, he turns to Laetitia who, finally able to see through to his egoism, turns him down until he agrees to marriage on her terms.

DALLOWAY, MRS. --(Two Cheers-Virginia)--The central fig-ure in the novel of the same name (1925) by Virginia Woolf (q. v.). Clarissa Dalloway is a woman in her 50's still chic, still attractive, but deeply disturbed by the direction her love and her life have taken. She senses that death is near and that growing old will be distasteful.

DALLOWAY, RICHARD--(Two Cheers-Virginia)--A character in the novel, Mrs. Dalloway (1925), by Virginia Woolf (q. v.). He is the husband of Clarissa Dalloway (see: Mrs. Dallo-way), a politician of the conservative persuasion who knows he will achieve nothing politically beyond his seat in Parlia-ment. He loves his wife deeply, but is incapable of dis-playing his affection for her.

DANCE OF DEATH--(AH-Proust)--Originating in 14th-cen-tury Germany, the Dance of Death is an allegorical represen-tation of Death, a skeletal figure, leading all manner of people in a dance to the grave. A type of morality play, it also became a popular subject in art. Holbein, among others, in a series of woodcuts represents the dance begin-ning with Adam and Eve.

DANIEL--(Alex II, 1)--A Hebrew prophet who was held prisoner in Babylon and who, eventually, was cast into a den of lions but was saved by God. His adventures are de-tailed in the Old Testament book of "Daniel."

DANTE--(AH-Adrift; AH-Cn; AH-Gem; AH-Marco; AH-My W; AH-Proust; Collect Ta-Celest; RWV V; Two Cheers-Bk; Two Cheers-Does; Two Cheers-Our; Two Cheers-Raison; Two Cheers-They; Two Cheers-Tol; Two Cheers-Two Bks; Two Cheers-What; WAFT II)--Dante Aleghieri, 1265-1321. An

Italian philosophical poet born in Florence but exiled from
his native city for siding with the wrong political faction.
He is best known for his long, poetical work which he titled
La Commedia (1300, 1308, 1311) and subsequent generations
have retitled La Divina Commedia. The poem, in terza
rima, details an imaginary journey through Hell, Purgatory
(conducted by Virgil) and Heaven (conducted by Beatrice, q.
v.). These regions are peopled with personages Dante knew
in life and are governed by his understanding of life and the
Deity. Another work, La Vita Nuova, is a series of 31
poems of love mostly in the sonnet form. Dante is also
credited with establishing the Tuscan dialect of Italian as
the standard in that language.

DARDANELLES--(PP-Return)--"The Hellespont," the narrow
strait which with the Bosporus to the NE separates European
Turkey from Asiatic Turkey and links the Black Sea with the
Aegean.

DARWIN--(LJ X; MT; Two Cheers-In)--Charles Robert Darwin, 1809-1882. Educated at Edinburgh and Cambridge, he
is most famous for a sea voyage which he took on the ship,
The Beagle, to the South Seas (Dec. 1831 to Oct. 1836), the
results of which have changed the direction of man's thoughts
and philosophy of life. The observations he made on that
voyage and other studies led to the formulation of his theory
of evolution. That theory, at first ridiculed and then, char-
acteristically, embraced fervently like a new faith, was detailed, especially with regard to man, in several works,
chiefly The Descent of Man (1871).

DA SAN GALLO, ANTONIA PICCONI--(Alex I, 1)--Original
name: Antonio Cordiani, 1483?-1546. He was an architect
and military engineer who worked with Raphael in directing
the building of St. Peter's Basilica in Rome. He also constructed many fortifications for the Pope. Forster refers
to da San Gallo as working with Michelangelo. In reality,
it was da San Gallo's uncle, Giuliano da San Gallo (orig.
name: Giuliano Giamberti, 1445-1516), who worked with
Michelangelo in competition with Raphael and Bramante for
control over the construction of St. Peter's.

DASHWOOD, JOHN--(AH-Notes)--A character in the novel,
Sense and Sensibility, by Jane Austen (q.v.). He is the
half-brother of Marianne (q.v.) and Elinor and the owner of
Norland. Though wealthy, he does nothing for his relatives.

DASHWOOD, MARIANNE--(AH-JA; Aspects IV)--A character
in the novel, Sense and Sensibility, by Jane Austen (q.v.).
She is the second daughter of Henry Dashwood.   Sensible
and clever, she is her sister Elinor's equal.   She is generous, amiable, and interesting; but she is not, like her sister, prudent.

DASHWOOD, MRS. JOHN--(AH-Notes)--A character in the
novel, Sense and Sensibility, by Jane Austen (q.v.).   Full
name: Fanny Ferrars Dashwood.   She is the wife of John
Dashwood (q.v.) and is instrumental in persuading him not
to help his half-sisters and stepmother.

DASHWOOD, OLD MR.--(AH Notes)--A character in the
novel Sense and Sensibility, by Jane Austen (q.v.).   On his
deathbed, he has his son, John (q.v.), promise to look after
the second Mrs. Dashwood and their three daughters.

DAULATABAD--(AH-Adrift)--A town in west-central Iran
about 44 miles SSE of Hamadan.

DAVID--(Hill; LJ VII)--A Biblical character, the shepherd-
king in the Old Testament.   (I Samuel xvi: I; II Kings.) He
is the conqueror of the giant Goliath and is thought by many
to be the composer of the Psalms.   He was secretly consecrated by Samuel as king when the Lord became displeased
with Saul.

DAVID--(Collect Ta-Coord)--Jacques Louis David, 1748-1825.
A French painter of the classical school who was once the
court painter of Louis XVI, but sided with the Revolution
and became, later (1804), court painter to Napoleon I (q.v.).
He was exiled when the Bourbons returned to the throne
(1815).

DAY LEWIS, C.--(Two Cheers-Raison)--Cecil Day Lewis,
1904.   Poet Laureate of England and writer of detective fiction [under the pseudonym of Nicholas Blake].   He has also
done some translations, e.g., Virgil's Georgics (1940).

DEAD CITY, THE--(Two Cheers-Whiff)--La Città Morta, a
tragedy in five acts by D'Annunzio (q.v.), translated into
English by Prof. G. Mantellini, Chicago; 1902.

DEBUSSY--(HE V; Two Cheers-Not Listening; Two Cheers-
Romain)--Claude Achille Debussy, 1862-1918.   A French
composer who broke from the conventions of the 19th cen-

tury to produce music which was, for his time, advanced.
He is now part of the standard repertory and is noted for
such works as "L'Après-Midi d'un Faun, " a symphonic poem
(1902); and Pelleas and Melisande, an opera (1902).

DECAMERON, THE--(RWV VI)--A collection of 100 tales
written by Boccaccio in 1353. The storytellers (ten) have
left Florence during a plague and each tells a story on each
day of their exile. The volume was widely read in its day
and is still relatively popular. It inspired many similar
works and influenced Chaucer (q. v.) in the creation of his
Canterbury Tales which uses a similar framework.

DE CHARLUS, M. --(AH-Proust; Aspects IV)--See: Charlus,
Baron de.

DECIUS--(Alex I, 2)--Gaius Messius Quintus Trajanus Decius,
A. D. 201-251. He was Roman emperor from 249-251. Born
in Pannonia, he commanded the troops of the Emperor Philip,
the Arab, on the Danube. His soldiers revolted and proclaimed him emperor against his will. He defeated and
killed Philip at Verona. He was responsible for a cruel
persecution of Christians, and died during a battle with the
Goths in Thrace.

DECLINE AND FALL--(AH-Capt; Two Cheers-Anon; Two
Cheers-Book; Two Cheers-Gibbon)--The Decline and Fall of
the Roman Empire by Edward Gibbon in six books: Vol. I,
published in 1776; II and III, 1781; and IV through VI, 1788.
It covers the period from the Emperor Trajan to the disin-
tegration of the empire in the west and, in the east, from
the reign of Justinian to the capture of Constantinople by the
Turks in 1453. Despite the fact that later historians have
disputed much of what Gibbon has written, the work, nevertheless, remains impressive in its scope and the quality of
its prose.

DEDALUS, STEPHEN--(Aspects VI)--A character in the
novel Ulysses (1922) by James Joyce (q. v.). He is a young
Irishman who is sensitive and proud and a writer who is
searching relentlessly for some meaning to life. His early
years were marked by poverty and privation. His devotion
to Ireland is as empty as is his faith. He finds a father,
for whom he is searching, symbolically, in Leopold Bloom
(q. v.) though he declines to live with Bloom and his wife,
Molly (q. v.).

DEDLOCK, LADY--(Aspects IV)--A character in the novel
Bleak House (q.v.) by Charles Dickens (q.v.). She has an
illegitimate child before her marriage to Sir Leicester Dedlock (q.v.). The family lawyer tries to blackmail her.
When he is killed, she is suspect. She is later found dead
at the gate of the cemetery in which her lover is buried.

DEDLOCK, SIR LEICESTER--(Aspects IV)--A character in
the novel Bleak House (q.v.) by Charles Dickens (q.v.). The
husband of Lady Dedlock, he is the head of a great family
and is conservative and reserved. He marries a woman of
no family. When he learns that she was the mother of an
illegitimate child born before their marriage, he forgives
her. Shocked when he hears of her death, he lives a broken
man.

DEFFAND, MME. DU--(AH-VO)--Born: Matie de Vichy-
Chamrond, 1697-1780. A French marquise, she corresponded
with Voltaire, Montesquieu, Horace Walpole and other lumi-
naries of her day. She also held a salon at which she
gathered the notables and intellectuals of France.

DEFOE--(AH-JA; Aspects I; Two Cheers-Lon)--Daniel Defoe,
1659?-1731. An English novelist noted for his novel Robinson Crusoe (1719) which, much altered, has become a children's classic and the subject of a motion picture. Defoe
was also a journalist. Much of his journalistic expertise is
evident in the prose style employed in his novel which is
marked by the accuracy of its observation and the clarity of
its prose. It is ironic that another of his novels, The Fortunes and Misfortunes of Moll Flanders, 1722, was long suppressed as pornography. He also wrote the intriguing
Journal of the Plague Year (1722).

DE LA MARE, WALTER--(Aspects VI; Two Cheers-Eng;
Two Cheers-Fo)--1873-1956. An English poet who worked
largely in traditional forms. Many of his poems, perhaps
because of their traditional approaches and their nostalgia
for the past, have found their way into anthologies, notably
his most quoted poem, "The Listeners." There is a collected edition (1920) of his poetry, 1910-1918.

DELONEY, THOMAS--(Aspects I)--1543?-1600?--An English
writer of prose tales. He is often considered an early
novelist in the broadest interpretation of that title. He was
a weaver of silk and also the author of many broadside ballads. He is, perhaps best known, and then only among stu-

dents of literature, for his stories of London craftsmen, notably The Gentle Craft (1597).

DELPHI--(Collect Ta-Road)--A town in Greece at the foot of
Mt. Parnassus which, in ancient times, was sacred to Apollo.
His major shrine was located there. The temple, now in
ruins, was also the location of the most famous of all ora-
cles. The oracle was silenced about A. D. 400.

DELPHI CHARIOTEER, THE--(GLD X)--A Greek statue in
bronze, c. 474 B. C., found at Delphi (q. v.) and now in its
museum. It was part of a group portraying a four-horse
chariot intended as a votive gift which stood in the shrine of
Apollo. It is fully clothed with an impressively modeled
gown.

DEMETER--(PP-Clement)--See: Demeter of Cnidus.

DEMETER OF CNIDUS--(AH-Cn; LJ XII)--In Greek myth,
Demeter was the goddess of fruits, crops, and vegetation
generally, and the protector of marriage. Her daughter was
Persephone. She is identified with the Roman goddess, Ce-
res. In citing the Demeter of Cnidus, Forster may, in his
essay on his visit to Cnidus, have mistaken the statue for
that of its more famous sister, the Aphrodite carved by
Praxiteles which stood in her temple at Cnidus, the location
of which, when Forster visited, was not known.

DEMIURGE--(Alex I, 3; Collect Ta-Eternal)--In Gnostic (q. v.)
belief, the creator of man and a deity lesser than God who
wrongly believes himself to be God. God took pity upon mankind and sent Christ to counteract the ignorance of the
Demiurge and to give us Gnosis [knowledge].

DE MORGAN, W. V. --(AH-Word)--William Frend de Morgan,
1839-1917. A friend of William Morris (q. v.), he first devoted his attention to art, producing stained glass and pottery. Ill health brought this to an end. He turned to writing fiction and completed several novels, the most successful of which is Joseph Vance (1906).

DENDYRA--(Alex I, 2)--Dendera. A village in Upper Egypt
on the left side of the Nile and the site of the temple dedicated to the worship of the goddess Hathor. The temple
was begun in the 1st century B. C. and added to by the Romans, especially Augustus and Domitian (q. v.).

DENHAM, LADY--(AH-JA)--The patroness of Clara Bereton in Sanditon a fragment of a novel by Jane Austen (q.v.). Though jolly, she tends to be domineering.

DENIS, SAINT--(AH-Vo; MT)--The patron saint of France and the apostle to the Gauls. He was martyred in Paris in A.D. 272 and legend has it that he picked up his severed head and walked with it to the site which is now his cathedral.

DEODATA, SAINT--(WAFT)--See: Fina, Santa.

DE QUINCY--(Two Cheers-Virginia)--Thomas De Quincy, 1785-1858. An English essayist and literary critic who is perhaps best known for his addiction to opium. The anguish that addiction caused is detailed in his Confessions of an English Opium Eater (1821). He was an excellent and important critic and had at his command a polished style which he called "impassioned prose."

DESCARTES--(AH-Vo)--Réné Descartes, 1595-1650. This French mathematician and philosopher who founded Cartesianism held that there is a possibility of mathematical exactitude in metaphysical reasoning. The method of reasoning he developed is discussed in his short work Discours de la Méthode (1639).

DESCRIPTION OF THE EAST--(Alex IV)--See: Pocock, Richard.

DESENCHANTÉES, LES--(AH-Salute)--A novel by Pierre Loti (q.v.). There is an English translation, The Disenchanted (1906), by Clara Bell.

"DESERTED VILLAGE, THE"--(Eng)--A poem (1770), by Oliver Goldsmith (q.v.) which describes the effects of the industrial revolution on village life in England.

DEVONSHIRE, THE DUKE OF--(MT)--Spencer Compton Cavendish (8th Duke of Devonshire), 1833-1908. He held a number of British government posts (e.g., War Secretary, Postmaster General) but declined the premiership. He was partly responsible for sending General Gordon (q.v.) to the Sudan and not supporting him. He was also, for a time, the leader of the Liberal party in the House of Commons.

DIANA OF THE CROSSWAYS--(AH-AB)--A novel (1885) by
George Meredith (q. v.).   After a brief introduction to English society, Diana Merion marries Augustus Warwick who
has leased her ancestral home, Crossways.   The marriage
breaks apart because of her innocent friendship with Lord
Dannisburgh.   Separated from her husband, Diana returns
to society after her vindication at a trial and becomes a
successful novelist and falls in love with Dannisburgh's nephew, Percy, only to lose him.   Broken-hearted, she turns
to Thomas Redworth, her long-time admirer and marries
him after Warwick's death.

DICKENS--(AH-Liberty; Aspects I; Two Cheers-Eng; Two
Cheers-Lon; Two Cheers-Our)--Charles John Huffman Dickens, 1812-1870.   An English novelist who used many of the
events of his early, poverty-stricken life for his novels.   He
became a reporter of the debates of the House of Commons
for several newspapers and periodicals and began writing
short sketches (the first was published Dec. 1833) which
were later collected into his first volume, Sketches by Boz
(1836).   From that publication rose a steady stream of
volumes, most of which have become endeared to the reading publics of the 19th and 20th centuries and have made
his name a household word.   Some of these works are
Oliver Twist (1837-39), A Christmas Carol (1843), and
David Copperfield (1849-50).   Though sociological in orien-
tation, they survive, nevertheless, because of their memorable characters.

DICKINSON, GOLDSWORTHY LOWES--See: Lowes Dickinson.

DICKINSON, JOSEPH--(GLD I)--1782-1849.   The grandfather of Goldsworthy Lowes Dickinson (q. v.), he came to
London at the beginning of the 19th century and set up a
print and lithography shop and photography business in Bond
Street.

DICKINSON, LOWES--(GLD; Hill; Two Cheers-Camb; Two
Cheers-Tol)--Goldsworthy Lowes Dickinson, 1862-1932, the
subject of a biography by Forster (Goldsworthy Lowes Dickinson).   He was an essayist, and the author of many works
on Greek literature, philosophy, and life.   His influence on
Forster's work has never been fully explored.

DICKINSON, LOWES CATO--(GLD I)--The father of Goldsworthy Lowes Dickinson (q. v.), he grew up in the shop of
his father, Joseph, and began as a lithographer.   In 1850,

he went to Italy to study art.   He came into contact with the Christian Socialist movement of F. D. Maurice (q. v.) and helped to found the Working Men's College where he taught drawing for years.

DICKINSON, MAY LOWES--(GLD-Intro)--The sister of Goldsworthy Lowes Dickinson (q. v.).

DICKINSON, WILLIAM--(GLD I)--1738-1819.   The great-grandfather of Goldsworthy Lowes Dickinson (q. v.).   He was a farmer who had land near Bardon Mill, Northumbria.

DICKINSON OF WHITFIELD, JACOB--(GLD I)--The great-great-grandfather of Goldsworthy Lowes Dickinson who may have taken his name from a farmer who adopted him.

DI CREDI, LORENZO--(WAFT VII)--1459-1537.   A Florentine painter and pupil of Verrocchio, his subjects are generally religious.   He is represented in most major collections including that of the National Gallery, London, and of course, the Uffizi in Florence.

DIDO--(LJ XI)--The name Virgil (q. v.) gives in The Aeneid (q. v.) to the founder of Carthage.   In his work, she falls in love with Aeneas (q. v.) who, when Mercury reminds him of his mission to found Rome, kills herself by casting herself on a funeral pyre when she realizes that she cannot keep him with her at Carthage.   The name Dido is Phoenician for Artarte (Artemis) the goddess of the moon whom the Romans called Diana.   She was the protectoress of Carthage.

DINAH--(Aspects VII)--A character in the novel, Adam Bede (1859), by George Eliot (q. v.).   She is a young Methodist preacher and a compassionate individual who tries to help all in need.   Seth, Adam's younger brother, is in love with her, but she refuses to marry him because of her vocation to the ministry.   Later, however, she falls in love with Adam and manages to overcome her scruples and marries him.

DINOCRATES--(Alex I, 1; PP-Return)--A Greek architect of the late 4th century B. C.   He designed for Alexander the Great (q. v.) the new city of Alexandria and built the great and famous funeral pyre of Hephaestion.

DIOCLETIAN--(Alex II, 1; PP-Clement)--Gaius Aurelius Valerius Diocletianus, surnamed Jovius, A. D. 245-313.   He

was Roman emperor (284-305). His name comes from his
birthplace, Dioclea in Dalmatia. He held command under
the emperors Probus, Aurelian, and Caius. He was proclaimed emperor on the death of Numerianus and adopted as
his co-ruler, Maximian who ruled in Gaul. Later because
of perilous times, he chose others, including Constantius
Chlorus (q.v.). He kept Asia and Egypt for his own and
parcelled out the remainder of the empire to his colleagues.
He proclaimed an edict against the Christians which resulted
in many martyrs for the early Church (303-313). He abdicated and retired to his palace in Dalamatia (now in Yugo-
slavia) which, in the Middle Ages, became the town of Split.
The remains of his huge public baths are still to be seen in
Rome; one room was made into a church by Michelangelo (q.v.).

DIONYSUS--(Alex I, 1)--In Greek myth the god of wine (Roman name: Bacchus). In the earliest times he was represented by a bearded man completely clothed, but after the
time of Praxitiles (q.v.), as a beautiful youth. The change
is, perhaps, ascribable to a change of philosophy of or
approach to the effects of wine. In peace, the god wore a
robe of purple; in times of war, it was replaced by a panther's skin. He was the son of Zeus and Semele and is
said to have married Adriane after her desertion by Theseus
in Naxos. His worshippers conducted a wild celebration in
his honor which Romantics and neo-pagans have since interpreted in a bowdlerized fashion to suit their pre-conceptions
of antiquity.

DIOSCURI--(PP-Ph)--[From Gk.: dios, "Zeus"; kouros,
"sons of."] In Greek legend they are Castor and Pollux
(q.v.) the sons of Zeus by Leda.

DIOSCURUS, PATRIARCH--(Alex I; 2)--The Founder of the
Coptic Church in the 5th century. The Council of Chalcedon
condemned his monophysite (q.v.) doctrines and, as a result, he was exiled from Alexandria, A.D. 451.

DISNEY, WALT--(AH-Our Div)--Walter E. Disney, 1901-
1966. One of the most successful American producers of
animated motion pictures. He is credited with the creation
of dozens of characters among which is the most famous
Mickey Mouse for whom he supplied the voice. Other notable creations are Minnie Mouse, Goofy, and Donald Duck.
He also produced, in addition to the short films in which
these characters appear, feature length motion pictures often

based on fairy tales and children's classics: Bambi, Sleeping Beauty, Snow White and the Seven Dwarfs, etc.

DISRAELI--(MT; Two Cheers-English)--Benjamin Disraeli (1st Earl of Beaconsfield), 1804-1881. He was a British statesman and a successful novelist. Prime Minister during the reign of Victoria (q. v.), he was responsible for having her proclaimed Empress of India. He is author of novels of a social nature (e. g., Coningsby, 1844, and Tancred, 1847).

DIVES--(AH-My Wood)--The name given to the rich man in the parable of the "Rich Man and Lazarus" in the Bible (Luke, xvi: 19).

"DIVINE BABIES WHOM NO CHEAP REPRODUCTIONS CAN EVER STALE"--(RWV II)--Forster is referring to the work of Lucca della Robbia (1399-1482), a series of terra cotta medallions of babies in swaddling clothes which adorn the façade of the Foundling Hospital in Florence.

DIVINE COMEDY, THE--(Two Cheers-Bk)--See: Dante.

DOBELL--(Two Cheers-Fo)--Sydney Thompson Dobell, 1824-1874. An English poet and critic, popular in his day but now of interest only to the literary historian, he wrote under the pen name of Sydney Yendys. He was an ardent liberal and staunch advocate of national causes especially that of Italian liberty. He was a member of the "spasmodic school" of poetry because of his "attitude of skeptical unrest." His works include The Roman (1850), and England in Time of War (1856).

DOBRÉE, BONAMY--(GLD XIV)--1891- . English editor and literary scholar most noted for his work in Restoration drama (Restoration Comedy, 1924, and Restoration Tragedy, 1929).

DODGE, WILLIAM--(Two Cheers-Virginia)--A character in the novel Between the Acts (1941) by Virginia Woolf. He is an unwanted and uninvited guest of the Olives; he finds solace in his rejection and loneliness as he talks with Isa.

DODSWORTH--(AH-Sin)--A novel (1929) by Sinclair Lewis (q. v.). Sam Dodsworth is the president of the Revelation Motor Co. He is a sincere and likable individual but restless and slightly dissatisfied with what he has made of his

life. His wife, Fran, urges him on a trip to Europe. That
trip results in their alienation and eventual separation. Fran,
a snob, is determined to become a member of European society. She has an affair, and then another which she hopes
will end in marriage. To effect it, she begins divorce proceedings against Sam. Hurt and lonely, he turns to Edith
Cortwright. But Fran, dropped by her lover, tries to win
him back. He resists and begins to build a new life for
himself.

DODSWORTH, SAMUEL--(AH-Sin)--See: Dodsworth.

DOLCE FAR NIENTE--(Collect Ta-Story)--[Ital. "the sweet
joy of doing nothing."] It is an embodiment of a philosophy
of life generally antithetical to that of the Anglo-Saxon but
eminently delicious and attractive to him because it appears
wicked since it implies that life is too precious and important to waste it on constantly directed activity or work.
Though Forster, like his fellow Englishmen, feels its allure-
ments, he, nevertheless, sniffs at it in slight disapproval
sensing, though never stating, the superiority of the North-
erners' stand on the question.

DOLCI, CARLO--(Collect Ta-Eternal)--1616-1688. A Florentine painter. He is especially known for his small religious paintings and for his portraits.

DOMITIAN--(Alex II, 1)--Titus Flavius Domitianus Augustus,
A. D. 51-96. The third of the Flavian line of emperors of
Rome. He reigned from 81 to 96. He was the second son
of Vespasian and brother of Titus. He recalled Agricola
from a successful campaign in Britain (84) because of jealousy and was murdered by a freedman as a result of a conspiracy by officers of his court and his wife, Domitia.

DONATIST--(PP-Tim)--The name given to a follower of a
schismatic Christian sect of North African origin (early A.
D. 300's) who rigorously refused to accept back into the
church those who had defected during the periods of persecution. They were led by Donatus the Great, the bishop of
Carthage. They also held that the validity of the sacraments rested upon the spiritual sanctity of the minister.

DONIZETTI--(Two Cheers-George; WAFT VI)--Gaetano Donizetti, 1797-1848. An Italian composer of superbly melodic
operas which necessitate the use of bel canto voices in the
leading roles. After the death of Bellini (q. v.), he was the

foremost composer of dramatic operas. Among his many
works in the repetoire, perhaps the most popular are Lucia
di Lammermoor (q. v.) and L'Elisir d'Amore (1832).

DONNE, JOHN--(AH-TS)--1573-1631. An English metaphysical poet raised as a Catholic, but turned to Anglicanism. He
took holy orders and preached before Charles I (q. v.). His
early works are extremely sensual and his later, pious.
Among his poetic works are Epithalamium (1613) and Cycle
of Holy Sonnets (1618).

DONWELL--(AH-JA)--Donwell Abbey. The estate of Mr.
Knightly in the parish of Donwell adjoining Highbury, in the
novel, Emma (q. v.), by Jane Austen (q. v.).

DORCAS--(LJ VII)--The Dorcas Society. The name given to
women's circles dedicated to making clothing for the poor.
They are named after Dorcas in the Bible (Acts, ix: 39)
who made garments as an act of charity for widows.

DORIAN HEXAPOLIS--(AH-Cn)--A league of six cities (Hex-
apolis) on the island of Rhodes by which Dorian colonists in
Asia hoped to protect themselves against non-Greeks.

DOSTOEVSKY--(AH-TS; Aspects I; GLD XI)--Fedor Mikhailo-
vitch Dostoevsky, 1821-1881. A Russian novelist who gave
up a military career for writing. He ran afoul of the
government and was condemned to death only to be reprieved
and sent to Siberia. His experiences there were turned into the substance of The House of Death (1861) and Letters
from the Underworld (1864). Perhaps the novels best known
to English speaking audiences are Crime and Punishment
(1866), The Idiot (1868-69), and The Brothers Karamazov
(1880).

DOUAMOUTEF--(Alex II, 1)--Duamutef. In Egyptian myth
the guardian of the East and canopic protector of the stomach.
The name means "protector of his mother."

DOUGHTY, CHARLES MONTAGU--(AH-Salute)--1843-1926.
An English writer of travel books, he studied at Caius College, Cambridge and, from his two years' travel and hard-
ship in Arabia (1875-77) grew his great book, Travels in
Arabia Deserta (1888), considered by many as a prose classic. He also wrote epics: Dawn in Britain (1906), and
Mansoul (1923). They are marked by a style similar to

that of his prose: austere, artificial, and archaic.   There
is a biography by D. G. Hogarth (1928).

DOUGLAS, NORMAN--(Aspects IV; Two Cheers-English)--
1868-1952.   English writer of travel books including South
Wind (1917) and Old Calabria (1928).   The latter is an Englishman's view of a region almost totally outside of his emotional ability to comprehend.   Non-Calabrians tend to consider it a classic work of its kind.

DOUSTERSWIVEL, HERMAN--(Aspects II)--A character in
the novel The Antiquary by Sir Walter Scott (q.v.).   He is
Sir Arthur Wardour's German agent who brought his patron
to the brink of financial ruin.   He is assumed to be skilled
in the black arts, and was malicious, ungrateful and super-
stitious.   He was finally outwitted and so roughly treated by
Ochiltree that he had to leave the country.

DOVEDALE--(AH-JA)--An aristocratic house mentioned in
the novel Pride and Prejudice by Jane Austen (q.v.).

DOYLE, CONAN--(Aspects V)--Sir Arthur Conan Doyle,
1859-1930.   A British physician best known as the creator
of Sherlock Holmes, the great detective, in such works as
The Hound of the Baskervilles and The Sign of the Four.
Dr. Watson, Holmes's confidant and sometimes considered
Doyle's alter ego, also appears in these tales.   Doyle also
wrote historical fiction (e.g., Micah Clarke, 1888, and Sir
Nigel, 1906).   In the latter part of his life, Doyle became
deeply interested in spiritualism.

DR. M. G. JONES'S EXCELLENT BOOK ON HANNAH MORE
--(MT)--The book Forster refers to is Hannah More, Cambridge, Eng.: University Press, 1952.   Mary G. Jones
is also the author of related volumes: The Charity School
Movement; A Study of 18th Century Puritainism in Action,
etc.

DRAKE--(AH-Consol; AH-Our D)--Francis Drake, 1540-1596.
A great English seaman or pirate, depending upon one's
point of view, of the Elizabethan period.   He circumnavi-
gated the world in his ship, The Golden Hind, and returned
from a voyage to Virginia with the first tobacco to infect
England.   He destroyed a Spanish fleet in the bay of Cadiz
(1587) and helped to defeat the Spanish Armada (1588).

DRAVIDIA--(PI XII)--or Dravidian. The name applied to the peoples of South and Middle India and those parts of Ceylon where a Dravidian language is spoken. The term is wholly linguistic and does not refer to a unified racial or national type.

DRAYTON--(HE XXXIII; Two Cheers-Stratford)--Michael Drayton, 1563-1631. An English poet and dramatist noted for his The Shepherd's Garland (1593), a cycle of 64 sonnets, and also for Polyolbion (1622), a description of England in verse, hence Forster's allusion in Howards End.

DRUIDS--(AH-Our D; HE XXVI)--Members of a pagan religion practiced in ancient Britain and, some say, still alive today. Their rites were conducted in groves of oak and the mistletoe was sacred to them. They believed in the transmigration of souls and in the powers of magic. Their sacred sign was a serpent's egg. The name, Druid, was originally applied only to their priests, teachers, magicians, or socerers. Now it is commonly applied to the members of the faith at large.

DRURY LANE--(Two Cheers-Stratford)--A street in the West End of London noted for its theater, the Drury Lane, the fourth on its site and one of the largest and most famous theatres in London. Benjamin Wyatt built the present theatre (1889-1912).

DRYAD--(Aspects VI; Collect Ta-Other; Collect Ta-Road; LJ-VII)--In classical myth, a dryad is a tree-nymph who was supposed to live in trees and die when the trees died.

DRYDEN--(Two Cheers-Bishop)--John Dryden, 1631-1700. One of the most influential of English poets of his time, he was also a dramatist, and was chosen Poet Laureate (1670). An Anglican, he became a Roman Catholic and defended his conversion in The Hind and the Panther (1687). He was also a skillful satirist ("MacFlecknoe," 1682) and translator (Juvenal, Virgil, et al.).

DUCHESS OF MALFI, THE--(Collect Ta-Celest)--The title of a tragic play by John Webster (c. 1618). The Duchess falls in love with her steward and runs afoul of her brother, a cardinal. She is condemned to strangulation, but first endures a series of tortures.

DUER, ANGUS--(AH-Sin)--A character in the novel, Arrowsmith (1924), by Sinclair Lewis (q.v.). He is a classmate
of Martin Arrowsmith's who is determined to make a great
deal of money from his profession as a doctor. As a result, he works at the fashionable Rouncefield Clinic.

DUFF-GORDON, LADY LUCIE--(AH-Salute)--1821-1869. An
English writer and childhood friend of John Stuart Mill, she
was the wife of Sir Alexander Cornewall Duff-Gordon. She
conducted a salon in which gathered the celebrities of her
day. She lived in Egypt from 1862 and died in Cairo and
was the author of Letters from Egypt (1863) and More Letters from Egypt (1875).

DUKE, THE--(MT)--See: The Duke of Wellington.

DUKE OF WELLINGTON, THE--(AH-Notes; MT)--Arthur
Wellesley (1st Duke of Wellington), 1769-1852. Known as
the Iron Duke, he was a British general and statesman noted
for his victory over Napoleon (q.v.) at Waterloo (q.v.) in
1815. He was Prime Minister (1828-30) and supported the
Catholic Emancipation Act (1829). He protected London during the Chartist uprising (1848). He was buried in St. Paul's
after a sumptuous public funeral. His London home (Hyde
Park Corner) has been turned into a museum.

DUNSTABLE, MISS--(Aspects VIII)--Emily Dunstable is a
character in the novel, Last Chronicle of Barset (1867), by
Anthony Trollope (q.v.). She is the cousin of Mrs. Martha
Dunstable Thorne and a wealthy heiress.

DURBAR, THE--(AH-Gem; Hill)--[From Persian: der,
"door"; bar, "admittance."] The word is used in India to
signify the council chamber of a ruler and for official re-
ceptions on a grand scale or state ceremonies.

DUSE, ELEANORA--(Two Cheers-Whiff)--1859-1924. An
Italian actress who began her career at the age of 13. She
made her American debut in 1893, and is known especially
for her interpretations of the tragic heroines of Dumas,
Sardou, Ibsen, and for her lover, D'Annunzio (q.v.).

DYNASTS, THE--(Aspects V; Two Cheers-Clouds)--A monu-
mentally long dramatic poem (1903-1908) on the Napoleonic
Wars by Thomas Hardy (q.v.).

E

EARNSHAW, CATHERINE--(Aspects VII)--One of the principal characters in the novel Wuthering Heights (1847), by Emily Brontë (q.v.). She is the wife of Edgar Linton and mother of Cathy Linton. When young, she was a beautiful, high spirited, headstrong, and selfish individual. She falls in love with Heathcliff, a young gypsy whom her father brings home one day. She refuses, however, to consider him as a suitable marriage partner because of her arrogance. Nevertheless, despite her marriage, she remains deeply drawn to him as he is to her. Their spirits are united after death.

EARNSHAW FAMILY--(Aspects VII)--Characters in Wuthering Heights (q.v.), by Emily Brontë (q.v.). The family consists of Mr. Earnshaw and his children: Catherine (q.v.) and Hindly. It also includes, by marriage to Catherine, Edgar Linton and their daughter Cathy Linton. Ultimately, it includes Heathcliff's son who marries the young Cathy.

ECBATANA--(PP-Ph)--An ancient city in Iran, the site of which is now occupied by the modern town of Hamadan. It was the capital of Media and the summer residence of the Achaenenid kings.

ECCLESIASTICUS--(AH-My Own)--One of the books of the Old Testament placed after the "Book of Proverbs." It was once attributed to King Solomon (q.v.).

ECLOGUES OF VIRGIL--(Collected Ta-Other)--A collection of pastoral poems by Virgil originally titled Bucolics. The collection was given the title "Eclogues" because the poems represented a selection of his poetry. Now the word "eclogue" has come to mean any pastoral or rustic dialogue in verse.

EDGAR, MASTER OF RAVENSWOOD--(Aspects II)--A character in The Bride of Lammermoor (q.v.) by Sir Walter Scott (q.v.). He is the son of Allan, Lord Ravenswood, who has sworn vengeance on the Ashwood family for the wrong it has done to his own. Edgar falls in love with Lucy Ashton, but she is to wed another. On the wedding day, she attempts to kill her fiancé and goes mad.

EDMUND--(Aspects IV)--A character in the novel Mansfield Park by Jane Austen (q.v.). Edmund Bertram is the younger

son of Sir Thomas and Lady Bertram.   He is sensible and
has an upright mind.

EDOUARD--(Aspects V)--A character in the novel The Counterfeiters (q.v.) by André Gide (q.v.).   He is a novelist and
is Gide's alter ego who observes and comments upon the
other characters.   He also serves as the link which connects
their stories.   He believes that an individual has, above all,
a duty to be himself.

EDWARD, KING--(AH-Me)--See: Edward VII.

EDWARD, KING--(Two Cheers-William)--1002?-1066.   Called
"The Confessor," the last Anglo-Saxon King of England.

EDWARD VI--(AH-Car)--1537-1553.   King of England and
Ireland and member of the house of Tudor.   He was the
only child of Henry VIII by Jane Seymour and his only surviving son.   He succeeded to the throne under a regency and
died of tuberculosis after a very undistinguished reign.   He
died childless thus clearing the path of his half-sister Elizabeth I (q.v.) to the throne.

EDWARD VII--(AH-Me; AH-Wil; Alex II, 4; Two Cheers-
Luncheon; Hill)--Edward Albert Christian George Andrew
Partick David, 1894-   .   After his abdication he became
known as the Duke of Windsor.   He was King of Great Britain and Ireland Jan. 20-Dec. 11, 1936.   The eldest son of
George V (q.v.) and Queen Mary (q.v.), he received some
naval training and served with the British Expeditionary
Forces during W.W. I.   He had the distinction of being the
first bachelor King in 176 years.   He ran into troubled
waters when he announced that he intended to marry a twice-
divorced woman and make her his queen.   Rather than give
her up, he chose to abdicate.   The woman, an American,
Mrs. Wallis Simpson, married him in June of 1937.

EGDON HEATH--(Aspects V)--The wild and gloomy scene
of much of The Return of the Native (q.v.) by Thomas
Hardy (q.v.).

EGOIST, THE--(Aspects I)--A novel by George Meredith (q.
v.) published in 1879.   Local gossips hope that Sir Willoughby Patterne, who has been jilted by Constance Durham, will
now marry the charming and talented Laetitia Dale, the
daughter of his invalid pensioner, but he falls in love with
Clara Middleton (see: Clara).   She agrees to marry him

after a whirlwind courtship. On a visit, before their marriage, to Patterne Hall, she meets Vernon Whitford, Patterne's cousin with whom she is later to fall in love and
marry. During the visit, she learns about her fiancé's ego-
tism and realizes that she cannot marry him. Disturbed
about the possibility of yet another jilting, Patterne convinces
himself that she is jealous of Laetitia. To save face, he
proposes to Laetitia, but her love for him has cooled and
turned to contempt. She refuses, but later she relents and
marries him on her own terms.

EIFFEL TOWER--(PP-Ph)--Erected by Alexander Gustave
Eiffel, a French engineer, in Paris, for the exposition of
1889. It is 984 feet high.

EINSTEIN--(Nordic; Two Cheers-English; Two Cheers-Racial;
Two-Cheers-What)--Albert Einstein, 1879-1955. A theoreti-
cal physicist born in Ulm, Germany, and a professor at
various European universities. When the Nazis deprived
him of his citizenship and property in 1934, he left Germany
and became a naturalized American citizen. He enunciated
the theory of relativity in 1905, and was awarded the Nobel
Prize in physics (1922). He was the author of many volumes
including The Meaning of Relativity (1923).

EKDAL, HJALMAR--(AH-Ibsen)--A character in the play,
The Wild Duck (1889) by Henrik Ibsen (q. v.). He is a pho-
tographer whose chief joy is his daughter. His happiness
is wrecked when he learns that his daughter is not his.

ELEPHANTA--(PI VII)--A small island in the harbor of
Bombay, India. It is famous for its cave temples carved
out of solid rock some 1200 years ago. A large stone ele-
phant (hence the name) which formerly stood at the landing
was removed in 1864 to Bombay.

ELGAR--(HE V)--Sir Edward Elgar, 1857-1934. Originally
the organist of St. George's Church (R. C.) in Worcester
1885-1890, he resigned and settled in Malverne to devote all
of his time to composition. Millions have been graduated from
school to the strains of his "Pomp and Circumstance," but
he has produced other works notably The Dream of Gerontius
(1900), In the South (1904) and symphonies, marches,
concert overtures, etc.

"ELIJAH"--(GLD V)--An oratorio by Mendelssohn (q.v.) first
performed at Birmingham, England, in 1846.

ELIOT, GEORGE--(AH-Ronald; PP-Poetry; Two Cheers-English; Two Cheers-Webb)--[Pen name of Mary Ann or Marian
Evans] 1819-1880. An English novelist. She was well educated having studied German, Italian and music. She fell in
love with George Henry Lewes who could not marry her because he already had a wife and divorce was not possible.
They lived together in what she regarded as a marriage.
She published her first story under her pseudonym in Black-
woods' Magazine and won acclaim with Adam Bede (1859),
and continued her success with The Millon the Floss (1860)
and Silas Marner (1861). Her last novel was Daniel Deronda
(1874-76). After Lewes' death (1878), she wrote no more.
She married a New York banker on May 6, 1880, and died
on the 22nd of December.

ELIOT, LORD--(Two Cheers-Lon Lib)--Edward Granville
Eliot (3rd Earl of St. Germans), 1798-1877. He was a
British diplomat who held several government posts including
that of chief Secretary for Ireland. He was confidential advisor to Queen Victoria (q.v.).

ELIOT, T. S.--(AH-Note; Aspects I; Two Cheers-India; Two
Cheers-Lon; Two Cheers-Two Bks)--Thomas Stearns Eliot,
1888-1965. He was a poet and critic born in America who
became a naturalized British citizen in 1927. He is the
author of works noted for the depth of their scholarship as
well as for their patina of modernity. Because he was a
convert to Anglo-Catholicism, they also reflect an absorption in spiritual matters. Prufrock and Other Observations
(1917) and The Wasteland (1922) are among the better known
of his poetical works; Eliot himself considered Four Quartets (1943) his finest achievement. The Sacred Wood (1920)
is a collection of critical essays. He also tried his hand at
drama (Murder in the Cathedral, 1935; The Cocktail Party,
(q.v.)).

ELIZABETH--(AH-AB; AH-Consol; Aspects I; MT; Two
Cheers-English; Two Cheers-John)--1533-1603. Elizabeth I,
Queen of England and Ireland 1558-1603. She was the
daughter of Henry VIII by his second wife, Anne Boleyn and
declared illegitimate by Parliament in favor of Edward VI
(q.v.), the son of Jane Seymour. Nevertheless, Elizabeth
succeeded to the throne having to wait only for the death of
her elder half-sister, Mary, daughter of Henry's first wife,
Catherine of Aragon. Elizabeth was a shrewd politician who,
by her wits and her promises of marriage never fulfilled
(she died never wedded), managed to steer her country to a

position of military and financial security. Sometimes ruthless (she had her rival, the Catholic Mary Stuart, murdered)
and sometimes human (she agonized over sending her favorite, Essex (q.v.) to the axman), she fostered the arts and
was responsible for what some call England's Golden Age.

ELIZABETH--(AH-JA)--Elizabeth Bennet is a character in
the novel, Pride and Prejudice, by Jane Austen (q.v.). She
is an intelligent girl who, in her dislike of Darcy, represents the "prejudice" of the title; he represents the "pride."
She at first refuses his proposal of marriage because of her
prejudice, but when he helps the Bennets in the affair of the
elopement of Lydia Bennet, Elizabeth sees her error and
consents to marry him.

ELLIOT, ANNE--(Aspects IV)--A character in the novel,
Persuasion, by Jane Austen (q.v.). She is the second daughter of Sir Walter and Lady Elliot. She has an elegant mind
and sweet character.

ELLIOT, ELIZABETH--(Aspects IV)--A character in the
novel, Persuasion, by Jane Austen (q.v.). She is the eldest
daughter of Sir Walter and Lady Elliot and the sister of
Anne (q.v.). She is beautiful and very much like her father
in disposition. At 16, she succeeded to "all that was possible of her mother's rights and consequences."

ELLIOT, FREDERICK--(LJ I)--Rickie, the central figure of
Forster's Longest Journey. The model is the author himself.

ELMER GANTRY--(AH-Sin)--A novel (1927) by Sinclair Lewis
in which he satirizes religious hypocrisy in America in the
form of Elmer Gantry, a preacher who does not practice
what he preaches.

ELOHIM--(Collect Ta-Mr)--[Plural of Hebrew: eloah, "God."]
The plural is used to denote heathen gods. In the singular,
it was used to denote God and His power.

ELSA--(LJ IX)--A character in the opera Lohengrin (1880)
by Richard Wagner (q.v.). She is the bride of Lohengrin
and the Princess of Brabant.

ELSTIR--(AH-Proust)--A character in the novel, Remembrance of Things Past (q.v.), by Proust (q.v.). He is a

gifted artist who meets Marcel, the central figure, at Ver-
duins'. He becomes a great painter.

ELTON, PROF. OLIVER--(Aspects I)--1861-1945. An English literary historian and educator. He was professor of
English literature at Liverpool. He wrote many volumes, including a history of English literature from 1730 to 1880, in
parts (1912-1928).

ELY--(LJ VII)--Urban district, Isle of Ely, in E England,
18 miles NNE of Cambridge.

ELYSIAN FIELDS--(AH-Mac; AH-Word; LJ XII; Two Cheers-
What)--In Greek myth, the home of the blessed, the Paradise or Happy Land. Elysian in Greek means happy, delightful.

EMERSON, RALPH WALDO--(GLD VIII; RWV X)--1803-1882.
An American poet, essayist, and, to some degree, a philosopher. He was trained for the ministry, but later resigned
his office because of problems of doctrine. In his travels
he came to know the great literatures of his day, English as
well as American. His first work, Nature (1836) contained
the germ of his philosophy which is termed "transcendental."
It borrows freely from the East and emphasizes the individual, self-reliance, and the value of the inner life. It is
rather difficult to penetrate to the heart of the philosophy because of its emotional rather than intellectual character.
Moreover, it is often contradictory, a position with which
Emerson did not feel ill at ease. His Essays, in two volumes (1841, 1844), secured his national and international
reputation.

EMMA--(Aspects I; Two Cheers-Virginia)--See: EMMA.

EMMA--(AH-Early; Two Cheers-Raison)--A novel by Jane
Austen (q. v.). Emma enjoys arranging the lives of her
friends and attempts to match the vicar and Harriet Smith.
Harriet is in love with a farmer, but is persuaded by Emma
to believe that she cannot be. Finally, after much difficulty,
Harriet marries her farmer. Emma also interferes in the
affairs of Jane Fairfax and Frank Churchill. Emma's con-
cern with the lives of others comes to an end when she
realizes that she is in love with John Knightly.

"EMPEDOCLES"--(AH-Note)--Full title: "Empedocles on
Etna. " A dramatic poem (1853) by Matthew Arnold (q. v.).

It deals with the tale of Empedocles, one of Pythagoras's scholars, who threw himself into the crater of Etna (Sicily) so that people would suppose that the gods had carried him to heaven. Unfortunately, one of his iron pattens was cast out with the lava and was recognized. His wish for immortality was at an end.

EMPEROR OF CONSTANTINOPLE--(AH-Gem)--Forster is referring to John VIII Palaeologus, 1391-1448. He was the son of Manuel II and was emperor of what was left of the Eastern Empire from 1425 to 1448. A cautious ruler, he did not try to oppose the Turks alone. He sought help from the West and, in a bid to attract that help, moved for a reconciliation of the Western (Roman Catholic) and his own (Orthodox) Eastern Church.

EMPEROR OF RUSSIA--(MT)--Forster refers to Alexander I (1777-1825) who was emperor from 1801 to 1825.

EMPOLI--(WAFT III)--A commune in the province of Firenze, Tuscany, central Italy. It is about 18 miles WSW of Florence and has an interesting 11th-century cathedral.

ENCHANTED FLOOD, THE--(Two Cheers-En)--Subtitled: or, the Romantic Iconography of the Sea, New York, 1950; London, 1951, by W. H. Auden (q.v.).

ENDYMION--(WAFT X)--In Greek myth, he is a beautiful young man who so moved the goddess of the moon, Selene, that she came down to earth while he slept on Mt. Latmus and kissed him. That kiss, and her lying at his side, produced beautiful dreams for him. When he awoke, the dreams so beguiled him that he begged Zeus (q.v.) for immortality. Keats (q.v.) used the tale as the foundation, for his long poem of the same name (1817).

"ENFANT, MACAO ETAIT UN SAGE, MAIS LE GOUVERNEUR AVAIT RAISON."--(AH-Hap)--French: "Child, Macao was a wise man, but the governor was right."

ENGLISH LOCAL GOVERNMENT--(Two Cheers-Webb)--By Beatrice and Sidney Webb (q.v.). A study in nine volumes (1906-1919) which ranges from the parish and the county (Vol. 1) to the history of the English Poor Law (Vols. 8-9).

ENNEADS--(Alex I, 3)--The title given to the philosophical writings of the neo-Platonist, Plotinus (q.v.), c. A.D. 205,

edited by his pupil, Porphyry. In part, they contain an explanation of Plotinus's understanding of the universe which
flows directly from the core of his philosophy: a desire to
escape from the material world. He comprehends the universe in terms of a hierarchy, the lowest level of which is
matter and the highest, God, Who is the final abstraction
without form or matter, i.e., pure existence.

EPHESUS--(AH-JA)--A major city in the ancient world in
Asia Minor near the Aegean Sea. It was the center of an
important cult of Diana (q.v.) and her temple. Artisans
who fashioned silver replicas of that building complained
against St. Paul and his preachings out of fear that the new
faith would extinguish that of Diana and put an end to their
trade.

EPICTETUS--(AH-Note)--A Greek Stoic philosopher: first a
slave who was freed by his master, he became a teacher in
Rome until A.D. 90 when he, and other teachers of philosophy, were expelled by order of the emperor Domitian (q.
v.). He left no writings; hence, his philosophy is known
only through those of his pupil, Flavius Arrian.

EPICUREAN PHILOSOPHY--(Alex I, 3)--A Greek philosophy
developed by Epicurus c. 340-270 B.C. He taught that happiness or enjoyment is the highest good in life. His disciples corrupted his teachings until the philosophy came to
mean that happiness and enjoyment should be sought for
themselves. An epicure has, from this corruption, come
to mean an individual devoted to pleasure of all shades but
most especially that of the table.

EPSOM--(HE XV)--EPSOM DOWNS, a popular racecourse in
Surrey, S. England, not far from London.

ERASISTRATUS--(Alex II, 1)--A Greek physician who founded
the school of anatomy (3rd century B.C.) at Alexandria.
Many hold that he is the first to have distinguished between
the motor and sensory nerves; the first to have traced veins
and arteries to the heart; and probably the first to reject
the widely held belief that humors cause disease.

ERASMUS--(AH-Car; Two Cheers-Tol; Two Cheers-What)--
Desiderus Erasmus (Gerhard Gerhards), 1466?-1536. He
was a Dutch scholar and author, who, for his time, traveled
widely. In England, he met and was a friend to Colet,
Thomas More, Linacre, and Grocyn. He taught Greek at

Cambridge. At first, he was in favor of the Reformation and then, seeing its excesses of destruction and the sourness of its adherents, refused to follow it and remained loyal to the Roman Church as did his friend, Thomas More. He did not, as More, suffer martyrdom for his belief. His most famous work is In Praise of Folly.

ERATOSTHENES--(Alex I, 1; PP-Ph)--A Greek astronomer and geographer (3rd century B.C.) in Cyrene and Africa who was called by Ptolemy III Euergetes (q.v.) to Alexandria to head his library. Among his accomplishments can be counted the establishment of a scientific chronology whereby dates were calculated from the conquest of Troy; and the measurement of the circumference of the earth.

ERDA--(LJ XIII)--In German myth, the goddess of the earth.

EREBUS--(GLD V)--In Greek myth, he is primeval darkness who sprung from Chaos and is the father of Day by his sister, Night.

EREWHON--(Two Cheers-Bk)--The title of the philosophical novel (1872) by Samuel Butler (q.v.) which treats of a visit to an ideal country which is described in detail. The name is an anagram for "nowhere."

ERINYES--(HE XLI)--In Greek myth, they are the Furies, daughters of the Earth whose duties involve avenging wrong-doing by tormenting the evil-doers.

ERNEST--(Aspects II)--A character in the novel, The Swiss Family Robinson (1813), by Johann Rudolf Wyss. He is the second son of the Robinsons who are shipwrecked on a deserted island. Because of his previous studies of natural histories and sciences, he is of immeasurable help to the family during their stay.

EROICA SYMPHONY--(Collect Ta-Co-ord)--The name given to his third symphony (1803-04) by Beethoven (q.v.). The "Heroic" symphony was written in celebration of Napoleon (q.v.) to whom the work was originally dedicated. Beethoven withdrew the dedication, however, when Napoleon assumed the title of emperor.

ERYX--(Alex I, 1)--The name of a mountain as well as the name of the lengendary king of that mountain in Sicily. In

ancient times, it was the location of an important center for
the worship of Venus, or Aphrodite (q. v.).

ESAU--(Aspects VII)--An individual named in the Old Testament. The son of Isaac and Rebecca, he was the twin
brother of Jacob to whom he sold his birth-right (see: "Genesis").

ESMOND--(Aspects I)--A character in the novel, Henry Esmond (1852) by William Thackeray (q. v.). Henry is an orphan and is believed to be the illegitimate son of Lord Castlewood. He is level-headed and intelligent and learns that he
is Castlewood's heir, but keeps this knowledge secret out of
affection for Castlewood's widow. He believes himself to be
in love with his cousin, Beatrix Esmond [see: Beatrix], and
as a result becomes involved in a plot to secure the throne
for the Stuart Pretender. He comes, however, to realize
that it is Beatrix's mother, Rachel, whom he loves. He
emigrates to America with her.

ESSEX--(Two Cheers-English)--Robert Devereux, 1506-1601.
The second Earl of Essex and the favorite of Elizabeth I
(q. v.) who was executed on her order when she learned of a
plot he led to usurp her throne.

ESTE, ISABELLA D'--(AH-For the Muse)--1474-1539.
Marchioness of Mantua, she was also noted for her beauty,
her patronage of learning, and her skill in diplomacy.

ETON--(AH-Note; AH-Ron; GLD VI; LJ XV; Two Cheers-
Mrs)--The site of a famous preparatory school founded by
Henry VI in 1440. It is opposite Windsor on the Thames.

ETRUSCAN LEAGUE--(WAFT II)--A league of cities formed
by the Etruscans, a people who inhabited the region of Italy
now known as Tuscany. Their origins are unknown as is
their language. Their art was highly developed and as a
result of this and other evidence, some historians claim
them as orientals who migrated from Asia Minor.

EUCLID--(Alex I, 1; GLD III; PP-Ph)--Fl. 300 B. C. A
Greek mathematician who founded a school in Alexandria.
His chief work, Elements, is the basis of many works by
others in geometry.

EUHEMERUS--(AH-Gem)--fl. 300 B. C. A Greek writer
(born in Sicily) who developed the theory in his Hierd Ana-

graphae (Sacred Scripture) that the exploits of the gods of the ancients were in fact those of mortal kings or heroes who were then deified by those over whom they reigned or by those whom they helped. The word "euhemerism" has come to mean the interpretation of myths as traditional accounts of historic events.

EUNOE--(Alex I, 1)--As Forster points out, a character in the 15th idyll of Theocritus. The name also appears in Dante's Divine Comedy (q.v.). It is the name given to a river in Purgatory. Drinking its waters makes one recall all the good one has done. It lies a bit beyond the river of forgetfulness, Lethe.

EUPHORION--(GLD VII)--b. c. 275 B.C. A Greek poet and grammarian who studied philosophy at Athens and was director of the royal library at Antioch in Syria. He wrote poetry on mythological themes, epigrams, a work on grammar, etc. Although much admired by the ancients, he was a plagiarist.

EUPHRATES--(AH-Vo)--A river in SW Asia about 1700 miles long. In antiquity, its waters helped give rise to the civilizations of Chaldea, Assyria, and Babylonia.

EURIPIDES--(AH-Troop; Alex II, 4; GLD VIII; LJ IX; Two Cheers-Bishop)--c. 484-406 B.C. A Greek tragic playwright who lived most of his life in retirement. His first play was produced in 455 B.C. and he is credited with writing some 90 plays, the central motivations of which generally involved men and women in stress because of passion or conflicting desires. Some of his more important plays are Alcestis (438), Medea (431), The Bacchae (405), and The Trojan Women (415).

EUROTAS--(Collect Ta-Road)--The major river of Laconia in Greece the capitol of which was Sparta.

EUTYCHIDES--(AH-Cn)--fl. early 3rd century B.C. Greek sculptor of the school of Argos and Sicyon, and a pupil of Lysippus, he created Fortune, a depiction of the city of Antioch as the goddess Tyche, a work much copied since in spirit.

EVELYN, JOHN--(AH-AB; Two Cheers-In)--An important English diarist. He was a Royalist and, after the restoration of Charles II (q.v.), was given several minor governmental

posts for his loyalty. He was the author of several volumes
on various subjects including architecture and landscape gar-
dening. He is most noted for his Diary (1640-1706) which
gives an important picture of the contemporary events.

F

F MAJOR QUARTET--(AH-Word)--By Beethoven (q. v.). The
second of 6 quartets composed for piano, flute, bassoon, two
violins, viola, and cello, between 1786-1790.

FABIANISM--(GLD X)--The name given to the social philosophy of the Fabian Society (1884) in England. The society
included in its membership George Bernard Shaw (q. v.), the
Webbs (q. v.) and, for a time, H. G. Wells (q. v.). It was
dedicated to the reorganization of society through freeing
land and industry from individual and class ownership for
the benefit of all.

FAFNIR--(Two Cheers-What)--In Norse myth, a poison-
breathing dragon and guardian of Andvari's gold. In Wagner's
Ring he is Fafner, one of the giants who built Valhalla for
Wotan and is killed by Siegfried.

FAIRFAX, JANE--(Aspects IV)--A character in the novel
Emma (q. v.) by Jane Austen (q. v.). She is the only child
of Mrs. Bate's daughter Jane, who married Lieutenant Fairfax and died of consumption and grief soon after the death
of her husband. Jane was very elegant and graceful, her
eyes a deep grey with dark lashes and brows and her skin
was clear. Emma admires her but cannot like her because
she finds her too reserved.

FALSTAFF--(AH-Ron; Aspects IV)--The most famous of
Shakespeare's comic characters. He appears in The Merry
Wives of Windsor, Henry IV Pts. I and II, and Henry V.
In the latter, he dies. He is fat, sensual, boastful, a liar,
and somewhat of a coward.

FANNY--(AH-JA; Aspects IV)--Fanny Price. The heroine of
the novel, Mansfield Park, by Jane Austen (q. v.). A poor
relation of the Bertrams who raise her, she is timid and
self-effacing. She has always loved Edmund Bertram (q. v.),
the second son. Henry Crawford falls in love with her, but
she refuses him. Sir Thomas Bertram is angry with her
believing that she has missed the only chance she will ever

be given for a good marriage.   After his daughters disgrace
him, however, her worth is clearly demonstrated to him.

FARRÈRE, CLAUDE--(AH-Salute)--Nom de plume of Frédéric Charles Bargone, 1876-1957.   A French writer and naval
officer, he is the author of Fumée d'Opium (1904), La
Bataille (1909), La Marche Funèbre (1929), and other works.

FATHER OF WILLIAM AND MATTHEW ARNOLD--(Two
Cheers-William)--See: Thomas Arnold.

FAUNS--(Aspects VI; Collect Ta-Other; LJ VII)--In Roman
myth, they are gods of the woodlands.   They are gifted with
prophecy and are guardians of crops and herds.

FAUNTLEROY, LORD--(Two Cheers-Anon)--The central
character in an immensely popular, but now largely forgotten, story by Frances Hodgson Burnett (1886).   He is seven
years old and the child of an English lord and an American
mother.   His adventures include winning the hearts of his
English relatives and securing his grandfather's inheritance.
The clothes he wore were rather distinctive and gave rise
to a style of boys's clothing which died slowly (black velvet,
lace collar, yellow curls).

FAUST--(GLD VII; Two Cheers-Mohammed; Two Cheers-
Raison)--A dramatic poem by Goethe (q.v.) based on the legend of an individual who sells his soul to the devil for
youth and wisdom.

FAUST--(AH-Word; HE V)--An opera by Gounod produced in
Paris, 1859.   It is based on the Goethe drama (see above)
with a libretto by J. Barbier and M. Carré.

FAUX MONNAYEURS, LES--(Aspects IV)--A novel (1925) by
André Gide (q.v.).   It has been translated into English as
The Counterfeiters.   Bernard Profitendieu discovers an old
love letter of his mother's and realizes that he is illegitimate.   This event begins a whole series of stories in which
the real and the counterfeit personalities of the characters
are investigated.

"FECEMI LA DIVINA POTESTATE/LA SOMMA SAPIENZA
E IL PRIMO AMORE"--(Two Cheers-Does)--Italian.   "The
Divine Power made me, /Supreme Wisdom and the First
Love."   ℓℓ. 5-6, Canto III, "The Inferno, The Divine Come-
dy, by Dante (q.v.).   The lines are part of those written

over the gates of Hell.

FEISUL--(AH-TE)--[Alt. spelling of Faisal I] 1885-1933.
King of Syria (1920) and Iraq (1921-1933). Born in Mecca
and raised among Bedouins, he was educated in Constantinople. World War I provided the opportunity for him to
realize his dreams of Arab independence. He took command of a group of Arab rebels and later joined with T. E.
Lawrence (q. v.) and General Allenby (q. v.) in a Cecil B.
DeMille-like campaign which wrested Jerusalem and Damascus from the Turks. After the war, he was proclaimed
King of Syria only to be deposed by the French. The British, nevertheless, made him King of Iraq.

FELIX THE CAT--(AH-Our Div)--A character of animated
cartoons and comic strips internationally popular during the
20's and 30's.

FERGHANA--(AH-Emp; PI IX)--[Fergana]. A region in W
central Asia now a division of Soviet Turkistan. It was
overrun by Arabs (719) and conquered by Genghis Khan (q. v.)
and Tamerlane (q. v.).

FEUCHTWANGER, LEON--(Nordic)--1884-1958. A German
novelist and playwright, he left his country before World
War II because of Nazi persecution and eventually made his
way to the U. S. (1940). His most familiar works are
Josephus (1932) and The Jew of Rome (1935).

FEVERAL, RICHARD--(HE XIV)--A character in the novel,
The Ordeal of Richard Feveral (1859), by George Meredith.
He is the heir of Sir Austin Feveral, a misogynist. Sir
Austin hopes to educate his son according to a system in
which women were to be excluded until the boy's 25th year.
Despite the rigidity of the system, Richard's humanity shines
through.

FICINO, MARSILIO--(AH-Gem)--1433-1499. An Italian philosopher and Platonist who was commissioned by the elder
Cosimo de' Medici to translate the works of Plato and some
neo-Platonists into Latin from the original Greek.

FIELDING, HENRY--(AH-Early; Aspects III; Reading; Two
Cheers-Anon)--1707-1754. An English novelist and playwright, he was a justice of the peace at Westminster and
chairman of quarter-sessions at Hicks Hall. He began his
career as a writer with comic plays (e. g., The Temple Beau,

1730; Tom Thumb, 1730) but gained real success with Joseph Andrews (1742) and Tom Jones (1749), novels which have become English classics.

FIESOLE--(RWV I)--A commune in the province of Firenze, Tuscany, Italy, some 4 miles N of Florence. It contains Etruscan and Roman ruins as well as a Romanesque Cathedral.

FINA, SANTA--(PP-Clement)--The model for the mythical Santa Deodata (q. v.) who Forster describes in Where Angels Fear to Tread. Forster, for obvious reasons, exaggerates in recording her life. St. Fina (also known as St. Seraphina, d. 1253) was a paralytic from childhood. She suffered also, from repulsive sores. Despite her extreme suffering, she showed infinite patience. She was born and died in San Geminiano, Italy.

FINSBURY CIRCUS; FINSBURY PARK--(HE V, XLI)--A section in London which preserves in its name the memory of the fens or marshes called Vynesbury Moor, which lay outside of the city wall until the 16th century when it was drained.

FIRBANK, RONALD--(AH-Ronald)--Arthur Annesley Ronald Firbank. An English author of sophisticated novels. He was born in London and was converted to the Roman Church in 1908. He was a rather sickly child who grew up in the same condition. He traveled on the continent extensively and is the author of rather short novels filled with crackling conversations, among which are The Flower Beneath the Foot (1922) and The Prancing Nigger (1924).

FITZGERALD, EDWARD--(Two Cheers-George)--1809-1883. An English translater and poet whose father was John Purcell. He assumed his wife's family name. His son is best known for his translation into English of the Persian poet, Omar Khayyám's, Rubáiyát (1859). Its rather sensuous philosophy shocked the Victorians and assured its popularity. He also translated two plays of Sophocles, six of Calderon, and others, all of which never attained the popularity of The Rubáiyát.

FLANDERS, MOLL--(Two Cheers-Bishop)--The central character and narrator of the novel (1722) of the same name by Daniel Defoe (q. v.). She relates in frank detail her rather sordid life from infancy, her first affair and her final repentance which comes only after a series of exhausting adventures which she has obviously enjoyed.

FLECKER'S MAGIC--(Aspects VI)--A novel by Norman Mat-
son.   For a good summary of its plot see: Aspects of the
Novel, Chapter VI.

FLODDEN--(Two Cheers-John)--A hill near the Scottish border which was the site of a battle (Sept. 9, 1513) in which
the English defeated the Scots under James IV who was killed.

FLUSH--(Two Cheers-Virginia)--A novel by Virginia Woolf
(called a biography), 1933, which re-tells the tale of Elizabeth Barrett (q. v.) and Robert Browning (q. v.) from the
point of view of Flush, Elizabeth's dog.

FLY--(HE XXXV)--A type of covered carriage pulled by one
or two horses, generally used for pleasure.

FOLKESTONE--(WAFT I)--Municipal borough in Kent, SE
England, on the Strait of Dover, dating back to Roman times.

FOLLOWING DARKNESS--(AH-Reid; Two Cheers-Fo)--A
novel by Forrest Reid, London: Edward Arnold, 1912.   It
is the first version of his Peter Waring.   The book is dedicated to "E. M. F."--obviously Edward Morgan Forster, who
has called it a "masterpiece."

"FOLLOWING DARKNESS LIKE A DREAM"--(Two Cheers-
Fo)--The quotation from which Forrest Reid drew the title
of his novel, Following Darkness (q. v.).   It is from A Midsummer Night's Dream, the play by William Shakespeare
(q. v.).   Act V, Sc. i, ℓ. 393.

FORD, HENRY--(GLD XII)--1863-1947.   A machinist by
trade, he invented an economical method of producing auto-
mobiles which was to make him a multi-millionaire and the
atmosphere polluted.   This assembly line method was adapted by other industries as well.   Ford organized and was
president of the Ford Motor Company.

FOUAD, KING--(Alex II, 1; Egypt)--See: Fuad I.

FOURTH SYMPHONY OF BRAHMS--(Two Cheers-Not Listening; Two Cheers-Raison)--The Symphony No. 4 in E minor,
Opus 98, completed in 1885.

FOURTH SYMPHONY OF TCHAIKOVSKY--(Two Cheers-Not
Listening)--The Symphony No. 4 in F minor, Opus 36, composed 1878, first performed in Moscow on March 4, 1878,
and dedicated to Nadezhda von Meck.

FOX--(MT)--Charles James Fox, 1749-1806. An English
statesman who led the opposition in Parliament to Lord
North's measures against the American Colonies.

FOXE'S BOOK OF MARTYRS--(MT)--The popular title for
Actes and Monuments (1563), a compilation of the lives of
those who died a martyr's death for their Protestant faith
during the reign of Queen Mary. It was assembled by John
Foxe (1516-1587). He was the tutor of the Earl of Surrey
and was ordained to the ministry in 1560. Later, he became prebendary [an honorary canon] in Salisbury Cathedral.

FOXE, JOHN--(Alex I, 4)--See: Foxe's Book of Martyrs.

FRANCE, ANATOLE--(Aspects VIII; Two Cheers-In)--The
nom de plume of Jacques Anatole François Thibault, 1844-
1924. Novelist, critic, poet, satirist, he was awarded the
Nobel Prize for literature in 1912. Perhaps the works best
known to his English reading audience are The Crime of
Sylvester Bonnard (1881), and Thaïs (1890).

FRANCIA, FRANCESCO--(RWV XV)--Francesco di Marco di
Giacomo Raibolini, 1450?-1517. He was an Italian goldsmith
and painter. Born at Bologna, he became master of its
mint.

FRANCIS JOSEPH--(Alex II, 3)--Francis Joseph I (1830-
1916), Emperor of Austria, 1848-1916. His empire, when
he ascended the throne, was in a state of revolution. Gradually, through repressive measures and through wars, he
pacified it. In an attempt to mollify Hungary, he was proclaimed its king. He brought his country into World War I
when his nephew and heir was assassinated at Sarajevo, June
28, 1914.

FRANCIS, SAINT--(HE XXII; Two Cheers-Fer; Two Cheers-
Henry; Two Cheers-Last)--There are several saints of that
name (of Paola, de Sales, Xavier, et al.). Forster, however, is probably referring to the most popular saint of that
name--most popular also to non-Catholics because of his
legendary exploits with the birds and his friendship for animals, qualities most beloved by the English. That Francis

is St. Francis of Assisi (Giovanni Francesco Bernardone),
1182-1226. He founded the Franciscan order and received
papal permission for it from Honorius III because of a
dream that pope had wherein he saw a man dressed in
brown (the Franciscan habit) supporting a falling church. In
1214, the wounds of Christ--the Stigmata--appeared on his
body. He was canonized in 1228.

FRANCISCO DE ASSIZ, DON--(AH-Wil)--Maria Fernando
Francisco de Asia, 1822-1902. The nephew of Ferdinand
VII of Spain, he married his cousin, Isabella II in 1846 and,
as a result, was granted no part in the administration of
the affairs of the kingdom of Spain. He left Spain when the
Queen was deposed in 1868, and was granted a separation
from her in 1870.

FRANCK, CÉSAR--(AH-Note; Two Cheers-Last; Two Cheers-
Not Listening)--César Auguste Franck, 1822-1890. He was
a Belgian-French composer and exponent of the cyclic form
of composition (i. e., the use of the same theme in more
than one part of the same work). He is credited by many
as the founder of the modern French instrumental school.
Born in Liege of a Belgian father and a German mother, he
studied in his native city and in Paris where he was appointed as organist at St. Clotilde. He was also appointed
professor of organ at the Paris Conservatory.

FRANCO--(Two Cheers-George)--Francisco Paulino Herene-
gildo Teódulo Franco-Bahamonde, 1892- . Born in Galicia,
he was educated in the military academy at Toledo. During
Spain's Civil War, he became the military leader of the in-
surgents and, at its end assumed the dictatorship though he
still maintains that the country is a monarchy. Spain remained neutral during World War II despite the aid supplied
him by Italy and Germany during the Civil War.

FRANZ, LITTLE--(Aspects II)--Francis Robinson, the youngest of the Robinson children who, with his family, is shipwrecked on a deserted island, in the novel, The Swiss Family Robinson (1813), by Johann Rudolf Wyss. Despite the
difficulties the family encounters, he loves his life on the
island.

FREDERICK THE GREAT--(AH-Vo; Two Cheers-Volt)--
Frederick II, (1712-1786), King of Prussia, 1740-1786. He
was the key figure in the rise of Prussia to the forefront
among the German states. A patron of literature and a

sometime friend of Voltaire (q.v.), he also encouraged art and music. He built the palace of Sans Souci, the only real rival to Versailles.

FREDERICK OF PRUSSIA, PRINCE--(AH-Vo)--See: Frederick the Great.

FREISCHUTZ--The central figure in the opera by Carl Maria von Weber, Der Freischutz (1820). The opera, with a libretto by F. Kind, is based on the legend of the "freeshooter" (der Freischutz), who is in league with the Devil. Satan gives him seven bullets with six of which he can hit anything at which he aims. The seventh is to be directed by Satan. In the opera, Satan intends the seventh for Max's (der Freischutz) sweetheart.

FRENCH REVOLUTION--(Collect Ta-Machine; MT; Two Cheers-Romain; Two Cheers-Tol)--A political upheaval which began in France in 1789 and which ultimately affected the whole world. There is disagreement as to its exact causes; some see it as the revolt of the underprivileged against the privileged, others as the logical outcome of the liberal "Enlightenment" of the 18th century. Whatever its causes, it never achieved its goal, the goal of all revolutions, heaven on earth, simply because it failed to take into account man's nature. It drowned in a pointless blood-bath.

FREUD--(Hill; MT; Nordic; Two Cheers-Ascent; Two Cheers-English; Two Cheers-George; Two Cheers-Racial; Two Cheers-What)--Sigmund Freud, 1856-1939. An Austrian regarded as the founder of psycho-analysis which developed from his experiments in treating hysterics and those suffering from severe neuroses. He was, naturally, condemned by his colleagues in his own day for his theories which base these maladies in the sex drive. But, just as naturally, as the 20th century grew up and people searched for ways out of their malaises, his ideas grew fashionable especially because he directed the blame for one's condition away from oneself and placed it upon one's parents or one's early training. In later life, Freud was lauded and worshipped and died in the odor of sanctity. He was much influenced by German Romantic philosophy and, in naming aspects of man's hidden and darker self, he made use of classical and literary allusions (e.g., Oedipal and Electra complexes and the ego). The treatment he used consisted in permitting the patient to speak freely about himself and his dreams. The latter were interpreted by the analyst.

FRITZ--(Aspects II)--Fritz Robinson, the eldest of the Robinson boys who, with their parents, are shipwrecked on a deserted island in the novel, The Swiss Family Robinson (1813),
by Johann Rudolf Wyss. He grows up to become a gentleman and to accept his responsibilities, nevertheless, he
wants to return to Europe. (See also: Franz, Little; and
Ernest.)

FROGS, THE--(Two Cheers-Raison)--A comic play (405 B. C.)
by Aristophanes (q. v.), in which he lampoons Euripides (q.
v.). Dionysus (q. v.) hungers for the plays of Euripides who
has just died. He is determined to follow him to Hades to
return him to Athens. In Hades, he finds Euripides trying
to usurp from Aeschylus (q. v.) the throne of premier dramatist. A trial is held with Dionysus as judge. The two de-
fend themselves vehemently, and the decision is awarded to
Aeschylus.

FROISSART--(Two Cheers-In)--Jean Froissart, 1333?-?1400.
A French chronicler who traveled widely and ultimately entered the Church. When in England, he became acquainted
with Chaucer (q. v.). He is most remembered for his
Chronique de France, d'Angleterre, d'Écosse, et d'Espagne
the date for which is uncertain. It treats of the historical
period beginning in 1325 and, in part, depicts the Hundred
Years' War.

FROM RITUAL TO ROMANCE--(AH-TS)--A study (1920) of
the legend of the Holy Grail by Jesse L. Weston in which
she attempts to support the theory that at its roots lies the
record of an ancient ritual which had as its end the initia-
tion of the individual into the secret of physical and spiritual life. The volume is, perhaps, best known as the inspiration for T. S. Eliot's (q. v.) Wasteland (q. v.).

FRONTO, SAINT--(Alex II, 7)--A hermit in the desert of
Nitra in Egypt in A. D. 100's(?).

FRY, ROGER--(AH-Roger; Collected Ta-Intro; GLD-Intro;
Two Cheers-Does; Two Cheers-Not)--Roger Eliot Fry, 1866-
1934. A friend of E. M. Forster, he was an English painter,
but was more successful as an art critic. For a time, he
held the post of curator of paintings at the Metropolitan
Museum of Art in New York. He produced many mono-
graphs on prominent artists including Bellini (q. v.) and
Cézanne (q. v.). He also wrote several volumes, e. g.,
Vision and Design (1920), a collection of his lectures.

FUAD I--(Alex II, 1; Egypt)--Ahmed Fuad Pasha, 1868-1936.
Sultan (1917-1922) and King (1922-1936) of Egypt.

FURIES--(AH-Word; Two Cheers-John; Two Cheers-Not Listening)--See: Erinyes.

G

G MAJOR PIANO CONCERTO--(AH-Word)--By Beethoven (q.
v.). The Pianoforte Concerto No. 4 in G Major, Opus 58
(1805-6), dedicated to the Archduke Rudolph and published in
1808.

GABLER, HEDDA--(AH-Ibsen)--Hedda Gabler Tessman, the
central figure in the play, Hedda Gabler (1890), by Henrik
Ibsen (q.v.). She has married a professor and life with
him bores her. Lövborg, a former lover, is now the tutor
to the step-children of Thea Elvsted. Under Thea's influence he reforms his life and writes a book which brings him
fame. Hedda, in a jealous determination to dominate him,
lures Lövborg back to the dissipations he had left behind.
When, by accident, the manuscript of his second book falls
into her hands, she burns it. Giving Lövborg a pistol, she
urges him to die beautifully. He does die, not beautifully
as she had wished, but rather in a brawl. Hedda shoots
herself when threatened with exposure.

GAINSBOROUGH--(Two Cheers-Stratford)--Thomas Gains-
borough, 1727-1788. An English painter noted for his portraits of the famous of his day, he was one of the founding
fathers of the Royal Academy (q.v.). His "Blue Boy" is
perhaps the best known of his works. Others are in the collections of the Metropolitan Museum of Art in New York,
and, of course, The National Gallery in London.

GALATEA--(GLD VI)--In Greek legend, a sea nymph who
was loved by Polyphemus but who, in turn, was in love with
Acis. Acis was crushed under a rock by the jealous giant
Polyphemus and in despair, Galatea threw herself into the
sea.

GALILEO--(Alex I, 1; PP-Ph)--Galileo Galilei, 1564-1642.
An Italian astronomer and physicist, he discovered the iso-
chromism of the pendulum; invented the hydrostatic balance;
demonstrated the laws of gravity; and conceived the three
laws of motion which were later to be formulated by Newton.

He also devised a simple thermometer and improved the telescope through which he discovered the mountains of the moon and the Milky Way. In short, he was a remarkable man.

GALLIPOLI--(AH-Our; Egypt)--Forster is referring to the Gallipoli Peninsula, the site of fierce battles during World War I between the Turks and the British forces and ending in the withdrawal of the latter. The peninsula is some 63 miles long and lies between the Dardanelles and the Aegean Sea.

GALSWORTHY--(Aspects VIII; Two Cheers-English)--John Sinjohn Galsworthy, 1867-1933. A popular English writer of the early part of this century who began his career with a training in the law, but never practiced it. He is perhaps best known for the novel-trilogy, The Forsyte Saga, which, in a televised series, has rescued him from oblivion. An excellent craftsman, he never became part of or was influenced by the experimentation conducted by other writers during his lifetime.

GAMBIER, JAMES--(MT)--(1st Baron Gambier) 1756-1833. A British naval man who led his nation's forces, as an admiral, in the bombardment of Copenhagen and the defeat of the Danish fleet (1807). As Commander of the Fleet, he blockaded Napoleon's (q.v.) navy in the Basque Roads. He was appointed as the commissioner who negotiated the peace with the United States after the War of 1812.

GAMP, MRS.--(Collect Ta-Celest)--A character in the novel, Martin Chuzzlewit, by Charles Dickens (q.v.). She is a midwife, fat and old and the possessor of a husky voice and an eye which had the remarkable power of turning upward showing only its white. She wore a rusty black dress besprinkled with snuff and a shawl and bonnet in no better condition. Her nose was somewhat red and swollen.

GANDHI--(AH-Mind; GLD XI; Hill; MT; Two Cheers-George) --Mohandas Karamchand Gandhi, 1869-1948. He was called Mahatma, ("great-souled"). Born in Western India, he studied law in England and practiced it in India and South Africa. He agitated, in a peaceful manner, for the expulsion of the British from India. He was imprisoned several times, and died from an assassin's bullet.

GANESH--(AH-Our Div)--Forster is alluding to Ganesha who,
in Indian myth, is the god of wisdom, son of Siva (q.v.) and
lord of the lesser dieties known as Ganas. A sacrifice is
made to him at the beginning of any important work.

GANTRY, ELMER--(AH-Sin)--See: Elmer Gantry.

GARDEN OF EDEN--(Two Cheers-Raison)--In the Old Testament (Genesis), the garden created by the Lord for Adam
and Eve and their progeny in which all of nature was sub-
ordinate to their wishes, and life was good.

GARDENS OF SHALIMAR--(PI XXIII)--They are located 6
miles E of Lahore in what is now West Pakistan. They were
laid out by the Mogul emperor Shah Jahan (q.v.), the creator of the Taj Mahal (q.v.), in 1637.

GARGERY--(Aspects I)--A character in the novel, Great
Expectations, by Charles Dickens (q.v.). Joe Gargery, the
husband of Pip's sister, is a fair-haired, mild-tempered
man, much abused by his wife. He was the son of a drunk-
en father and the best friend Pip ever had. After his wife's
death, he marries Biddy and produces a Pip of his own.

GARIBALDI--(Aspects I; Two Cheers-Last; WAFT II)--
Giuseppe Garibaldi, 1807-1882. He is called, by those who
sympathize with his cause, "The Liberator of Italy." He
was associated with Mazzini who agitated for the union of
Italy. For a time, he was forced to flee Italy and lived in
various places including the United States where he made his
living in Staten Island and became a naturalized citizen. He returned to Italy in 1854 and commanded an army which was
named "the Redshirts" after a prominent part of its uniform.
With that army he captured Sicily and marched against Rome
twice only to be defeated by a French army. He lived to
see a united Italy and was elected deputy for Rome in the
new government.

GARNETT, DAVID--(AH-Ron)--1892- . An English novelist,
for a time he was the partner of Francis Meynell in the
Nonesuch Press. His most popular work, which won him
the Hawthornden and James Tait Black Memorial Prize
(1923), is Lady into Fox (1922).

GARRICK--(AH-Mrs; Two Cheers-Stratford)--David Garrick,
1717-1779. He was an English actor--some say the greatest
English actor--and a close friend of Dr. Samuel Johnson and

once his pupil at Litchfield. He came to London with Johnson and made his reputation in Richard III. He amassed a
great fortune from his career and retired to a comfortable
life in Hampton.

GARVICE, CHARLES--(Two Cheers-Anon)--1833-1920. An
English novelist, journalist, and playwright.

GAZPACHO--(Aspects I)--Subtitled: Or Summer Months in
Spain, a book of description and travel by William George
Clark, London: J. W. Parker, 1850. It takes its title
from a cold soup favored by the Spanish which consists of
finely chopped tomatoes, onions, cucumbers, garlic, etc.

"GEATE A-VALLENTO, THE"--(Two Cheers-William)--A
poem by William Barnes (1801-1886) in Poems Grave and
Gay, edited by Giles Dugdale.

GENESIS--(LJX)--The first book of the Old Testament. It
treats of the creation of the world and other matters.

GENGHIS KHAN--(AH-Emp)--[Orig. name: Temyin] 1162-
1227. The great Mongol conqueror of China, much of Asia,
and part of Europe. He was proclaimed Khan of all the
Mongols in 1206 and took as his capital the city of Kara-
koum. He conquered China (1213), Korea (1218), and
Northern India. His huge empire fell apart at his death.

GENLIS--(MT)--Comtesse de Genlis, née Stéphanie Félicité
du Crest de Saint Aubin, 1746-1830. A French author
whose husband was guillotined during the French Revolution
(q. v.), she was forced to flee France. She returned in
1802 and found favor with Napoleon (q. v.). Among her
many works are Madame de Maintenon (1806) and her
Mémoires (1825).

GENNADIUS II--(AH-Gem)--Georgios Scholarios. An Orthodox theologian, Greek scholar, and Patriarch of Constantinople, 1453-1459.

GEORGE--(AH-HOS)--A character in Belchamber by Howard
Overing Sturgis (q. v.).

GEORGE II--(AH-Capt)--George Augustus of the House of
Hanover (1683-1760), King of Great Britain and Ireland,
1727-1760. He was the son of George I. He became involved in European politics and wars because of his desire

to safeguard Hanover, his German state.   As a result, he
allied himself with Frederick the Great (q.v.) of Prussia.
In his declining years, his empire grew to include Canada,
a foothold in India, and success on the high seas.   He fought
with his son Frederick Louis and, as a result, was succeeded
by his grandson, George III (q.v.).

GEORGE III--(MT)--George William Frederick (1738-1820),
King of Britain and Ireland and elector and King of Hanover,
1760-1820.   He suffered from what was believed to be a
form of insanity which has since been diagnosed as a rare
vitamin deficiency.   It was during his reign that Britain lost
her colonies in America.   His son, later George IV (q.v.),
ruled as regent from 1811 because of the advanced state of
his father's illness.

GEORGE IV--(Aspects I)--George Augustus Frederick (1762-
1830), son of George III (q.v.), King of Great Britain and
Ireland and King of Hanover, 1820-1830.   He married Mrs.
Fitzherbert, his mistress, illegally (1785) and finally deserted her in 1794 to marry Caroline of Brunswick from
whom he became estranged.   He refused to have her present at his coronation and initiated proceedings for divorce.
The suit had to be dropped for lack of evidence.   He had no
legitimate children and was succeeded by his brother, William IV (q.v.).

GEORGE V--(AH-My Own; Aspects I)--George Frederick
Ernest Albert, 1865-1936.   Son of Edward VII (q.v.) and
grandson of Queen Victoria (q.v.), he became heir to the
throne because of the death of his elder brother.   He married Princess Victoria Mary of Teck (see: Queen Mary).
The chief event of his reign was World War I.

GEORGE AND MARY--(Hill)--King George V (q.v.) and
Queen Mary (q.v.).

GEORGE, HENRY--(GLD VII)--1839-1887.   An American
economist who developed the idea of a "single-tax."   His
pamphlet, Our Land and Land Policy discusses his contention that land values represent monopoly power and that the
entire tax burden should therefore be upon land.   His son
has written his biography (1910).

GEORGE, STEPHAN (STEFAN)--(Two Cheers-G&G)--1868-
1933.   A German poet associated with the Pre-Raphaelites
(q.v.), and in France with Beaudelaire and Mallarmé.   He

was the leader, in Germany, of the "art for art's sake" school of poetry.

GEORGE, KING--(Two Cheers-Madan)--Forster is alluding to George III (q. v.).

GEORGE, KING--(AH-Mind)--Forster is alluding to George V (q. v.).

GEORGE, ST. --(AH-Notes; Two Cheers-Not)--The patron saint of England. He is depicted as a Knight in armor slaying a dragon (Satan). The Vatican has recently [1969] declared him non-existent.

GEORGES--(Aspects V)--A character in the novel, The Counterfeiters (q. v.), by André Gide (q. v.). He is Olivier Molinier's younger brother who passes counterfeit money and is instrumental in the death by suicide of a friend from school.

GERASIM--(Two Cheers-Three)--A servant of Ilyich in "The Death of Ivan Ilyich" by Leo Tolstoy (q. v.).

GERD--(AH-Ibsen)--A character in the play, Brand, by Henrik Ibsen (q. v.). A gypsy girl, she follows Brand up the mountain on the top of which, she sees him as Lord and Redeemer.

GERETH, MRS. --(Aspects VIII)--A character in the novel, The Spoils of Poynton (1897), by Henry James (q. v.). She is the owner of Poynton, a mansion which she has filled with beautiful objects. She is worried that her son will not properly cherish the house and its contents. An accidental fire burns the building to the ground.

GERMAN EMPEROR--(AH-Jo)--Forster is alluding to William II (q. v.).

GERUSALEMME LIBERATA--(Two Cheers-Raison)--1580-81. Jerusalem Delivered (q. v.) by Torquato Tasso (q. v.). The tale in 24 cantos of the capture of Jerusalem from the Saracens.

GHOSTS--(AH-Ibsen)--A play (1881) by Henrik Ibsen (q. v.). Mrs. Alving has built an orphanage in memory of her husband. Her only son, Oswald, has come from Paris for its dedication. Regina, her maid, is her husband's illegitimate

daughter and Oswald's half-sister.   Oswald flirts with her
not knowing of their relationship.   Mrs. Alving sees them
as ghosts of her husband and Regina's mother.   She plots to
remove Regina from the house.   Oswald, meanwhile, deteriorates rapidly from an un-named disease, doubtless syphilis,
which he has inherited from his father.   He tells his mother
of his determination to marry Regina.   His mother reveals
their relationship.   Oswald asks Regina to live with him as
his sister, but she leaves in disgust.   Having begged his
mother's assistance, Oswald takes an overdose of morphine
and dies.

GIB--(Two Cheers-John)--The cat who ate Jane's (q. v.) sparrow in the poem "Philip Sparrow" by John Skelton (q. v.).

GIBBON--(AH-Capt; AH-Gem; AH-Roger; Two Cheers-Bk;
Two Cheers-Gibbon; Two Cheers-In; RWV II)--Edward Gibbon, 1737-1794.   An English historian and master of English prose.   Time has proven him a better stylist than historian.   He left England to live in Lausanne, Switzerland.
His masterpiece is, of course, The History of the Decline
and Fall of the Roman Empire which Forster, like many,
calls The Decline and Fall (q. v.).

GIBBON'S "TIRESOME OLD AUNT"--(Two Cheers-Gibbon)--
Forster is referring to Miss Hester Gibbon who, at the time
Gibbon wrote his Autobiography (1795), was still alive at the
age of 84 and living at Cliffe in Northamptonshire.

GIBBS, JAMES--(Two Cheers-Camb)--1682-1754.   An English architect.

GIDE, ANDRÉ--(AH-TS; Aspects IV; Two Cheers G&G; Two
Cheers-Gide; Two Cheers-In)--1869-1951.   A French novelist,
satirist, and critic.   He attacked Puritanism and defended
homosexuality in his semi-autobiographical works such as
The Immoralist (1902) and La Porte Étroite (1907).   For a
time he was associated with the Symbolist movement.   During the 20's he was the leader of the young and radical
French writers.   He received the Nobel Prize for literature
in 1947.   See also: Les Faux-Monayeurs.

GILBERT AND SULLIVAN--(AH-Mind; LJ X)--Sir William
Schwenk Gilbert (1836-1911) and Sir Arthur Seymour Sullivan
(1842-1900).   They were collaborators in a series of comic-
satiric operas which have never been equaled in the English
language.   They were, surprisingly enough, enormously pop-

ular when first performed and have increased in popularity
since.   Rarely does a season go by when one of their oper-
ettas is not produced.   The best productions are still those
of the company formed by their original producer, D'Oyly
Carte, and named after him.   Some of the more memorable
of the group written by Gilbert (lyrics) and Sullivan (music)
are this writer's favorites, H. M. S. Pinafore (1878), The
Pirates of Penzance (1879), and The Mikado (1885).

GILES, HERBERT ALAN--(GLD XI)--1845-1935.   Author,
translator, and Sinologist.   He has written: Gems of Chinese
Literature, London: Quaritch, 1883; and a Chinese-English
Dictionary, 1892; and edited: Chinese Fairy Tales, 1911,
and Chinese Poetry, 1898.

GILLRAY--(HE XVIII)--James Gillray, 1757-1815.   An English political cartoonist; some of the more biting of his cartoons were aimed at the King (George III, q. v.) whom he
called "Farmer George."

GIONO, JEAN--(Two Cheers-Post)--1895-   . A French
novelist noted for depicting the peasant life in the remote
districts of the Basses-Alpes.   He is the author of Harvest
(English edition, 1939).

GIORGIONE--(RWV IV; Two Cheers-Not)--Giorgio Barbarelli,
1478?-1511.   A Venetian painter who influenced many of his
contemporaries, including Titian.   His pictures are extremely rare.   He was a pupil of Giovanni Bellini (q. v.).

GIOTTO--(Aspects VI; Collect Ta-Eternal; RWV II; Two
Cheers-India; WAFT VI)--Giotto di Bondone, 1276?-?1337.
A Florentine painter, architect, and sculptor, and pupil of
Cimabue, he is especially noted for the design of the cam-
panile [bell tower] of Santa Maria della Fiore, the cathedral
(Il Duomo) of Florence.

GIRNAR--(PI XXIII)--A sacred mountain in India about 240
miles NW of Bombay.

GITANJALI--(AH-Two)--[Bengali: song offerings.]   The collection was translated by its author, Tagore (q. v.), into
English from the original Bengali, 1913.   The volume has
an introduction by W. B. Yeats (q. v.).

GLADSTONE--(AH-Wil; Aspects I; Egypt; MT; Two Cheers-
Lon Lib)--William Ewart Gladstone, 1809-1898.   A British

statesman who held a number of government posts but is
most known for his Prime Ministry on four different occasions: 1868-74; 1880-85; 1886; 1892-94; and the dubious
honor of having a type of suitcase named after him. He
was also the originator of a landbill, and an attempted reform of the Irish government with a provision for home-rule.

GLASTONBURY TOR--(AH-Mrs)--A curious hill in the town
of Glastonbury in the South of England. It is crowned with
ruins of a medieval chapel. The area is drenched in history. It was the scene of the Roman occupation, and the
home of St. Joseph of Atimathea, and the site of a Benedic-
tine Abbey suppressed by Henry VIII, the ruins of which are
still visible. It is curious that, while the stones of the Abbey were used by the people as a quarry, the Lady Chapel
dedicated to the Virgin was never touched by the townspeople.

GLENALLEN, THE COUNTESS OF--(Aspects II)--A character in the novel, The Antiquary, by Sir Walter Scott (q.v.).
She is the mother of the Earl of Glenallen. Her burial at
midnight in the ruins of St. Ruth's priory causes terror to
the treasure seekers. In life, she was anxious to prevent
the marriage of her son to Eveline Neville and unaware that
they were already married. She convinces him that Eveline
was the illegitimate daughter of his father.

GLOBE SHAKESPEARE--(Aspects I)--Published in 1864, it
is a one-volume edition of Shakespeare's plays edited by W.
G. Clark, J. Glover, and W. A. Wright who used the text
of the Cambridge Shakespeare (q.v.). The Globe edition is
important because it established the standard for the num-
bering of the lines of the play.

GLUCK--(AH-Word; GLD IX; RWV XV; Two Cheers-Not Listening)--Christopher Willibald von Gluck, 1714-1787. A
German composer of opera and other musical pieces. He is
noted as a reformer of opera stressing the importance of
subordinating the music to the needs of the drama. Some of
his better known works are Alcestis (1767), and Iphigenia in
Aulis.

GNOSTICISM--(Alex I, 3)--A Christian heresy of the first
six centuries of the Christian era. It taught that knowledge
rather than mere faith is the key to salvation. Christ, it
held, was an "eon" or divine attribute personified like Mind,
Truth, Logos, etc. The totality of "eons" make up the divine fullness.

GOBINEAU--(GLD X)--Comte Joseph Arthur de Gobineau,
1816-1882. French writer, orientalist, and diplomat most
noted for a strange work which presented the theory (later
developed by Hitler) that the Aryan or Teuton is superior to
any race of man. The title of the work in which this odd
concept appeared is Essai sur l'Inégalité des Races Humaines
(1854, 1884).

GODWIN--(GLD VII)--William Godwin, 1756-1836. An English writer and a leading radical of the day. He preached
for the overthrow of all governments and all institutions including that of marriage. In terms of the latter, he practiced what he preached with Mary Wollstonecraft whom he
met in 1791 and had a child by (named Fanny); but later
(1797) inexplicably he married her. Obviously influenced by
Jean Jacques Rousseau, he in turn influenced the English
Romantics and, in particular, Wordsworth, Coleridge, Byron
and Shelley; his daughter, Mary, the creator of Frankenstein
married Shelley in 1816. A stepdaughter of a later marriage
was briefly Byron's mistress. Godwin, other than for the
peculiarities of his domestic arrangements, is best known
for his novel, Caleb Williams (1794).

GOEBBELS--(Nordic; Two Cheers-G&G; Two Cheers-Ter;
Two Cheers-What Would)--Joseph Paul Goebbels, 1897-1945.
He was Hitler's propaganda minister (1933-1945) who was
instrumental in setting into motion the horrifying persecu-
tion of the Jews. He died a suicide when it was clear that
Germany was about to lose World War II.

GOETHE--(AH-Reid; GLD VI; LJ IX; Nordic; Reading; Two
Cheers-Fer; Two Cheers-Gide; Two Cheers-Mohammed; Two
Cheers-Raison; Two Cheers-Tol; Two Cheers-What)--Johann
Wolfgang von Goethe, 1749-1832. The greatest German exponent of the Romantic school of writing and one of the most
important of all German poets. He began his maturity with
a study of law and was eventually licensed to practice it,
but he turned from it to writing and began publishing a long
series of poems. These poems inaugurated a German literary period which has become known as "Sturm und Drang"
[storm and stress]. His most famous work is Faust (q. v.)
(Pt. I, 1808; Pt. II, 1832). His works wielded a strong
influence on the direction German literature was to take.

GOG MAGOGS--(AH-Wil; LJ VII)--GOG AND MAGOG--In
English legend, they are the only survivors of the 33 infamous daughters of Diocletian who murdered their husbands.

They were set adrift in a ship for their sins and reached
Albion (England) where they took up life with a number of
demons.   Their descendants, a race of giants, were wiped
out by Brute except for Gog and Magog who were brought to
London in chains and made porters at the royal palace, now
the site of the Guidhall.   Their effigies remained there until
the great fire and were replaced in 1717.

GOLDBERG VARIATIONS, THE--(AH-Word; Two Cheers-Not
Listening)--Goldberg (Johann Gottlieb Goldberg, 1727-1756)
was a German clavier player and a pupil of Johann Sebastian
Bach (q.v.).   On commission from Count von Kaiserling,
the patron of Goldberg, Bach composed 30 variations for a
double harpsichord.   Their structure reveals that Bach was
writing for a very skillful performer.

GOLDSMITH--(Aspects V)--Oliver Goldsmith, 1728-1774.   An
English poet, novelist, essayist, and dramatist, born in Ireland.   He belonged to the literary circle which gathered
about Dr. Samuel Johnson.   Some of his better known works
are the play, She Stoops to Conquer (1773); the novel, The
Vicar of Wakefield (1766); and the poem, "The Deserted Village" (q.v.), 1770.

GOPHER PRAIRIE--(AH-Sin)--The small town in Minnesota
which Sinclair Lewis (q.v.) associated with all the negative
values of small-town American life.   It is the scene of his
satirical novel, Main Street.

GORDIUS--(PP-Return)--The name of a peasant who was
made king of Phyrigia and, as a consequence, dedicated his
wagon to Jupiter.   He tied its yoke to a beam in Jupiter's
temple with a knot which no one could untie.   A legend grew
that he who could undo it would become master of the East.
Alexander (q.v.) hearing of the legend, cut the knot with his
sword.

GORDON, GENERAL--(Egypt; GLD I; Two Cheers-English)--
Charles George Gordon, 1833-1885.   A strange individual
called Chinese Gordon.   He was an Englishman, one could
call him a soldier of fortune, who commanded a Chinese
army which suppressed the Taiping rebellion against the
Emperor of China (1863-64).   He also served under the
Khedive of Egypt as governor of the Sudan and the Equatorial Provinces.   While governor, he suppressed the slave
trade.   He was killed at Khartoum when the Mahdi's (q.v.)
forces overwhelmed its garrison.

GORGO--(Alex I, 1)--A female character in the 15th Idyl of
Theocritus (q. v.). She is a friend of Praxinoe.

GÖRING--(Nordic)--Hermann Göring, 1893-1946. He served
in the German air force in World War I and became involved
with Hitler (q. v.). In 1933, Hitler appointed him as a cabinet minister for air forces. From 1940 he was the president of the council for war economy. He committed suicide
in jail while on trial for his war crimes.

GOSTREY, MARIA--(Aspects VIII)--A character in the novel,
The Ambassadors (q. v.), by Henry James (q. v.). An "in-
troducer" and tour director, she is a chance acquaintance of
Lambert Strether. She is sensitive and understanding.

GOTTERDAMMERUNG--(LJ IX; RWV XII; Two Cheers-C)--
[German: literally, "the twilight of the gods."] The title of
the fourth of a series of four operas, by Richard Wagner
(q. v.), called the "Ring" series.

GOURMONT, RÉMY DE--(Two Cheers-Post)--1858-1915. A
French writer whose work is sensual, fantastic, and ironic.
He was, in the early portion of his career, a member of the
Symbolist movement. His face was disfigured by an unwhole-
some looking growth and, as a result, he lived much of his
life as a recluse. He dressed in the habit of a Trappist
monk, but there is no record of his having lived as one.
Two of his works which have been translated into English
are A Night at Luxembourg (1906) and The Virgin Heart
(1907).

GRACCHI, THE--(Two Cheers-Ascent)--Two brothers, Tiberius Sempronius Gracchus (d. 133 B. C.) and Gaius Sempronius Gracchus (d. 121 B. C.). Their mother was the
famous Cornelia. Their fame rests on their attempts to
solve the economic depression of Rome brought about by the
state's failure to administrate its land on sound principles.

GRAHAM--(Aspects V)--Dr. John Graham Bretton, a character in the novel, Villette (1853), by Charlotte Brontë (q. v.).
He is the son of Lucy's godmother. Kind-hearted, young
and handsome, for a time it seems that a romance between
him and Lucy is developing. However, he gives his heart
to Pauline whom he eventually marries.

GRAND CANAL, THE--(PI XXXI)--The largest of Venice's
many canals, its "main street" so to speak.

"GRANDE JATTE, LA"--(Two Cheers-Art)--Full title: "Un Dimanche [Sunday] à la Grande Jatte." It is a painting [1887] by Georges Seurat (1859-1891), a co-founder of the Impressionist school of French painting in the pointillist style he perfected.

GRANDE MADEMOISELLE, LA--(MT)--See: Mademoiselle de Montpensier.

GRANT, ALEXANDER--(MT)--Sir Alexander Grant, 1826-1884. A British educator and principal of Edinburgh University from 1868 to 1884.

GRANT, DUNCAN--(Tribute)--Duncan James Corrour Grant, 1885- . Born in Inverness, Scotland, he is a painter best known for his decorative work.

GRANVILLE, LORD--(Egypt)--Granville George Leveson-Gower, (2nd Earl Granville), 1815-1891. A British statesman who held a number of government posts including foreign secretary under Gladstone (q. v.). In the latter office, he was unable to take effective measures against the troubles in Egypt and the Sudan among other matters.

GRASMERE--(HE XIX; PI XIV)--One of the lakes in England's Lake District in Westmorland (NW England). The community, which takes its name from the lake, was once the home of Wordsworth (q. v.).

GRAVES, ROBERT--(GLD V)--1895- . An English novelist and poet who first came to the public's eye through his poetry about the horrors of World War I. His works include two remarkable novels, I, Claudius (1934) and Claudius the God (1934).

GRAY--(Two Cheers-Stratford)--Thomas Gray, 1716-1771. An English poet whose modern reputation rests upon his "Elegy in a Country Churchyard" considered the poem which foreshadowed the Romantic school of English poetry. There is in it a melancholy and imaginative approach to nature which reflects the tenets of that school.

GREAT BOYG, THE--(AH-Ibsen)--A character in the play, Peer Gynt (q. v.), by Henrik Ibsen (q. v.). He is a monster identified only as a voice in the darkness who claims to conquer though he does not fight.

GREAT EXPECTATIONS--(Aspects V)--A novel (1860) by
Charles Dickens (q. v.).   Pip is raised by a sister and her
husband, Gargery (q. v.).   He is told, one day, that he is to
be raised as a gentleman by means of money supplied by an
unknown benefactor whom he thinks is the recluse, Miss
Havisham.   In reality, the benefactor is Magwitch, an escaped convict, whom Pip had helped.   Magwitch has made a
fortune in New South Wales.   When he returns to England,
he is arrested and his wealth is confiscated.   Thus ends
Pip's great expectations.   He also loses in love when Estella,
Miss Havisham's ward, refuses to marry him.

GREAT FIRE, THE--(Two Cheers-London)--In September,
1666, a huge conflagration destroyed most of the City of
London including the Gothic St. Paul's Cathedral.   A monument marking where it was finally brought under control is
dedicated to the memory of the destruction it wrought.

GREAT ORMOND STREET--(AH-Early)--A street in London
which leads West from Milliman St.   Several important hospitals are located along its length including the Hospital for
Sick Children, the largest hospital of its kind.   It was
founded in 1852.

GREAT WESTERN--(HE XXVIII)--A wooden paddle steamer
built in 1837 by Isambard Kingdom Brunel.   It was the first
successful transatlantic steamship.

GREEK VIEW OF LIFE, THE--(GLD X)--By Goldsworthy
Lowes Dickinson (1896) (q. v.), it is "an introduction to translations from the Greek, " and an "attempt to demonstrate to the
non-expert the character and environment of hidden treasures
and to leave him among them."

GREEN MANSIONS--(Aspects I)--A romance (1916) by W. H.
Hudson and set in the jungles of South America.   Mr. Abel,
the narrator, tells the story of his tragic love for Rima,
the "bird girl, " who lives in the jungles and dies there.

GREENE, GRAHAM--(Two Cheers-Eng)--1904-   .   An English novelist, critic, dramatist, essayist, his more important work consists chiefly in probing the psychology of sin.
Perhaps his best novel is The Power and the Glory, in
America called The Labyrinthine Ways (1940).

GREENWICH VILLAGE--(Two Cheers-Mount)--The area of
New York roughly W of Fifth Avenue to the Hudson River,

S of 14th St. and N of Houston Street. It is more a state
of mind than a clearly defined section of the city. It is the
playground of the Bohemian, the would-be Bohemian, and the
derelict of all ages.

GREY, SIR EDWARD--(GLD XII)--Viscount Grey of Fallodon,
1862-1933. A British statesman who held several government posts including that of Secretary of State for foreign
affairs (1905-16). During the course of his tenure in that
office, he consolidated the triple entente which united the efforts of France, Russia and Great Britain during World War
I. He also played an important role in the Peace Conference
in London (1912-1913). He was a chancellor of Oxford (1928).

GRIEG--(HE VI)--Edvard Hagerup Grieg, 1843-1907. A Norwegian composer noted for the ethnic character of his music.
He studied in Leipzig and Copenhagen. One of his more familiar compositions is the music for the play, Peer Gynt
(q. v.). He has also created many Norwegian dances, folk-
songs, and orchestral pieces.

GRIGSON, GEOFFREY--(Two Cheers-Outsider)--b. 1905. A
British critic, poet, and editor. Born in Cornwall, he was
a contemporary of Auden (q. v.), and MacNiece at Oxford,
but did not know them. After college, he turned to journalism. Some of his works are The Arts Now (1935), Selected
Poems of William Barnes (1950), and Selected Poems of John
Clare (1950).

GRIMES, PETER--(Two Cheers-George C)--See: Peter
Grimes.

GROPIUS--(Nordic)--Walter Gropius, 1883- . Born in Berlin, he had to flee from persecution by the Nazi party. He
is an architect and founder of the Bauhaus school of architecture which has had enormous and not always happy influence upon modern architecture in the United States. Gropius based his architectural principles upon the philosophy of
functionalism. It resulted in some beautiful structures, but
all too often it produced soulless, inhuman, and cheap buildings. It is the latter quality which has made the style so
popular.

GROTE, GEORGE--(Two Cheers-Lon Lib)--1794-1871. An
English historian and vice-chancellor of London University
(1862). His major work is a history of Greece in eight
volumes (1846-56). His biography (Personal Life of George

Grote, 1873) was written by his wife.

GUBBIO--(WAFT I)--A city in the province of Perugia, Italy, noted for its cathedral (13th century) and its church of St. Francis (14th century) as well as other important tourist attractions.

GUELFS--(RWV I)--The party opposed to the Ghibellines (12th-14th centuries) whose conflicts in Italy and Germany shaped the history of those areas. The Guelfs were supporters of the papacy and the Ghibellines, the German emperors.

GRUNDY, MRS.--(AH-Mrs G; Nordic; RWV II)--Originally a character in the play, Speed the Plough (1798), by Thomas Morton. The Grundys are neighbors of the Ashfields and Mrs. Ashfield is jealous of them. Her husband, a farmer, remonstrates with her because she is continuously measuring their actions against "What Mrs. Grundy will say." The name has since become associated with somewhat humorous arbiters of morals, especially those dealing with sex, tending toward repression.

GRUYÈRE--(HE XVII)--A kind of cheese produced in Switzerland and France which gets its name from the district in the Canton Friburg, Switzerland. Pale yellow in color, the cheese is soft to the palate.

GUERMANTES, DUCHESSE DE--(Two Cheers-Our)--A character in the novel, Remembrance of Things Past (q.v.), by Marcel Proust (q.v.). She is a member of an aristocratic family who once shuns Odette as a vulgar social climber, but then becomes pleased to attend her salon.

"GUERNICA"--(Two Cheers-Last)--The title of a painting (1937) by Pablo Picasso which attempts to depict, symbolically, the horrors of the Spanish Civil War, and all wars, in terms of the bombing of Guernica. The large painting, in black, white, and shades of grey, hangs in the Museum of Modern Art in New York.

GUINEVERE--(Collected Ta-Other)--The wife of King Arthur. She was passionately in love with Sir Lancelot, a member of Arthur's Round Table. She was seduced by Modred, the King's nephew and usurper of his kingdom. Arthur battled him, killing him and dying himself. Guinevere became a nun and legend says she is buried at Glastonbury (q.v.).

GULLIVER'S TRAVELS--(Two Cheers-Bk)--The masterpiece (1726) of Jonathan Swift (q.v.), titled Travels Into Several Remote Nations of the World, by Lemuel Gulliver. It treats of Gulliver's journeys to such lands as Lilliput whose inhabitants are six inches high; Brobdingnag, the land of giants; and finally to a country where Houyhnhnms (thoroughly rational horses) govern the Yahoos (degenerate reasonless human beings). The work is a bitter satire against man and his institutions.

GURNEY, SIR GOLDSWORTHY--(GLD I)--1793-1875. An English inventor responsible for the steam jet and the oxyhydrogen blowpipe. He also invented a steam-driven carriage.

GURNEY'S METHOD--(MT)--A system of short-hand.

GYNT, PEER--(AH-Ibsen; Two Cheers-Ascent; Two Cheers-Mohammed)--See: Peer Gynt.

H

HADES--(AH-Cn)--The home of departed spirits in Latin and Greek myth. It is gloomy, but not a place of torture even though it has come to be synonymous with the Judeo-Christian Hell. In Homer, the name Hades refers to the god Pluto who rules over the dead.

HADRIAN--(Alex II, 1)--Publius Aelius Hadrianus, A.D. 76-138. A Roman emperor (117-138), he was born in Rome, was a nephew of Trajan and married a grandniece of that emperor. He accompanied Trajan on many of his expeditions. When he came to the throne, he established the river Euphrates as the eastern boundary of the Roman empire. He was fond of traveling and visited much of the empire including Britain where he caused a wall to be built from Solway Firth to the mouth of the Tyne. He beautified Rome with many buildings and monuments including his tomb now known as the Castel Sant'Angelo.

HAECKEL--(AH-Wil)--Ernst Heinrich Haeckel, 1834-1919. A German philosopher and biologist and the first German to advocate the teaching of evolution. He is also responsible for the definition of the now-discarded biogenetic law which states that the stages through which a species has passed in its evolution (phylogeny) are recapitulated in each individual's

development (ontogeny--a word Haeckel coined). He was also the first to construct the genealogical tree which relates
the evolutionary development of various orders of animals.

HAFIZ--(PI II)--Shams ud-din Mohammed Hafiz, fl. 14th
century. A Persian lyric poet, he was also a philosopher
of the mystic persuasion and chief of an order of dervishes.
He became a professor of exegesis of the Koran. His chief
work is Divan, a collection of short odes (gazels).

HAGEN--(Nordic)--A Burgundian knight in the Nibelungenlied
and Norse sagas. He is liegeman to Gunther, the king.

HAGGARD, RIDER--(Hill)--Sir Henry Rider Haggard, 1856-
1925. An English novelist, immensely popular in his day,
now fallen into the limbo of the half-forgotten. He was in
the service of the government in South Africa and the more
popular of his romance-adventures are set in one or another
part of that continent, e.g., King Solomon's Mines (1885);
Alan Quartermain (1887); and She (1887).

HA-HA--(LJ XI)--A ditch used on English estates to serve
as a protection for property and live-stock, like a hedge,
without spoiling the view.

HALKETT, CECELIA--(Aspects VIII)--A character in the
novel, Beauchamp's Career (1874-75). She is the daughter
of Col. Halkett and falls in love with Beauchamp (q.v.).
She thinks him courageous and honorable. But finally, she
bows to the will of her father and marries a more suitable
young man.

HALLAM, ARTHUR--(Two Cheers-Lon Lib)--Arthur Henry
Hallam. 1811-1833. He was a close friend of Tennyson who
dedicated his long poem, In Memoriam, to him. He was
also engaged to Tennyson's sister.

HAMLET--(GLD XI; Two Cheers-Jul; Two Cheers-Stratford)
--The Prince of Denmark and chief character in the play of
the same name (1600-1601) by William Shakespeare (q.v.).
It is difficult to sum up his character because it has become embedded under tons of scholarly and pseudo-scholarly
commentary. He is torn by grief for the death of his father
and the hasty marriage of his mother to his uncle, his father's brother. He sees the ghost of his father who tells
his son that he was murdered by his brother. That death,
he insists, must be avenged. Hamlet is not content to do

justice to his uncle by killing him. He wants his uncle's soul to be condemned to hell, a prerogative not his, but God's. This desire to usurp divinity is the essential problem in the play and the source of all the difficulties depicted.

"HAMLET AND HIS PROBLEMS"--(AH-TS)--An essay by T. S. Eliot (q. v.) first published in 1919 and appearing in his Selected Essays, 1950 and in other editions of his work. He calls Shakespeare's play an "artistic failure. "

HAMPSTEAD--(PI XXXI)--A borough of London of some 2, 265 acres containing Hampstead Heath, a beautifully uncivilized park with a splendid view, from its hills, of the dome of St. Paul's and the City of London. It was also the home of the poet Keats (q. v.) whose house is preserved and open to view.

HAMPTON COURT--(Two Cheers-John)--A palace near London erected by Cardinal Wolsey (1514) and given as a "gift" to Henry VIII (q. v.) in 1529. The King added a great hall and a chapel. For 200 years, it was the favorite residence of the kings. Now part is open to the public and part is occupied by aristocratic pensioners of the crown.

HANDEL--(AH-Word; Two Cheers-Romain)--George Frederick Handel, 1685-1759. A German composer who became a citizen of Great Britain in 1726. He composed operas, oratorios and other concert pieces by the score. He was director of the Royal Academy of Music (1720-28) and director of the King's Theatre, Covent Garden (q. v.), 1728-34. The Messiah (1742), an oratorio is, perhaps, his most famous work.

HANLEY, JAMES--(AH-Liberty)--1901- . He is an English novelist, writer of short stories, journalist, seaman and railwayman.

HANNIBAL--(AH-Vo)--247-183 B. C. He was a Carthaginian general who became commander-in-chief of Carthage's army in Spain and a sworn enemy of Rome. He fought Rome in Spain and then, in a magnificent gesture, crossed the Alps into Italy with his elephants. He marched against Rome. Carthage was eventually defeated by Scipio Africanus. Hannibal was recalled to Carthage, and committed suicide there in 183 B. C.

HANUMAN--(PI XXXVII)--The monkey general, in Hindu myth, and faithful ally of Rama in his war with Ravana and the Rakghasas. He was rewarded with immortality for his courage and loyalty. He is as tall as a mountain and has enormous strength and agility as well as learning.

HAPI--(Alex II, 1)--The Egyptian god of the Nile and one of the four sons of Horus (q. v.) or of Osiris (q. v.). The others are Amset (q. v.), Qebhsneuf (Forster spells it Kebehsenouf, q. v.), Duamutef (Forster: Douamoutef, q. v.). Hapi is also the god of the north cardinal point and the Canopic god protecting the lungs. After death, the corpse's lungs were removed, mumified and placed in a jar with a cover in the form of Hapi's head.

HARCOURT, SIR WILLIAM VERNON--(AH-Wil)--1827-1904. A British statesman of the liberal persuasion. Born in York, he was educated at Cambridge and acquired a reputation by his articles in The Saturday Review and by his letters to the London Times signed "Historicus. " He was given a professorship of international law at Cambridge in 1869, and held various government posts, including that of Solicitor-General and Home Secretary under Gladstone (q. v.).

HARDINGE, LORD--(Hill)--Charles Hardinge (1st Baron Hardinge of Penhurst), 1858-1944. He was a member of the British diplomatic service from 1880 and ambassador to Russia (1904-06). He became Viceroy of India (1910-16) and ambassador to France (1920-23).

HARDY, THOMAS--(AH-Sin; Aspects I; GLD IX; MT; Two Cheers-Clouds; Two Cheers-Fer)--1840-1928. An English novelist who began his career as an architect, but from 1867 he devoted himself to writing. He produced a series of fatalistic works set in the mythical Wessex, but revealing all of the miseries of the real world. These bleak works climaxed with the bitter and dark Jude the Obscure (1895). American high school students of a certain vintage will recall with a shudder other of his novels which they were forced to read: The Return of the Native (1878) and Tess of the D'Urbervilles (1891). Hardy novels, these students will forever remember, need hardy readers. The author turned from the novel to the production of poetry equally bleak and hopeless in more than one way. The Dynasts (q. v.) is the chief work of this period of his life.

HARE, AUGUSTUS WILLIAM--(MT-On; Two Cheers-Virginia) --1792-1834. An English clergyman and writer who held the living at Alton-Barnes. Much of his writing was done in collaboration with his brother, Julius Charles Hare.

HARPOCRATES--(Alex II, 1)--The Greek equivalent of the Egyptian god Harpechrat (Horus, the sun-god as a child). He is represented as a boy with a finger in his mouth.

HARRINGTON, EVAN--(Aspects IV)--The principal character in the novel (1861) of the same name by George Meredith (q.v.). He is the son of a tailor who accepts his responsibilities to those whom he loves. Eventually, he marries Rose Jocelyn, an heiress.

HARROD'S--(HE X)--It is the block-long department store of the better kind located in The Brompton Road, Knightsbridge, London.

HARROW--(LJ XVI)--One of England's great public [i.e., private] schools. Located in Harrow-on-the-Hill near St. Albans, its charter was granted by Elizabeth I (q.v.) in 1572 to John Lyon. Winston Churchill (q.v.) was one of its more famous students.

HARRY RICHMOND--(Aspects V)--The Adventures of Harry Richmond (1871) by George Meredith (q.v.). Harry's father has one ambition: that his son obtain an exalted position. Harry falls in love with Princess Ottilia. His pursuit of her is the central plot of the novel.

HASTINGS, WARREN--(AH-JA)--1732-1818. An English statesman, governor of Bengal, India (1772) and governor general of India (1773). He was impeached for corruption and cruelty in 1788 and was acquitted after a spectacular trial.

HAUSSMANN--(GLD IX; PP-Bet)--Baron George Eugène Haussmann, 1809-1891. Perfect of the Seine (1853-70), he literally reconstructed Paris giving it not only sewers but wide, new boulevards and parks including the Bois de Boulogne among others.

HAWTHORNE, NATHANIEL--(AH-Reid; Aspects VII)--1804-1864. An American novelist born (as Nathaniel Hathorne) in Salem, Mass., he graduated from Bowdoin (whereupon he added the "w" to his name), and began writing immediately.

He was most interested in the psychology of sin and its effects on more than one generation. His most famous work
is The Scarlet Letter (1850).

HAYDN--(Two Cheers-Raison)--Franz Josef Haydn, 1732-
1809. Austrian composer of music in the service of the
Esterházy family. He is noted for his masses, overtures,
operas, sonatas, and symphonies.

HAYMARKET STORES--(HE X)--Lower Regent Street, London, named after the location of a market for hay and straw.

HEARD, GERALD--(AH-Vo; New Disorder)--Henry Fitzgerald Heard, 1889- . An English writer and editor. See:
Pain, Sex, and Time.

HEARN, LAFCADIO--(Collected Ta-Machine)--Patricio Lafcadio Tessima Carlos Hearn, 1850-1904. The son of a
British army surgeon, he came to America (1869) and worked
on several newspapers. He then went to Japan in 1890 and
taught English, finally becoming a Japanese citizen. His major work is devoted to interpreting Japan to English-speaking
peoples. Glimpses of Unfamiliar Japan (1894), and Japan,
An Attempt at Interpretation (1904).

HEART OF MIDLOTHIAN, THE--(Aspects I)--A novel (1816)
by Sir Walter Scott (q.v.). Effie Deans is confined in Tol-
booth, the jail which is the stone heart of Midlothian. She
is accused of murdering her illegitimate baby. Her half-
sister cannot bring herself to utter the half-truth which will
free her even though she knows Effie to be innocent. Nevertheless, Effie is freed from prison, and elopes with Staunton,
her seducer and the son of a nobleman. Years later, she
learns that her husband has been shot by a vagabond who is
actually her child, not murdered but kidnapped by Madge
Wildfire.

HEATHCLIFF--(Aspects VII)--The hero of the novel Wuthering Heights by Emile Brontë (q.v.). He is a gypsy raised
by Mr. Earnshawe, Catherine's father. He falls in love
with her, but she cannot consider him a suitable husband because of his birth.

HECTOR--(AH-Consol)--A character in the play Troilus and
Cressida (1601-02) by William Shakespeare (q.v.). He is
the chief of Priam's sons and the primary defender of Troy.
Troilus accuses him of being too merciful to the fallen ene-

my. Achilles and his band kill him when he is unarmed.

HECUBA--(Alex I, 1)--The second wife of Priam of Troy
and mother of 19 children including Paris and Hector. When
Troy fell, she became part of Ulysses's spoils. Afterwards,
she was metamorphosed into a dog and threw herself into the
sea.

HEEP, URIAH--(Aspects VII)--A character in the novel David
Copperfield (q.v.), by Charles Dickens (q.v.). He is a hyp-
ocritical clerk in the office of Mr. Wickfield who worms his
way into his employer's confidence only to ruin him. He is
exposed by Mr. Micawber.

HEGEL--(GLD IX)--Georg Wilhelm Friedrich Hegel, 1770-
1831. A German philosopher who formulated a system of
philosophy--in reality, a world view--of vast and complicated
proportions based on the Absolute and known as Hegelianism.
It provides for a dialectic which procedes from thesis to an-
tithesis. The system proved important for Marxism.

HEINE--(GLD IX; Reading; Two Cheers-What)--Heinrich
Heine, 1797-1856. A German lyric poet of Jewish parentage.
He became a Christian and lived in Paris. Three of his
works (Neue Gedichte, 1844; Buch der Lieder, 1827; Roman-
zen, 1851) contain some of the best known and best loved
German lyrics including "Die Lorelei."

HELEN--(GLD VII)--In Faust (q.v.) by Goethe (q.v.), she
is Helen of Troy who appears to Faust first as a spirit then
in bodily form and is sent by Satan to tempt him. She almost succeeds in seducing him, but like Gretchen, she fails.

HELEN--(Alex I, 1; Collect Ta-Point; PP-Ph)--Helen of
Troy. In Greek legend, daughter of Zeus and Leda and wife
of Menelaos, king of Sparta. She eloped with Paris and
thus brought about the Trojan War.

HELICON--(Aspects I)--A mountain which, in Greek myth,
was sacred to the Muses (q.v.).

HELIOPOLIS--(Alex I, 2)--An ancient city in Egypt some 6
miles NE of Cairo. It was dedicated to the worship of the
god of the sun, Ra.

HELLESPONT--(AH-Troop)--See: Dardanelles. It was
named after Helle, the daughter of the king of Thebes who

drowned there while fleeing the anger of her step-mother.

HELMERS, THE--(AH-Ibsen)--Nora and Towald Helmer.
Characters in the play, The Doll House by Henrik Ibsen (q. v.).
Towald treats Nora as a doll not conceiving that she has any
sense at all.

HÉLOÏSE--(GLD X)--Late 11th and early 12th century.   She
was the beloved of Pierre Abélard and niece of the Canon
Fulbert of Notre Dame, Paris.   They were secretly married.
In anger, Fulbert emasculated Abélard.   Abélard entered a
monastery and Héloïse died a nun.

HELVELLYN--(AH-Ibsen)--A mountain 3118 feet high in NW
England, in the Lake District.

HEMINGWAY, ERNEST--(Two Cheers-English)--1889-1961.
An American novelist, writer of short stories, and journalist.   He was born in Oak Park, Illinois and served in an
American ambulance unit during World War I and later with
an Italian Arditi in the same war.   He was later to use his
experiences as the basis for some of his writings.   After
the war, he became one of the "Lost Generation" and lived
in Paris where he came under the influence of Gertrude
Stein.   He produced a number of novels, some more successful than others, including: The Sun Also Rises (1926), A
Farewell to Arms (1929), and For Whom the Bell Tolls
(1940).   His latest work, Islands in the Sun, was published
posthumously in 1970.

HENRY, PRINCE--(AH-Ron)--A character in the plays
Henry IV, Parts I and II, by William Shakespeare (q. v.).
He appears also as Henry V (q. v.), by Shakespeare. Henry,
Prince of Wales, Prince Hal, Harry Monmouth is a boister-
ous young man who is led by bad companions into mischief.
He matures rapidly, however, when responsibility comes
his way.   He saves his father in battle and kills the rebel,
Hotspur.   In Henry V he repudiates his wild friends, notably
Falstaff (q. v.).

HENRY V--(GLD XII)--A play by William Shakespeare (q. v.).
Its action covers the opening of Parliament (1414), Henry's
battles in France for his French possessions, and his marriage to Katherine, daughter of the French king, in 1420.

HENRY V--(AH-Emp)--See: Prince Henry.

HENRY VI--(GLD IX)--Son of Henry V (q.v.) and Catherine
of Valois, whose marriage Shakespeare (q.v.) makes the subject of his play, Henry V (q.v.). When he was an infant,
his father died. He succeeded to the throne under the pro-
tectorship of his uncles and was crowned King of France
(Dec. 16, 1431). However, the success of Joan of Arc and
Charles VII expelled the English from France. The struggle
between the two houses of York and Lancaster for power began in his reign and resulted in the War of the Roses. He
was deposed in favor of the Duke of York (Edward IV) and
was killed in the Tower of London. The events of his life
are depicted in Shakespeare plays, Henry VI, Parts I, II,
and III.

HENRY VII--(Two Cheers-John)--Henry Tudor (1457-1509),
King of England, 1485-1509. He was the first king of the
house of Tudor. The unrest caused by the excesses of
Richard III called him back to England from exile in Brit-
tany. He defeated and killed Richard III at Bosworth Field,
and married Elizabeth, eldest daughter of Edward IV thus
uniting the houses of York and Lancaster and ending the devastating War of the Roses.

HENRY VIII--(Two Cheers-John)--1491-1547. King of England, 1509-1547. The son of Henry VII (q.v.), he married
Catherine of Aragon, the widow of his brother, Arthur, later divorcing her for Anne Boleyn. She, in turn, was deposed and beheaded for another wife, etc. His reign was
marked by the growing power of his country and the difficulties which resulted from the divorce. These led to a
break with Rome and suppression of the monasteries which
added considerably to the wealth of the nation.

HENSHAW, ROBERT--(AH-HOS)--A character in All That
Was Possible by H. O. Sturgis (q.v.). Sibyl Crofts falls in
love with him.

HEPHAESTION--(Alex I, 1; PP-Ph)--The temple of Hephaes-
tus, the Greek god of fire and those arts which employ fire.
He was the son of Zeus and Hera and is represented by
Homer as being lame. Hera is said to have thrown him
out of heaven in shame at his deformity. In revenge, he
sent her a golden chair in which she was trapped. Only he
could release her, but he refused until he was returned to
heaven. According to another story, his lameness stemed
from a quarrel between his mother and father. Zeus, in
anger, seized him by the foot and hurled him down to earth.

HEPPLEWHITE--(GLD II)--George Hepplewhite, d. 1786. He
was an English maker of furniture which is noted for its
lightness of design and delicate beauty. His work is marked
by slight tapering legs, and chair backs of shields, ovals,
hoops, and hearts.

HERACLES--(AH-Mac)--See: Hercules.

HERACLIUS--(Alex I, 2)--A. D. 575?-641. Emperor of the
Eastern Roman Empire, 610-641. He was the son of a general and was born in Cappodocia. Emperor Mauricias appointed him exarch of Africa. With his father's help, he
dethroned Phocas (610) and was proclaimed emperor. He
defeated the Persians (622) but was unsuccessful in a second
campaign against them. Later, he routed them completely
recovering the Holy Cross of Christ in the process and restoring it to Jerusalem (629). Under his reign, the Saracens took much of the empire.

HERAT--(PI XIV)--A city and province in NW Afghanistan
noted for its defensive walls and its ruins of palaces and
mosques. At the height of its prosperity, it was an important way station on the trade route to India. It was twice
destroyed by the Mongols.

HERCULES--(Alex I, 1; RWV V)--In Greek legend, a hero
possessed of great strength and represented as a brawny,
muscular, shortnecked individual of huge proportions. The
Pythian oracle told him that if he would serve Eurystheus for
12 years he would become immortal. He bound himself to
that king who commanded that he do 12 tasks of great difficulty and danger. He did so successfully. When he died he
was made into a constellation.

HEREDIA--(Two Cheers-In)--A province and town in central
Costa Rica NW of San Jose. It is the center of the country's coffee industry.

HERMES--(AH-For the Muse; Aspects VI; Collected Tales-
Intro; LJ III)--The Greek name for the Roman god Mercury.
He was the son of Maia and Zeus for whom he served as
messenger. He was also the god of science and commerce,
patron of travelers, vagabonds, thieves.

HERMES OF PRAXITILES--(AH-For the Muse; LJ III)--The
statue is in the museum at Olympia. It is assigned to
Praxitiles (q. v.) because it reflects characteristics of his

work: softness of modeling and effeminate features.   See
also: Hermes.

HERMES PSYCHOPOMPUS--(Collect Ta-Intro)--The Greek
god Hermes (q. v.) in his manifestation as conductor of the
souls of the dead to Hades (q. v.).   As such, Lucian includes
him in his "Dialogues of the Dead."

HERODOTUS--(AH-Marco; PP-Tim; Two Cheers-Clouds)--A
Greek historian of the 5th century B. C., his masterpiece is
a history of the Greek-Persian wars from 500-479 B. C.   He
is also credited with the invention of a systematic treatment
of historical facts and events which has caused him to be
titled the "father of history."

HERTFORDSHIRE--(HE X; Two Cheers-Lon)--A county in the
SE region of England, the chief town of which is St. Albans.
It consists of some 632 square miles.

HETTY--(Aspects VII)--A character in the 1859 novel Adam
Bede (q. v.) by George Eliot (q. v.).   Although Hetty (Hester
Sorrel) is the niece of a dairy farmer, she is fond of the
finer things in life.   She is, consequently, an easy conquest
for Donnithorne, who, of course, seduces her.   When she
realizes that he will not marry her, she becomes engaged to
Bede.   She is convicted of killing her infant when she aban-
dons it while searching for her lover whose regiment has
gone to Ireland.

"HIC VER ASSIDUUM ATQUE ALIENIS MENSIBUS AESTAS"--
(MT)--Latin: The memory of spring and summer will be
present all the months of the year.

HIGHGATE--(AH-Early)--The name of a district, of a cemetery, and of a hill in the environs of London.   The cemetery was laid out in 1838 and contains, among other tourist
attractions, a circular, sunken catacomb vaguely Egyptian in
style with the chancel of the church above it.   The cemetery
contains the grave of Karl Marx (q. v.).

"HINC ILLAE LACRIMAE"--(GLD VII)--Latin: Hence those
tears.   From Terrence's Andria, Book I, ℓ. 126 (166 B. C.).
It was quoted by Horace, Cicero, and others.

HINDEMITH--(Nordic)--Paul Hindemith, 1895-1963.   A German composer of music and a concert violinist.   He came
to the U. S. as a result of the Nazi persecutions of the Jews.

He was one of the principal exponents of ultra-modern music.

HINDENBURG--(AH-Our Div)--Paul Ludwig Hans Anton von
Beneckendorff und von Hindenberg, 1847-1934. A general
and president of Germany. He fought in the Franco-Prussian
War and commanded an army on the East Prussian front during World War I. In 1916, he was made chief of the general
staff. He was elected president of Germany (1925-32) and
re-elected (1932-34), but was forced to yield to Hitler.

HINDU HOLIDAY--(GLD XI)--See: J. R. Ackerley.

HINDUISM--(Alex I, 3)--A complicated polytheistic faith and
social system of India. It is based squarely upon the concept of function (dharma) and observance of rather rigidly
conceived castes into which are placed its believers. It is
not a unified faith; there exist many sects and variations,
almost as many as its gods.

HIPPODROME--(HE XVII)--The Hippodrome Theatre (1900)
at Charing Cross Road and Cranbourn St., London.

HISTORY OF THE STANDARD OIL COMPANY--(GLD XI)--
See: I. M. Tarbell.

HITCHIN--(LJ VI)--An urban district in Hertfordshire, SE
England, some 32 miles N of London.

HITLER--(AH-Roger; GLD XIII; MT; Nordic; Reading; Two
Cheers-Bk; Two Cheers-Camb; Two Cheers-Cul; Two Cheers-
G&G; Two Cheers-Post; Two Cheers-Romain; Two Cheers-
Volt)--1889-1945. A German dictator whose family name is
said to have been Schiklgruber. He wanted desperately to
become a painter, but authorities discovered a notable lack
of talent in his work. He served in World War I and, after
its end, took advantage of Germany's economic and moral
depression to rise to power. As his position became more
secure, his megalomania grew. His strange ideas on racial
purity resulted in the death of millions of Jews, and his
dreams of empire resulted in World War II. When it was
clear that Germany would be defeated, he took his own life.

HOBBES--(AH-Capt; AH-TS)--Thomas Hobbes, 1588-1679.
An English philosopher who originated the theory of the social contract which undertook to examine the source of the
power of governments. His most famous work is Leviathan;

or, The Matter, Form, and Power of a Commonwealth, Ecclesiastical and Civil (1651), in which he explains his theory.

HOGG--(GLD VII)--Thomas Jefferson Hogg, 1792-1862.   An
English lawyer and friend of the poet Shelley (q. v.).   He
wrote a two-volume biography of his friend (1858).

HOLKAR--(AH-Mind)--The name of the Maratha dynasty of
the native Indian State of Indore which ruled until the state
was merged with the Republic of India in 1948.   The family
was founded by Malhar Rao Holkar (1693-1766).

HOLY GRAIL, THE--(LJ XVI)--The cup traditionally considered to have been used by Christ at the Last Supper and
which has become the center of a vast body of legend.   One
legend has it that Joseph of Arimathea took it to England
and it can be seen only by the purest of knights.

HOLY ROMAN EMPIRE--(Two Cheers-Challenge)--The name
given to a confederation of the states of Central Europe from
A. D. 800 until 1806.   It suggested the interdependence of
Church and State.   As a result, the emperors, beginning
with Charlemagne, received the title and their crown from
the popes.

HOME AND THE WORLD, THE--(AH-Two)--A novel (1919)
by Rabindranath Tagore (q. v.).   There is an edition (1919)
in English translated by Surendranath Tagore with a revision,
in English, by the author.

HOMER--(AH-Note; Alex I, 1; Aspects VI; Collect Ta-Celest;
Two Cheers-Anon; Two Cheers-In)--The name given to the
unknown poet or group of poets responsible for the Illiad (q.
v.) and The Odyssey (q. v.).   Some critics consider Homer
to be a mythical figure, but modern scholarship tends to
attribute the works to a blind man, Homer, who lived sometime between 1200 and 850 B. C.

HONEYCHURCH, MRS. --(RWV I)--A character in Room with
a View.   Wilfred Stone in his study of E. M. Forster, The
Cave and the Mountain, claims Forster's maternal grandmother, Louisa Graham Wichelo, as the original of the
character.

HOOGLI--(Two Cheers-India)--The most important and most
westerly channel of the Ganges River delta in India.

HOPKINS, GERARD--(AH-HOS; AH-TS)--1892-   . An English novelist (e. g. , A City in the Foreground, 1921), translator (Balzac, Mauriac, Proust (q. v.), Sartre, et al.) and editor.

HOPPNER--(AH-Ba; MT; Two Cheers-Henry)--John Hoppner, 1758-1810. A popular painter of portraits of English-German parentage.

HORACE--(GLD IV; Two Cheers-What)--Quintus Horatius Flaccus, 65-8 B. C. A Roman satirist who was educated in Rome and Athens and who commanded a legion in the battle of Philippi. Maecenas was his patron and he was favored by Augustus (q. v.). He produced odes, satires, epodes, letters, and a study of the art of poetry.

HORUS--(Alex I, 3)--One of the major gods of Egyptian myth. He is a blending of Horus the Elder, the sun god (corresponding to the Greek Apollo) and Horus, the child, the son of Osiris (q. v.) and Isis (q. v.). He was represented hieroglyphically by a hawk which was sacred to him or as a hawk-headed man. His emblem was the winged sun-disk. In many myths he is indistinguishable from Ra (q. v.).

HOUSE OF GUERMANTES--(AH-Proust)--Forster refers to a family in the novel, Remembrance of Things Past (q. v.), by Proust (q. v.). They are French noblemen and inheritors of a distinguished past but have little culture and less intelligence. They are interested only in maintaining their social superiority. The leading members are the Duc de Guermantes, the Duchess (q. v.), The Prince and Princess, Baron de Charlus (q. v.), and Robert de Saint-Loup.

HOUSMAN, A. E. --(AH-Note; RWV XII; Two Cheers-William) --Alfred Edward Housman, 1859-1936. An English scholar and poet known for a small quantity of rather depressing lyrics clearly showing the influence of the traditional English ballads and classical verse set against a background of the countryside. They are notable for their economy of language, directness and dramatic simplicity, and are ironic and fatalistic. His volumes include A Shropshire Lad (1896), Last Poems (1922), and the posthumous More Poems (1936).

HOUYHNHNMS--(GLD XI)--Characters in Gulliver's Travels (q. v.) by Swift (q. v.). They are a race of horses who have superintellects and the ability to control their passions by reason.

"HOW MANY AGES HENCE SHALL THIS OUR LOFTY SCENE
BE ACTED O'ER/ etc. --(Two Cheers-Jul)--From the play
Julius Caesar, by William Shakespeare. Act III, Sc. 1, 11.
111-112.

HOWARDS END--(HE I, MT)--A small house which figures
prominently in Forster's novel, Howards End (q.v.). It is
described in detail in the first chapter of that novel. The
house is based on Rooksrest, Stevenge, Hertfordshire, Forster's childhood home.

HOWARDS END--(Two Cheers-Gide)--A novel by E. M. Forster first published in London, 1910. For Summary see:
An E. M. Forster Dictionary.

HUMAYUN, EMPEROR--(Two Cheers-India)--1508-1556. The
second Mogul emperor of Hindustan, and son of Babur (q.v.).
He was driven from India by his enemies, but returned in
1555, re-conquered Delhi and died shortly thereafter.

HUNDING--(Nordic)--The husband of Sieglunde in the opera,
Die Walkure, by Wagner (q.v.).

HUTTON--(MT)--Richard Holt Hutton, 1826-1899. Principal
of University Hall, London and editor of The Enquirer, a
Unitarian magazine. He was also joint editor of The National Review, assistant editor of The Economist, and joint
editor of The Spectator.

HUXLEY, ALDOUS--(AH-Liberty; AH-Vo; Aspects I; Two
Cheers-English)--Aldous Leonard Huxley, 1894-1963. An
English critic and novelist. He experimented with several
forms of mysticism, notably Indian, and that so-called form
induced by certain fungi. He was also interested in the
supernatural. He is perhaps best known for his bitingly satiric novels: Chrome Yellow (1921), Antic Hay (1923), Point
Counter Point (1928), and his most popular, Brave New
World (1932).

HUXLEY, PROFESSOR--(Two Cheers-Webb)--Forster alludes
to Thomas Henry Huxley, 1825-1895. A biologist, professor, and staunchest defender and advocate of Darwin's theory
of evolution. He is the grandfather of Aldous Huxley (q.v.).

HUYSMAN, J. K.--(AH-Note)--1848-1907. A French novelist
of Dutch ancestry and a Décadent who finally became a convert to Catholicism. His style is highly vivid and marked by

concrete figures, fantastic descriptions, and grotesqueries.
His books include Marthe (1876); A Rébours [Against the
Grain], (1884); and La-Bas (1891).

HYDE PARK--(GLD III)--The largest of London's Royal Parks
first acquired by Henry VII as his private hunting preserve.
It is located in W central London.   One part (Speakers' Corner) is a long-time favorite location for open-air meetings
and speeches on any conceivable subject.

HYDERABAD--(PI XXVII)--A former Indian State which,
since 1956, is a part of Andhra Pradesh in S central India.

                                    I

"I BELIEVE A LEAF OF GRASS IS NO LESS THAN THE
JOURNEY WORK [sic] OF THE STARS, " etc. --(LJ XXIX)--
ℓℓ. 1-4, Stanza 31 of "Song of Myself" by Walt Whitman
from Vol. I of his Complete Works, New York: Putnam,
1902.

"I SHOULD HAVE BEEN A PAIR OF RAGGED CLAWS/
SCUTTLING ACROSS THE FLOORS OF SILENT SEAS. "--
(AH-TS)--ℓℓ. 74-75, "The Love Song of J. Alfred Pru-
frock, " by T. S. Eliot (q.v.) in The Complete Poems and
Plays 1904-1950, New York: Harcourt Brace, 1950.

"I WANDER THRO' EACH CHARTER'D STREET/etc. "--(Two
Cheers-Lon)--First stanza of "London" by William Blake
(q. v.).

IAGO--(Two Cheers-George)--The ancient [ensign] of Othello
(q.v.) in the play, Othello, by William Shakespeare (q. v.).
Envious of his commander, he plans to destroy Othello
through the Moor's wife, Desdemona.   He has Othello believe that Desdemona has been unfaithful to him with Cassio.
As a result, in a fit of rage, Othello kills his wife.

IBSEN, HENRIK--(AH-Ibsen; HE XVI; LJ XIII; Two Cheers-
Bishop; Two Cheers-En; Two Cheers-Mohammed)--1826-1906.
A Norwegian dramatist and poet, often called the "father" of
modern drama.   He began life as a chemist's assistant.   He
eventually became the director of the Norwegian Theater in
Oslo (1857-67).   By 1866, he was given a government pension.   He spent much of his life in Italy and Germany because of dissatisfaction with the political complexion of his

country. As a playwright, he is especially effective in his
socio-psychological plays which influenced so many dramatists including George Bernard Shaw (q. v.). Some of his
plays are A Doll's House (1879), Hedda Gabler (1894), and
Ghosts (q. v.), 1881.

IDA--(Two Cheers-Anon)--A mountain in the NW region of
Asia Minor which, in Homeric legend, is the home of the
gods. It is also the name of a mountain in Crete connected
in ancient times with the worship of Zeus (q. v.).

IDALIUM--(Alex I, 1)--Now called Dali, a village in E central Cyprus on the Yalias River. It is the site of an ancient temple of Aphrodite (q. v.).

IDES OF MARCH--(MT)--In the Roman calendar, the 15th
of March. The date is important in that it is connected with
the death of Julius Caesar. It is reported that a soothsayer
warned him that he would be in danger on that day. He,
nevertheless, went to the Senate and was murdered. The
scene is reported in the play, Julius Caesar, by Shakespeare
(q. v.).

IDOLINO--(RWV IV)--[Ital., diminutive for "idol."] It is
the name given to a bronze statue of a standing boy which
is a Romanesque copy of a Greek work. The statue is in
Florence.

IKHNATON--(Aspects VIII)--died c. 1454 B. C. King of
Egypt of the XVIII dynasty. He changed his name to Ikhnaton when he changed the polytheistic faith of Egypt to monotheism. He built a new capital in which Aton, the one god
he believed in, was to be worshipped. When he died, poly-
theism was restored. His reign is also marked by a break
with the traditional canons of Egyptian art.

ILFRACOMBE--(HE XLII; LJ XIX)--A seaside resort in SW
England on the Bristol Channel some 57 miles N of Plymouth.

ILISSUS--(LJ XX)--A stream flowing SE of Athens. The
river bed, as it nears the city, is generally dry. The
name is obviously used symbolically by Forster to under-
score his point.

IL PENSEROSO--(GLD IX)--A long poem (1632) by John
Milton (q. v.) in celebration of melancholy, solitude, contemplation, study. It has a companion piece, L'Allegro, de-

lineating the pleasures of joy and happiness.

IMAGINARY CONVERSATIONS--(HE II)--See: Walter Savage
Landor.

IMOGEN--(WAFT IV)--The daughter of Cymbeline in the play,
Cymbeline (1609) by William Shakespeare (q. v.). She is the
daughter of his former queen and, for part of the play, is
disguised as Fidele, a boy. She is faithful, courageous and
forgiving. Nevertheless, she is the object of a plot by her
husband to kill her.

INCHBALD, MRS. --(AH-JA)--Elizabeth Inchbald, née Simpson, 1753-1823. English author and actress. She wrote
comedies and farces which were generally adapted from
French originals. She is, perhaps, best known for two
tales: A Simple Story (1791), and Nature and Art (1796).

INDEX--(AH-Car)--Forster is referring to the list--actually
two lists--now abolished, of books which the Roman Catholic Church forbade its members to read. The first of these,
the Index Librorum Prohibitorum, consisted of the names of
works unconditionally forbidden, and the Index Expurgatorius,
which listed titles forbidden until changes were made or
parts excised. The first index was promulgated in 1564 as
a reaction to the Protestant revolt.

INDRA--(PI XXXVI)--In Indian [Hindu] myth, the god of warriors and of nature. He is a mixture of Hercules (q. v.)
and Zeus (q. v.). Sometimes, he is depicted with two arms,
one holding the thunderbolt and the other, the spear. He is
also depicted with four arms, the two additional are usually
holding lances.

INDUSTRIAL REVOLUTION--(AH-Notes)--The name applied
to the economic and social changes wrought in Britain from
the late 18th to the mid-19th centuries when machinery and
railways literally revolutionized the agrarian way of life essentially unchanged for over a 1000 years.

INFERNO, DANTE'S--(PP-Cotton; Two Cheers-Our)--See:
Dante.

INGLESE ITALIANATO E UN DIAVOLO INCARNATO--(RWV
IX)--Italian: An Italianate Englishman is the devil incarnate.

INQUISITION--(AH-Car)--An arm of the Church established by Gregory IX in 1229. It was a court instituted to inquire into offenses against the Church. Those found guilty were handed over to secular authorities for punishment.

INTERMEDIATE SEX, THE--(Two Cheers-Edward)--A study of sexual inversion by Edward Carpenter (q. v., London: S. Sonnenschein, 1909). Forster praises it in his essay on Carpenter.

IQBAL, SIR MUHAMMED--(Hill; PI I; Two Cheers-India; Two Cheers-Muhammed)--1873-1938. A Muslim Indian poet who wrote largely in Persian. He was also a philosopher speculating on the dynamic spirit of Islam which he held was a struggle for spiritual freedom. He was educated in Europe and the East.

IRVING, EDWARD--(MT)--1792-1834. Scottish clergyman who emigrated to London and was noted as a preacher but was forced to resign his livelihood because of his enthusiastic acceptance of the phenomena of the Pentecost (i. e., prophesying and "speaking in tongues.") His followers were known as Irvingites. They later took the name of The Holy Catholic Apostolic Church.

ISABELLA--(AH-JA)--A character in the novel, The Castle of Otranto (1764), by Horace Walpole. She is the daughter of the Marquis of Vicenza and Conrad's fiancée. Manfred, Prince of Otranto, and the villain, plans to marry her after Conrad's death. She manages, however, to elude him, and marries her love and true heir to Otranto.

ISABELLA II--(AH-Wil)--Maria Isabella Louisa. 1830-1904. She became Queen of Spain on the death of her father, Ferdinand VII. Her reign was marked by political unrest and wars. In 1868, her reign was overthrown by a revolution and she abdicated in favor of her son, Alfonso XII.

ISABELLA--(Aspects II)--Isabel Wardour. A character in the novel, The Antiquary, by Sir Walter Scott (q. v.). She is the beautiful and devoted daughter of Sir Arthur Wardour. When she learns that her lover, Lovel, was supposed to be illegitimate and that her father disapproved of him, she discouraged his advances, as she always obeyed her father.

ISCHYRION, ST. --(Alex II, 7)--He was a Roman martyr who died by impalement (A. D. 250). He was an Egyptian official and his feast day is Dec. 22.

ISEULT--(Alex I, 1)--[Also: Isolt, Yseult, or Isolde.] The
name of two characters in the Arthurian legend: Isolt the
fair, wife of King Mark and the lover of Tristan; and Isolt
of the White Hands, wife of Tristan. Wagner based his
opera, Tristan und Isolde on the former.

ISHERWOOD--(Two Cheers-Ascent; Two Cheers-English; Two
Cheers-Virginia)--1904- . An English novelist, writer of
short stories, etc. One of a group of Marxist-oriented
writers of the 1930's (others: Auden, C. Day Lewis, Stephen Spender). For a time, he collaborated with Auden
(q.v.) on several works including the verse play (1936) The
Ascent of F 6. (q.v.). He also has done some translating.

ISHMAEL--(AH-TE; Aspects VIII; Two Cheers-En)--A principal character and narrator of the novel, Moby Dick (q.v.)
by Herman Melville (q.v.). He is a young teacher who, becoming restless and dissatisfied with the world, ships aboard
the Pequod, a whaler. There he meets Ahab (q.v.) who has
pledged to revenge himself on the white whale which took
his leg. His quest results in the destruction of himself, his
ship, and all aboard except Ishmael.

ISIS--(AH-Salute; Alex II, 1; HE XXXIII)--The principal goddess of Egypt, wife and sister of Osiris (q.v.) and the mother of Horus. She is identified with the moon and the cow
was sacred to her. Its horns represented the crescent
moon. Her chief temples were at Abydos, Busiris, Philae.
She is represented as a queen, her head surmounted with
horns and the solar disc, or by a double crown.

ISKENDER--(AH-Salute)--A character in the novel, The Valley of the Kings, by Pickthall (q.v.).

ISMAIL, KHEDIVE--(Alex II, 3)--Ishmail Pasha [Ismail I]
(1830-1895), Khedive of Egypt, 1863-1879. He was proclaimed Viceroy of Egypt on the death of his uncle and received the title, Khedive, from the Sultan of Turkey (1867).
He rebuilt Cairo, improved Alexandria, and strongly encouraged the building of the Suez Canal. He was forced to
abdicate by his European creditors in favor of his son Tewik
Pasha (q.v.).

"IT SEEMS TO ME MOST STRANGE THAT MEN SHOULD
FEAR/etc."--(Two Cheers-Jul)--Act II, Sc. ii, ℓℓ. 43 ff.,

<u>Julius Caesar</u>, by William Shakespeare (q. v.).

<u>J</u>

JACK--(Aspects II)--Jack Robinson, the third of the Robinson boys in <u>Swiss Family Robinson</u> (q. v.). He helps his mother tend the animals.

JACOB--(AH-Early)--The principal character in <u>Jacob's Room</u> (1922) by Virginia Woolf (q. v.). Jacob <u>Flanders</u> is a young Englishman of the middle class. The volume tells of his boyhood at Cornwall, his days in Cambridge, his love affairs, his travels on the continent, and his death in World War I.

JACOB--(PP-Eliza)--A patriarch in the Old Testament ("Genesis") who had 12 sons, each the founder of one of the 12 tribes of Israel. He bought his birthright from his brother, Essau, for a mess of pottage and received from his blind father, Isaac, the blessing intended for Essau.

<u>JACOB'S ROOM</u>--(AH-Early; GLD XII; Two Cheers-Camb)--See: Jacob--(AH-Early).

JACQUEMANT, HENRI ALFRED--(Alex II, 1)--1824-1895. A French sculptor.

JAEL--(AH-Consol; WAFT VIII)--In the Old Testament, a woman who offered Sisera refuge from the pursuing Deborah and Barak, and then killed him with a tent-pin.

JAIN--(PI XXIV)--A member of a heretic sect of the Hindu (q. v.) faith. The origin of the group dates from at least the 5th century B. C. Jains are largely traders and the sect is relatively wealthy.

JAMES I--(Two Cheers-Anon; Two Cheers-Art)--1566-1625. He was the King of Scotland as James IV (1567-1625) and of Great Britain as James I (1603-1625). He was the son of Mary, Queen of Scots, who was executed by Elizabeth I (q. v.) and great-grandson of Henry VII. He sought to assert the divine right of kings.

JAMES IV OF SCOTLAND--(Two Cheers)--See: James I.

JAMES, HENRY--(AH-HOS; AH-Jo; AH-Reid; AH-Sin; Aspects I; LJ-II; Two Cheers-Anon; Two Cheers-Does; Two
Cheers-Fo; Two Cheers-Virginia)--1843-1916.   An American
novelist, writer of short stories, and unsuccessful dramatist.
He was born in New York and attended law school, but from
1865 he devoted his life to literature.   From 1876, he was
an expatriate and lived in Paris, London, and Rye.   In 1915,
he became a naturalized citizen of Great Britain.   Never
truly a popular author, he is, nevertheless recognized by
professors of literature and others as a master novelist for
such works as The American (1877), The Wings of the Dove
(1902), The Golden Bowl (1902) and The Ambassadors (q.v.,
1903), all of which never gained the wide, public approval of
the novellas Daisy Miller (1878), and The Turn of the Screw
(1898).

JAMES, SAINT--(AH-Ab)--There are two major saints of
that name: 1) "The Greater," one of the apostles, brother
of John and son of Zebedee (New Testament).   He and John
were the only two disciples with Jesus as He prayed on the
eve of His death.   Tradition has it that he preached the gospel in Spain then returned to Judea where he was put to
death by order of Herod.   According to one legend his body,
set adrift on a raft, washed up on the Spanish coast and interred at Compostella.   2) St. James the Less another
apostle, the son of Alphaeus (New Testament), and Jesus'
cousin (through the relation of their mothers).   In A.D. 62
he was stoned to death for violating Jewish law.

JAMES AT COMPOSTELLA, SAINT--Spanish shrine built at
Santiago de Compostella in honor of Saint James the Greater
(q.v.).

JANE--(Two Cheers-John)--The young owner of the sparrow
eaten by Gib (q.v.), the cat, in the poem "Philip Sparrow"
by John Skelton (q.v.).

JANE EYRE--(Aspects I)--A novel (1847) by Charlotte Brontë
(q.v.).   The story is narrated by Jane who tells of her unhappy childhood and generally unhappy life which after she
meets Rochester who engages her as a governess for his
daughter, ends in happiness and their marriage.

JANUS--(LJ XXIX)--The ancient Roman god who was the
gatekeeper of heaven, hence: the guardian of gates and
doors.   He was represented with two faces: one in front,
the other behind.   The doors of his temple were open in

times of war and closed in times of peace.

JASON--(AH-Mac; Alex I, 1)--In Greek legend the hero who led the Argonauts in quest of the golden fleece. He was the son of Archon, king of Ioclus, and raised by the centaur, Chiron. When he demanded his kingdom from his half-brother, he was told he could have it in return for the golden fleece, hence the quest. To obtain it, he married Medea, a sorceress, but only to desert her whereupon she killed their two sons. In some versions of the legend, he killed himself from grief; in others, he was crushed by the keel of his ship.

JATS--(PI XX)--A people who inhabit the region about Agra and Mathura in India. They are probably of foreign origin and had no state prior to the 18th century when they revolted against Aurangzebe (q. v.). Eventually, they were given a state called Bharatper. In 1826, the state was conquered by the British.

JAURÈS, JEAN LÉON--(AS)--1859-1914. A French socialist and politician. He was a deputy from Tarn, but retired to teach and write essays on philosophy. He became interested in socialism and was returned as a deputy. He fought militaristic legislation and, on the eve of World War I was assassinated.

JAXARTES--(AH-Emp)--A river in Russia (central Asia).

JEANS--(AH-Vo)--Forster is alluding to Sir James Hopwood Jeans, 1877-1946. An English astronomer, physicist, and writer, his major work was devoted to the kinetic theory of gasses and radiation. He was the author of Through Space and Time (1934) and other popular as well as scholarly volumes.

JEHOVAH--(Collect Ta-Mr; PI XXIV; PP-Ph)--In the Old Testament, the sacred name of God.

JENKS, EDWARD--(GLD X)--1861-1939. An English educator, lawyer, and writer. He was a professor of law, London University, and the director and principal of legal studies for the Law Society.

JENNINGS, MRS. --(AH-JA)--A character in the novel Sense and Sensibility (1811) by Jane Austen (q.v.). She is the mother of Lady Middleton, and is a silly, but kindly old lady.

JERUSALEM DELIVERED--See: Gerusalemme Liberata.

JESUITS--(AH-Car)--The popular name given to members of
the Roman Catholic order of priests founded by St. Ignatius
Loyola in 1533, the Society of Jesus. It was founded to re-
verse the effects of the Protestant revolt and to propagate
the Faith. The order was organized along military lines.
Because of its discipline, the secrecy of its methods, and
its efficacy, it was for a time suppressed.

JESUS COLLEGE--(AH-Troop; GLD X)--A residential college,
founded 1496, of Cambridge University (q. v.).

JEZABEL--(HE XVI)--In the Old Testament, the wife of Ahab
(q. v.). She was known for her wanton ways.

JINN--(Alex II, 1)--In Arabian myth, demons who were
created from fire some 2000 years before Adam and governed
by a race of kings named Suleyman one of whom was credited with building the pyramids. Their chief home was the
mountain Kâf and they were said to assume the forms of
snakes, dogs, cats, monsters, or humans. They could also
become invisible at pleasure. The evil jinn are ugly, but
the good are beautiful. The word is plural; the singular is
"jinnee."

JOACHIM--(Nordic)--Joseph Joachim, 1831-1907. A Hungar-
ian composer and violinist of Jewish parents. He was director of the Musical Hochschule at Berlin where he formed the
Joachim quartet in 1869.

JOAN OF ARC--(AH-Notes; AH-Proust; AH-Vo)--1412-1431.
The national heroine and patroness of France who, at the
age of 13 heard heavenly voices which directed her to save
France. She led the French armies to victory and saw
Charles VII crowned King of France. She was burned at the
stake as a witch, May 30, 1431 and was proclaimed a saint
on April 11, 1909.

JOB--(Collect Ta-Word; GLD XIV)--A patriarch of the Old
Testament ("Book of Job") who bore up under afflictions with
fortitude and faith in God.

JOCASTA--(Two Cheers-Ascent)--In Greek legend, the mother of Oedipus whom she marries after he kills his father,
her husband. The story is told in the play, Oedipus Rex,
by Sophocles (q. v.).

JOHN, DR. --(Aspects V)--A character in the novel, Villette (1853), by Charlotte Brontë (q.v.). He is the son of Lucy Snowe's godmother. Now living in Villette, he is the kind-hearted, handsome young doctor who attends Mme. Beck's children. Lucy had known him in early life as a mischievous boy who had little time for girls. His recognition of Lucy comes when he is called to serve her after she has fainted while leaving a church. For a time, romance seems to flower between them, but Dr. John falls in love with Pauline and eventually marries her.

JOHN--(AH-Mr.)--See: John Keats.

JOHN THE BAPTIST--(MT; Two Cheers-Lon)--In the New Testament, the son of Elizabeth, the cousin of the Virgin Mary, and Zacharius. He baptized Jesus and is known as His precursor. He was executed by Herod.

JOHN BULL--(AH-Notes; MT)--The national symbol of England. He is a rather kind-hearted, bull-headed, no-nonsense, well-fed character.

JOHN CHRISTOPHER--(Two Cheers-Romain)--JEAN CHRISTOPHE, 1904-1912. A novel in three volumes by Romain Rolland. It is the spiritual biography of a German musician who escapes from Germany and lives in Paris. He has a miserable childhood and struggles through a long life finally achieving success.

JOHN GABRIEL BORKMAN--(AH-Ibsen)--A play (1890) by Ibsen (q.v.) which treats of a man of the "most energetic imagination whose illusions feed on his misfortunes."

JOHN, KING--(AH-Ab; Two Cheers-Last)--1167?-1216. Called John Lackland of the house of Plantagenet. King of England, 1199-1216. He was the son of Henry II and brother of Richard the Lionhearted (Richard I). He is, perhaps, most famous as the signer of the Magna Carta (June 15, 1215) which laid the foundation of English freedom.

JOHN, SAINT--(Alex II, 7; PP-Clement)--The Evangelist, one of the 12 apostles and brother of James the Greater (q.v.) and son of Zebedee. He is the author of the fourth gospel and the Epistles of John, as well as the "Revelation of John," all part of the New Testament.

JOHNSON, MRS. --(Aspects I)--A character in the novel, The History of Mr. Polly (1909), by H. G. Wells (q. v.). She is the rather vulgar wife of Howard Johnson, Mr. Polly's cousin who urges him to buy a shop.

JOHNSON, DR. SAMUEL--(Aspects VI; GLD IX; MT; Two Cheers-Bishop; Two Cheers-English; Two Cheers-Stratford)-- 1709-1784. One of the most important literary figures and arbiters of literary taste in the 18th century. A master conversationalist, it is said that, had he spoken less and written more, his reputation would have been far greater. Educated at Oxford, he never took a degree there but, after he had secured a reputation, was granted an honorary doctorate. His most important work, by far, is his Dictonary, the project of years of single-handed work--an enormous accomplishment--published in 1755 after many delays.

JONAH--(Aspects VII)--In the Old Testament, a prophet of God, who, disobeying God's command to preach in Ninevah, was swallowed by a huge fish and remained inside it for three days.

JONATHAN--(LJ VII)--In the Old Testament (Samuel), the eldest son of King Saul, friend of David, and killed at the battle of Mt. Gilboa.

JONDET--(Alex II, 1)--Gaston Jondet. In addition to Les Ports Submergés de l'Ancienne Isle de Pharos (1916), he is also the author of Atlas Historique de la Ville et des Ports d'Alexandrie (1921), among other works.

JONES, DR. M. G. --See under DR. M. G. JONES.

JONES, TOM--(Aspects IV; Collect Ta-Celest; HE XVII)-- The principal character in The History of Tom Jones, A Foundling (1749), a novel commonly called Tom Jones, by Henry Fielding (q. v.). He is a fundamentally good individual, manly, generous, but inclined to the weaknesses of humanity. He finally marries and, hopefully, reforms his life after a series of comic adventures.

JONSON, BEN--(AH-TS; GLD VII; Two Cheers-Stratford)-- 1572-1637. An English playwright and poet. He is especially known for his strict observance of classical principles in his plays despite the romantic approach used by his contemporaries such as Shakespeare (q. v.). He is best known for his comedies of humor: Every Man in His Humour (1598)

Volpone (1606), and The Alchemist (1610).

JOSEPH--(AH-Wil; MT; PP-Eliza)--A patriarch of the Old
Testament ("Genesis"). The youngest son and favorite of his
father who was hated by his 11 older brothers and sold by
them as a slave to a caravan going to Egypt. In Egypt he
rose to a position of trust under the Pharoah and saved his
people from a famine.

JOSEPH ANDREWS--(Aspects VI)--A novel (1742) by Henry
Fielding (q.v.). The title-character is a footman who marries a maid and is vigorously pursued by Lady Booby who
has evil designs upon him. The novel was intended as a
burlesque of Pamela by Samuel Richardson, in which the
situation is reversed.

JOSEPH OF ARIMATHEA--(Two Cheers-Not)--In the New
Testament, the rich Jew and member of the Sanhedrin who
believed in Christ and who, after the crucifixion, asked Pilate for His body burying It in his own tomb. He is also
the subject of many legends one of which takes him to England with the Holy Grail (q.v.).

JOSEPH VANCE--(AH-Word)--A novel (1906) by W. F. de
Morgan (q.v.) considered by many to be his masterpiece.

JOSIAH--(Two Cheers-Anon)--In the Old Testament ("Kings,"
"Jeremiah"), he was the king of Judah 638?-608? B.C.
During his reign, "Deuteronomy," the book of law, was
found in the temple at Jerusalem. He was also responsible
for a reform movement.

JOSIPOVICI, ALBERT--(AH-Salute)--1892- . An Egyptian
writer of Greek heritage. He is co-author with Albert Adès
of Le Livre de Goha le Simple (Paris, 1919). He also co-
authored, again with Adès, Les Inquiets (Paris, 1921).

JOURNAL OF THE PLAGUE YEAR, THE--(Aspects I)--By
Daniel Defoe (1722), a ficticious account of the bubonic plague
which swept England in 1665.

JOVE--(Collect Ta-Celest)--Another name for the Roman
god Jupiter (equivalent of the Greek deity, Zeus, q.v.).

JOYCE--(AH-Early; Aspects III; Two Cheers-English)--James
Joyce. 1882-1941. An Irish novelist, writer of short stories, and verbal experimentalist. He used the stream of

consciousness technique and, as a consequence, some believed that he pushed the novel to its outer limits in such
works as Ulysses and Finnegans Wake.

JUAN, DON--(Two Cheers-George)--Don Juan Tenorio, the
hero of a number of poems (e.g., Byron's Don Juan, 1819-
24), plays, and an opera, Don Giovanni by Mozart. He was
a citizen of Seville in the 14th century who was killed for
seducing the young daughter of the commandant of the city
whom he had killed. His name has become a synonym for
a seducer and libertine.

JUDE THE OBSCURE--(Aspects V)--A novel by Thomas
Hardy (q.v.). (1895). It tells of the love of Jude Fawley
for his cousin. Both marry others, but obtain divorces and
finally live together. Jude's son by his former wife murders Jude's two younger children and hangs himself. Shat-
tered by the tragedy, Jude and his cousin return to their
spouses.

JUDITH--(RWV V; Two Cheers-Stratford; RWV V; WAFT
VIII)--In the Old Testament. She is a beautiful widow who
saved her people by killing the enemy general, Holofernes,
who had invaded Israel.

JUGGERNAUT CAR--(HE XLI)--Juggernaut is a Hindu (Indian) god, called the "lord of the world." His statue is
generally on view for three days when it is washed and
taken in a car to the nearest temple. Fanatics used to
throw themselves under the wheels of the car that bore him
in the belief that they could gain heaven by such an act.

JULIAN--(Alex I, 2; PP-St A; Two Cheers-John)--Flavius
Claudius Julianus (A.D. 331-363), called "The Apostate,"
Roman emperor, 361-363. He was the youngest son of
Julius Constantius who was half-brother of Constantine the
Great (q.v.), and escaped the general massacre of the Fla-
vian family (337). He was well educated and studied in the
schools of Athens. He was the persistant enemy of the
Christians and sought to revive the worship of the ancient
gods, hence the name he received. There is a biography
by Giuseppe Ricciotti (Milwaukee, 1960).

JULIET--(GLD XI; WAFT VI)--One of the principals in the
play, Romeo and Juliet (1594-96). She is the only daughter
of old Capulet who falls in love with Romeo, a member of
a family, the Montagues, who were sworn enemies of the

Capulets.   Their love leads to their deaths.

JULIUS CAESAR--(Two Cheers-Anon; Two Cheers-Jul)--A
play (1601) by William Shakespeare (q. v.) which records the
death of Caesar at Brutus's hand, and the final destruction
of Brutus at Phillippi.

JUMMA--(AH-Emp)--An 860 mile-long river in N central
India that flows into the Ganges.

JUNO--(Collect Ta-Other)--The wife of Jupiter (q.v.) and
queen of heaven in Roman myth.   She is equivalent of Hera
in Greek myth.

JUPITER--(Collect Ta-Other; Two Cheers-John)--See: Zeus.

JUVENAL--(Aspects II)--Decimus Junius Juvenalis, A. D.
60?-140?   A Roman satirist and lawyer.   He satirized the
vices of the Romans under the empire.   Five books (16
satires) are extant.

K

KABUL--(AH-Emp)--The name of a city and the river on
which it is located in Afghanistan.   The city is now the
capital of Afghanistan.   It was part of the Indian empire
when Babur (q.v.) recaptured it in 1526.

KAISER--(MT; Nordic; Two Cheers-Cul)--The German form
of the Latin title, Caesar.   It was the title of the emperor
of the Holy Roman Empire and the emperors of Germany
and Austria.   Forster is, of course, referring to a specific
Kaiser, William II (1859-1941), emperor of Germany and
king of Prussia, 1888-1918.

KALIDAS--(AH-Adrift)--Kalidasa, A. D. 400's.   He is called
"the prince of poets."   Tradition has it that he was the
court poet of King Vikramaditya.   Some of his works are
Raghuvamsa (an epic poem), and Sakuntala (a drama).

KAMES, LORD--(Two Cheers-Raison)--Henry Home, 1696-
1782, Scottish philosopher and jurist.   He is the author of
several philosophical works including Essays on the Principles of Morality and Natural Religion (1751).

KANSA, KING--(Hill; PI XXXIII)--The demon-king, in Hindu myth, of Mathura who committed great evils. Brahma, witnessing his acts, prayed to Vishnu to relieve the world of him. Vishnu plucked two hairs from his own head, one white and the other black. Vishnu pledged that the two hairs would revenge the wrongs done. The black hair became Krishna (q. v.).

KASHMIR--(PI XXIII)--A region on the NW frontier of India and bounded by Afghanistan, Tibet, and China.

KAVAPHES, KONSTANTINOS PETROU--(Alex I, 4; PP-Poetry)--[Cavafy] 1868-1933. An Alexandrian poet of Greek origin. There has been a recent translation of his complete poems by Rae Dalven with an introduction by W. H. Auden (New York: Harcourt, Brace and World, 1961). The volume also contains an extensive bibliography. Other than Forster, the following have done critical studies of Cavafy: Sir Cecil Maurice Bowra, The Creative Experiment, New York, 1958; Margarite Yourcenar; and Pierre Seghers.

KEATS--(AH-JA; AH-Mr; Aspects III; Collect Ta-Celest; GLD VII; LJ II; Two Cheers-George; Two Cheers-Raison; Two Cheers-Snow)--1795-1821. One of the greatest of English Romantic poets. He studied medicine, but never practiced. He was first published in Leigh Hunt's Examiner (May 5, 1816). This was followed by "On First Looking Into Chapman's Homer" and other sonnets and poems which have made him and his work household words in English-speaking circles. He died in Rome.

KEBEHSENOUF--(Alex II, 2)--The Son of Horus (q. v.), in Egyptian myth, guardian of the West, and canopic protector of the intestines of the mummy which were preserved apart from the body in a jar bearing the god's head. His name means pleaser of his brethren.

KENNICOTT, CAROL--(AH-Sin)--One of the principal characters in the novel, Main Street (1920), by Sinclair Lewis (q. v.). She is idealistic and eager to reform the world especially that portion known as Gopher Prairie, the town to which her husband, a doctor, takes her. The town, located in America's Midwest, is not about to be reformed. Her efforts fail.

KENSINGTON GARDENS--(AH-My Own)--Conterminus with Hyde Park (q. v.) in London. The gardens were once the

private domain of Kensington Palace. The gardens owe
their present appearance to Queen Caroline (1730) the wife
of George II (q. v.).

"KEW GARDENS"--(AH-Early; Two Cheers-Virginia)--A short
story by Virginia Woolf (q. v.) in Monday or Tuesday (q. v.).
Called a "postimpressionistic painting in prose," it is the
story of a snail crawling across a flower.

KEYES, SIDNEY--(Two Cheers-Outsider)--1922-1943. An
English poet of great originality and promise, killed in
World War II. His work includes: The Iron Laurel (1942),
The Cruel Solstice (1943), and Collected Poems (1946).

KEYNES, MAYNARD--(Tribute)--John Maynard Keynes, 1883-
1940. An English economist who was director of the Bank
of England. He wrote many volumes on economics including
The Economic Consequences of the Peace (1919).

KHAJRAHA--(PI XXIII)--Khairagaah. A former Indian state
now part of the Eastern States, NE Indian Union.

KHARTOUM--(GLD I)--A city in the Sudan which, in 1885,
was besieged by the forces of the Mahdi (q. v.), a Moslem
fanatic. He and his forces captured the city putting to
death its defenders including General Gordon (q. v.). Gordon's death caused a furor in England. An Anglo-Egyptian
force was raised and the city was recaptured in 1898.

KHAYYAM, OMAR--(GLD X; Two Cheers-In)--See: Omar
Khayyam.

KIERKEGAARD--(Two Cheers)--Søren Aabye Kierkegaard,
1813-1855. A Danish philosopher and theologian. He was
opposed to Hegel (q. v.) and his objective philosophy on faith.
He held that religion is an individual matter and that the
relation of the individual to God involves suffering.

KING, THE--(AH-Capt)--Forster is referring to George II
(q. v.).

KING, THE--(AH-Mrs. Grundy)--Forster is referring to
George V (1865-1936), King of Great Britain and Northern
Ireland and Emperor of India, 1910-1936.

KING LEAR--(Aspects I)--A play (1605) by William Shakespeare (q. v.). Lear, an old man, is determined to divide

his kingdom among his three daughters. As a guide to the
size of the portions, he asks each to tell him how much they
love him. His two eldest daughters flatter him, but his
youngest, Cordelia, refuses and is cut off with nothing thus
beginning a series of events which end in her's and Lear's.
death.

KING OF SPAIN, THE--(Two Cheers-Not)--Forster is referring to Philip IV (1605-1665), King of Spain, 1621-1665.

KING'S COLLEGE--(GLD II)--A residential college, founded
in 1441, of Cambridge University.

KING'S CROSS--(HE II; Two Cheers-Lon)--The location in
London of the principal terminus of the Eastern Region for
long distance trains to the north.

KING'S PARADE--(LJ VI)--See: Pettycury.

KINGLAKE, ALEXANDER WILLIAM--(AH-Salute)--1809-1891.
An English historian. He traveled in the East (1835) and
wrote Eothen or Traces of Travel Brought Home from the
East (1854). He also wrote Invasion of the Crimea (8 vols.,
1863-1887).

KINGSLEY, CHARLES--(AH-Vo; GLD IV)--1819-1875. He
was an English clergyman and novelist deeply interested in
the social reform movements of his time which was reflected
in his novels, two of which are Yeast (1850), Alton Locke
(1855).

KIPLING--(AH-Liberty; AH-New Disorder; Aspects I; HE
XVII; New Disorder)--Rudyard Kipling, 1865-1936. An English novelist, writer of short stories, poet. His work generally reflects a glorification of British Imperialism especially
in India. Kipling was extremely popular at the turn of the
century and his popularity has been declining ever since.
His technique is essentially a mixture of romanticism and
realistic details. Plain Tales from the Hills (1887) is a
collection of short stories; Barrack-Room Ballads (1892) is
perhaps the best known collection of his verse. His novels
include The Light that Failed (1890) and Captains Courageous
(1897).

KIPPS--(AH-Salute; Aspects IV)--A semi-autobiographical
novel (1905) by H. G. Wells (q.v.). It tells of a fortune

inherited by a poor draper's assistant, Kipps, and his struggle to live up to it.

KIRKUP, JAMES--(Two Cheers-Outsider)--1918- . An English poet (The Prodigal Son, 1959; etc.), novelist (Love of Others, 1962; etc.), and author of travel books (Hong Kong and Macao, etc.).

KITTY--(AH-JA)--A character in Pride and Prejudice (1813) by Jane Austen (q. v.). Her full name is Catherine Bennet, younger sister to Elizabeth, and daughter of Mr. and Mrs. Bennet.

KLEE--(Nordic)--Paul Klee, 1879-1940. Swiss modernist painter and representative of the modern German school of painting. His work is an attempt to fuse the subconscious and the fantastic.

KNIGHT, FANNY--(AH-JA)--Lady Fanny Catherine Knight Knatchbull (1793-1882), the niece of Jane Austen (q. v.).

KNOWLES, JAMES--(MT)--Sir James Thomas Knowles, 1831-1908. An English architect and editor. For 30 years he practiced architecture in London. He founded the Metaphysical Society (1869), edited The Contemporary Review (1870-77), and founded and edited The Nineteenth Century (1877-1908).

KNOX--(MT)--John Knox, 1505-1572. Scottish reformer, writer, and statesman. Preached against Roman Catholicism, and against Mary, Queen of Scots. He organized the Presbyterian Church in Scotland.

KOLCHAK--(AH-Voter's)--Aleksander Vasilievich Kolchak, 1874-1920. Russian adventurer and counter-revolutionist. He was a rear-admiral in World War I. After the Russian Revolution (1917), he organized the White Army in Siberia. He was captured and shot by the Reds.

KON-TIKI EXPEDITION--(Two Cheers-En)--Organized by Thor Heyerdahl, the expedition hoped to prove that it was possible for the people of ancient Peru to have populated the islands of the South Seas. The group, led by Heyerdahl, left Peru on a balsa raft, April 23, 1947, and arrived at the island of Raroia, August 7, 1947.

KORAN--(AH-Adrift; PI XIV)--[Arabic, "reading."] The sacred book of Islam and considered by the faithful as the revelations of God to Mohammed (A. D. 651-652).

KOUSSEWITSKY, SERGE--(Two Cheers-George)--Serge Kous-
sevitsky, 1874-1951. Russian-American conductor. He began his musical career playing the double bass. He debuted
as a conductor in Berlin, 1908, and conducted the Boston
Symphony, 1924-49. He was also the director of the Berkshire Festival after 1936.

KREUTZER SONATA, THE--(Two Cheers-C; Two Cheers-
Not Listening)--Sonata in A for violin and piano (1803) by
Beethoven (q. v.) and dedicated to Rudolphe Kreutzer (1766-
1831), a French violinist and composer.

KRISHNA--(AH-Hymn; Hill; GLD X)--[Hindu, "The Black
One."] In Hindu myth, he is one of the greatest deities, the
god of fire, of the heavens, storms, lightning, etc. He is
considered as the 8th avatar [i. e., incarnation] of Vishnu.

"KUBLA KHAN"--(Two Cheers-Raison)--An unfinished poem
(1797) by Samuel Taylor Coleridge (q. v.). What exists is a
description of Kubla Khan's (q. v.) palace which the poet
claims to have written after awakening from a narcotic-in-
duced dream.

KUBLAI KHAN--(AH-Marco; Two Cheers-Raison)--1216-1294.
The Mongol emperor of China and founder of its Yuan dynasty (1279-1368). He was a humane ruler.

                              L
                              =

LADY FROM THE SEA, THE--(AH-Ibsen)--A drama (1889)
by Henrik Ibsen (q. v.) concerning the struggle in the heroine, Ellida, between the love she has for her husband, Dr.
Wrangel, and an infatuation for a strange seaman to whom
she had once been engaged. Her husband's love wins out.

LADY INTO FOX--(Aspects VI)--A short novel (1922) by
David Garnett. The setting is England in 1880. Silvia Fox
Tebrick is transformed into a fox. Her husband tries to
keep up appearances, nevertheless, her nature asserts itself. People begin to think her mad. She is finally attacked
by hounds and dies in her husband's arms.

LADY OF THE LAKE--(AH-JA)--Vivien or Nimuë in Arthurian legend. She is Merlin's mistress and lives in an imaginary lake surrounded by ladies and knights. She is the individual who gives Arthur his sword, Excalibur.

LAGERKVIST, PÄR--(Nordic)--A Swedish poet, dramatist,
and novelist perhaps best known for his novel, Barabbas (1950)
and the motion picture from which it was made (1962). His
central interest, however, is in political and social problems. These are generally reflected in his work.

LAGO MAGGIORE--(WAFT I)--A lake of 81 square miles in
Northern Italy and Southern Switzerland. There are many
resorts in the area.

LAKE DISTRICT--(Two Cheers-William)--A mountainous region in NW England within the Cumberland, Westmoreland,
and Furness districts in Lancashire which contains many
lakes and peaks. Notable among the lakes are Grasmere
and Windermere. The area was the home of many poets of
the Romantic period of English Literature.

LAKE OF GARDA--(HE XXXI)--A lake in N Italy of about
143 square miles.

LAKE POETS--(AH-Notes)--See: Lake School.

LAKE SCHOOL--(AH-TS)--The name attached by the Edinburgh Review to Wadsworth (q.v.), Coleridge (q.v.) and
Southy (q.v.) who lived in the Lake District (q.v.).

LAKES, THE--(Two Cheers-William)--See: Lake District.

LAKSHMI--(PI XXIV)--One of the wives of the Vishnu in
Hindu myth. She is the mother of Kama and is the goddess
of beauty, pleasure, and wealth and, like Aphrodite (q.v.),
she is associated with the sea-foam.

LAMB, CHARLES--(Two Cheers-Anon; Two Cheers-Virginia)
--1775-1834. An English essayist and schoolmate of Coleridge as well as friend of many individuals involved in the
Romantic movement of English Literature. He developed the
personal essay to superb heights. His essays are contained
in two series Essays of Elia (1820, 1833). His most famous essay is the delightful "A Dissertation upon Roast
Pig."

LAMMLE, MR. AND MRS. --(Aspects III)--Characters in the
novel Our Mutual Friend (1864) by Charles Dickens (q. v.).
Mrs. Lammle (née Miss Sophronia Akershen) married Alfred
Lammle in the belief that he was wealthy, while Alfred believed the same of her.   When they discover their error,
they agree to join forces and prey upon their friends.

LANCASHIRE--(HE XXVII)--A county in NW England.   Its
principal urban centers are Liverpool and Manchester.   It
was part of the Anglo-Saxon kingdom of Northumbria.

LANCASTER--See: Bell and Lancaster.

LANDAU--(MT)--A four-wheeled covered carriage with a
divided top which can be lowered.   The name is also applied
to an automobile the rear quarter of which can be opened.

LANDOR, WALTER SAVAGE--(HE II; PP-Return)--1775-1864.
English poet, literary critic, and writer of prose.   He is
noted for the intellectuality of his verses many of which were
written in imitation of Latin and Greek forms thus reflecting
his general interest in the ancient classics.   In his youth he
was a revolutionary raising an army to fight Napoleon in
Spain.   His chief work, other than his poetry which was
little read in his own time and less now, is a series of
imaginary discussions between historical figures (Imaginary
Conversations, 1824-1853).

LANG, ANDREW--(GLD X)--1844-1912.   Scottish literateur,
and scholar.   He held that literary myth is the outgrowth of
anonymous folklore.   He translated Homer and edited volumes
of fairy tales.

LANGTON, STEPHAN--(AH-Ab)--1150?-1228.   He was the
Archbishop of Canterbury whose see was denied him by King
John (q. v.) and, as a result he became leader of the barons
who forced John to sign the Magna Carta.

LANSDOWNE, LORD--(Egypt)--Henry Charles Keith Petty-
Fitzmaurice, 5th Marquis Lansdowne, 1845-1927.   He held
minor political posts under Gladstone (q. v.) then was appointed Governor General of Canada (1883-1888), and then
Viceroy of India (1888-1893) where he stabilized the rupee.
He was also Secretary of War (1895-1900) and Foreign Secretary (1900-05).

LAOCOÖN--(AH-For the Muse)--He was, in Greek legend, the son of Priam and priest of Apollo of Troy. His fame rests on his tragic fate. He and his two sons were crushed to death by a serpent while he was sacrificing to Poseidon because he had offended Apollo. In 1506, a sculpture depicting his death agony was unearthed in Rome and is now in the Vatican Museum.

"LASCIATE OGNI BALDANZA [sic] VOI CHE ENTRATE"-- (Collect Ta-Celest)--Mr. Bons's misreading of ℓ. 9, Canto III of the Inferno (Book I of Dante's Divine Comedy, q.v.). The line is "lasciate ogni speranza, voi ch'entrate" ("relinquish hope all who enter here.") The words are part of the inscription over the gates of Hell. In Mr. Bons's version it becomes "Abandon haughty pride all who enter here."

LAST BEETHOVEN SONATA--(Two Cheers-Not Listening)-- See: LAST PIANO SONATA of Beethoven.

LAST CHRONICLE OF BARSET--(Aspects III)--A novel (1867) by Anthony Trollope (q.v.). It is the last novel in the Chronicles of Barsetshire, a series which treats of the life of the ficticious cathedral town of Barchester. The same characters appear in most of the novels.

LAST PIANO SONATA OF BEETHOVEN--(Two Cheers-C)-- The sonata in C minor, Opus 111, composed in 1822 and dedicated, by the publisher, to the Archduke Rudolph.

LAST DAYS OF POMPEII, THE--(Aspects I)--A novel (1834) by Bulwer Lytton which tells of the love of Glaucus for the beautiful Ione and her guardian's attempt to thwart the romance. The plot unwinds against the backdrop of Pompeii just before and during its destruction by Vesuvius.

LAURA--(Aspects V)--A character in The Counterfeiters (q.v.) by André Gide (q.v.). Laura Douviers is a friend of Edouard (q.v.) and the pregnant ex-mistress of Vincent. She meets Edouard when both were patients in a sanitorium.

LAURA--(Collect Ta-Celest)--Laure de Noves, 1308-1348. She was married and the mother of 11 children and was loved by Petrarch (q.v.) who, it is said, on first seeing her determined to become a poet. He wrote a large number of love sonnets dedicated to her.

LAURA DE NAZIANZI, SAINT--(AH-Ron)--Her "story" is
told in The Flower Beneath the Foot, a novel (1923) by
Ronald Firbank (q. v.).

LAWRENCE, COL. --(Two Cheers-Ascent)--See: T. E.
Lawrence.

LAWRENCE, D. H. --(AH-Liberty; Aspects IV; GLD VII;
Two Cheers-English)--David Herbert Lawrence, 1885-1930.
An English novelist who used many of the themes of Freud
(q. v.) in his work and produced what was, for his time,
"liberated" novels of the workings of sexual passion in sensitive beings. His Lady Chatterly's Lover (1928) which
seems tame in the light of recent publications was the cause
célèbre of the period. It was, of course, proscribed and,
as a result, Lawrence's fame skyrocketed among those who
saw the court action as a destruction of liberty, the voyeurs,
and professors of literature. He is still much admired today.

LAWRENCE, T. E. --(AH-Liberty; Collect Ta-Intro; Two
Cheers-Clouds; Two Cheers-En; Two Cheers-English; Two
Cheers-Whiff)--Thomas Edward Lawrence, 1888-1935. A
British archeologist, writer, and soldier of fortune who is
best known for his exploits as the leader of the Arab revolt
(1917-18) against the Turks during World War I which he
described in his book, Seven Pillars of Wisdom (1926) and
its shorter version, Revolt in the Desert (1926). He spent
the remainder of his life seeking the anonymity he had lost
because of his deeds.

"LAY OF THE LAST MINSTREL, THE"--(MT)--A long narrative poem (1805) by Sir Walter Scott (q. v.). Baron Henry
of Cranston loves Lady Margaret, but a feud exists between
their families. The poem describes the difficulties he over-
comes to win her.

LEAGUE OF NATIONS--(AH-Note; Egypt; GLD-Intro; New
Disorder; Two Cheers-Art; Two Cheers-Menace; Two Cheers-
Romain; Two Cheers-What)--The League was formed after
World War I largely through the efforts of Woodrow Wilson
(q. v.) although the United States was never a member. Its
headquarters were in Geneva. The League guaranteed the
territorial integrity and existing political independence of all
members and, in cases of dispute, arbitration with a time
limit was agreed on. During the 1920's it was able to settle minor disputes between nations and made a considerable

contribution in the fields of refugee rehabilitation, public
health, and international labor problems. However, it had
no power to enforce its policies in cases of war. It failed
at the invasion of China by Japan (1937) and of Ethiopia by
Italy (1934). The Civil War in Spain (1936-1939) is another
League failure. The League came to an end with the beginning of World War II (1939) and was formally dissolved
April 18, 1946.

LEANING TOWER--(Two Cheers-Virginia)--Forster is alluding to the most famous of all leaning towers [there are
many], that of Pisa. It is part of Pisa's cathedral complex
and leans some 14 feet out of perpendicular.

LEAR--(Two Cheers-En)--Edward Lear, 1812-1888. An English writer of nonsense verse and landscape painter. He was
the friend of Tennyson and had a studio in Rome. His written works include Book of Nonsense (1846), Nonsense Songs,
Stories and Botany (1870).

LEAR, KING--(AH-Our Div; Two Cheers-En; Two Cheers-
Jul)--See: King Lear.

LEDA--(Alex II, 1)--In Greek myth, she was the mother, by
Zeus who came to her as a swan, of two eggs one of which
became Castor and Clytemnestra, and the other Pollux and
Helen.

LEE, ANNE--(Two Cheers-Mount)--1736-1784. Religious
mystic and foundress of the Shaker society in America. Born
in England, she came to America in 1774 with followers and
settled in what is now Watervliet, New York. She was arrested for treason in 1780 but was released.

LEE, VERNON--(GLD XII)--Pseudonym of Violet Paget,
1856-1935. English essayist and critic, author of Studies of
the Eighteenth Century in Italy (1880), Satan, the Waster
(1920), etc.

LEMAN, LAKE--(AH-Vo)--The Lake of Geneva in SW Switzerland and E France of 225 square miles.

LENIN--(Two Cheers-Muhammed)--Nikolai Ilich Ulyanov,
1870-1924. Russian communist leader. He was exiled to
Siberia (1897) and there he completed The Development of
Capitalism in Russia (1899). In 1900 he went to Switzerland
and worked for a Marxist-inspired revolution. In February

1917, the Germans, hoping to undermine the Russian war effort, permitted him to travel to Russia. There, he soon overthrew the moderate Kerensky government and installed himself as dictator, the position he held until his death. His embalmed body is now on view in a mausoleum in Red Square.

LEO--(PP-Tim)--Leo I, called the Great (400?-474), Emperor of the Eastern Roman Empire, 457-474.

LEOPOLD, UNCLE--(Two Cheers-English)--Leopold I (Georges Chrétian Frédéric of the House of Saxe-Coburg), 1790-1865. The first king of independent Belgium and uncle of Queen Victoria (q. v.).

LES AMOURS QUI SUIVENT SONT MOINS INVOLUNTAIRES--(LJ XXIV)--French: The loves which follow are less involuntary.

LESBIA--(Two Cheers-John)--Referring to the Island of Lesbos and particularly to Sappho, its famous poetess.

LESLIE, SIR--(Two Cheers-Virginia)--See: Leslie Stephen.

LESSEPS, DE--(AH-Salute)--Vicomte Ferdinand Marie de Lesseps, 1805-1894. A French diplomat and promoter of the Suez Canal.

LEVANT, THE--(HE XVII)--The name given to the Eastern shores of the Mediterreanean Sea.

LEVENS, THE--(MT)--The earldom (Leven) held from the 15th century by the Scottish family Leslie, or Lesly, or Lesley. The family originated in the pastoral parish of Lesslyn or Leslie in Aberdeenshire. It was ennobled when George Leslie of Rothes was made Earl of Rothes and Lord Leslie (1457). He held the earldom of Len, and baronies of Belgonie, Lindoies, and Newark.

LEWES, GEORGE HENRY--(GLD XI; Hill)--1817-1878. English literary critic and philosopher now most remembered as the common-law husband of Marian Evans [George Eliot (q. v.)] with whom he lived until his death.

LEWIS, SINCLAIR--(AH-Sin; Two Cheers-Does)--American novelist and playwright born in Sauk Centre, Minnesota, which he excoriated in his novels as Gopher Prairie. He

began his career as a journalist and editor. His best works
(Main Street, 1920; Babbitt, 1922, etc.) were done in the
1920's.

LIBŬSE--(Nordic)--A little-known opera (1881) by Smetana (q.v.). It is the story of Libŭse, the Queen of Bohemia,
who intends to vacate her throne in favor of a man who can
rule with an iron hand.

LIFE AS WE HAVE KNOWN IT--(Two Cheers-Virginia)--Sub-
titled: By Co-operative Working Women (London: Hogarth
Press, 1931), edited by Margaret Llewelyn Davis, with an
introductory letter by Virginia Woolf (q.v.). The volume is
a collection of autobiographies of working class women.

LIMBO--(AH-Cn)--A type of spiritual "half-way" house between this world and Heaven in which the patriarchs and the
prophets who died before Christ's death awaited the opening
of the gates of Heaven.

LINCOLNSHIRE--(HE XXVII)--A county in E England. Its
largest urban center is the city of Lincoln.

LINSCHOTEN, JAN HUYGEN--(AH-Adrift)--A Dutch traveler
and explorer. He promoted attempts by the Dutch to find a
northeast passage to the East Indies.

LINTON FAMILY--(Aspects VII)--Characters in the novel
Wuthering Heights by Emily Brontë (q.v.). They are Edgar
Linton, husband of Catherine Earnshaw (q.v.); Isabella Linton, his sister and the wife of Heathcliff (q.v.); Cathy Linton, his daughter by Catherine Earnshaw; Linton Heathcliff,
son of Heathcliff and Isabella Linton.

LIPS, EVA--(Nordic)--Wife of the pre-1940 director of the
Cologne Museum of Ethnology, Julius Lips. She wrote of
her experiences under the Nazis in What Hitler Did to Us
(q.v.) and Savage Symphony. She has also edited a life of
her husband and a collection of his works.

LITTLE EYOLF--(AH-Ibsen)--The name of a character and
the title of a play (1894) by Henrik Ibsen (q.v.). He is the
crippled son of Mr. and Mrs. Allmers (q.v.) who is tor-
mented by an old hag known only as the Rat Wife. The father awakens to his parental responsibility, which he has
shirked, only after the child's death.

LIVINGSTONE--(AH-Our Div)--David Livingstone, 1813-1873.
Scottish missionary and explorer in Africa.   He was the subject of a rescue by a journalist, Stanley, and the object of
an historical question posed by his rescuer: "Dr. Livingstone, I presume?"

LIVRE DE GOHA LE SIMPLE, LE--(AH-Salute; AH-Wil)--
See: Albert Adès; Albert Josipovici.

LIVY--(AH-Vo)--Titus Livius, 59 B. C. -A. D. 17.   Roman
historian born in Padua.   His most important work is The
Annals of the Roman People under the patronage of the Emperor Augustus.

LLOYD GEORGE, DAVID--(AH-Our Div; AS)--1863-1945.
1st Earl of Droyton, he was a solicitor and a member of
Parliament, where he won recognition through his brilliant
debates; he held several government posts including Chancellor of the Exchequer, Minister of Munitions, and Secretary of State for War.   He replaced Lord Asquith (q. v.) as
Prime Minister (1916-22) and, as virtual dictator, directed
Britain's policies to victory in World War I and in the peace
settlement.

LOCKE, JOHN--(Two Cheers-Tol)--1632-1704.   An English
philosopher.   His work, An Essay Concerning Human Understanding (1690), was an attempt to settle what questions the
human understanding is or is not capable of dealing with.
He is known as the father of English empiricism.

LOCKWOOD--(Aspects VII)--A character in the novel Wuthering Heights (q. v.), by Emily Brontë (q. v.).   He is Heathcliff's tenant at Wuthering Heights and the first narrator in
the novel.   It is to him that Mrs. Dean tells the story of
Cathy and Heathcliff.

LOGGIA DE'LANZI--(PI VII; RWV IV)--The Loggia dei Lanzi
or Loggia della Signoria.   Built 1378-1381 by Benci di Cione
and Simone Talenti.   It is a masterpiece of late Florentine
Gothic and is located on the Piazza della Signoria in Florence.

LOHENGRIN--(LJ IX)--An opera (1850) by Richard Wagner
(q. v.) with libretto by the composer.   It tells the story of
Lohengrin, knight of the Holy Grail, and son of Parsifal.

LONDON BRIDGE--(Two Cheers-Lon)--The name of a series
of bridges which connect Southwark with London and span the

Thames.   The latest is a replacement for one which was sold to an American city.

LONG AND IMPORTANT WORK ON BEETHOVEN, A--(Two Cheers-Romain)--Romain Rolland's Beethoven, Paris, 1903. Forster exaggerates the length.

LONG AND IMPORTANT WORK ON HANDEL, A--(Two Cheers-Romain)--Romain Rolland's Handel, translated into English by A. E. Hull, New York, 1916.

LONGINUS--(Alex I, 3)--Dionysius Cassius, A.D. 200's.   A Greek Platonic philosopher and rhetorician, he studied in Alexandria and taught in Athens.   He was tutor to the children of Queen Zenobia of Palmyra and her political advisor. He was beheaded in 273 by order of the Emperor Aurelian after Zenobia's fall.   Some of his works are On the Chief End, On First Principles, and Philosophical Discourse.

LORCA--(Two Cheers-They)--Frederico Garcia Lorca, 1899-1936.   Spanish poet and playwright.   Perhaps the play best known to English-speaking audiences is the tragedy, Blood Wedding (1939), an earlier (1935) version of which was called Bitter Oleander.

LORENZO IL MAGNIFICO--(RWV VI)--Lorenzo de' Medici (called the "Magnificent"), 1449-1492.   One of the greatest of the Renaissance princes.   He was ruler of Florence and more significantly the patron of the arts the products of which now are recognized as the greatest works of man.   He also did much to make Tuscan the national dialect of Italy.

LORENZO THE POET--(RWV VI)--See: Lorenzo il Magnifico.

LOTI, PIERRE--(AH-Salute; Aspects I)--The pseudonym of Louis Marie Julien Viaud, 1850-1923.   He was a French naval officer and novelist.   He is most known for his stories with exotic backgrounds of the near and far East: Fantôme d'Orient (1892), La Galilée (1895), etc.

LOUIS--(Two Cheers-Virginia)--A character in the novel The Waves (1931) by Virginia Woolf.   He is the son of a Brisbane banker, and is a self-conscious outcast of the society of his friends.   He is, nevertheless, the most brilliant and egotistical of his group.

LOUIS OF FRANCE, SAINT--(Alex II, 7)--Louis IX (1214-
1270), King of France, 1226-1270. His reign was long and
peaceful. He went on the sixth Crusade and was noted for
his piety.

LOUIS XIII--(MT)--1601-1643. King of France, 1610-1643.
For most of his reign he was under the influence of Cardinal
Richelieu, his chief advisor. He warred against the Hugue-
nots (1622-28) in the South of France.

LOUIS XIV--(GLD X; New Disorder; Two Cheers-Art)--1638-
1715. King of France, 1643-1715, he was called "le Grand
Monarque," "le Roi Soleil" (the Sun King). He succeeded
his father, Louis XIII (q.v.), when only five under a regency
of his mother, Anne of Austria. During the course of his
long reign, he brought France to the zenith of its reputation,
power, and culture. He created the greatest palace Europe
had ever seen, Versailles, as a golden prison for the nobility whose power he hoped to check by demanding that they
live there rather than on their estates.

LOUIS XV--(New Disorder)--1710-1774. King of France
1715-1774, ironically called "le Bien-Aimé" ("the Well-
Beloved"), he was the great grandson of Louis XIV (q.v.),
but was never as effective. He disordered the finances and
was hated by the masses.

LOUIS XVI--(MT)--1754-1793. King of France, 1774-1792.
Son of Louis XV and husband of Marie Antoinette, the French
Revolution toppled him from his throne and cost him and his
wife their heads.

LOUIS XVIII--(MT)--Louis Xavier Stanislaus, Louis "le De-
siré" (1755-1824), King of France 1814-15; 1815-1824.
Grandson of Louis XV (q.v.) and brother of Louis XVI (q.v.)
and Charles X. He lived in Germany after the French Revolution drove him out of France. He was also in exile
during Napoleon's reign. He became king after Napoleon's
defeat but was forced to flee Paris during Napoleon's "Hundred Days" return to France (1815). He was restored to
the throne once again upon Napoleon's final defeat at Waterloo.

LOUVAIN--(Two Cheers-John)--A commune in Belgium in
the province of Brabant. It was the center of the wool
trade in the 14th century and became the seat of a university founded in 1425.

LOVE AND MR. LEWISHAM--(AH-Sin)--A novel (1900) by
H. G. Wells (q. v.). Subtitled: The Story of a Very Young
Couple. The hero tries to live his life according to a plan,
but fails.

LOVEL, MR. --(Aspects II)--A character in Sir Walter Scott's
The Antiquary (q. v.). It is eventually discovered that he is
Lord William Geraldier, heir to the Earl of Glenallen. This
discovery removes the barriers to his marriage to Isabella
Wardour.

LOVELACE--(Aspects VII)--Robert Lovelace, a character in
the novel Clarissa Harlowe (1747-1748), by Samuel Richardson (q. v.). He is a young English nobleman brought into
the Harlowe household as suitor of Arabella, but he falls in
love with Clarissa. He seduces her and deserts her only to
discover that he is really in love with her and offers her
marriage.

LOVE'S COMING OF AGE--(Two Cheers-Edward)--By Edward
Carpenter (q. v.), and first printed at his expense in 1896.
It treats of the "sex-passion," man the "un-grown," woman
the "serf" and other aspects of humanity as a sexual force.

LOWES, JANE--(GLD I)--1749-1811. The great-grandmother
of Goldsworthy Lowes Dickinson (q. v.).

LOWES, LIVINGSTON--(Two Cheers-Eng; Two Cheers-Raison)
--John Livingston Lowes, 1867-1945. An American educator
and scholar, he was professor of English at Harvard and author of many scholarly works including The Road to Xanadu
(1927), The Art of Geoffrey Chaucer (1931), and Essays in
Appreciation (1936).

LOWES, MRS. --(GLD I)--Hattie Dickinson Lowes, the sister
of Goldsworthy Lowes Dickinson (q. v.).

LUBBOCK, PERCY--(AH-HOS; Aspects IV)--1879-1965. An
English literary critic and essayist. He is best known for
his The Craft of Fiction (1921), a study of the techniques of
the novel which has become a classic.

LUCAS, CHARLOTTE--(Aspects IV)--A character in the novel Pride and Prejudice, by Jane Austen (q. v.). She is the
eldest child of Sir William and Lady Lucas and a sensible
girl of about 27. She is Elizabeth Bennet's intimate friend.

LUCAS, E. V.--(HE XIV)--Edward Verrall Lucas, 1868-
1938. An English publisher and writer. He was on the
staffs of The Globe, and Punch and was chairman of Methuen
and Co., publishers. He was the author of many works including Old Lamps for New (1911), and the novel, Over Be-
merton's (1908).

LUCAS, F. L.--(Two Cheers-Raison)--Francis Laurence
Lucas, 1894-1967. An English writer and educator, author
of the novels The River Flows, and Cecile, and the plays
The Bear Dances (1932), and Land's End (1938), as well as
Poems (1935).

LUCIA DI LAMMERMOOR--(Two Cheers-George; WAFT VI)--
An opera (1835) by Donizetti with a libretto by S. Camma-
rano closely based on The Bride of Lammermoor (q. v.) by
Sir Walter Scott (q. v.).

LUCIFER--(Aspects VI; New Disorder)--The name applied to
Satan.

LUCRETIUS--(AH-Vo)--Titus Lucretius Caius, 96?-55 B. C.
Roman philosophical poet and disciple of Epicurus (q. v.).
His chief work is De Rerum Natura in six books, a didactic
poem which treats, according to the philosophy of Epicurus,
physics, ethics, and psychology.

LUCY--(Aspects II)--Lucy Ashton, a character in The Bride
of Lammermoor (q. v.) by Sir Walter Scott (q. v.). She is
the daughter of Sir William Ashton. Gentle, timid, and com-
pliant, she falls in love with Edgar Ravenswood, the enemy
of her family. Forced into another marriage, she dies mad.

LUDWIG, EMIL--(Nordic)--[Orig. name: Emil Cohn] 1881-
1848. He was a German writer and biographer noted for
his biographies of Goethe (1920) and Napoleon (1924).

LUGANO--(WAFT I)--A commune in the Ticino Canton of
Switzerland and located on the northern shore of Lake Lugano.
It is famous as a tourist center and for its silk and choco-
late.

LUGARD, SIR FREDERICK--(AH-Mind)--Frederick Dealtry
Lugard (created 1st Baron Lugard of Abinger in 1928), 1858-
1945. A British soldier and colonial administrator born in
Madras, India. Among others of his posts, he was high
Commissioner and Commander-in-Chief of Northern Nigeria

(1900-06), Governor of Hong Kong (1907-1912), and Governor General of Nigeria (1914-1919).

LUPESCU, MADAME--(Two Cheers-Jew)--Magda Lupescu, b. 1904. A Rumanian adventuress and mistress of King Carol of Rumania (q. v.).

LUTHER--(AH-Adrift; AH-Notes; LJ VI)--Martin Luther, 1483-1546. A German ex-Roman Catholic monk and founder of Lutheranism. He was excommunicated by Pope Leo X, Jan. 15, 1520, and married a former nun, translated the Bible, and was intolerant of those who did not agree with him.

LUXEMBOURG--(GLD IX)--The Grand Duchy of Luxembourg (998 square miles) in W Europe between SE Belgium and W Germany. Its inhabitants are of German origin but largely speak French.

LYCURGUS--(AH-Gem)--396?-?323 B. C. An Athenian financier and orator who favored the anti-Macedonian policy of Demosthenes.

LYDIA--(AH-JA)--A character in the novel Pride and Prejudice by Jane Austen (q. v.). She is the youngest of the Bennet daughters, and elopes at 15. Mr. Darcy helps her and her lover to marry by paying her lover's debts. Their marriage is never really happy.

LYME REGIS--(AH-JA; AH-My W)--A municipal borough in Dorchestshire, SE England.

LYONS MAIL--(GLD V)--A melodrama by Charles Reade originally titled The Courier of Lyons. It was first produced in 1854.

LYSISTRATA--(Two Cheers-Virginia)--The heroine of a comic play, Lysistrata (ca. 415 B. C.) by Aristophanes (q. v.). She persuades the wives of Athens to shut themselves in the Acropolis (q. v.) and have nothing to do with their husbands until they end the Peloponnesian War which was in its 21st year.

M

MAAT--(Alex II, 3)--In Egyptian myth, the goddess of truth.

MACARIUS, SAINT--(Alex II, 7)--Sometimes called Saint
Mercury. His identification is not entirely clear. The Roman martyrology places him and others (Rufinus, Justus,
Theophilus), potters by trade, at Alexandria where they were
martyred under the Emperor Decius (q. v.). Either February 28 or October 30 is their feast date. Butler, however,
lists him as a confectioner (A. D. 394) who forsook the
world and spent 60 years in the desert. He gives Macarius's feast date as January 2.

MACAULAY, ROSE--(Two Cheers-Eng)--Dame Rose Macaulay, 1881-1958. English author of ironic and satiric works
notably Potterism (1920) which is similar in intent to Sinclair Lewis's Babbitt (q. v.). She was also an essayist (A
Casual Commentary, 1925) and critic (e. g., Some Religious
Elements in English Literature, 1931; John Milton, 1933),
she also wrote extended essays on Keats (q. v.) and Forster.

MACAULAY, THOMAS BABINGTON--(AH-Mrs; MT; Two
Cheers-English; Two Cheers-Gibbon)--1809-1859. He was
the son of Zachary Macaulay (q. v.) and Selina Mills [sister
of Hannah More, q. v.]. He was created 1st Baron Macaulay in 1857. He was an English writer and statesman who
held several government posts including Secretary of War,
Paymaster of the Forces, etc. He is, of course, best
known for his writing which includes poetry (Lays of Ancient
Rome, 1842) and history (History of England, 1848, 1855).
His complete works were edited by his sister, Lady Treve-
leyan (Hannah More Macaulay), in 1876.

MACAULAY, ZACHARY--(AH-Ba; AH-Mrs; MT)--1768-1838.
Father of Thomas Babington Macaulay (q. v.) and great-
grandfather of R. C. Trevelyan (q. v.). He was an English
philanthropist who helped to suppress the slave trade. He
was Governor of Sierra Leone and editor of The Christian
Observer (1802-1816), an abolitionist journal.

MACBETH--(Two Cheers-Art; Two Cheers-George; Two
Cheers-Jul)--A play (1600) by William Shakespeare (q. v.)
which records Macbeth's rise to power in Scotland through
murder and his subsequent fall. He meets three witches
who prophesy his rise and he uses what they say as a spur
to his own ambition. He learns only too late that they tell

only half-truths.

MACCARTHY, DESMOND--(Tribute)--1878-1952.   British
writer, critic, and editor.   Author of The Court Theatre
Portraits, Leslie Stephen, and other works.

MACDONALD, RAMSAY--(Hill)--James Ramsay MacDonald,
1866-1937.   British statesman and leader of the Labour Party.   He was Prime Minister (1906-18; Jan. -Oct. 1924; 1929-
31; 1931-1935).   A pacifist, he opposed Britain's entry into
World War I.   He organized the first Labour ministry in the
history of Britain, January to October, 1924.

MACDOWELL--(HE IX)--Edward Alexander MacDowell,
1861-1908.   An American composer and protégé of Franz
Liszt.   He was professor of music at Columbia University,
1896-1904.   He composed symphonic poems, piano sonatas,
etc., and the popular "Woodland Sketches."

MACFLECKNOE--(EK)--The central character in a poetic
satire (1682) by John Dryden (q. v.).   He is in reality
Thomas Shadwell who, despite his shortcomings as a poet,
was made laureate.   The purpose of the poem is to satirize
the conferring of the office on individuals of little or no merit.

MACHA, K. H. --(Nordic)--Karl Hynek Macha, 1810-1836.
Czech lyric poet and novelist.   He is representative of
nationalism.

MACHIAVELLI--(AH-Emp; GLD X; Two Cheers-Books)--
Niccolò Machiavelli, 1469-1527.   An Italian statesman and
author of a guide for unscrupulous politicians, Il Principe
(1513).   The aim of the volume is to demonstrate that
rulers are free to do whatever they please to gain their
ends.

MACINTOSH, SIR JAMES--(MT; Two Cheers-Snow)--1765-
1832.   Scottish historian, philosopher, member of parliament,
professor of law, holder of several government offices, and
author (e.g., Dissertation on the Progress of Ethical Philosophy, 1830).

MCINTYRE, HECTOR--(Aspects II)--Captain Hector McIntyre, a character in Scott's The Antiquary (q. v.).   He is the
nephew of the antiquary who astonishes his uncle by his military efficiency.   He is a good lad.

MACLEOD, FIONA--(Aspects I)--Pseudonym of William
Sharp, 1856?-1905.   Scottish poet, biographer, essayist.
He helped to promote a revival of interest in Celtic literature and customs.   He wrote biographies of Dante Gabriel
Rossetti (q. v.), Shelley (q. v.), Heine (q. v.), etc.   Under
his pseudonym he wrote mystical stories and poetic prose
about the Celtic world (e. g., The Winged Destiny, 1904;
and Green Fire, 1896).

MADAN, MARTIN--(Two Cheers-Madan)--1726-1790.   English barrister and Methodist divine.   He was chaplain of
Lock Hospital, London and stirred up a protest with his
Thelyphithora (Ruination of Women, 1780) advocating polygamy as a remedy for prostitution.

MADARIAGA, SALVADOR DE--(Nordic)--1886- .   Salvador
de Madariaga y Rojo.   A Spanish diplomat and writer.   He
was Spanish ambassador to Washington (1931), on the League
of Nations Council (1931-36), etc.   Wrote Shelley and Cal-
deròn (1937), The World's Design (1938), etc.

MADEIRA--(HE XV)--The largest island of a group 440
miles W of Morocco.   It has deep ravines and rugged
mountains and produces a famous wine (Madeira).   Its capital is the city of Funchal.

MAESTOSO--(Two Cheers-C)--[Ital., "majestic, dignified."]
A word used to direct the playing of a musical composition
in a stately manner.

MAETERLINCK--(Collect Ta-Eternal)--Count Maurice Maeterlinck, 1862-1949.   Belgian essayist, novelist, poet, dramatist born in Ghent of Flemish origin.   He settled in Paris
(1896) where he became involved in the French Symbolist
movement.   He received the Nobel Prize for literature in
1911.   His Pelléas et Mélisande was adapted for operas
(1902) by his friend Debussy (q. v.).   The Blue Bird (1909)
is perhaps best known to English-reading audiences.

MAGDALENE--(Two Cheers-Not)--St. Mary Magdalene.   In
the New Testament she is a woman whom Jesus cured of sin
and who followed Him.   She was present at His crucifixion
and came to His tomb on the third day only to find it empty.

MAGIC FLUTE, THE--(Aspects I; GLD IX)--Die Zauberflöte,
an opera by Mozart (q. v.), in two acts composed in 1791.

Tamino falls in love with Pamina, the daughter of the Queen of the Night, who is kidnapped by the wicked magician, Sarastro (q. v.).

MAGIC FLUTE, THE--(Aspects VI; GLD IX)--Subtitled: A Fantasia (1920) by Goldsworthy Lowes Dickinson (q. v.). The author uses characters from the opera (q. v.).

MAGNUS THE MARTYR, ST. --(Two Cheers-Lon)--See: Saint Magnus the Martyr.

MAHDI--(AH-Wil)--Mohammed Ahmed, 1843?-1885. A Moslem agitator born in the province of Dongola, the Egyptian Sudan; proclaimed himself Mahdi (c. 1880) and overran the Egyptian Sudan. He besieged and captured Khartoum in 1885 and died that year at Omdurman on June 22.

MAHLER--(Nordic)--Gustav Mahler, 1860-1911. Bohemian composer and conductor. He was the director of the Imperial Opera in Vienna (1897-1907) and conducted in the United States (1907-10). He composed ten symphonies and many lesser compositions.

MAILLET--(AH-Vo)--Jacques Léonard Maillet, 1823-1894. French sculptor.

MAIN STREET--(AH-Sin)--A novel (1920) by Sinclair Lewis (q. v.). It is the story of a small, smug, mid-Western American town interested only in getting on with life in terms acceptable to its own prejudices. Carol Kennicott (q. v.), wife of the doctor, tries to change the town and fails.

MAIS C'EST UNE MAUVAISE PLAISANTERIE--(Two Cheers-Gibbon)--French: But it is a bad joke.

MALACHI--(Two Cheers-Jews)--The author of the Old Testament "Book of Malachi." c. 464-424 B. C. The book records reproofs of the priests for their laxity in serving the temple and reproofs of the people for foreign marriages.

MALATESTA, SISMONDO--(AH-For the Muse; AH-Gem)--d. 1468. Of Rimini. He was patron of the arts and of literature as well as an accomplished soldier. He warred against the Pope and was excommunicated.

MALEA--(RWV XX)--A cape at the extremity of the E peninsula of the Peloponnesus in southern Greece.

MALL, THE--(England's)--Pall Mall [pron. "pell mell"], a street in London which takes its name from an old French game resembling croquet, "paille-maille." It crosses the once fashionable district of St. James.

MALMAISON--(MT)--The small palace in France, and the town from which it takes its name, of Josephine, first wife of Napoleon (q. v.).

MALORY--(Two Cheers-In)--Sir Thomas Malory, 1394?-1471. An English knight and compiler of Le Morte D'Arthur printed in 1471. He was a rather strange individual, a soldier in the Hundred Years' War, who, in 1451, raided a monastery for which he was imprisoned. He wrote the volume in his cell, which he left only with his death.

MALRAUX, ANDRÉ--(Two Cheers-Gide)--1901- . A French novelist, essayist, statesman, and art historian, he was awarded the Prix Goncourt for his novel, La Condition Humaine (1931). In the Fifth Republic he was minister for culture.

MALTHUS--(AH-Troop; GLD X; Two Cheers-Camb)--Thomas Robert Malthus, 1766-1834. An English economist who formulated the theory named after him which states that population, when unchecked, tends to increase in a geometric ratio, while the food supply increases only arithmetically. Hence, there is an implication in the theory that checks on population are necessary if man is to survive. The theory is still popular today.

MAN FRIDAY--(Aspects III)--The faithful servant of Robinson Crusoe in the novel of the same name by Daniel Defoe (q. v.).

MAN WITHOUT A SOUL, THE--(Nordic)--Mannen utan Själ, 1936, a play by Pär Lagerkvist (q. v.).

MANICHAEAN--(PP-Tim)--Referring to a religion founded by Mani (c. A. D. 216-c. 277), a Persian sage, based on the belief that there exist two equal and opposing principles of good and evil in the world. For eight centuries this religion was a serious rival to Christianity, spreading from France to China. For nine years St. Augustine (q. v.) was a believer, before becoming a Christian.

MANN, HEINRICH--(Nordic)--1871-1950. Older brother of
Thomas Mann (q. v.), Heinrich was a German writer who
lived in exile in France (1933-1940), and was interned by
the Nazis (1940). He managed to escape to the United States.
He was the author of novels, short stories, plays and essays.
The Blue Angel (1932) is, perhaps, his best known work. It
was made into a film which gave Marlene Dietrich her start
as a motion picture star.

MANN, THOMAS--(Nordic; Two Cheers-What)--1875-1955.
Author and winner of the Nobel Prize for literature in 1929.
He was a refugee from Nazi Germany and came to the United
States in 1938 where he became a naturalized citizen in 1944.
Some of his more important works are Buddenbrooks (1901),
which made him famous, Death in Venice (1912), The Magic
Mountain (1924), and Joseph in Egypt (1938).

MANSFIELD PARK--(AH-JA; Aspects IV; MT)--A novel (1814)
by Jane Austen (q. v.). Self-effacing Fanny Price is adopted
by a rich and frivolous family. Her character is tested before her genuineness is recognized by her cousin, Edmond.

MANSFIELD RECTORY--(AH-JA)--Forster is more correctly
referring to Mansfield Parsonage in Jane Austen's Mansfield
Park (q. v.). It is, at first, the home of Mr. and Mrs.
Norris, later that of Dr. and Mrs. Grant.

MARABAR CAVES--(PI I)--There are no caves of such a
name in existence in India. There do exist, however, in
the Barabar Hills, Bihan, India, the Sophi and Vakuyaka
caves which are similar. The similarity of "Marabar" to
"Barabar" would suggest that Forster used those caves as
the models for his own. This contention is supported by
Wilfred Stone in his study, The Cave and the Mountain: A
Study on E. M. Forster, Stanford University Press, 1969.

MARATHAS--(PI XX)--The name of a people occupying the
region of the Western Ghats in India.

MARATHON--(PP-Return)--In Greece, the location of the
Battle of Marathon (490 B.C.), the result of which was announced at Athens by a runner who fell dead on his arrival
with the news of the Greek victory. It is also a race of
approximately 26 miles and one of the events of the modern
Olympic games.

MARCUS AURELIUS--(Alex II, 1)--Marcus Aurelius Antoninus
(orig.: Marcus Annius Verus), A.D. 121-180.   Emperor of
Rome, 161-180.   He was the nephew of Antonius Pius by
whom he was adopted.   He was, perhaps, the most eminent
of all Stoic (q.v.) philosophers.   He was gentle of character
and possessed of a broad and deep learning.   Nevertheless,
he vigorously supported the persecutions of Christians.   He
is the author of Meditations, a collection of precepts of practical morality and much admired by latter-day pagans.

MARGATE--(LJ IX)--A municipal borough and popular watering place in Kent, SE England, on the coast of the Isle of
Thanet about 65 miles E of London.

MARIE ANTOINETTE--(AH-Consol; MT)--Josèphe Jeanne
Marie Antoinette, 1755-1793.   The daughter of Francis I
and Maria Theresa of Austria, and wife of Louis XVI (q.v.).
She was extremely unpopular at the French court and made
many enemies because of her love of luxury and extrava-
gance.   She was executed by the revolutionary mob, but
went to her death with courage and dignity.

MARIE LOUISE--(Collect Ta-Coord)--1791-1847.   Second
wife of Napoleon I (q.v.) and daughter of Francis I and
Maria Theresa of Austria.

MARIUS THE EPICUREAN--(Aspects I)--A philosophical novel (1885) by Walter Pater.   The central figure is a young
Roman nobleman of the time of Marcus Aurelius (q.v.).   He
is drawn to Christianity, but makes no move to formally
embrace it.   His death, nevertheless, is such that the
Christians consider him a martyr.

MARK, SAINT--(Alex I, 2; PI XXXI; PP-St A)--John Mark,
the Evangelist, fellow worker with Paul and Barnabas
("Acts," "Colossians," "Philemon") and traditionally regarded as the author of the second gospel of the New Testament.   His body was said to have been buried at Alexandria
and stolen by the Venetians who placed it in the Cathedral
of Saint Mark.

"MARK ON THE WALL, THE"--A short story by Virginia
Woolf (q.v.) appearing in her collection Monday or Tuesday
(q.v.).   It is, as one critic [James Hafley, The Glass Roof,
1954] puts it "a story about a person thinking about thinking
about thinking."   The central figure concentrates upon a
mark on a wall left by a snail.

MARLBOROUGH--(LJ I)--John Churchill (1st Duke of Marlborough), 1650-1722. An English military man who rose in
the ranks with the help of his sister, the mistress of the
Duke of York [later James II]. He led a complicated life
suited to the political involvements of the times but was careful enough to choose the correct side and subsequently was
created Duke of Marlborough by Queen Anne.

MARLOW--(Aspects VII)--A character appearing in two books
by Joseph Conrad (q.v.): Lord Jim (1900) and Heart of
Darkness (1902). In the second he is an impartial observer
who learns about himself by analyzing Kurtz and, in the
first, he sympathizes with Jim's plight and tries to help him.

MARS--(LJ XIII)--Mars, the Roman god of war. He is identified with the Greek Ares. He was also worshipped as the
patron of farmers.

MARS--(AH-My W)--One of the planets revolving about the
Sun so called because of its reddish color suggesting war
and the shedding of blood appropriate to the god of war.

MARSYAS--(GLD XII)--In Greek myth, a flute player who
challenged Apollo (q.v.) to a contest of skill and was beaten
by the god. For his presumption, he was skinned alive.
The river Marsyas arose from his flowing blood.

MARVELL--(AH-TS)--Andrew Marvell, 1621-1678. English
poet of the Metaphysical School of poetry noted for his ability to combine intellectualism with lyricism. He was one
time assistant to Milton (q.v.) who was then Latin secretary
to the Commonwealth. T. S. Eliot (q.v.) is responsible for
awakening interest in his work in the 20th century. Some
of his better known poems are "To His Coy Mistress" and
"The Garden."

MARX--(AH-Roger; Two Cheers-Bishop; Two Cheers-George)
--Karl Marx, 1818-1883. A German political philosopher
who formulated the philosophical basis for communism in
his three volume Das Kapital (1867, 1855, 1895) which was
completed by Frederick Engels.

MARXISM--(Two Cheers-Last)--Generally the name applied
to the doctrine of philosophical socialism taught by Karl
Marx (q.v.).

MARY--(Alex I, 2)--The virgin mother of Jesus Christ and premier saint of the Roman Catholic and Orthodox Faiths.

MARY, QUEEN--(AH-Our Div)--The individual Forster alludes to is Victoria Mary of Teck, the wife of George V (q.v.) and grandmother of Queen Elizabeth II.

MASARYK--(Nordic)--Thomas Garrigue Masaryk, 1850-1937. Czechoslovak statesman and philosopher. He was a professor at the University of Prague and agitated for the independence of his country from Austria. He gained his dream at the end of World War I and was elected its first President, 1918-1935.

MASEFIELD--(Reading)--John Masefield, 1878-1967. English poet, playwright and writer of fiction. He was England's laureate from 1930. Perhaps his most notable work is his Salt Water Ballads (1902).

MASOOD, SYED ROSS--(Hill; Two Cheers-Syed)--See: Forster's essay, "Syed Ross Masood," in Two Cheers for Democracy.

MASTER OF BALLANTRAE, THE--(Aspects I)--A novel (1889) by Robert Louis Stevenson. It is the story of the hatred which exists between two brothers narrated by John Mackellar, steward of Ballantrae.

MASTER BUILDER, THE--(AH-Ibsen)--A play (1892) by Henrik Ibsen (q.v.). Halvard Solness is the "Master Builder." He is drunk with the success he has achieved yet fearful of the rivalry of younger and better-trained men. In an attempt to out-distance them, he completes the best building he is capable of and dies when he falls from one of its towers.

MATILDA, COUNTESS--(WAFT II)--Matilda of Tuscany, 1046 1115. She was known as the "great countess." At the height of her power, she ruled over much of Northern Italy as well as Tuscany. She supported the Pope in his struggle with the emperor of the Holy Roman Empire (q.v.).

MAU--(PI XX)--A town in Eastern Uttar Pradesh, India on a tributary of the Ganges River some 55 miles NE of Varanasi [Bengres, q.v.].

MAUGHAM--(Two Cheers-English)--William Somerset Maugham, 1874-1965. English novelist, writer of short stories, playwright and critic. He studied medicine but never practiced it. Despite a rather austere beginning, he was a generally popular and well-paid author whose popularity, though it has waned, is once again on the rise. Some of his more popular works are Of Human Bondage (1915), The Moon and Sixpence (1919), and The Razor's Edge (1944). There is also a collected edition of his short stories.

MAUGRAS--(Two Cheers-Fer)--Gaston Maugras, 1850-1927. Co-author (with L. Perey) of La Vie Intime de Voltaire.

MAURICE, FREDERICK DENISON--(Aspects VI; GLD)--John Frederick Denison Maurice, 1805-1872. An English theologian of the Broad Church party and founder of Christian Socialism.

MAUROIS, ANDRÉ--(Aspects III)--Pseudonym of Emile Salomon Wilhelm Herzog, 1885-1967. A French writer who worked with the British forces during World War I, he is especially known for his biographies of Shelley (1923) and Byron (1930).

MAURON, CHARLES--(Aspects; Two Cheers-Fer; Two Cheers-Not)--Forster's "friend" in the essay, "Ferney" (Two Cheers for Democracy); he is also the Charles Mauron to whom Forster dedicated his Aspects of the Novel. He is an author (e.g., Aesthetics and Psychology, 1935) and translator of English works into French.

MAX--(AH-Ron)--See: Max Beerbohm.

MAXWELL, GENERAL--(Egypt)--Sir John Grenfell Maxwell, 1859-1929. A British officer who saw service under Kitchener in Egypt (1892-1900). He was also military Governor of Pretoria in South Africa.

MAZZINI, GIUSEPPE--(AS; GLD VIII)--1805-1872. An Italian patriot who struggled for the unification of Italy into a republic. He suffered exile and imprisonment for his activities and, when Italy was united as a kingdom, he refused a seat in its parliament remaining a republican to the end.

MEAKINS, ALICE--(AH-HOS)--A character in Belchamber by H. O. Sturgis. She is a governess who marries well.

MEDEA--(Alex I, 1; LJ IV)--In Greek legend, a sorceress, daughter of Ates, king of Colchis. She married Jason (q. v.), the leader of the Argonauts, whom she helped to obtain the golden fleece, and was the mother of Medus whom the Greeks regarded as the ancestor of the Medes.

MEDICI--(AH-Capt)--In Italian, the name means doctors or physicians. It is the name of a powerful Italian family which ruled Florence from the 14th to the 16th centuries. They were patrons of art and literature.

MEDICI, CATHERINE DE'--(Hill; MT)--1519-1589. The daughter of Lorenzo de' Medici (q. v.) she married Henry of France and became his queen (1547). She had four sons, three of whom became kings. She exerted great influence during the reigns of her sons.

MEDICI, COSIMO DE'--(AH-Gem)--1389-1464. The son of Giovanni de' Medici and patron of the arts. He gave refuge in Florence, where he ruled for some 30 years, to Greek scholars who fled Constantinople after its fall (1453). He is the grandfather of Lorenzo il Magnifico (q. v.).

MEDICI, LORENZO DE'--(RWV VI)--See: Lorenzo il Magnifico.

MEDICI, PIERO DE'--(AH-Jo)--1414-1469. Son of Cosimo (q. v.) and father of Lorenzo il Magnifico (q. v.).

MEDUSA--(LJ XX; Two Cheers-John)--In Greek myth, she is the child of the Gorgons. Legend says that she was a beautiful maiden, especially famous for her hair. She violated the temple of Athene (q. v.). In anger, the goddess transformed her hair into serpents and made her face so horrible that all who looked upon it were turned to stone. Assisted by Athene, Perseus struck off her head and rescued Andromeda. Medusa was the mother of Poseidon, of Chrysaor, and Pegasus.

MEDWAY, THE--(AH-Consol)--A river in SE England about 60 miles long which flows into the Thames.

MEISTERSINGER--(AH-Word)--Die Meistersinger von Nürnberg (1868). An opera by Richard Wagner (q. v.). The daughter of the town goldsmith is promised in marriage to the winner of the singing contest. Walter is loved by the maid, but is hampered because he is unaware of the petty rules which govern the contest. Hans Sachs, the cobbler, helps him and he wins the song-fest and the girl.

MELCHITE--(PP-Tim)--The name of a rite used by the Byzantine Catholics. They are found (the Melkites) mainly in Egypt, Syria and Israel.

MELETIUS--(PP-St. A)--d. A.D. 381. He was bishop of Antioch and orthodox in doctrine. As a result, he was attacked by the Arians (q.v.). He died while presiding over the Council of Constantinople.

MELPOMENE--(Two Cheers-John)--In Greek myth, the muse of tragedy. See: Muses.

MELVILLE, HERMAN--(Aspects I; AH-TE; Hill; Two Cheers-Enchanted; Two Cheers-English)--1819-1891. An American novelist, he shipped to the South Seas and deserted at the Marquesa Islands. He found refuge among cannibals. He also enlisted in the United States Navy. These experiences he wove into Typee (1846), Omoo (1847), Mardi (1849), Redburn (1849), White-Jacket (1850), and his 1851 masterpiece, Moby Dick (q.v.).

MEMENTO MORI--(Two Cheers-Anon)--Latin: "remember that you must die"; also, an object serving as a reminder of death.

MENAS, SAINT--(Alex I, 2; PP-Sol)--A young Egyptian officer who was martyred during his service in Asia Minor because he would not abandon his faith in Christ (A.D. 298). When the army moved back to Egypt, some of his friends brought his ashes with them. At the entrance to the Libyan desert, a miracle occurred. The camel carrying the ashes would go no farther. The saint was buried and forgotten. A shepherd later observed that a sick lamb which had crossed a certain spot became well. Then a sick princess was healed. The remains were exhumed and a church built over them.

MENDEL, GREGOR--(Two Cheers-Racial)--Gregor Johann Mendel, 1822-1884. An Austrian botanist and Augustinian priest. He is known for the discovery and formulation of the law, named after him, which governs inherited characteristics.

MENDELSSOHN--(Collect Ta-Celest; HE V; Nordic; Two
Cheers-Raison)--Jacob Ludwig Felix Mendelssohn-Bartholdy,
1809-1847.   Known as Felix Mendelssohn.   He added the
name Bartholdy after his conversion to Christianity.   He
was a German composer, pianist, and conductor.   He gave
impetus to the revival of interest in Bach (q.v.) and composed five symphonies as well as many overtures, concertos, operas, and other works.

MENDELSSOHN, ERICH--(Nordic)--1887-1953.   German Ex-
pressionistic architect whose buildings' forms symbolized
their purposes.   He settled in England after being driven
from Germany by the Nazis (q.v.).

MENELAUS--(PP-Ph)--In Greek legend, the son of Arteus
and brother of Agamemnon (q.v.) and husband of Helen (q.v.)
whose desertion of him led to the Trojan War.   He was king
of Sparta or Lacedaemon.

MENES--(AH-Gem)--c. 3400 B.C.   First king of the first
Egyptian dynasty.   He united upper and lower Egypt into one
kingdom.

"MENINAS, LAS"--(Two Cheers-Not)--The title of a painting
("The Maids of Honor," 1656) by Diego Rodriguez de Silva
y Velásquez.   It hangs in the Prado Museum, Madrid, and
is considered the supreme masterpiece in group painting.

MENOU, GENERAL--(Alex II, 1)--Baron Jacques François
de Menou, 1750-1810.   French soldier in the revolution and
officer in Napoleon's army.   After the death of Kleber (1800),
he commanded the Napoleonic army in Egypt, but was defeated at Alexandria by the British, March 1, 1801.

MEPHISTOPHELES--(Collect Ta-Co-ord; GLD IX; Two
Cheers-Raison)--Another name for Satan.   The name appears
in the German Faustbuch of 1587.   Faust sells his soul to
the evil spirit who bears that name.

MERCHANT OF VENICE, THE--(Reading)--A play (1600) by
William Shakespeare (q.v.).   Antonio pledges a pound of his
flesh to Shylock as a bond to aid his friend, Bassanio.   When
the loan cannot be repaid, Shylock demands Antonio forfeit
the bond.   Antonio is saved by Portia's shrewd argument at
court.

MEREDITH--(AH-Ab; AH-HOS; AH-TS; Aspects III; GLD X;
LJ VII; New Disorder; Two Cheers-Art; Two Cheers-Last;
Two Cheers-Virginia)--1828-1909. An English novelist,
grandson of a prosperous tailor, he was articled to a solicitor but turned to journalism instead of the law. In 1858,
his wife, the daughter of Thomas Love Peacock, deserted
him. His first great novel was The Ordeal of Richard
Feverel (q. v.). He soon became acquainted with the great
writers of the day and was employed as a reader for Chapman and Hall, the publishers, remaining with them until
1894. Some of his other novels are The Egoist (q. v.), and
Diana of the Crossways (q. v.).

MERIMÉE, PROSPER--(Two Cheers-George)--1803-1870.
French dramatist and novelist. He is, perhaps, best known
as the author of Carmen which inspired Bizet's opera.

MERLIN--(Collect-Ta-Road)--A magician in the Arthurian
legend. His mother was a nun. He made the Round Table
for Uther Pendragon, Arthur's father, and was Arthur's tutor.

MERRILIES, MEG--(MT)--An old gypsy in Guy Mannering
(1815) by Sir Walter Scott (q. v.). She plays a major role
in the kidnapping which is crucial to the plot.

MESSIAH--(GLD V)--An oratorio by Handel (q. v.), first performed in Dublin in 1742. It has a libretto, drawn from the
Bible, by C. Jennens.

MEYERBEER--(Nordic)--Giacomo Meyerbeer, 1791-1864. An
opera composer of Jewish descent born in Berlin. His most
successful works are Les Huguenots (1836), Le Prophète
(1842), and L'Africaine (1865).

MIAMI, EDNA--(AH-Ron)--A character in Prancing Nigger
(1924) by Ronald Firbank (q. v.).

MICAWBER, MR.--(Aspects IV)--A character in the novel
David Copperfield (1849-50), by Charles Dickens (q. v.). He
is the agent for Mudstone and Grinley. He is good natured
and stout and is possessed of an enormous family. David
boards with him and his family which is always on the verge
of utter ruin. Mr. Micawber, however, is perpetually waiting for "something to come up." He is the individual who
exposes the machinations of Uriah Heep (q. v.). Many critics
consider him the masterpiece of Dicken's comic characters.

MICAWBER, MRS.--(Aspects IV)--A character in David Copperfield (1849-50) by Charles Dickens (q.v.). She is the
wife of Mr. Micawber (q.v.). She is a trim and faded lady,
not at all young, who dotes upon her husband and presents
him with a great number of children.

MICHAEL, SAINT--(Alex II, 4)--An archangel, the warrior
of God. He is most often depicted with wings and sword in
hand slaying a dragon, Satan.

MICHEL, LOUISE--(AH-Wil)--Clémence Louise Michel, 1830-
1905. A French anarchist, she took an active part in the
Commune of Paris in 1871 and, as a result, was deported
to New Caledonia. She returned to Paris in 1880 and once
again took up her subversive activities. She received a
prison term of six years.

MICHELANGELO--(AH-Car; AH-Jo; Alex I, 1; Two Cheers-
Not)--Michelangelo Buonarroti, 1475-1564. An Italian painter
sculptor, architect, poet. He was apprenticed to Ghirlandaio
and lived in the palace of Lorenzo de' Medici (q.v.) for a
time. His most important works, e.g., the paintings in the
Sistine Chapel and the plans for St. Peter's, were done for
Pope Julius II.

MICKEY MOUSE--(AH-Our Div)--The hero of a long series
of animated cartoons by Walt Disney (q.v.). He is a self-
confident, sprightly, level-headed mouse. His leading lady
is Minnie Mouse.

MINNIE MOUSE--(AH-Our Div)--See: Mickey Mouse.

MICROMEGAS--(AH-Vo)--A philosophical tale by Voltaire
(q.v.) in imitation of Swift's Gulliver's Travels (q.v.).

MIDAS--(Collect Ta-Other)--A semi-legendary king of Phry-
gia who, having entertained Silenus well, was asked by the
god Dionysius (q.v.) what gift he wished as a reward. He
begged that everything he touched would turn to gold. His
prayer was answered, but soon he begged the god to be relieved of the gift.

MIDDLETON, CLARA--(Aspects VIII; LJ IX)--See: Clara.

MIDDLETON, LADY--(AH-JA)--A character in Sense and
Sensibility (1811) by Jane Austen (q.v.). She is the wife of
Sir John Middleton and kind to the Dashwoods.

MILK OF PARADISE--(Two Cheers-Fo)--Subtitled: Some
Thoughts on Poetry, London: Faber and Faber, 1946. The
last book by Forrest Reid (q. v.). It consists of a series of
informal discussions of poetry with extensive attention to the
poetry of A. E. (q. v.), John Clare, and Wordsworth (q. v.),
among others.

MILL, JOHN STUART--(GLD IX; Two Cheers-Henry)--1806-
1873. An English economist-philosopher. He was a junior
clerk in India House and an early disciple of the principle of
Utilitarianism formulated by Jeremy Bentham (q. v.). He later modified his views on that philosophy. His chief works
are "System of Logic" (1843) and Principles of Political
Economy (1848).

MILL ON THE FLOSS, THE--(Aspects I)--A novel (1860) by
George Eliot (q. v.). Tom and Maggie are the children of
the miller of Dorlcotte Mill on the Floss. Maggie falls in
love with Philip Wakem, the deformed son of a neighboring
lawyer. Their father dislikes the elder Wakem, and when,
through a law suit, he becomes a bankrupt, his feelings for
Wakem Senior turn to hatred. This hatred forces Maggie
and Philip to part and leads to a rupture in her affections
for her brother. Tom recognizes her true worth only moments before the two are drowned in a flood.

MILLS, SELINA--(AH-Mrs)--Sister of Hannah More (q. v.),
wife of Zachary Macaulay (q. v.).

MILLY--(Aspects VIII)--A character in Wings of the Dove
(1902) by Henry James (q. v.). Bright, vivacious, and
charming, Mildred Theale is the "dove" who comes to
Europe to learn how to live. She dies there of an incur-
able disease, the only surviving member of a wealthy New
York family of six.

MILNER, ALFRED--(Egypt)--1st Viscount Milner, 1854-1925.
A British statesman. He was administrator in South Africa,
Governor of the Cape of Good Hope (1897-1901), Governor of
the Transvaal and Orange River Colonies (1902-05), among
other posts. He was created a baron (1901) and subsequently a viscount (1919). He headed the mission to Egypt which
recommended independence for that country (1919).

MILNES, MONCKTON--(Two Cheers-Lon Lib)--Richard
Monkton Milnes, (1st Baron Houghton), 1809-1885. An English writer and editor, he was educated at Trinity College,

Cambridge where he was the friend of Tennyson (q.v.), Hallam (q.v.), and Thackeray (q.v.). He became active politically and wrote on political subjects. He also wrote poetry (Poetical Works, 1876) and was the first to champion Keats (q.v.) as a great poet.

MILTON--(AH-Liberty; Aspects III; LJ X; MT; Nordic; Two Cheers-Bishop; Two Cheers-In; Two Cheers-Raison; Two Cheers-Ter)--John Milton, 1608-1674. One of England's greatest poets. He was educated at Christ's College, Cambridge where he wrote the remarkable "Ode on the Morning of Christ's Nativity" (1629) and other poems of almost equal merit. In 1632 he produced "L'Allegro" and "Il Penseroso" (q.v.). He plunged into the politics of the day which were chiefly religious in nature. He wrote the famous Areopagitica, (q.v.), (1644) on liberty of the press and cast his lot in with the Parliamentarians, becoming Latin Secretary to the Commonwealth. He retired, completely blind, at the Restoration. He completed his masterpiece, Paradise Lost (1667, 1674) during this period.

MINIVER, MRS.--(Two Cheers-Mrs.)--Central figure in the novel of the same name (q.v.) by Jan Struther (q.v.).

MIRABEAU--(Collect Ta-Machine; GLD IX)--Honoré Gabriel Victor Ricqueti (Comte de Mirabeau), 1749-1791. French Revolutionary hero and orator. He was, perhaps, the most important individual in the first two years of the Revolution (q.v.). He exerted great influence in the National Assembly through his oratory and believed strongly in a limited or constitutional monarchy.

MIRBEAU, OCTAVE--(AH-Salute)--1850-1917. A French dramatist, novelist, and journalist. He was a radical who attracted attention by the violence in his writings. His Oeuvres Complêtes (9 vols., 1934-1936) were published in Paris. There is a study by M. Renon, Paris, 1924.

MITFORD, MARY RUSSELL--(AH-Troop)--1786-1855. Born in Hampshire, her father was a doctor fallen on financial troubles. She turned to writing for financial stability and wrote copiously (poetry, tragedies: Julian, 1823; Rienzi, 1828; etc.; essays). Her Life appeared in 1870.

MITYA--(Aspects VII)--A character in The Brothers Karamazov (q.v.), by Feodor Dostoevsky (q.v.). It is the diminutive used for Dimitri Karamazov, the oldest son of

Feodor Pavlovitch Karamazov.   He most resembles his father in temperament.   He fears his own heredity and broods
upon the wrongs done to him and his mother by his father.

MOBY DICK--(AH-TE; Aspects I; Two Cheers-Eng)--A novel
(1851) by Herman Melville (q.v.) which tells of one, Ahab,
who seeks to revenge himself upon the white whale which
took his leg.   As a consequence, he destroys himself, his
ship, and all of his crew saving Ishmael (q.v.), the narrator.

MODENA--(RWV III)--A city 200 miles NNW of Rome known
for its manufacture of silks, woolens, leather, and glass.
An ancient Etruscan city, it was a colony of Rome in 183
B.C.

MODERN EGYPT--(Egypt)--A history of Egypt in the 19th
century in two volumes (London, 1908) by Lord Cromer (q.v.).

MOGUL EMPIRE--(PI VII)--An empire located in northern
India and ruled by the Mogul (Mughul) dynasty (1526-1858).

MOHAMMED--(AH-Wil; Alex I)--A.C. 570-632.   The founder
of the Islam faith who was born in Mecca.   He married a
rich widow and became a merchant.   He was disturbed about
the condition of the Arabs: their superstition and ignorance.
After years of meditation, he had a call as a prophet and
teacher of his people.   His followers were persecuted, but
the faith spread.   His teaching is embodied in the Koran
(q.v.).

MOHAMMED ALI--(Alex I, 5; Egypt)--1769-1849.   This is
the individual Forster is referring to when he talks of the
founder of the reigning Egyptian house.   He was born in
Kavalla, Rumelia, of Albanian parents.   He was appointed
Viceroy of Egypt (1805-1848).   To secure his position, he
massacred the Mameluks and, as a result, was left without
a rival.   His declining years were marked by a weakening
of his mind.   More of him and his exploits are recorded
in Cairo: Biography of a City (Boston, 1969) by James Al-
drige.

MOLL FLANDERS--(Aspects III; Two Cheers-Lon)--An excellent summary of the plot of this novel by Daniel Defoe
(q.v.) is offered in the third chapter of Aspects of the Novel.
(See also: Flanders, Moll.)

MONASTERIES OF THE LEVANT--(Alex II, 7)--By Robert
Curzon, 14th Baron Zouche (q. v.). The full title: Visits to
Monasteries in the Levant, it is a "gentleman's book" des-
cribing the author's visits to the Convent of the Pulley, the
White Monastery, the monasteries on the Island of Philae,
the Monastery of St. Saba (Jerusalem), the monasteries of
Meteora, and the monasteries of Mt. Athos. The volume
was first published in 1849 and reprinted five times.

MONCRIEFF, SCOTT--(AH-Proust)--Charles Kenneth Michael
Scott-Moncrieff, 1889-1930. Scottish translator and officer
in the Scottish Borderers during World War I. His translations include Song of Roland (1914), Beowulf (1921), and the
works of Stendhal, Pirandello, as well as Proust (q. v.), to
which Forster refers.

MONDAY OR TUESDAY--(Two Cheers-Virginia)--A collection
(1921) of eight short stories by Virginia Woolf: "Kew Gardens (q. v.)," "A Society," "The Mark on the Wall (q. v.)," "An
Unwritten Novel," "A Haunted House," "Blue and Green,"
"Monday or Tuesday," and "The String Quartet."

MONET--(HE V; Two Cheers-Not Looking)--Claude Monet,
1840-1926. A French Impressionist painter of landscapes
recognized as the greatest painter of the school. His studies
of water lilies, executed late in his career, hang in New
York's Museum of Modern Art. Examples of his work are
in any museum worthy of the name.

MONISM--(AH-Wil)--A religious and a philosophical doctrine
which holds that there exists only one form of ultimate reality or substance: mind or matter.

MONOPHYSITE--(PP-Tim)--See: Monophysitism.

MONOPHYSITISM--(Alex I, 3)--The religious and the philosophical doctrine that the divine and the human in Christ
constitute only one nature, either composite or thoroughly
unified.

MOSQUE OF AMR--(Two Cheers-Last)--The Amr Ibn el 'As
Mosque in the old section of Cairo. It was built by Amr
(q. v.) in the A. D. 600's.

MONTAGU, MRS. --(AH-Mrs; MT)--Elizabeth Montagu, née
Robinson, 1720-1800. An English writer, she maintained a
salon in Mayfair which became the center of the literary and

social life of London.   Dr. Johnson (q.v.) praised her con-
versation.   Her chief work is Writings and Genius of Shakespeare (1769).

MONTAIGNE--(Nordic; Two Cheers-Tol; Two Cheers-What)--
Michel Eyquem de Montaigne, 1533-1592.   A French writer
who developed the form known as the essay, named after his
work Essais (1571-1580).   These essays reflect a spirit of
scepticism and wielded an important influence on French and
English literature, serving as a rallying point for those of
similar mind.

MONTERIANO--(WAFT I)--A fictional Italian town, the scene
of much of the action of Forster's novel Where Angels Fear
to Tread.   Wilfred Stone (The Cave and the Mountain, 1966)
credits San Gimignano as the original.

MONTEVERDI--(Two Cheers-Raison)--Claudio Monteverdi,
1567-1643.   An Italian composer of music who became a
priest (1633).   He made many innovations in musical composition including the development and elaboration of the reci-
tative in opera.   He wrote many operas including Orfeo
(1607), and L'Incoronazione di Poppea (1642).

MONTGOMERY, ROBERT--(MT)--1807-1855.   An English
poet who wrote Omnipresence of the Deity (1828) and other
works of not much merit.   He owes much to the fact
that Macaulay (q.v.) gave him a type of immortality by trying to destroy his reputation as a poet in the pages of The
Edinburgh Review.

MONTHELITISM--(Alex I, 3)--A religious and philosophical
doctrine related to monophysitism (q.v.) which asserts that
the human and divine natures of Christ are united in a single
will.

MOTHER, THE--(Nordic)--Matka (1938), an anti-fascist
Czech play by Karel Capek (q.v.).

MONTPENSIER, MADEMOISELLE DE--(MT)--Anne Marie
Louise d'Orleans (Duchesse de Montpensier), 1627-1693.
She was known as la Grande Mademoiselle.   The daughter
of Gaston d'Orleans and opposed by Cardinal Mazarin, she
aided Condé in the revolt of the Fronde (1651-1652), and
commanded one of the armies.   As a result, she was banished from court.   She also had a somewhat violent love

affair with the Duc de Lauzun.   Her Mémoirs were published
in 1729.

"MOONLIGHT SONATA"--(GLD II)--The popular name for
Beethoven's (q.v.) piano sonata in C sharp minor, Opus 27,
no. 2 (1801), not applied by him, and, some musicologists
maintain, suiting only the first movement.

MOORE, G. E.--(GLD X)--George Edward Moore, 1873-
1958.   An English philosopher and author of Principia Ethica
(1903), Philosophical Studies (1903) and other works on philosophy.

MOORE, GEORGE--(Two Cheers-English)--1852-1933.   An
Irish novelist who studied art in Paris but left it for poetry
(Pagan Poems, 1882) and journalism.   His first novels
showed the strong influence of Flaubert and Zola: e.g., A
Modern Lover, 1883; and A Mummer's Wife, 1885.   His
first real recognition came with Esther Waters (1894).

MORE, MRS. HANNAH--(AH-Ba; AH-JA; AH-Mrs; MT)--
1745-1833.   An English writer of religious works.   She first
came to the attention of readers with The Search After Happiness (1762), a pastoral drama.   She came to London (1774)
and became part of the circle of Dr. Johnson (q.v.).   She
wrote two dramas produced by Garrick (q.v.), but after his
death came to believe that drama was evil and turned to
writing tracts, chiefly social and religious.   She joined with
Zachary Macaulay (q.v.) and William Wilberforce (q.v.) in
their evangelical views.

MORGAN, PIERPONT--(HE XXVII)--John Pierpont Morgan,
1837-1913.   An American banker and financier, he was a
lover of art and a collector of rare books housed in an ex-
quisite library in New York's Murray Hill district.   In the
world of finance, he is best known for his railroad financing
after the crash of 1893 on behalf of the government.

MORGAN, WILLIAM FREND DE--(AH-Word-Making)--1839-
1917.   An English novelist and artist in association with the
Pre-Raphaelite circle.   He experimented with stained glass
and other decorative arts.   He also devoted himself to cer-
amics and rediscovered the process of making brilliant blue
and green glazes.   On his retirement, he turned to writing
novels (e.g., Joseph Vance, 1906; Somehow Good, 1908; and
When Ghost Meets Ghost, 1914).   He was called the "modern
Dickens."

MORIAH--(Two Cheers-What)--The mountain upon which Isaac
was to be sacrificed ("Genesis" xxii:2). Its meaning is uncertain. It is probably not a name but merely a description,
i. e., "high land" or a "high place." It is also the name of
the hill upon which Solomon built his temple.

MORLAND, CATHERINE--(AH-JA)--A character in Northanger Abbey (1818), by Jane Austen (q. v.). She is a young
impressionable girl who has read too many Gothic novels.
Filled with these romances, she makes many humorous mistakes when she is visiting Northanger Abbey.

MORMONISM--(Two Cheers-Mount)--The name given to the
religious and social system of the Latter Day Saints (Mor-
mons).

MORRIS, WILLIAM--(AH-Note; Two Cheers-Does)--1834-
1896. An English writer, socialist, fine arts craftsman,
typographer, and member of the Pre-Raphaelite (q. v.) group.
His first book of poetry was The Defence of Guenevere and
Other Poems (1858). His prose was filled with more social
consciousness. There has been a recent study of him by
Philip Henderson (New York, 1967).

MOSES--(PP-Eliza; Two Cheers-Duke)--The Hebrew prophet
and law-giver of the Bible who led the Israelites out of
Egypt to the promised land (Exodus).

MOSLEY, SIR OSWALD--(AH-Liberty)--Sir Oswald Ernald
Mosley, 1896- . He is the organizer of the British Union
of Fascists. He was placed in protective custody by the
British government during World War II.

MOUSEION [MUSEUM] OF ALEXANDRIA--(Alex I, 1)--It
was established by Ptolemy Soter (q. v.) along the lines of
the Athenian Mouseion which had contained the library of
Aristotle. Its first librarian was Demitrius Palerius, an
Aristotelian. It soon diverged widely from its model, being
richer and larger, and became essentially an institution of
the royal court. In some ways it resembled a modern university with the exception that its scientists and literary men
were never obliged to teach. Their only obligation was the
pursuit of their studies. The most famous division of the
mouseion was its library of some 500,000 books which were
catalogued in 120 volumes.

MOUTH FAMILY--(AH-Ron)--Characters in the novel, The Prancing Nigger (1924), by Ronald Firbank (q. v.).

MOZART--(Aspects VI; GLD V; RWV XVIII; Two Cheers-C; Two Cheers-Virginia)--Wolfgang Amadeus Mozart, 1756-1791. An Austrian composer of operas, symphonies, concerti, etc. His best known operas are Don Giovanni, Le Nozze di Figaro (The Marriage of Figaro), and the Magic Flute.

"MR. BENNETT AND MRS. BROWN"--(AH-Early)--An essay (1924) by Virginia Woolf (q. v.) which originated as "a paper to be read to the Heretics, Cambridge, on May 18, 1924." Essentially, it is an attack on the methods of H. G. Wells (q. v.) and Arnold Bennett (q. v.), and other popular novelists.

MRS. DALLOWAY--(AH-Early)--An almost plotless novel (1925) by Virginia Woolf (q. v.) set in London on a June day, 1923.   The novel records the emotions and memories of the characters within the framework of a party which Mrs. Dalloway is giving.

MUCKLEBACKIT, ELSPETH--(Aspects II)--A character in the novel, The Antiquary (q. v.), by Sir Walter Scott (q. v.). She was the mother of Saunders and a confidential servant of the countess of Glenallen.   Hating what was hated by her mistress, it was she who suggested the lie by which the countess ruined her son's life.

MUSES--(Aspects V; Two Cheers-Duty; Two Cheers-Raison)-- In Greek myth, the name given to the nine virginal daughters of Zeus (q. v.) and Mnemosyne each of whom is identified with, and is the protectress and the source of, inspiration of an art or science: Calliope, chief of the muses and muse of epic or heroic poetry; Clio, heroic exploits and history; Euteyne, Dionysian music and the double flute; Thalia, gaiety, comedy, pastoral life; Melpomene, song, harmony, tragedy; Terpsichore, choral dance and song; Erato, lyric and erotic poetry and the lyre; Polyhymnia, the stately hymn; Urania, astronomy.

MUSEUM OF ALEXANDRIA--(PP-Ph)--See: Mouseion.

MUSGROVE, LUISA [LOUISA]--(Aspects IV)--A character in the novel Persuasion by Jane Austen (q. v.).   She is the fashionable, happy, and merry, 20-year old sister of Charles Musgrove.   It appears that she will marry Wentworth, especially after she is injured in an accident that he considers his fault.   But, in the end, she marries Captain Benwick instead.

MUSOORIE--(PI XXXI)--A Hill station and sanitorium in Northern Ultar Pradash in India about 135 miles from Delhi. It was once the chief resort of the British during their occupation of India.

MUSSET, ALFRED DE--(Two Cheers-Syed)--Louis Charles Alfred de Musset, 1810-1857.   A French poet who began publishing at an early age.   Like Chopin, he had a grand passion for George Sand (q.v.).

MUSSOLINI--(GLD XIII; Nordic; Two Cheers-Challenge; Two Cheers-Jul; Two Cheers-Letter)--Benito Mussolini, 1883-1945.   An Italian dictator who organized the Fascist party in Italy in 1921 and supervised its growth.   In 1922, he was summoned by the King to form a ministry and, from that point on he ruled as dictator.   He entered World War II on the side of Hitler (q.v.) in May 1940 and was assassinated by Italian partisans, April 28, 1945.   Besides extensive political writings, he was the author of a work on John Huss, a novel, a play, and two volumes of autobiography.

MY DAYS AND DREAMS--(Two Cheers-Edward)--The autobiography of Edward Carpenter (q.v.).   Chapter XI is devoted to his books.

MY GRANDFATHER--(Two Cheers-Bishop)--Forster is referring to Henry Thornton.

MYSHKIN--(Aspects VII)--A character in The Idiot (1868-69) by Feodor Dostoevsky (q.v.).   Prince Nicolaievitch Myshkin is a nobleman whose mind deteriorates during the course of the book.   As it deteriorates, he loses all the petty prejudices which separate men and comes to love all despite their faults.   As a result, he is destroyed by those whom he most loves.

N

NAIAD--(Collect Ta-Other; Collect Ta-Road)--In Greek myth, a nymph of lake, fountain, river, or stream.

NAPIER, SIR CHARLES--(Alex I, 5)--1760-1860. A British naval officer who was influential in bringing to an end the Spanish Civil War by raising the siege of Oporto (1834) and restoring Maria II to the Spanish throne. In 1840, he concluded a convention, on behalf of the British, with Mohammed Ali (q. v.). He commanded the Baltic fleet in the Crimean War (1854), but was removed for his failure to storm Kronshtadt.

NAPLES--(HE VIII)--A city in southern Italy.

NAPOLÉON--(AH-Ba; AH-Notes; AH-Wil; Alex I, 5; Collect Ta-Coord; Egypt; HE XXVII)--Napoléon Bonaparte, 1769-1821. Born a Corsican, he attended military school in Paris and was commissioned a second lieutenant. He played an active role in the French Revolution (q. v.). He married Josephine de Beauharnais by whom he had no children. He was crowned Emperor of France on December 2, 1804, and assumed the title of King of Italy in 1805. As emperor, he planned and executed military campaigns to extend his empire including the ill-fated invasion of Russia. He divorced Josephine and married Marie Louise (q. v.) of Austria. They had one child who was titled Napoléon II. Ultimately, the senior Napoléon was defeated at Waterloo, Belgium, in 1815, by a multinational coalition of European troops led by Wellington (q. v.).

NASH--(Two Cheers-London)--Thomas Nash, 1567-1602. English dramatist and writer of prose noted especially for his participation in the many controversies of the Elizabethan period. In these, he attacked the Puritans. He was one of the "University Wits" and an important personality of his day. Two of his works are Christ's Tears Over Jerusalem (1593), and Lenten Stuff (1599).

NATASHA--(AH-Proust; Aspects II)--A character in the novel War and Peace by Leo Tolstoy. Princess Natasha Rostova is the beautiful daughter of Count Rostov. She becomes engaged to Prince Bolkonsky, but the marriage is postponed. She ruins her prospects for marriage when she attempts to elope with Kuragin. When Bolkonsky is mortally wounded, she nurses him and receives his forgiveness. She later marries Bezuhov.

NATIONAL GALLERY--(HE XLI; RWV X; Two Cheers-Anon)--Located on the north side of Trafalgar Square, London, the main portion of the museum was built 1834-37 from designs by William Wilkers. It houses one of the greatest, richest, and most extensive collections of paintings in the world arranged by national schools.

NATIONAL SOCIALISTS--(Two Cheers-G&G)--See: Nazis.

NAUTILUS--(AH-Sin)--A fictional city in Iowa. Martin Arrowsmith (Arrowsmith, by Sinclair Lewis, q.v.) is forced to accept a post in its health department.

NAZARITES--(MT)--The name given to those among the Hebrews who had taken vows of abstinence. Samson was a Nazarite.

NAZI[S]--(Nordic; Reading; Two Cheers-Volt)--An abbreviation of the German "Nazionalsozialist," the National Socialist German Worker's Party which, with Hitler, seized power in 1933. It is also the name by which its members were known.

NEITH--(Alex II, 1)--In Egyptian myth, a sun-goddess.

NEKHT HERU HEBT--(Alex II, 3)--The name of a native Egyptian pharoah, c. 378 B.C.

NELSON--(AH-TE; Alex I, 5)--Horatio Viscount Nelson, 1758-1805. He entered the British navy in 1770 and lost his right eye in the battle of Calvi, Corsica. He lost his right arm, also in battle, at Santa Cruz. In 1778, he destroyed the French fleet in Abukir Bay. In 1801, he commanded the attack on Copenhagen and was killed at Trafalgar, 1805.

NEPHTYS--(Alex II, 3)--The Greek rendering of the name of the Egyptian goddess Nebthet, "Mistress of the Palace." She was the second daughter of Geb and Nut. From a union with Osiris, her eldest brother, Anubis (q.v.) was born. Nephtys is designated as protectress of the dead.

NEPTUNE--(Alex II, 1; PP-St. A; RWV IV; Two Cheers-Enchanted)--The Roman god of the sea, corresponding to the Greek god, Poseidon. He is generally represented as an elderly and dignified old man, bearded and carrying a trident. Sometimes he is astride a dolphin or a horse.

NERBUDDA--(AH-Emp)--or Narbada. A river about 800 miles in length in central India. It flows W to the Gulf of

Cambay through Bombay. It is second only to the Ganges in
holiness.

NEREID--(AH-JA; Collect Ta-Other; Collect Ta-Story)--In
Greek myth, one of the 50 daughters of Nereus and Doris
who were sea-nymphs (q. v.). The best known of them is
Amphitrit, wife of Poseidon [i. e., Neptune].

NERO--(Two Cheers-John)--Nero Claudius Caesar Drusus
Germanicus (orig.: Lucius Domitius Ahenobarbus), A. D. 37-
68. Roman emperor, 54-68. He was adopted by the Emperor Claudius in the year 50. His mother, Agrippina,
poisoned his step-father, thus permitting him to succeed.
His early years as a ruler were marked by peace and stability. Soon, however, his latent madness began to assert
itself. He murdered his wife and was suspected of burning
Rome. He died a suicide.

NESTORIAN--(PP-Tim; Two Cheers-John)--The name given
to a follower of Nestorius, patriarch of Constantinople (A. D.
428-431) who maintained that Christ had two distinct natures
and that Mary was mother only of His human nature. Nes-
torianism spread as far as China.

"NEVER WILL BE PERFECT" etc. --(Two Cheers-Outsider)--
ℓ ℓ. 12 ff. "Sonnet XXVII" by W. H. Auden (q. v.) as reprinted in Poets of the Present, edited by Geoffrey Grigson
(q. v.), pp. 40-41.

NEVILE, EVELINA--(Aspects II)--A character in The Antiquary (q. v.), by Sir Walter Scott (q. v.). She is the daughter of a cousin of the countess of Glenallan's husband. She
was brought up by the countess and is her intimate friend.
She tries to drown herself after hearing the countess's tale
of her parentage.

NEVILLE--(Two Cheers-Virginia)--A character in The Waves
(1931) by Virginia Woolf. He is a poet and a sensitive genius. He finds it difficult to survive the death of his lover,
Percival.

NEVISON, HENRY--(Two Cheers-Kidd)--Henry W. Nevison, 1856-1941. A British journalist and essayist, and
foreign correspondent of the London Daily Chronicle (1897).
His A Modern Slavery (1906) exposed the slave trade in
Portuguese Angola.

NEWBY, GERALD--(AH-HOS)--A young Cambridge (q.v.)
don in Belchamber by H. O. Sturgis (q.v.).

NEWCASTLE, DUKE OF--(AH-Capt)--Forster is referring to
Thomas Pelham-Holles (1693-1768), 1st Duke of Newcastle
(1715) and son of Sir Thomas Pelham.

THE NEWCOMES--(MT)--A novel (1853-55) by W. M. Thackeray (q.v.). The story revolves about the career of Clive
Newcome, a generous individual, who falls in love with his
cousin, but her grandmother, the countess of Kew, has other
plans for her. In despair, he marries Rosey Mackenzie.
The marriage is a failure. His father's fortune is lost and
the family is reduced to poverty. The book ends with Rosey's
death.

NEWGATE--(Aspects III)--Once the principal western gate of
the City of London. Its gate house was used as a prison
from the 12th century. In 1780, it was rebuilt and, in 1902,
was replaced by the Central Criminal Court.

NEWSOME, MRS.--(Aspects VIII)--The mother of Chadwick
(Chad, q.v.) Newsome in The Ambassadors (q.v.) by Henry
James (q.v.). It is she who sends Strether to Paris to her
son to negotiate his return to the United States.

NEWTON--(AH-Vo)--Sir Isaac Newton, 1642-1727. An English philosopher, physicist, and mathematician who discovered
and codified the laws of gravity about which he wrote in his
Philosophiae Naturalis Principia Mathematica (1687). He was
knighted in 1705 and buried in Westminster.

NICAEA--(Alex I, 2; PP-St. A)--An ancient city in Asia
Minor and the site of the Council of Nicaea (325) which settled the problem of Arianism (q.v.) and developed the creed
known as the Nicene Creed.

NICHOLAS, GRAND DUKE OF RUSSIA--(AH-Jo)--Forster
refers to Nikolai Nikolaevich (1831-1891), Russian grand
duke and third son of Czar Nicholas I. He commanded the
Russian Army of the Danube in the Russo-Turkish War.

NICHOLS, ROBERT--(GLD XIV)--Robert Malise Bowyer
Nichols, 1893-1944. English poet and dramatist. Author of
three volumes of poetry: Invocation (1915), Ardours and
Endurances (1917), and Aurelia (1920); of plays including
Guilty Souls (1922); of philosophical tales, and other works.

NICHOLSON, WILLIAM--(Two Cheers-Webb)--1781-1844.
Scottish portrait painter and etcher.

NICIAS--(Aspects VIII)--A character in Thais (q. v.).

NICOLAY--(AH-Proust; Aspects II)--Count Nikolay Rostov,
the handsome brother of Natasha (q. v.) in War and Peace
(q. v.) by Leo Tolstoy (q. v.). He marries Princess Marya
Bolkonskaya and not Sonya as everyone expects.

NIEBELUNG'S RING--(Nordic; Two Cheers-What)--See: Ring
of the Niebelung.

NIETZSCHE--(AH-Two; Aspects V; HE XXVII; RWV XII; Two
Cheers-Mohammed; Two Cheers-What)--Friedrich Wilhelm
Nietzsche, 1844-1900. German poet and philosopher. He
was professor of classical philology at Basel, and an opponent of Schopenhauer and Wagner (q. v.). He denounced religion and developed the doctrine of the perfectibility of man
through forcible self-assertion and glorification of the super-
man. His theories influenced the Nazis.

NIGERIA--(HE III)--At the time Forster wrote Howards End,
Nigeria (Western Africa) was a British colony and protecto-
rate. It became a dominion in the British Commonwealth,
October 1, 1960.

NIGHT AND DAY--(AH-Early; Two Cheers-Vir)--The least
experimental novel (1919) of Virginia Woolf (q. v.). It is
also her longest novel. Set in upper-middle class London,
the work treats of Katherine Hilbery's decision not to marry
William Rodney and her deliberate overturning of the mores
of her society to marry the lower-middle class Ralph Denham.

NIGHTINGALE, FLORENCE--(MT)--1820-1910. The founder
of modern nursing. She is famous for the nursing services
she provided during the Crimean War and the revolutionary
reforms she instituted in Army hospitals.

"NIL MIHI RESCRIBERIS ALTERAM IPSE VENI"--(MT)--
Latin: You would not have answered my letter, so I came.

1984--(Two Cheers-George)--A novel (1949) by George Orwell. It is a story of totalitarianism in the future and one
man's futile struggle against it and his subsequent defeat.

NINTH SYMPHONY--(AH-My Own; AH-Word)--The "Choral Symphony" by Beethoven (q.v.), No. 9 in D minor, first performed in 1824. It has three purely orchestral movements followed by a setting of "Ode to Joy" by Schiller, for four solo singers, chorus, and orchestra.

NIOBE--(LJ XIX)--The personification, in Greek legend, of maternal sorrow. Niobe was the daughter of Tantalus and the wife of Amphion, king of Thebes. She was the mother of 12 children and taunted Latona who had only two: Apollo (q.v.) and Diana (q.v.). Latona commanded her children to avenge the insult and they caused Niobe's children to die. As a result of her sorrow, she wept herself to death. The gods, taking pity on her, changed her into a stone from which water ran.

NIRVANA--(AH-Two)--Literally "nothingness." In Buddhist myth, it is the end of personal existence and the absorption of the soul into the supreme spirit.

NOAH--(AH-Vo)--The Hebrew patriarch, son of Lamech, and hero of the deluge ("Genesis" v:29 ff).

NOAKS--(Aspects VI)--A poor student in Zuleika Dobson (1911) by Max Beerbohm (q.v.). Zuleika thinks that she can love him because he does not love her. He is in love with Katie Batch for whom he kills himself when he thinks she does not love him.

"NON FATE GUERRA AL MAGGIO"--(RWV VI)--Italian: Do not make war with May.

NORTHAMPTONSHIRE--(PI XXVIII)--A county in central England. Its chief urban center is Northampton.

NORTH DOWNS--(HE XIV)--A range of low hills across south central England. Leith Hill is the highest point.

NORTHANGER ABBEY--(Two Cheers-Anon)--A novel (1818) by Jane Austen (q.v.). Catherine Moreland (q.v.), daughter of a well-to-do clergyman, falls in love with Henry Tilney whose father, thinking she is a wealthy heiress, encourages the match. He invites her to his family seat, Northanger Abbey. Catherine, whose head is filled with the nonsense of Gothic romances she has read, is delighted. She persuades herself that the senior Tilney is the culprit in a mystery. When Henry's father learns that she is not wealthy, he sends her back to her family and forbids his son to see her. Henry disobeys, proposes to Catherine and is accepted.

NORTON, ELIOT--(GLD X)--Charles Eliot Norton, 1827-1908. Professor of fine arts at Harvard and a leading intellectual in America, he saw as his mission the awakening of his countrymen to the values and achievements of the past. He was joint editor of the North America Review (1864-68).

NOSNIBOR, MR.--(Two Cheers-Bk)--A character in Erewhon (q.v.) by Samuel Butler (q.v.). He is a leading merchant in Erewhon and is recovering from a severe case of embezzlement. He has been assigned to teach Strong the customs of the land.

NOTES ON LIFE AND LETTERS--(AH-JA)--A volume of essays (1921) by Joseph Conrad (q.v.). It contains essays on authors: James (q.v.), Daudet, Anatole, France (q.v.), etc., and on such varying topics as "Confidence," "On the Loss of the Titanic," etc.

NOTES TOWARD THE DEFINITION OF CULTURE--(Two Cheers-Two Bks)--A collection of essays (1948) by T. S. Eliot (q.v.). He treats such aspects of his subject as "the three senses of 'culture,'" "culture and politics," etc.

NOUS AVONS CHANGÉ TOUT CELA--(LJ XXIX)--French: We have changed all of that.

NUBAR PASHA--(Alex II, 3)--1825-1899. Premier of Egypt 1878-79; 1884-88; 1894-95.

NYMPH--(MT)--Female personification, in Greek myth, of a mountain, spring, river, or tree.

O

"O CITY, CITY, I CAN SOMETIMES HEAR/etc."--(Two Cheers-Lon)--$\ell\ell$. 259-265 of "The Wasteland" by T. S. Eliot in his Complete Poems and Plays 1909-1950, New York: 1952.

"O JULIUS CAESAR! THOU ART MIGHTY YET" etc.--(Two Cheers-Jul)--From the play Julius Caesar (q.v.) by William Shakespeare (q.v.), Act V, Sc. iii, ℓ. 94.

OAKLEY STREET--(HE XV)--A street in the Chelsea (q.v.) section of London. It leads north from Albert Bridge to King's Road.

OANNES--(AH-Vo)--A god, in Babylonian myth, with the body of a fish and the head of a man, he is credited with having appeared from the Persian Gulf to give civilization to the Babylonians.

OCEANIA--(Two Cheers-George)--The name that Orwell (q.v.) gives to the world state in his novel, 1984.

OCHILTREE, EDIE--(Aspects II, MT)--A character in The Antiquary (q.v.) by Sir Walter Scott (q.v.). He is a beggar who was once a soldier. He plays an important role in bringing the love affair of Lovel and Miss Wardour to a happy end.

OCTAVIAN--(Alex I, 1)--Augustus, Gaius Octavius, Caesar Octavianus, Ceasar Augustus. See under Augustus.

ODETTE--(AH-Proust; Two Cheers-Our)--A character in the novel, Recherche du Temps Perdus, by Proust (q.v.).

ODYSSEY--(Alex I, 2; Aspects V)--A poem by Homer (q.v.) describing the adventures of Odysseus and his men on their return from the Trojan War.

OEDIPUS--(AH-Troop)--The common name for Oedipus Rex (sometimes: Oedipus Tyrannus) a play (first produced, 429 B.C.) by Sophocles (q.v.). See: Oedipus.

OEDIPUS--(Collect Ta-Road)--In Greek legend, the son of Laius, King of Thebes. He is fated to kill his father and marry his mother, Jocasta. He does so without knowing it is his father he has killed or his mother he has wed. When he learns what he has done, he gouges out his own eyes in horror. His story was used as the basis for several plays, of which only those of Sophocles (q.v.) remain.

OEDIPUS COLONUS [sic]--(Collect Ta-Other)--Oedipus Coloneus, a play by Sophocles (q.v.) (in 402 B.C.) after his death by his grandson. It treats of the blind and banished Oedipus, attended by his daughter-sister, Antigone, at Colonus.

OENANTHE--(PP-Epiph)--Mother of Agathocles (q.v.) and Agathoclea (q.v.).

OFFENBACH--(Nordic)--Jacques Offenbach, 1819-1880. Born at Cologne, he is noted as the creator of French comic opera which attained great popularity. He is best known for his Contes d'Hoffman and Orphée aux Enfers.

OLD SARUM--(LJ XI)--Two miles N of Salisbury (q. v.), in Witshire, England. No longer inhabited, it was a highly prosperous city and once the seat of the Kings of Wessex.

OLD TESTAMENT--(HE XVI)--The Hebrew Bible and the older portion of the Christian Bible. It consists of a varying number of books in varying order.

"OLD, UNHAPPY, FAR-OFF THINGS /AND BATTLES LONG AGO"--(Reading)--ℓℓ. 19-20, from the poem "The Solitary Reaper," by William Wordsworth (q. v.). The first line, in most editions of the poem, reads: "For old, unhappy, far-off things."

OLD WIVES' TALE, THE--(Two Cheers-Virginia)--A novel (1908) by E. A. Bennett concerning the lives of two sisters, daughters of a draper, from their girlhood through disillusioned maturity and death.

OLDBUCK, JONATHAN--(Aspects II)--Oldenbuck, Oldinbuck. A character in The Antiquary (q. v.) by Sir Walter Scott (q. v.). He also appears in the introduction to The Betrothed by the same author. He is Laird of Monkbarns and a bachelor. He is witty, kind, and is possessed of some learning.

OLIPHANT, MRS. --(GLD VII)--Margaret Oliphant, née Wilson, 1828-1897. An English novelist who married her cousin, a painter. She was extremely popular in her day and published many novels among the most popular of which were Salem Chapel, The Perpetual Curate, Miss Majoribanks, and Phoebe Junior. She has since slipped into that limbo where all popular novelists must go and whence only a few are ever resurrected. That fortunate event seems unlikely in her case.

OLIVIER--(Aspects V)--Olivier Molinier, the nephew of Edouard (q. v.) in The Counterfeiters (q. v.) by André Gide (q. v.). He is jealous of his uncle's interest in Bernard. He falls temporarily under Passavant's influence but escapes and attempts suicide, which Edouard thwarts.

OLYMPIA--(Collect Ta-Road)--A plain and sanctuary in S
Greece at one time a center of religious worship with a special festival, the Olympiads. The temple contained the famous statue by Phidias known as the Olympian Zeus (q.v.).

OLYMPUS, MOUNT--(Collect Ta-Other)--The highest peak
of a mountain range in NE Greece. In Greek myth, it was
known as the home of the gods.

OMAR KHAYYAM--(GLD X; LJ I; Two Cheers-In)--died
1123. A Persian poet and astronomer. He was one of the
scholars appointed by the sultan Malik Shah to reform the
Moslem calender. He published a treatise on algebra, but
is best known for his Rubáiyát, a collection of quatrains of
rather worldly philosophy, known to English readers through
the translation of Edward Fitzgerald (q.v.).

ON BEING ILL--(Two Cheers-Virginia)--A short essay (34
p.) by Virginia Woolf. It was published in a limited edition
(250 copies) by the Hogarth Press (1930).

ON HEROES AND HERO WORSHIP--(Two Cheers-Bk)--A col-
lection of essays (1841) by Thomas Carlyle (q.v.): "The
Hero as Divinity," Odin; "The Hero as Prophet," Mohammet;
"The Hero as Poet," Dante (q.v.) and Shakespeare (q.v.);
"The Hero as Priest," Luther and Knox; "The Hero as a
Man of Letters," Samuel Johnson (q.v.), Rousseau (q.v.),
and Robert Burns (q.v.); "The Hero as King," Cromwell
(q.v.) and Napoleon (q.v.).

"ONCE DID SHE HOLD THE GOLDEN EAST IN FEE"--
(Collect Ta-Co-ord)--Line 1 from the sonnet "On the Ex-
tinction of the Venetian Republic" by William Wordsworth
(q.v.).

ONE THOUSAND AND ONE NIGHTS--(Aspects II)--The Arabian Nights' Entertainment. A collection of stories in Arabic first translated into English in an expurgated edition by
Edward William Lane (1839-1841) and then in an unexpur-
gated edition by Sir Richard Burton (q.v.) 1885-1888.

ONITON--(HE XVII)--Wilfred Stone, in his study of Forster's
work, The Cave and the Mountain, holds that Clun Castle,
Shropshire, is the original of Mrs. Wilcox's home.

OOM PAUL--(Two Cheers-Luncheon)--Stephanus Johannes
Kruger, 1840-1926. A South African statesman and a founder

of the Transvaal State. When it was annexed by the British, he was dismissed as general of its forces. In the Boer rebellion (1880), he was a leader, and after it, became president of Transvaal (1883-1900). During the Boer War (q. v.) 1899-1902, he tried vainly to get help from European powers.

OPEN ROAD--(HE XIV)--An anthology (1899, revised 1905) by E. V. Lucas (q. v.).

OPHELIA--(HE XI)--The daughter of Polonius in Hamlet (q. v.) by William Shakespeare (q. v.).

OPUS III--(RWV III)--By Beethoven (q. v.). The trio in E flat major for violin, viola, and cello, published February 8, 1797.

OPUS 20--(Two Cheers-Raison)--By Beethoven (q. v.). The septet in E flat major for clarinet, horn, bassoon, violin, viola, and double bass, composed 1799-1800 and dedicated to Empress Maria Theresa.

ORDEAL OF RICHARD FEVERAL, THE--(HE XIV)--A novel (1859) by George Meredith (q. v.). Sir Austin Feveral has been deserted by his wife and, as a result, decides to raise his son, Richard, in strict accordance with a system the chief point of which is no contact with women. He hopes, in this way, to avoid corruption for his son. The system breaks down, however, during his son's adolescence. The boy falls in love with Lucy, the niece of a farmer.

"ORDINA QUESTO AMOR, O TU CHE M'AMI"--(Two Cheers-Art)--Italian: Order this love, O you who love me.

OREADS--(Collect Ta-Other; Collect Ta-Story)--In Greek myth, mountain nymphs (q. v.).

ORFORD, ELLEN--(Two Cheers-George)--A character in the opera, Peter Grimes (q. v.), by Sir Benjamin Britten (q. v.).

ORIGEN--(Alex I, 3; PP-Clement)--Origines Adamantius. A. D. 185-254. Christian apologist and writer of Alexandria. He is one of the Greek Fathers of the Church. He was head of the catechetical school in Alexandria and later founded a school in Caesarea. He wrote many works on the Old Testament, a treatise on prayer, and a defense of Christianity.

ORIGIN OF THE SPECIES--(MT)--By Charles Darwin (q.v.).
Full title: On the Origin of the Species by Means of Natural
Selection, or the Preservation of Favoured Races in the
Struggle for Life, published in London in 1859, and creating
thereupon a storm of controversy.

ORIGINAL LETTERS FROM INDIA OF MRS. ELIZA FAY,
THE--(PP-Eliza)--Published by the Calcutta Historical Society with an introduction by E. M. Forster.

ORION--(Collect Ta-Point; LJ XXIII)--A stellar constellation
which used to set about November and consequently was associated with rain and storms.   In Greek myth, Orion was
a giant hunter and the subject of a number of legends.   After his death, the gods placed him among the stars.

ORLANDO--(Two Cheers-Virginia)--A character in the novel
(1928) of the same name by Virginia Woolf (q.v.).   He is a
young English nobleman living during the reign of Elizabeth
I, who doesn't die.   During the time of Charles II, he sleeps
an entire week and changes into a woman.   Despite the
change, he/she is still a restless soul.   During the Victorian period, he/she marries and returns to his/her earlier
love of literature.   In the 1920's he/she is a woman of 36.

ORMUS--(AH-Conso)--Hormuz, Ormuz.   An ancient town on
the coast of Persia near the modern Bandar Abbas on the
Straits of Ormuz, S Iran.

ORONTES--(AH-Cn)--A river in W Syria.

ORPHEUS--(AH-Word; Two Cheers-Not Listening)--In Greek
myth, a poet and son of the muse (q.v.) Calliope, and a
follower of Dionysus.   He was a skilled player of the lyre.
He so loved his wife, Eurydice, that he successfully be-
seeched the underworld to release her after her death;
bringing her up again to sunlight he disobeyed an injunction
not to look back, and lost her forever.

ORWELL, GEORGE--(Two Cheers-George)--Pen-name of
Eric Blair, 1903-1950.   He was an English novelist, essayist, political satirist, etc., born in Bengal, but educated in
England.   He considered himself a democratic socialist, and
hated totalitarianism.   Perhaps his most famous works are
those aimed against totalitarianism: Animal Farm (1945)
and 1984, published in 1949 (both q.v.).

OSIRIS--(AH-For the Muse; Alex I, 1; Aspects II; Two Cheers-They)--One of the chief gods in Egyptian myth. He was judge of the dead and ruler of the kingdom of ghosts; the creator, the god of the Nile and constant foe of his brother, Set, the principle of evil. His wife is his sister, Isis (q.v.). He represents the setting sun (Ra). He was slain and his body was cut up and distributed throughout Egypt. Isis helped restore him to life and was revenged on his slayer by Horus and Toth.

O THAT 'TWERE POSSIBLE/AFTER LONG GRIEF AND PAIN--(AH-HOS)--From Tennyson's "Maude." The quotation is the source of Sturgis's All That Was Possible.

OTHELLO--(GLD IV; Two Cheers-Jul)--Othello, the Moor of Venice, a play by Shakespeare (q.v.) was first printed in 1622. Married to Desdemona, the Moor is made jealous of her by Iago who hates him. Othello kills his wife, thinking her unfaithful to him. When he realizes his error, he kills himself.

OTELLO--(Two Cheers-C; Two Cheers-George)--An opera by Verdi first produced in Milan (1887) with a libretto by A. Boito. It is based on Othello (q.v.) by Shakespeare (q.v.).

OUR VILLAGE--(AH-Troop)--Sketches of "rural character and scenery" in five volumes (London, 1824-1832), by Mary Russell Mitford (q.v.).

OUTLINE OF HISTORY--(GLD XII)--A "history" (1920 and revised several times) of the world from the origin of the earth to the period after World War I, by H. G. Wells (q.v.).

OVID--(MT)--Publius Ovidius Naso. 43 B.C.-A.D. 18. A Roman poet banished from Rome by Augustus (q.v.) because of his scandalous Ars Amatoria and his involvement with unsavory members of the court.

OWEN, WILFRED--(Reading)--1893-1918. An English poet who was killed in action in France a week before the armistice. In 1920, his friend Siegfried Sassoon collected his poetry in a single volume and his reputation grew slowly but steadily.

OXFORD--(AH-Consol; Aspects I; HE XII; Nordic; Two Cheers-Camb; Two Cheers-Gibbon; Two Cheers-John; Two

Cheers-Mount; Two Cheers-William)--A town in the county
of Oxfordshire, central England and seat of the famous university of the same name founded in the Middle Ages.

OXFORD CIRCUS--(Two Cheers-Lon)--The crossing, in
London's West End, of Regent and Oxford Streets.

OXUS--(AH-Emp)--The Amy Darya River in central and W
Asia some 1500 miles long. It empties into Lake Aral.

P

P. E. N. --(New Disorder)--An international association of
poets, playwrights, editors, essayists, and novelists founded
in 1921 by Mrs. Dawson Scott to promote cooperation among
writers all over the world. Its first president was John
Galsworthy (q. v.).

PADDINGTON STATION--(HE II)--The chief terminus in London of the Western Region located in Edgeware Road.

PADEREWSKI--(Two Cheers-Whiff)--Jan Ignace Paderewski,
1860-1941. A Polish statesman and pianist who studied
piano in Warsaw and Vienna and made his debut in Vienna
in 1887. His debut as a statesman was made during World
War I when he campaigned for the cause of a free Poland.
After the war, he formed a coalition ministry in the new
state of Poland. In it he was Prime Minister and Foreign
Minister. The ministry held office for ten months.

PAIN, SEX AND TIME--(Two Cheers-Ger)--Full title: Pain,
Sex and Time: A New Hypothesis of Evolution by Gerald
Heard (q. v., London, 1939). A discussion of evolution
through the physique and through the psyche. Heard holds
that the processes of evolution are culminating in the modern
period, and as a consequence, we are part of an evolutionary
crisis.

PAIX SUCCÈDE À LA PENSÉE, LA--(Two Cheers-Anon)--
French: Peace follows thought.

PALAEOLOGUS FAMILY--(AH-Gem)--A Greek Byzantine
family which furnished the last eight emperors of the Eastern Roman Empire, from 1259 to 1453. Branch families
ruled in the Italian marquisate of Montferrat, 1305-1533,
and in the Morea, 1383-1460.

PALATINE--(AH-Mac)--One of the seven hills of Rome on which was located the palace of the Caesars.

PALAZZO FARNESE--(Alex II, 1)--A Renaissance palace of the Farnese family, the work of the architect Antonio da San Gallo the Younger. It is now the French embassy.

PALERUS, DEMETRIUS--(Alex I, 1)--A follower of Aristotle who was summoned by Ptolemy Soter (q. v.) to Alexandria and ordered to organize an institution along the lines of the Athenian Mouseion, a philosophical establishment which had contained the library of Aristotle (q. v.). The result was the museum of Alexandria.

PALLADIO, ANDREA--(LJ XI)--1518-1580. An Italian archi-tect who adapted the principles of Roman architecture to the taste of his time. Inigo Jones imported his classic style to England and later, architects of the Georgian period founded on it designs which have since come to be named "Palladian."

PALLAS ATHENE--The Greek goddess Athene (q. v.). The meaning of the appellation "Pallas" is not known. Some le-gends have it that Athene slew a giant of that name.

PALLONE--(WAFT II)--Forster uses the Italian word as the name of a game at which Gino Carella excels. It means "balloon" and carries the suggestion when used with the ad-jective "gonfiato, " that the individual to whom it is applied is a "wind-bag" or pretentious non-entity. The context in which Forster applies the word suggests that this meaning is intended.

PALMER--(AH-Vo)--A pilgrim who, in the Middle Ages, wore two palm leaves crossed as a symbol that he had been to the Holy Land.

PALMERSTON, LORD--(Two Cheers-England)--Henry John Temple (3rd Viscount Palmerston), 1784-1865. An English Tory statesman who held numerous government posts in-cluding that of Prime Minister (1855-65). He supported the movement for Catholic emancipation and advocated indepen-dence for Italy.

PALMYRA--(Two Cheers-Duty)--An ancient ruined city 135 miles NE of Damascus, Syria. It became prosperous at the beginning of the Christian era because of its location on the trade route from Persia to Egypt. It was destroyed by

Rome in A. D. 273.

PAMELA--(Aspects VI)--A character in the novel (1740-41) of the same name by Samuel Richardson. She is a virtuous serving girl of Lady B. whose son attempts to seduce her. When she resists, he is so impressed by her virtue that he offers her marriage which she accepts.

PAMINA--(GLD XII)--A character in the opera, Die Zauberflöte (The Magic Flute), by Mozart (q. v.).

PAN--(AH-Mac; Aspects VI; Collect Ta-Other; Collect Ta-Story; HE XIII; LJ XIII; RWV VII)--In Greek myth, the god of pastures, forests, flocks, and herds. His lower half was that of a goat and his upper, that of a man. He is also the personification of deity displayed in creation and pervading all. His lustful nature symbolized the spermatic principle in the world.

PAN, PETER--(Collect Ta-Coord)--The boy who wouldn't grow up in Barrie's play (1904) of the same name. Peter takes the Darling children to Never-Never land where they meet Captain Hook and have interesting adventures.

PAN PIPES--(LJ XV)--The title Forster has his character Rickie, in The Longest Journey, give to his collection of short stories.

PANDAVA WARS--(PI XXXIII)--The Pandavas were five sons, in Indian myth, of Pandu about whose rivalries the great epic Mahabharata was written.

PANTHEON--(Two Cheers-Last)--A Roman temple, now the church of All Saints. It was erected in 27 B. C. by Agrippa and restored, after a fire, by Hadrian.

PANTRY, BISHOP--(AH-Ron)--A character in the first novel of Ronald Firbank (q. v.), Vainglory (1915).

PANZA, SANCHO--(MT)--A paunchy rustic whom Quixote persuades to follow him in the novel Don Quixote (Part I, 1605; Part II, 1615), by Miguel de Cervantes.

PAPHNUCE--(Aspects VIII)--A character in Thais (1890) by Anatole France (q. v.). His name is actually Paphnutius. He is a monk of Alexandria in the early Christian era, who longs to convert the courtesan, Thais. She enters a nunnery,

but he finds himself stirred by her beauty.   He cannot fight
his love for her and goes to her cell only to find her wrapped
in visions which he cannot share, her love given to God.

PARFENOVITCH, NIKOLAY--(Aspects VII)--A character in
The Brothers Karamazov (q. v.) by Feodor Dostoevsky (q. v.).

PARKER, MR. AND MRS. --(AH-JA)--Characters in the fragment, Sanditon, by Jane Austen (q. v.).

PARK LANE--(LJ VII)--A street in London near Hyde Park
(q. v.); Disraeli (q. v.) lived at No. 93.

PARNASSUS--(Aspects I; GLD IX)--A mountain in Greece
several miles N of Delphi.   It was sacred to the Muses (q.
v.).

PARRY, HUBERT--(MT)--Charles Hubert Hastings Parry,
1848-1918.   An English composer of choral works and many
solo settings of English verse.   He also wrote symphonies,
an opera, etc.

PARSIFAL--(RWV XV)--The title of an opera (1882) by
Richard Wagner (q. v.) based on the legend of the Holy Grail.

PARTHENON FRIEZE--(LJ XX)--The frieze on the Parthenon in Athens depicting the festal procession of the Athenians
every four years to honor Athene (q. v.), to whom the temple was dedicated.   Much of it is now in the British Museum (q. v.).

PARVATE--(PI VII)--In Indian myth, the feminine deity who
personifies the power of Siva.   She is the daughter of the
Himalayas and is also known as Uma (the gracious), Kali
(the black), Bhairavi (the terrible), Gauvi (the brilliant),
and by other names.

PASSAGE TO INDIA, A--(Hill; Two Cheers-Syed)--A novel
(1924) by E. M. Forster.

PATER, WALTER--(GLD X)--Walter Horatio Pater, 1839-
1894.   Educated at Queen's College, Oxford, he was associated with the Pre-Raphaelites (q. v.).   His Studies in the
History of the Renaissance (1873) brought him into the public eye.   It was followed by perhaps his most famous work,
Marius the Epicurean (q. v.).

PATHANS--(PI XX)--The tribal peoples inhabiting the frontier region between India and Afghanistan.

PATHETIC SONATA [sic]--(Two Cheers-C)--The piano sonata in C minor, Opus 13 (c. 1798), by Beethoven (q. v.), more often called "The Pathétique."

PATRAS--(Collect Ta-Road)--A seaport city of Greece in the NW Peloponnesus (q. v.) on the Gulf of Patras.

PATROCLUS--(Alex I, 1)--The son of Menoetius and a character in the Iliad (q. v.) by Homer (q. v.). He was the favorite companion of Achilles.

PAUL, SAINT--(AH-JA; Two Cheers-Tol; Two Cheers-What) --[Orig.: Saul.] A Jew of Tarsus and persecutor of the Christians. He was converted to Christianity when Christ appeared to him (Acts). Christ designated him as the apostle to the gentiles. He made several journeys to found churches among them. He was martyred at Rome c. A. D. 67.

PAVIA--(AH-Car)--A province in N Italy.

PAX ROMANA--(WAFT II)--Latin: Roman Peace, i. e., the order Rome established during the reign of Augustus (q. v.).

PEACOCK--(Aspects VI; MT)--Thomas Love Peacock, 1785-1866. An English novelist and poet. He produced satirical romances, the most famous of which are Nightmare Abbey (1818) and Crotchet Castle (1831).

PEACOCK THRONE--(PI VII)--The throne of the Mogul (q. v.) emperors of India. It was studded with gems.

PECKHAM--(LJ VII)--A district in London.

PECKHAM, JOHN--(AH-Car)--d. 1292. An English churchman who taught in Oxford. He was made archbishop of Canterbury in 1279. He wrote many works on scriptual and moral subjects as well as on science.

PEEL, ROBERT--(MT)--1788-1850. A British statesman who held various public offices including that of prime minister. He helped to defeat the movement toward Catholic emancipation and established a constabulary first known as "Peelers" then the more familiar "Bobbies."

PEER GYNT--(AH-Ibsen)--A play (1867) by Henrik Ibsen (q.
v.) which has as its hero the legendary Peer Gynt of Norse
folklore.   He is a braggart and an egotist who avoids any
issue.   He has a long series of wild adventures which take
him over the face of the earth.   These reveal his real character.   He returns to Norway to find Death, the Button Mol-
der, waiting to melt him back to the nothing from which he
came.   Edvard Grieg (q.v.) wrote incidental music for the
play.

PEGASUS--(LJ I)--In Greek myth, a winged horse which
sprang from the blood of Medusa (q.v.) when Pereseus (q.v.)
cut off her head.

PELAGIAN--(Collect Ta-Curate; MT)--The name of a Christian heresy which denied that original sin (Adam's sin) affected humanity.   Hence, it held, man has no need of God's
grace for salvation.   It takes its name from Pelagius, the
monk who preached it.

PELOPONNESUS--(AH-Gem)--A peninsula forming the southern part of Greece attached slenderly to the mainland by the
Isthmus of Corinth.

PEMBERLEY--(AH-JA)--Pemberley House.   The estate of
Darcy in Derbyshire, in Pride and Prejudice (q.v.) by Jane
Austen (q.v.).   It is a large, handsome stone building,
standing well on rising ground and backed by a ridge of high,
woody hills.

PENELOPE--(Aspects VI)--The wife of Odysseus in The
Odyssey (q.v.).

PENSIONE BERTOLINI--(RWV I)--The pension in which Lucy
and Charlotte stay in A Room With A View.   It is on the
Arno in Florence.   It could very well be modeled upon the
Berchielli, a similar establishment, occupying roughly the
same position at the time Forster wrote the novel.

PENTATEUCH--(WAFT I)--The first five books of the Old
Testament.   The word is from Greek penta (five) and
tench(os) (tool, implement).

PENTONVILLE--(Two Cheers-Lon)--The word was first applied to houses built about 1773 on the land in Clerkenwell
by Henry Penton.   It is now the name of a road in London
leading east to Islington, and also the name of a prison.

PEPYS--(GLD IX)--Samuel Pepys, 1633-1703. Known chiefly for his Diary (January 1, 1660 to May 31, 1669) which he
wrote in cipher. It describes graphically the London of his
day. It was first deciphered in 1825 by John Smith and
edited by Lord Braybrooke. Since then, many editions have
appeared.

PERCIVAL--(Two Cheers-Virginia)--A character in the novel,
The Waves (1931), by Virginia Woolf. He is the childhood
friend of the central characters who respect, admire and
love him. He symbolizes the ordinary man, the conventional figure. Though rather awkward, he is pleasant and is
accepted everywhere.

PERCY CIRCUS--(Two Cheers-London)--Forster may be referring to Percy Street, in London, which leads to Tottenham Court Road. It was opened and built upon 1764-70.

PEREY, KUICAN--(Two Cheers-Fer)--The pseudonym of
Clara Adele Luce Herpin, 1845-1914. A French writer of
biography and historical studies of the 18th century. She
co-authored with Maugras La Vie Intime de Voltaire.

"PERISH EACH LAGGARD! LET IT NOT BE SAID/THAT
SAWSTON SUCH WITHIN HER WALLS HATH BRED. "--(LJ
XVI)--Two lines from the Sawston School (q. v.) anthem
composed by the organist.

PERSEPHONE--(AH-Cn; PI XXIV; RWV VI)--In English,
sometimes referred to as Proserpine. In Greek myth, the
daughter of Zeus (q. v.) and Demeter (q. v.). She was carried off by Pluto (q. v.) and made queen of the underworld.
Demeter prayed to Zeus and he allowed Persephone to spend
spring and summer of each year on earth and autumn and
winter with Pluto; the story of Demeter (goddess of Agricul-
ture) and Persephone is acknowledged to be an interpretation
of the course of seasons--Nature's fruits disappear with
Persephone and reappear with her.

PERSEUS--(RWV V)--In Greek myth, the son of Zeus (q. v.)
and Danae. Polydectes, in love with Danae, tried to rid
himself of her son by sending him to fetch Medusa's head
(q. v.). Pluto (q. v.) loaned him a helmet which would ren-
der him invisible, Athene (q. v.) gave him a buckler like a
mirror, and Hermes (q. v.) wings for his feet. With these,
he destroys Medusa.

PERSIA--(PI IX)--The name once applied to Iran.

PERSONAL RECORD, A--(AH-Jo)--A book of reminiscence and philosophy by Joseph Conrad.

PERSUASION--(AH-JA, Aspects IV)--A novel (1818) by Jane Austen.   Anne Elliot and her lover, Wentworth, have been engaged for eight years, but Anne has broken the engagement because of her family and friends.   Upon his return, he finds her changed.   After overcoming numerous obstacles, the two are happily married.

PERUGIA--(RWV III)--A city 85 miles N of Rome.   It was one of the cities of Etruria captured by Rome in 309 B.C. In the 16th century it became part of the Papal States and was annexed to the kingdom of Italy in 1860.

PETER--(Alex I, II)--[Orig.: Simon.] Son of John and a disciple of John the Baptist who left to become an apostle of Christ.   After the Resurrection, he made Jerusalem his headquarters.   Thence he traveled to Rome where he was martyred c. A.D. 67.   He is recognized as the first pope by the Catholic Church.

"PETER GRIMES"--(Two Cheers-George C)--The poem by George Crabbe, as well as the opera by Sir Benjamin Britten, both discussed at length in Forster's essay "George Crabbe and Peter Grimes" in Two Cheers for Democracy, 1951.

PETER DES ROCHES--(AH-Ab)--d. 1238.   He was an English churchman and the bishop of Winchester (1203).   He took up the cause of King John (q.v.) against the barons.

PETER WARING--(Two Cheers-Fo)--A novel (1937) by Forrest Reid (q.v.).   The first version was published in 1912 under the title Following Darkness.   It was entirely rewritten and dedicated to E. M. Forster.

PETERLOO MASSACRE--(MT)--Also known as the Manchester massacre.   A meeting was held August 16, 1819 in St. Peter's Fields, Manchester, as a protest against the exceptionally high price of foods.   It had as its objective the reformation of Parliament.   About 60,000 people were present. None was armed.   The yeomanry were expected to keep order.   They were bitter oponents of the "radicals" and made a general attack upon the crowd.   Almost 500 people were killed or wounded.

PETESOUCHOS--(Alex II, 1)--In Egyptian myth, the crocodile god.

PHAEDO--(GLD VI)--By Plato (q.v.) translated into English by Benjamin Jowett (Waltham St. Lawrence, Berkshire: The Golden Cockerel Press, 1930). Initial letters were designed by Eric Gill.

PHAEDRA--(LJ XIX)--In Greek legend, the daughter of King Minos. She fell in love with Hippolytus and, when he did not return her love, she accused him to his father of raping her. He was put to death. Her story is told by Seneca, Euripides (q.v.), and Racine (q.v.).

PHAEDRUS--(AH-Early; Two Cheers-Duty)--A freedman in the household of the Roman emperor Augustus (q.v.). He was the author of a collection of fables based on those of Aesop.

PHAETHON--(RWV II)--The son of Phoebus. He begged his father to be permitted to drive the chariot of the sun. When he could not control the horses, Zeus sent a thunderbolt which hurled him into the Po River.

PHARILLON--(PP-Eliza)--The Arabic successor to the Pharos (q.v.) lighthouse.

PHAROS--(Alex I, 1; PP-Eliza; PP-Ph)--One of the seven wonders of the world, a lighthouse built by Ptolemy Philadelphus (q.v.) on the island of Pharos off Alexandria, Egypt.

PHÈDRE--(New Disorder; Two Cheers-Art)--A play by Racine based on the legend of Phaedra (q.v.).

PHILAE--(Alex I, 2)--An island in the Nile River, the site of many temples.

PHILIP--(MT)--Philip II, King of Macedonia, 382-336 B.C. He succeeded his father in 359 B.C. and was considered a military genius. He waged war in and conquered Greece. He was succeeded by his son, Alexander the Great (q.v.).

"PHILIP SPARROW"--(Two Cheers-John)--A poem by John Skelton amply discussed by Forster in his essay "John Skelton" in Two Cheers for Democracy, 1951.

PHILIPPI--(Two Cheers-Jul)--A ruined city in Macedonia
(q. v. under Augustus), the site of the battle of the same
name in which Octavian and Mark Antony (q. v.) defeated
Brutus and Cassius.

PHILISTINE--(Collect Ta-Celest; Collect Ta-Story)--In the
Old Testament, the enemies of the Israelites. In modern
times, the word has come to mean the ignorant and those
who lack culture or those who are directed only by materialistic desires.

PHILO--(Alex I, 3; PP-Philo)--Philo Judaens, or Philo of
Alexandria, b. about 20 B. C., d. not later than A. D. 54.
A Hellenized Jewish philosopher known as the "Jewish Plato,"
he tried to harmonize the philosophies of such men as Aristotle and Plato with that of the Pentateuch (q. v.).

PHILOCTETES--(LJ XIX)--The most famous archer in the
Trojan War. Hercules gave him his arrows. It was he who
slew Paris and brought about the fall of Troy (q. v.).

PHLEGETHON--(Two Cheers-They)--In classical myth it is
the name of a river of fire in Hades. It flows directly into
the river Acheron. From the Greek phlego (to burn).

PHOCAS--(Alex II, 1)--d. A. D. 610. Emperor of the Eastern Roman Empire, 602-610. He was a centurian who was
raised to the throne by mutinous soldiers. He was noted for
his cruelty. He was overthrown, tortured and beheaded by
Heraclius (q. v.), the Exarch of North Africa, who took the
throne for himself.

PIANO CONCERTO IN B FLAT MINOR--(Two Cheers-Raison)
--by Tchaikovsky (q. v.). The Concerto No. 1 for Piano in
B flat Minor, Opus 23, composed 1874-5 and first performed
in Boston, 1875.

PIANO SONATA--(Two Cheers-C)--Forster refers to the
piano sonata in F minor (Opus 21) by Beethoven (q. v.) composed in 1795, dedicated to Haydn (q. v.), and published 9
March 1796.

PIAZZA SIGNORIA--(RWV IV)--The main square in Florence,
Italy.

PICASSO--(Nordic; Two Cheers-Last)--1881- . A Spanish
artist of the modern school who lives in France. Highly

experimental, his art falls into several periods reflecting
that experimentation. He is, perhaps, best known for his
"Cubist" period. He is equally well known for his business
acumen.

PICCADILLY CIRCUS--(Two Cheers-Lon)--In London's West
End. The origin of its name is uncertain.

PICKTHALL, MARMADUKE--(AH-Salute)--1875-1936. English novelist and orientalist. He spent three years in the
Near East learning Arabic and Arabian philosophy. In 1913,
he took the Turkish point of view and wrote a series of articles which were collected in With the Turk In War-Time
(1913). He began to write fiction at an early age. Critics
tend to agree that his first novel, Said the Fisherman (1913),
is his best. Other works are Oriental Encounters (1911),
The Valley of the Kings (1909), and The Children of the Nile
(1908).

PILATE--(GLD XII)--Pontius Pilate. The procurator of Judea (A.D. 26 to 36) under the emperor Tiberius. He tried
and condemned Christ to death.

PILGRIM'S PROGRESS, THE--(Aspects I; MT)--The Pilgrim's
Progress from This World to That Which is to Come (1678).
A prose allegory in the form of a dream by John Bunyan
(q.v.). It details the journey of Christian through life.

PILLARS OF HERCULES--(PI XXXI)--Also called Pillars of
Melkart. The peaks on either side of Gibraltar.

PINDAR--(Collect Ta-Celest)--522?-443 B.C. A Greek lyric
poet born near Thebes. Little is known of his life, but
there are extant some 44 Odes of Victory (Epincia) which
celebrate victories in national games. There also exist
fragments of other works.

PIO NONO--(MT)--Giovanni Maria Mastai-Ferrati (1792-1878),
Pope Pius IX, 1846-1878. He is, perhaps, best known for
the Vatican Council (1869-70) which promulgated the dogma
of papal infallibility.

PIP--(Aspects IV)--The central figure in Great Expectations
(q.v.) by Charles Dickens (q.v.). He is an orphan raised
by his sister. She treats him unkindly, but also treats her
husband in the same fashion. Pip and he become good
friends despite the difference in their ages. While still a

child, Pip meets an escaped convict who forces him to secure food for him and a file.   Some time after, Pip goes to
Miss Havisham's house to play.   Later, an unknown benefactor bestowes upon him a large allowance with a promise
of "greater expectations."   He drifts away from the friends
of his youth and, much to his surprise, discovers that it is
not Miss Havisham, the recluse, who has helped him, but
the convict.   That convict returns to England, is captured
and, as a result, Pip loses all hope of wealth.

PIQUET--(AH-Our D)--A game of cards.

PIRAEUS--(GLD X)--The Greek seaport city serving Athens,
about five miles SW of that city.

PIRATES OF THE SPRING--(AH-Fo)--A novel (1919) by Forrest Reid.

PIRELLI, CARDINAL--(AH-Ron)--A character in the novel
The Eccentricities of Cardinal Pirelli (1925) by Ronald Firbank (q. v.).

PISGAH--(Aspects I)--A mountain in ancient Palestine E of
the N end of the Dead Sea.

PITT, WILLIAM--(AH-Ba; AH-Capt; MT; Two Cheers-Henry)
--1759-1806.   Called the "Younger Pitt" he is considered the
greatest of England's Prime Ministers.

PITTI--(RWV IV)--Forster is referring to the Palazzo Pitti
in Florence.   The palace was begun in 1458 and has under-
gone many alterations.   It is the home of one of the more
important collections of paintings in Italy.

PLACE, FRANCIS--(MT)--1771-1854.   An English reformer
who led the successful campaign to repeal the laws forbid-
ding unionism.

PLASSEY--(AH-Our Div; PI XXXIV)--A village in W Bengal,
India about 90 miles N of Calcutta.   It was the scene on
June 23, 1757 of the victory of Clive (q. v.) with a British
force of 3, 000, against the 80, 000 man army of Siraj-ud-
daula.   The victory marks the beginning of the British Empire in the East.

PLATO--(AH-Early; AH-Gem; Alex I, 3; GLD II; Hill; LJ
IV; PP-Clement; Two Cheers-Duty)--[Orig.: Aristocles]

428/427-348/347 B.C.   A Greek philosopher, disciple of
Socrates, and teacher of Aristotle.   He studied under and
with Socrates until the latter's trial and death (399 B.C.).

PLEIADES--(Two Cheers-George)--A stellar constellation.
In Greek myth they are the daughters of Atlas who, after
their death, were placed among the stars.

PLESIOSAURUS--(Two Cheers-Not)--The word refers to ma-
rine reptiles of the Mesozoic era which have a very long
neck, small head, and four paddle-like limbs.

PLETHO, GEMISTUS--(AH-Gem; RWV VI)--Georgius Gemistus Pletho [or Plethon], 1355?-?1450.   He was a Byzantine
Platonic philosopher and regarded as one of the foremost
figures in the revival of learning in Western Europe.

PLOMER, WILLIAM--(Two Cheers-Virginia)--William Charles
Franklyn Plomer, 1903- .   A South African novelist.   The
author of many novels with an African setting, including Tur-
bott Wolfe (1926).   He has also written a biography of Cecil
Rhodes (1933) and some poetry.

PLOTINUS--(AH-Gem; Alex I, 3; GLD VII)--A.D. 205?-270.
A Neo-Platonic philosopher born in Egypt of Roman parents.
He studied at Alexandria under Ammonius Sciccas (q.v.) and
lectured in Rome.   He is the chief exponent of Neo-Platonism.

PLUTARCH--(Alex I, 1; GLD I; Two Cheers-Jul)--Born c.
A.D. 46, d. between 120 and 127.   A Greek biographer who
was educated in Athens and traveled widely.   He taught in
Rome.   He is best known for his Parallel Lives in which he
offers character studies of great Greeks and Romans in
pairs.

PLUTO--(Alex I, 1; Two Cheers-John)--In Roman myth, the
god of Hades.   Son of Saturn, he is the brother of Jupiter
and Neptune.   His wife is Persephone (q.v.).

PLUTO--(AH-Our Div)--The dog of Mickey Mouse (q.v.).

POCOCK, RICHARD--(Alex I, 4)--1704-1785.   An English
traveler who published accounts of his travels up the Nile,
in Greece, and the Near East.

POE--(AH-Reid; Aspects VII; GLD II; Two Cheers-Fo)--Edgar Allan Poe, 1809-1849. An American writer of short stories and poems. His stories are generally filled with grotesquery and fantasy. He is credited with influencing the growth of the Symbolist Movement in France. Among his best known stories are "The Murders in the Rue Morgue," 1841; "The Masque of the Red Death," 1842; and "The Fall of the House of Usher," 1839. His most famous poem is "The Raven," 1845.

POETRY OF THE PRESENT--(Two Cheers-Outsider)--Subtitled: An Anthology of the Thirties and After, London: Phoenix House, 1949. Compiled with an introduction by Geoffrey Grigson (q. v.).

POGGIBONSI--(WAFT II)--A small town in the province of Siena, Italy, about 16 miles NW of Siena.

POLITICS--(Hill)--A treatise (c. 4th century B. C.) by Aristotle (q. v.) on the philosophy of the state. He begins with a discussion of the nature of the state economy. He rejects Platonic communism. He classifies the forms of states noting that monarchy is the best but indicating that, because of the lack of good leaders, a constitutional republic is more practical. The purpose of the state, he notes, is the good of its citizens.

POLLUX--(AH-Mac)--See: Castor and Pollux.

POLLY--(Aspects I)--The central character in the novel, The History of Mr. Polly (q. v.) by H. G. Wells (q. v.).

POLO, MARCO--(AH-Adrift; AH-Marco)--1254-1324. An aristocratic Venetian merchant who, with his father and uncle, visited China and wrote about his travels; he stayed for 17 years and held several high government posts under the Great Kublai Khan.

POMERANIA--(HE XII)--A region on the Baltic Sea. In the 12th century, the Germans established it as a duchy.

POMPEY--(Alex I, 1; PP-Eliza)--Gnaeus Pompeius Magnus, 106-48 B. C. A Roman general and statesman and rival of Julius Caesar (q. v.). Because he was the champion of the Senate and the conservative party which sought to block Caesar's move to control the country, a civil war developed. He was defeated and fled to Egypt for protection where

Ptolemy, its king, had him killed.

PONSONBY, LORD--(GLD XI)--Arthur Augustus William
Harry (1st Baron Ponsonby of Shulbrede), 1871-1946. He
was a page to Queen Victoria (q.v.) and was educated at
Oxford. For a time he was in the diplomatic service. He
was also an author and wrote biographies of Pepys (1928)
and Queen Victoria (1933), among other works.

POPE, ALEXANDER--(Two Cheers-Bishop)--1688-1744. The
most influential poet of the 18th century in England. Using
the rather limited heroic couplet, he produced brilliant poetry, e.g., The Rape of the Lock (1712), a translation of
The Iliad (1715-1720) The Dunciad (1728; rev. 1743), and
the Essay on Man (1733).

POPILIUS--(Alex I, 4)--Popilus Laenas, a general and the
Roman envoy to Egypt (2nd century B.C.). He successfully
repulsed an invasion of Egypt by the armies of Syria.

PORPHYRY--(Alex I, 3)--Porphyrius [orig.: Malchus] A.D.
232?-?304. A pupil of Plotinus (q.v.), he was a Greek
scholar and Neo-Platonic philosopher. He also studied under Cassius Longinus and lectured on philosophy in Rome.
He vigorously defended paganism against Christianity.

PORTMAN SQUARE--(GLD III)--A square in London off Oxford Street. It is a fashionable quarter laid out after 1761
and still has many of the fine 18th-century buildings.

PORT SAID--(PI XXVIII)--A seaport on the Mediterranean
at the N end of the Suez Canal.

PORTRAIT OF THE ARTIST AS A YOUNG MAN, A--(Aspects VI)--A novel (1916) by James Joyce (q.v.) which details the youth of Stephen Dedalus.

"PORTRAIT OF A LADY, THE"--(AH-TS)--A poem by T. S.
Eliot, in Complete Poems and Plays 1909-1950 (New York:
Harcourt Brace, 1950) p. 8-11.

POSEIDON--(AH-Cn; Alex II, 1; PP-Ph)--In Greek myth, the
god of the sea [Latin: Neptune]. The son of Cronos and
Rhea, brother of Zeus (q.v.) and Pluto (q.v.) and husband
of Amphitrite.

POST-IMPRESSIONISM--(GLD IX; PI VII)--The term, invented by Roger Fry (q. v.) is used to describe a period of
French painting from the 1880's to 1905, initiated by Cézanne,
and including Van Gogh, Gauguin, and Seurat.   The period
followed impressionism and preceded Fauvism.

POTIPHAR--(AH-Salute)--The Egyptian husband of the woman who tempted Joseph ("Genesis").   He was an officer of
the Pharoah and bought Joseph as a slave from the Midian-
ites and made him his major-domo.

POTIPHAR'S WIFE--(AH-For the Muse)--See: Potiphar.

POTTER, RICHARD--(Two Cheers-Webb)--The father of
Beatrice Webb (q. v.).

PRAETERITA--(Two Cheers-In)--Subtitled: Outlines of Scenes
and Thoughts Perhaps Worthy of Memory in My Past Life
(1885-1889).   The unfinished autobiography of John Ruskin
(q. v.).

PRANCING NIGGER--(AH-Ron)--A novel by Ronald Firbank
(q. v.).   For an outline of its plot see Forster's essay,
"Ronald Firbank, " in Abinger Harvest.

PRAXINOE--(Alex I, 1)--A middle-class visitor to the festival of Adonis at Alexandria.   She behaves as do all matrons
of her class in all ages.   She appears in the 15th Idyl, the
"Adoniazusae, " of Theocritus (q. v.).

PRAXITILES--(AH-For the Muse; LJ III; WAFT V)--One of
the most famous of ancient Greek sculptors born at Athens
about 390 B. C.   Only one original work of his is extant,
the Hermes (q. v.) with the infant Dionysus (q. v.).   The
Aphrodite of Cnidus (q. v.), the most famous of his works,
is known only through Roman reproductions, though recently
(1970) there has been speculation that its head has been discovered in the basement of the British Museum (q. v.).

"PRAYER TO THE FATHER OF HEAVEN"--(Two Cheers-
John)--A poem by John Skelton (q. v.) set to music by
Vaughan Williams (q. v.).

PRE-RAPHAELITES--(AH-Wil; MT)--A group of artists and
critics who called themselves the "Pre-Raphaelite Brotherhood. "   They sought to infuse art with a careful study of
nature and the depiction of morally elevating subjects.   They

published their ideas in The Germ.   Some of their number were D. G. Rossetti (q. v.), John Everett Millais, and William Holman Hunt.

PRIAM--(PP-Return)--The last king of Troy and father of some 50 sons as well as several daughters.   Hector, Paris, and Cassandra were the most famous of his children.   He was slain when the Greeks took the city.

PRICE, FANNY--(AH-JA)--A character in Austen's Masefield Park.   She is the eldest daughter of Lieutenant and Mrs. Price.   She is timid, awkward, yet sweet.

PRIDE AND PREJUDICE--(AH-JA)--A novel (1813) by Jane Austen (q. v.).   Mr. and Mrs. Bennet have five daughters of marriageable age.   One of them, Elizabeth, is attracted to and by Darcy, the proud and wealthy nephew of Lady Catherine de Bough, but her prejudice against his pride blinds her to his finer qualities.   When he helps her younger sister who has eloped with a n'er-do-well, she sees him as he really is.   They become engaged.

PRIG, MRS. BETSY--(Collect Ta-Celest)--A character in the novel Martin Chuzzlewit by Charles Dickens (q. v.).   She is nurse and a companion character to Mrs. Gamp, but not so fat.

PRIMROSE, MRS. --(Aspects V)--The wife of Dr. Primrose, the vicar of The Vicar of Wakefield (1766) by Oliver Goldsmith (q. v.).   She is an ambitious woman who is determined to get her daughters married well.

PRINCE, THE--(AH-Emp; Two Cheers-Bk)--A handbook (1513) of advice for the acquisition, maintenance, and use of power by Machiavelli (q. v.).

PRINCE OF ASTURIAS--(AH-Wil)--Francisco de Asís Fernando Pio Juan María Gregorio Pelayo.   1857-1885.   He succeeded his mother, Isabella II, on the throne of Spain as Alfonso XII, 1874-1885.

PRINCE CONSORT--(Two Cheers-English)--See: Albert.

PRINCE OTTO--(HE XIV)--A novel by Robert Louis Stevenson (q. v.).

PRINCE REGENT--(AH-JA; Two Cheers-Lon)--See: George IV.

PRINCE OF WALES--(AH-Adrift)--See: Edward VII.

PRINCESS OF PARMA--(Aspects IV)--A character in À la
Recherche du Temps Perdu by Proust (q.v.).

PRINCESS ROYAL--(Two Cheers-Eng)--Victoria Alexandra
Alice Mary, The Princess Royal of England, daughter of
Queen Victoria (q.v.).

PROCUSTUS--(Two Cheers-Raison)--See: Bed of Procustus.

PROGRESS AND POVERTY--(GLD VII)--By Henry George
(q.v.).

PROMESSI SPOSI, I--(Collect Ta-Eternal)--A novel (1825) by
Alessandro Manzoni.   Title in English: The Betrothed.
Renzo and Lucia, two Lombardy peasants in the 17th century, are thwarted in marriage by the plans of Don Rodrigo
who wants Lucia for himself.   Fortunately, a powerful Sig-
nore comes to the rescue of the lovers.

PROMETHEUS--(AH-TS; GLD VI)--Prometheus Unbound
(1820) by Shelley (q.v.).   A poetic drama in four acts.
Prometheus is at once an ideal and allegorical representation of man's desire for spiritual liberty and the fulfillment
of his intellect.

PROSPERO--(GLD V; HE XXVI)--A character in The Tempest
(first presented in 1611) by Shakespeare (q.v.).   The rightful Duke of Milan, exiled by his usurping brother, lives
on a distant island and has at his command magical powers
and a spirit, Ariel.   He regains his rightful place.

PROTEUS--(Alex I, 1; PP-Ph)--In the Odyssey, "the old
man of the sea."   He herded the seals and knew all things;
had the power of prophecy, and could change himself instant-
ly into any form he might wish (hence the adjective "protean").

PROTEUS--(PP-Tim)--A patriarch of Alexandria murdered
by the Alexandrians.

PROTO--(RWV II)--Proto in Toscana, a commune in the
province of Firenze, Italy some 11 miles NW of Florence.

PROUDIE, MRS.--(Aspects III)--A character in Barchester
Towers (1857) by Anthony Trollope.   She is the agressive
wife of the bishop of Barchester who tries her best to control the diocese.

PROUST, MARCEL--(AH-Proust; Aspects I; GLD XIV; Two Cheers-Anon; Two Cheers-English; Two Cheers-In; Two Cheers-Raison; Two Cheers-Romain; Two Cheers-Virginia)--1871-1922. Perhaps one of the most important of modern French writers or at the very least, having that reputation. He is most known for his huge seven-part novel (1913-1928) À la Recherche du Temps Perdu (q. v.).

PRUFROCK--The first volume of verse by T. S. Eliot (q. v.). Full title: Prufrock and Other Observations (1917).

PSCHOI, ST. --(Alex II, 7)--Also known as Besa or Isaiah, d. A. D. 250. A martyr during the persecution of Decius (q. v.). A mob killed him for attempting to protect Sts. Julian and Cronion from them.

PTOLEMIES--(Two Cheers-Racial)--A Greek family which ruled Egypt from the 4th to the 1st centuries B. C. See following entries.

PTOLEMY I SOTER--(Alex I, 1)--? 367-281 B. C. Surnamed Soter, the savior or preserver. King of Egypt, 323-285 B. C. He founded the dynasty which ruled over Egypt after it was conquered by Alexander the Great (q. v.). He was reputed to be the son of Arisone, a concubine of Philip II of Macedonia (q. v.), Alexander's father. He married his half-sister Berenice. He was a general in Alexander's army and received Egypt and Libya as his share of the empire Alexander had built. He made Alexandria his capital, established the museum and library of Alexandria, wrote a life of Alexander and resigned his throne in favor of his son Ptolemy II Philadelphus (q. v.).

PTOLEMY II PHILADELPHUS--(Alex I, 2; PP-Ph)--309-246 B. C. King of Egypt, 285-246 B. C. Surnamed Philadelphus, i. e., friend of his sister. He was the son of Ptolemy I Soter (q. v.). He married Arisone I, the daughter of the king of Thrace, and then his sister, Arisone II. His was a relatively peaceful reign. He built a canal from the Nile to the Red Sea and the lighthouse on Pharos. He also caused, according to tradition, the translation of the Hebrew Bible into Greek, i. e., the Septuagent.

PTOLEMY III EUERGETES--(Alex I, 1)--282?-222 B. C. King of Egypt, 246-222 B. C. Surnamed Euergetes, i. e., the well-doer or benefactor. He was the son of Ptolemy I. He married Berenice II of Cyrene. Other than a war against Syria, his reign was relatively peaceful. He was a patron of the arts and added a great number of books to the Alexandrine library. He was also a great builder of temples.

PTOLEMY IV PHILOPATER--(Alex I, 1)--244?-203 B.C. King of Egypt, 221?-203 B.C. He was the son of Ptolemy II (q.v.) and married his sister Arisone III. He was a weak ruler who early fell under the control of court favorites. He composed a tragedy and built a temple dedicated to Homer.

PTOLEMY V EPIPHANES--(PP-Epiph)--210?-181 B.C. King of Egypt, 203-181 B.C. The kingdom, during his reign, was menaced by Syria but saved by the intervention of Rome. He was poisoned by a member of his court.

PTOLEMY VII--(Alex I, 1)--161-144 B.C. King of Egypt, 145-144 B.C. Called Neos Philopater, i.e., to distinguish him from Ptolemy IV Philopater (q.v.). He was the son of Ptolemy VI and was murdered by his uncle who assumed the title of Ptolemy VIII.

PTOLEMY XIII--(Alex I, 1)--[According to some authorities his is the XII or the XIV of that name] 61-48 B.C. King of Egypt, 51-48 B.C. He married his sister, Cleopatra VII the Great (q.v.), and ruled jointly with her from 51-49 B.C. She expelled him, however, and he, in turn, waged war against her. She called on Julius Caesar for help, which was willingly supplied--and thereby hangs a tale. Ptolemy was drowned during a battle.

PTOLEMY XIV (OR XIII OR XV)--58?-44 B.C. King of Egypt, 47?-44 B.C. He was the youngest brother of Cleopatra VII the Great (q.v.) and also her brother-in-law since she was married to their brother Ptolemy XIII (q.v.). They ruled jointly until she murdered him to make room for her son by Julius Caesar, Caesarion.

PTOLEMY XV (OR XIV OR XVI)--(Alex I, 1)--47-30 B.C. Called Ptolemy Philomentor Caesar or, more commonly, Caesarion. Co-regent with his mother, Cleopatra VII the Great, of Egypt 44?-30 B.C. After the battle of Actium (q.v.), he was put to death by Octavius (q.v. under Augustus).

PTOLEMY XVI--(Alex I, 1)--See: Ptolemy XV.

PTOLEMY, CLAUDIUS--(Alex I, 1)--[Claudius Ptolemoeus] c. A.D. 100-170. An astronomer, geographer, and mathe-

matician of Alexandria. His compendius 13-volume Megale
Syntaxis tes Astronomias (Great System of Astronomy) described what is commonly known as the Ptolemaic System.
When translated into Arabic it received the prefix "al" and
has since widely been known by the contracted title Almagest.
Essentially, the theory held that the planets and the stars
revolve about the earth; also he insisted on accurate longi-
tude and latitude measurements before maps were made.

PUCCINI--(Two Cheers-Raison)--Giacomo Puccini, 1858-1924.
One of the most celebrated composers of Italian opera.
Among his most popular works are La Bohème (1896), Tosca
(1900) and Madame Butterfly (1904).

PUCK--(Two Cheers-Fo)--A mischievous goblin in the play
A Midsummer Night's Dream by William Shakespeare (q.v.).

PUMBLECHOOK--(Aspects I)--A character in Great Expectations (q.v.) by Charles Dickens (q.v.). Uncle Pumblechook
is a relative of Joe Gargery (q.v.) who constantly offers
platitudes as advice.

PUNCH--(AH-Notes)--An illustrated comic weekly magazine
founded in London in 1841 and still publishing.

PUNJABI--(PI XX)--Natives of the Punjab, a region in NW
India.

PUNJABI--(Two Cheers-William)--The pseudonym of William
Arnold (q.v.) under which he wrote Oakfield, or Fellowship
in the East.

PYM, DOROTHY--(MT)--The author of Battersea Rise (London, 1934). She was a cousin of Forster.

PYRAMUS AND THISBE--(Two Cheers-John)--Characters in
the play within the play in A Midsummer Night's Dream by
Shakespeare (q.v.).

PYRRHUS--(Alex I, 1)--318?-272 B.C. King of Epirus who
lost his throne and was then restored with the help of
Ptolemy I Soter (q.v.). He went to Italy to aid Tarentun
against the Romans and defeated them but, on being con-
gratulated for his victories, noted saltily that "one more
such victory and we are utterly undone." The cost of the
victory was so great that it was closer to a defeat, hence
the phrase a "Pyrrhic victory."

PYTHAGORAS--(AH-Gem)--fl. 565-495 B.C. A Greek philosopher and mathematician who traveled widely in search of
wisdom. He assigned a mathematical basis to the universe
and is said to have discovered the mathematical theorum
named after him.

PYTHO--(PP-Clement)--The original name of Delphi (q.v.).
It was given the name after the giant python which was slain
by Apollo.

Q

QUAKERS--(GLD XII)--The name commonly applied to members of the Society of Friends, a religious group founded in
1648-1650 by George Fox.

QUALITY STREET--(PI V)--A play (1901) by J. M. Barrie
(q.v.). Phoebe Throssel sets out to reconquer the heart of
Valentine Brown who, after his return from a long absence
finds her changed.

QUEEN, THE--(MT-East)--Queen Victoria (q.v.).

QUEEN'S ACRE--(AH-HOS)--The house of Howard Overing
Sturgis near Windsor.

QUEEN OF THE NIGHT--(Aspects VI; GLD X)--A character
in The Magic Flute (q.v.) by Mozart.

QUEEN OF PTOLEMY IV--(PP-Epiph)--Arisone III.

QUEEN OF SPAIN, THE--(Two Cheers-Not)--Jean Mariana
of Austria, wife of Philip IV. She served as regent for her
son Charles II.

QUEEN VICTORIA--(Two Cheers-Eng)--A biography (1921) by
Lytton Strachey.

QUEEN'S HALL--(HE V)--The "dreariest music-room" in
London where Aunt Juley, Meg and Helen go to hear Beethoven's Fifth Symphony.

QUEEQUEG--(Aspects VII)--A character in Moby Dick (q.v.)
by Herman Melville (q.v.). He is a Polynesian prince who
ships as a harpooner aboard Ahab's (q.v.) ill-fated whaler.

QUESTIONS OF THE ENCYCLOPEDIA--(AH-Vo)--by Voltaire (q.v.).

QUIPS, THE--(AH-Our D)--British "performers" in Egypt.

QUISLING--(Nordic)--Vidkun Quisling, 1887-1945. A Norwegian official who was a willing and active collaborator in
Germany's conquest of his country (1940). He was made
head of the puppet state council. After the war, he was
executed as a traitor.

QUIXOTE, DON--(Two Cheers-En)--The central figure in the
novel, Don Quixote de la Mancha (q.v.), by Miguel de Cervantes. He is a gentle, dignified, good, but slightly mad
individual who, through his reading, comes to think of himself as a knight of old. This mild madness leads him into
a series of humorous incidents.

                                R

RABELAIS--(MT)--François Rabelais, 1494?[1483? 1490?]-
1553. A French scholar, writer, satirist, physician, and
monk. He is most known for his Gargantua and Pantagruel
(1533) a satire of pedantry, religion, politics, etc.

RACHEL--(AH-Early; Two Cheers-Virginia)--The central figure in The Voyage Out (1915) a novel by Virginia Woolf (q.
v.). She is a young and unexperienced girl who falls in love
only to die of a tropical fever before she can live the life of
a normal young woman.

RACINE--(Aspects VIII; Nordic; Two Cheers-Cul; Two Cheers-
Does; Two Cheers-Raison)--Jean Baptiste Racine, 1639-1699.
A French playwright known for the psychological portrayal of
character. Phèdre (q.v.) is considered his chef d'oeuvre.

RADCLIFFE, MRS.--(AH-JA)--Mrs. Ann Radcliffe, née Ward,
1764-1823. An English Gothic novelist whose most popular
work is her Mysteries of Udolpho (1794). She specialized in
offering natural explanations of the supposed supernatural
events she depicted.

RAEMAKERS--(AH-TS)--A character in the novel À Rebours
(Against the Grain) 1884 by J. K. Huysmans.

RAINBOW, THE--(AH-Liberty)--A novel (1915) by D. H.
Lawrence (q. v.).   The work is ostensibly a study of three
generations of a family, the Brangwens.

RAJ PUTANA--(PI XXIII)--Literally: the country of the Raj-
puts, i. e. , NW India.

RALEIGH, SIR WALTER--(AH-Capt)--1552? -1618.   An Elizabethan adventurer, soldier of fortune, poet, writer, etc.
He was twice sent to the Tower, first by Elizabeth I (q. v.)
and then by James I.   He never came out the second time.

RALEIGH, SIR WALTER--(Aspects I)--1861-1922.   A professor of English at Oxford from 1904.   He wrote biographies
of Milton (1900), Wordsworth (1903), etc.

RAMESES [sic]--(Alex II, 1)--Or Ramses.   The name of 12 kings
of the XIXth and XXth dynasties of ancient Egypt.   Forster
is referring to the most famous of these, Ramses II (q. v.).

RAMSES II--(Alex II, 1)--Reigned 1292-1225 B. C.   The
fourth king of the 19th dynasty of Ancient Egypt.   He enlarged his kingdom in the early part of his reign and his
rule was generally marked by peace and prosperity.   He
caused a great number of temples to be built including addi-
tions to the Karnak complex and the Rameseum, a great
mortuary temple.   He is held to be the pharoah of the op-
pression ("Genesis, " "Exodus").

RAMSEY, MR. AND MRS. --(Two Cheers-Virginia)--Chief
characters in To the Lighthouse (1927) by Virginia Woolf
(q. v.).   He is a professor of philosophy, an author, and
the father of eight children.   She is a beautiful, warm, and
compassionate woman.

RANDOLPH--(AH-HOS)--A character in the novel, Belchamber, by Howard Overing Sturgis.

RANSOM, MICHAEL--(Two Cheers-Ascent)--A character in
The Ascent of F6, by W. H. Auden (q. v.) and Christopher
Isherwood (q. v.).   For a description see Forster's essay
"The Ascent of F. 6" [sic] in Two Cheers for Democracy.

RANSON, MRS. --(Two Cheers-Ascent)--The mother of Michael Ranson (q. v.).

RAPE OF THE LOCK, THE--(Aspects VI)--A comic-satiric poem in five cantos (1714) by Alexander Pope (q. v.). Lord Petrie has forcibly and willfully cut off a lock of Miss Fermor's hair and has thereby precipitated a quarrel between their families.

RAPHAEL--(Collect Ta-Celest)--Raffaello Santi. 1483-1520. An Italian painter most known for his madonnas and for the decorations of the Stanze in the Vatican. He was also one of the architects of St. Peter's Basilica.

RAPHAEL--(Collect Ta-Wood)--An archangel mentioned in the Book of Tobit.

RASKOLNIKOV--(Aspects VII)--Rodion Romanovich Raskolnikov, the chief character in Crime and Punishment (1866), by Dostoevsky (q. v.). He is a complex, introspective young student who murders an old money lender and, through that crime, confronts himself.

RASOUMOVSKY QUARTET--(Two Cheers-C)--The name given to three Beethoven (q. v.) string quartets, Opus 59, in F, E minor, and C (1806-07).

RASSELAS--(Aspects I)--The History of Rasselas, Prince of Abissinia (1759) by Samuel Johnson (q. v.), a "didactic romance." The Prince, weary of the pleasures and the comforts of the court of his father, escapes to Egypt and proceeds to study the various conditions of the life of mankind.

RAT WIFE, THE--(AH-Ibsen)--A character in Ibsen's (q. v.) Little Eyolf who is responsible for the death of Little Eyolf (q. v.).

RAWLINGS, MRS. --(AH-Mr.)--Frances Jennings Keats Rawlings, d. 1810. The mother of the Keats children, she married William Rawlings two months after the death of her first husband, but left him soon after.

READING, LORD--(Hill)--Rufus Daniel Isaacs, (1st Marquess of Reading), 1860-1935. A British statesman and jurist, he was Viceroy and Governor General of India, 1921-26.

REBOURS, À--(AH-TS)--A novel (1884) by J. K. Huysmans. Eng. title: Against the Grain. It is the story of Jean Esseintes, an effeminate descendant of warrior ancestors, who has a series of mistresses which results in the loss of

his virility.   He retires from the world and devotes himself
to a life of culture and refinement.   He is forced to return
to the world he hates on the advice of his physician.

RECHERCHE DU TEMPS PERDUS, À LA--(Two Cheers-Our)
--[Literally, "In Search of Time Lost."] See: Remembrance
of Things Past.

REFORM BILL OF 1832--(AH-Notes)--Designed by the English Parliament to widen its franchise and to remove abuses
in the system of representation.

REFORMATION--(AH-Notes)--The 16th-century movement
which attempted to change the doctrines of the Roman Catholic Church and resulted in the establishment of a series of
"Protestant" churches, more or less along national lines, in
Northern Europe.

REGENT STREET--(Two Cheers-London)--Designed (1813) by
John Nash to connect the London home of the Prince Regent
(q. v.) with Regent's Park (q. v.).   It was rebuilt 1922-26.

REID, FORREST--(AH-Fo; GLD XIV; Two Cheers-Last)--
1876-1946.   An Irish novelist, critic, and biographer, and
student of abnormal psychology.   His best novels are Spring
Song (1916) and its sequel Pirates of the Spring (1919).   He
has also written biographies of de la Mare and Yeats.

REMARQUE, ERIC [sic] MARIA--(Nordic; Two Cheers-What)--
[Orig. name: Erich Paul Remark] 1898-1970.   A German
novelist who made his international reputation with his anti-
war novel All Quiet on the Western Front (1929).   He became an American citizen in 1947.

REMEMBRANCE OF THINGS PAST--(Two Cheers-Our)--[À
la Recherche du Temps Perdu.] A novel (1913-1927) in
seven parts by Marcel Proust (q. v.).   Essentially, it re-
creates an epoch using over 200 characters.   Part I (1922)
is titled Swann's Way (Du Côté de chez Swann, French publication 1913).   In it Marcel recalls his days as a child and
the tenderness he desired from his mother but never received.   When he is older, it is clear to him that this
childhood longing for his mother is psychopathological.   There
is also a hint of homosexuality about it as well.   Swann, after whom the volume is named, is a neighbor and friend of
Marcel's family who, though gifted and fashionable, is essentially a philanderer.   Part II (1924), Within a Budding

Grove (Al'Ombre des Jennes Filles en Fleur, 1918), treats
of Marcel's love for Swann's daughter.   In Part III (1925),
The Guermantes Way (Le Côté de Guermantes, 1920-21),
Marcel's next love affair is treated: he falls in love with
the beautiful Duchesse de Guermantes.   In Part IV (1927),
Cities of the Plain (Sodom et Gomorrhe, 1921-22), Marcel
becomes involved with Albertine, a lesbian, who causes him
endless torment.   In Part V (1929), The Captive (La Prison-
nière, 1924), Marcel is determined to marry Albertine, thus,
he hopes, putting an end to his emotional malaise, but his
suspicions and jealousies drive her from him.   Part VI
(1930), The Sweet Cheat Gone (Albertine Disparu, 1925), is
a deeper investigation of Marcel's desire for Albertine.   Now
that she has gone from him, he desires to have her back.
He receives word that she is dead and, months later, a
telegram telling him that she is alive.   Marcel realizes,
however, that Albertine no longer means anything to him.
Part VII (1932), The Past Recaptured (Le Temps Retrouvé,
1927), merges the memories with the present, the author
with the hero, and self-chronology with self-realization.

REMUS--(Two Cheers-Fo)--The name of Forrest Reid's (q.
v.) dog.

RENAN, ERNEST--(LJ X)--Joseph Ernest Renan, 1823-1892.
A French philosopher and historian.   He was the leader of
the French school of critical philosophy.   His most famous
works are those in the series Histôires des Origines du
Christianisme including La Vie de Jésus (1863) and Les
Apôtres (1866).

RENI, GUIDO--(RWV IV)--1575-1642.   An Italian Eclectic
painter born near Bologna.   He worked for a time in Rome
until jealous rivals forced him to return to Bologna.

"REQUIEM"--(GLD X)--By Mozart (q. v.), who left it unfinished.   It was completed by Süsmayr.

RETURN OF THE NATIVE, THE--(Aspects V)--A novel
(1878) by Thomas Hardy (q. v.).   The novel is set on Egdon
Heath (q. v.) as sombre as the events it records.   Wildeve,
an engineer turned publican, is involved with two women who
love him: the gentle Thomasina and the wild Eustacia.   Dig-
gory Venn loves Thomasina but is rejected by her.   The two,
however, marry when Wildeve and Eustacia drown.

REUTER--(GLD XII)--Baron Paul Julius von Reuter (orig.:
Israel Beer Josaphat), 1816-1899. A German journalist who
in 1851 founded a bureau for collecting and transmitting news.
He transferred his operation to England where he became a
naturalized citizen.

REVOLT IN THE DESERT--(AH-Jo)--By T. E. Lawrence
(q. v.). It is a narration of Lawrence's efforts to stir the
Arabs into revolt against their Turkish masters during
World War I.

RHAKOTIS--(Alex I, 1)--A small Egyptian town, c. 3000
B. C. which once occupied the rise of ground in Alexandria
where new "Pompey's Pillar" stands.

RHINEGOLD--(LJ I)--An opera by Wagner (q. v.), one of the
Ring series. The king of the Nibelungs steals the gold of
the Rhine maidens and forges a magic ring with which he
hopes to become the master of the world.

RHODA--(Two Cheers-Virginia)--A character in The Waves
(1931) by Virginia Woolf (q. v.). She is the plain, clumsy
misfit who is despised by the world.

RIAZ PASHA--(AH-Wil)--1835?-1911. An Egyptian statesman and Prime Minister of Egypt for a number of years
(1879-81; 1888-1891; 1892-1894).

RICARDO--(Two Cheers-Henry)--David Ricardo, 1772-1823.
An English economist who published in 1817, Principles of
Political Economy and Taxation, his major work, which dis-
cusses the causes that determine the distribution of wealth.

RICHARD II--(GLD II)--1367-1400. King of England 1377-
1399. He was the son of the Black Prince. He set in motion his own tragic end when he banished Henry Bolingbroke
(later Henry IV) who was to depose him in 1399. He was
murdered in prison. He is the subject of a play by Shakespeare (q. v.).

RICHARD III--(Two Cheers-George)--A play (printed in 1597)
by Shakespeare (q. v.). It treats of the life of Richard of
Gloucester who murdered his way to the throne only to be
killed at Bosworth. The play ends the cycle dealing with
the War of the Roses (q. v.).

RICHARD FEVEREL--(Aspects I)--See: Feverel, Richard.

RICHARDS, I. A.--(Aspects IX)--Ivor Armstrong Richards, 1893- . An English literary critic and authority on semantics. His most popular work is his Practical Criticism (1929).

RICHARDSON, DOROTHY--(Two Cheers-Eng)--1873-1957. An English novelist and a pioneer in the development of the "stream-of-consciousness" technique used by James Joyce (q. v.) and Virginia Woolf (q. v.). She wrote a roman fleuve, comprising several volumes, Pilgrimage (1915-1938).

RICHARDSON, SAMUEL--(Aspects I)--1689-1761. An English novelist of little formal education who nevertheless was able to produce such novels as Pamela (1740-41) and Clarissa Harlowe (1747-48) which have become classics of their kind.

RICHMOND, GEORGE--(MT; Two Cheers-Bishop)--1809-1896. An English painter of portraits and a member of the Royal Academy (q. v.). He completed over 300 portraits in his lifetime.

RICKETTS--(HE V)--Charles Ricketts, 1866-1931. English painter, sculptor, and writer on art. He was originally trained as an illustrator and founded the Vale Press (1896) for which he designed type faces, initials, etc., in the spirit of William Morris.

RICKIE--(LJ I)--See: Frederick Elliot.

RIDGE, PETT--(Aspects I)--William Pett Ridge, 1860?-1930. An English novelist.

RIMBAUD--(Two Cheers-En)--Arthur Rimbaud, 1854-1891. A French Symbolist poet. He abandoned literature when still quite young and passed much of the remainder of his life as an explorer.

"RIME OF THE ANCIENT MARINER, THE"--(Two Cheers-Anon)--A long, narrative poem (1798) by Coleridge. It treats of an ancient mariner who has killed an albatross and is condemned to tell his story, as a form of penance, and thereby teach all to love and reverence life.

RIMINI--(AH-Gem)--A seaport in the province of Emilia (N Italy).

RING AND THE BOOK, THE--(Two Cheers-Snow)--A long
poem (1868-69) by Robert Browning based on a Roman murder case. The poem tells the story of Guido Franceschini,
a nobleman, who is arrested and executed for the murder of
his wife, Pompilia.

RING, THE--(GLD V)--Der Ring des Nibelungen. A four-
opera cycle by Richard Wagner (q. v.): Das Rheingold (q. v.,
"Rhinegold") Die Walküre, Siegfried, and Götterdämmerung.

RIPON--(HE X)--A city in Yorkshire, England about 23 miles
N of Leeds. It contains a 12th-century Norman cathedral.

RISORGIMENTO--(AH-Consol)--[Ital., "resurrection."] The
word is used as a name for the revolutionary movement of
the 19th century which had as its goal the unification of Italy.

ROBERTS, LORD--(LJ I; Two Cheers-Duke; Two Cheers-
English)--Frederick Sleigh Roberts (1st Earl Roberts of
Kandahar, Pretoria, and Waterford), 1832-1914. A British
soldier born in India, he served during the Sepoy Mutiny
and other campaigns in which he distinguished himself. He
was made commander in chief in India (1885-93), in Ireland
(1895-99) and in South Africa (1899).

ROBINSON CRUSOE--(Aspects I; MT)--The Life and Strange
Surprising Adventures of Robinson Crusoe (1719) by Daniel
Defoe (q. v.). The shipwrecked Crusoe successfully makes a
life for himself on a deserted island with the help of a poor
savage whom he names Friday.

ROCH, SAINT--(PP-Clement)--1295?-?1327. A French
Franciscan monk who worked among those striken by the
plague.

ROCKEFELLER--(GLD XI)--John Davison Rockefeller (I),
1839-1937. An American multi-millionaire oil magnate. He
organized the Standard Oil Company and was its first president. He also established four great charities.

RODD, SIR RENNELL--(Egypt)--James Rennell Rodd (1st
Baron Rennell), 1858-1941. English writer and diplomat.
He was minister to Sweden and ambassador to Italy. He began his diplomatic career with an appointment as secretary
at Cairo (1894-1901).

ROGER FRY--(Two Cheers-Virginia)--A biography of Fry (q.v.) by Virginia Woolf (q.v.), 1940.

ROLLAND, ROMAIN--(Two Cheers-Romain)--1866-1944. A French novelist, historian, music critic, etc. He is best known as the author of the ten-volume novel, Jean Christophe (q.v.). He also wrote a biography of Beethoven (q.v.).

ROMAN ANGLAIS DE NÔTRE TEMPS, LE--(Aspects I)--See: Chevalley, Abel.

ROMAN PICTURES--(Aspects VIII)--A novel by Percy Lubbock (q.v.).

ROMEO AND JULIET--(Two Cheers-Stratford)--A romantic tragedy by Shakespeare (q.v.). The play was probably written in 1595. The Montagues and Capulets are mortal enemies. Romeo, a Montague, falls in love with Juliet, a Capulet. Their love leads to their tragic death.

ROMFREY, EVERARD--(Aspects V)--A character in Beauchamp's Career (1874-75) by George Meredith (q.v.). He is Beauchamp's (q.v.) uncle and a conservative. He dislikes Dr. Shrapnel and approves of the match between his nephew and Cecilia.

ROOM OF ONE'S OWN, A--(Two Cheers-Virginia)--By Virginia Woolf (q.v.), 1921.

ROOSEVELT, PRESIDENT--(HE V)--Theodore Roosevelt, 1858-1919. The 26th president of the United States.

ROSAMUND--(Aspects V)--A character in Beauchamp's Career (1874-75). Mrs. Rosamund Culling, Romfrey's (q.v.) housekeeper, whom he finally marries.

ROSENBERG, ALFRED--(Nordic)--1893-1946. A Nazi leader and writer, editor, and director of the foreign policy office of the Nazi Party. He was also the founder of the Kampfbund for German culture.

ROSSETTI--(HE V)--Dante Gabriel Rossetti, 1828-1882. English poet and painter and one of the founders of the Pre-Raphaelite Brotherhood (q.v.).

ROSSETTI, CHRISTINA--(GLD IX)--Christina Georgina Rossetti, 1830-1894. A poet and sister of Dante Gabriel Rossetti (q.v.).

ROSMER--(AH-Ibsen)--The central character of <u>Rosmersholm</u> (q. v.) by Ibsen (q. v.).

<u>ROSMERSHOLM</u>--(AH-Ibsen)--A play (1886) by Ibsen (q. v.). Beata, married to Rosmer, commits suicide and, under the direction of Rebecca West, Rosmer becomes a free-thinker. When he learns that Rebecca has planned his wife's misery, Rosmer rebels against her tutelage.   They both go to their deaths in the mill stream.

ROSTOV, NATASHA--(AH-JA)--See: Natasha.

ROTHERHITHE CHURCH--(Two Cheers-Lon)--St. Mary's Church, Rotherhithe St.   It is the parish church, built in 1715, of Rotherhithe on the S bank of the Thames.

ROUSSEAU--(AH-Ab; Two Cheers-Enchanted; Two Cheers-Fer; Two Cheers-Menace)--Jean-Jacques Rousseau, 1712-1778.   A Swiss philosopher and writer, he led a rather erratic life and lived for 25 years with a kitchen maid by whom he had five children which he left at a foundling hospital.   He describes his rather disoriented life in his <u>Confessions</u>.   In a novel, <u>La Nouvelle Héloïse</u> he advocated a return to nature.   In other works, he attributed evil not to sin but to a departure from the "natural state" in which man is essentially good.   His philosophy, needless to say, proved very popular.

ROXANA--(Aspects III)--A character in <u>Roxana; or, the Fortunate Mistress</u> (1724) by Daniel Defoe (q. v.).   It is the purported autobiography of Mlle. Belear, later to be called Roxana, who is married to and deserted by a London brewer. She enters a life of prostitution and, true to the motion picture code of a later age, she dies repentant, but not until she has had a wild series of sexual adventures.

ROYAL ACADEMY--(AH-Me; LJ XI; MT)--Founded in 1768 under the patronage of George III (q. v.) for the annual exhibition of works of contemporary artists.   It was moved from the National Gallery (q. v.) to Burlington House, its present home, in 1869.   Joshua Reynolds was its first president.

ROYAL OPERA--(HE V)--See: Covent Garden.

<u>RUBÁIYÁT</u>--(Two Cheers-In)--See: Omar Khayyam.

RUBEKS, THE--(AH-Ibsen)--Arnold and Maria Rubek. Characters in the play, When We Dead Awaken (1900) by Ibsen
(q. v.). He is a sculptor once in love with Irene. He finds
life with Maria, his wife, impossible and goes in search of
Irene. Both die.

RUGBY--(AH-Ron; Two Cheers-William)--A school founded
in 1567. The game of the same name originated there.

"RUINS OF ATHENS, THE"--(RWV III)--Incidental music
(1812) by Beethoven (q. v.) for a play by Kotzebue. The play
was produced for the opening of the German Theatre at Pest
in Hungary.

RUINS OF HAMPI, THE--(PI XXIII)--The city of the Vijayan-
agar, a Hindu kingdom, destroyed in 1565. The ruins are
located near the modern city of Hampi in SW Andhra Pradesh, Indian Union.

RUMMING, ELINOR--(Two Cheers-John)--See: Forster's
essay "John Skelton" in Two Cheers for Democracy.

RUNES--(Two Cheers-Raison)--Letters or characters of the
earliest Teutonic alphabet used by the Anglo-Saxons.

RUSÉ--(Two Cheers-Raison)--French: artful, crafty, sly.

RUSHDI PASHA--(Egypt)--1864?-1928. He was Prime Minister of Egypt through the difficult period of World War I
and its immediate aftermath.

RUSHWORTH, MRS. --(AH-JA)--Née Maria Bertram. A
character in Mansfield Park (1814) by Jane Austen (q. v.).
She is the granddaughter of the wealthy baronet, Sir Thomas
Bertram and the older daughter of Edmund, his second son.
Spoiled and selfish, she marries the wealthy Mr. Rushworth
but tires of him and runs off with Henry Crawford. As a
result she is disgraced.

RUSK, HUBERT--(AH-Fo)--A character in Forrest Reid's
novel, The Bracknells.

RUSKIN--(GLD I; HE VI; RWV II; Two Cheers-Does; Two
Cheers-In)--John Ruskin, 1819-1900. An English writer,
art critic. The work which brought him into the public's
eye was Modern Painters; the first volume was issued in
1843. The five volumes which comprise it took some 17

years to produce.   He is also known for his Seven Lamps of
Architecture (1849) and Stones of Venice (1851-53).   He
championed the cause of the painter Turner, of Gothic Art,
and of the Pre-Raphaelite Brotherhood (q. v.).

RUSSELL, BERTRAND--(GLD XI; Hill; Two Cheers-English)
--Bertrand Arthur William Russell (3rd Earl Russell), 1872-
1970.   An English philosopher, logician, educator, etc.   He
is the author of many volumes many of which were propaganda for the causes he championed.   Like many very vocal
people, he was dedicated but rather petulant.   He is the author of Human Knowledge, Its Scope and Limits (1948).

RUSSELL, GEORGE WILLIAM--See: A. E.

RUTHERFORD, MARK--(Aspects VIII)--The pseudonym of
William Hale White, 1831-1913.   An English writer, book-
seller, and doorkeeper of the House of Commons.   He wrote
many volumes among which are The Autobiography of Mark
Rutherford and its sequel.   Both are intimately self-revela-
tory.

RUTLAND, THE DUKE OF--(Two Cheers-George)--Charles
Manners (4th Duke of Rutland), 1754-1787.   He protested in
Parliament the government policy of taxing the American
Colonies.   He was Lord Lieutenant of Ireland (1784).

RYLAND--(GLD XIV)--Henry Ryland, 1856-1924.   An English water-colorist.

                              S
                              ‾

SAAD ZAGLOUL PASHA--(Egypt)--See: Zagloul.

SABAEAN--(PP-Tim)--Inhabitants of the Biblical kingdom of
Sheba in Southern Arabia.

SABOATH--(Alex II, 1)--Hebrew: armies, hosts.

SACCO--(AH-Car)--A river in central Italy.

SACRED WOOD, THE--A book of critical essays by T. S.
Eliot (q. v.).

SAID PASHA--(Alex I, 5; Egypt)--1822-1863.   Viceroy of
Egypt (1854-63).   He was the fourth son of Mohammed Ali

(q. v.). He granted concessions to de Lesseps to build the Suez Canal.

SAINT-EUVERTE, MME. --(AH-Proust)--A character in Remembrance of Things Past (q. v.), by Marcel Proust (q. v.). She is a hostess whose parties are attended by the new and old friends of Swann (q. v.).

ST. HELENA--(Collect Ta-Co-ord)--A British island in the South Atlantic some 1200 miles from the W coast of Africa. It was Napoleon's (q. v.) place of exile from 1815-21.

SAINT JOAN--(Two Cheers-Clouds)--A play (1923) by George Bernard Shaw (q. v.). It tells the story of the saint's struggle to end England's control of France, but in the slightly irreverent style which is typically Shaw's.

SAINT LOUP--(AH-Proust; Aspects IV)--A character in Remembrance of Things Past (q. v.) by Marcel Proust (q. v.). He is the nephew of Baron de Charlus (q. v.) and the friend of Marcel (q. v.). Aristocratic society and his experiences in the army turn him from an innocent into a sophisticate.

ST. MAGNUS THE MARTYR--(Two Cheers-Lon)--A church designed by Christopher Wren (q. v.) and built from 1671-87, with one of his finest steeples. Located near London Bridge (q. v.), it was damaged in World War II and was rebuilt in 1951.

ST. MARGARET'S WESTMINSTER--(GLD I)--The mother church of the city of Westminster, London and the parish church since 1614 of the House of Commons. It was founded in the 11th or 12th century and rebuilt in the perpendicular style 1504-23.

ST. MARY'S--(LJ VI)--The Roman Catholic Church in Cambridge (q. v.).

ST. PANCRAS--(HE II)--A London borough, the name of a church and a railroad station.

ST. PAUL'S--(Two Cheers-Lon)--The cathedral of London and the seat of its bishop. The present church is a replacement for the gothic structure destroyed in the Great Fire (q. v.), 1666. It was begun in 1675 and completed in 1710 and was designed by Christopher Wren (q. v.).

SAINTY--(AH-HOS)--A character in the novel, Belchamber, by Howard Overing Sturgis. He is a misfit who, though bored by his class, remains an aristocrat.

SALAMIS--(PP-Return)--In ancient times, the chief city of Cyprus on its east coast.

SALEH AGHA TOUNMAKSIS--(Alex II, 7)--The builder of Toumaksis Mosque in Rosetta (1694).

SALISBURY--(LJ XI)--A town in S England on the Avon containing a famous and beautiful gothic cathedral.

SALISBURY, LORD--(MT)--Robert Albert Talbot Cascoyne-Cecil (3rd Marquis of Salisbury), 1830-1903. Prime Minister and Foreign Secretary (1885-86; 1886-92; 1895-1902). He followed an imperialist policy.

SAMARKAND--(AH-Emp; PI XXX)--The name of a city as well as a province in Uzbek SSR. The city contains the tomb of Tamerlane.

SANDOW, EUGENE--(LJ XII)--1867-1925. A professional strongman and exponent of physical culture. He was born in Königsberg, Germany and exhibited his feats of strength at the Chicago World's Fair (1893).

SALTER, SIR ARTHUR--(GLD XII)--Sir James Arthur Salter, 1881- . An English economist and professor of political theory and institutions at Oxford since 1934. He was general secretary of the Reparation Commission 1920-22, as well as director of the economic and finance section of the League of Nations (q. v.) 1919-20; 1922-31.

SALUTE--(PI XXX)--[Ital.:   health.] Santa Maria della Salute, a church in Venice across the Grand Canal from the Piazza San Marco.

SAND, GEORGE--(Aspects VI)--Pseudonym of Amatine Lucille Aurore Dupin, 1804-1876. A French novelist known more for the male clothing she wore, the cigars she smoked, and the lovers she had (de Musset, Chopin, etc.) than for her novels which were influenced, logically, by the philosophy of Rousseau (q. v.).

SANDYS, JOHN--(Alex I, 4)--[Forster is in error in Sandys' given name. It is George, not John] 1578-1644. He was a traveler and translator, son of an archbishop of York and educated at Oxford. In 1615 he published an account of his journey to the East.

SAN GIMIGNANO--(WAFT I)--A hill town in the province of Siena. It contains many towers of the 13th and 14th century and other remains of the Middle Ages and of the Renaissance.

SAN GIORGIO--(PI XXXI)--A church in Venice located on an island of the same name.

SAN GOTHARD TUNNEL--(WAFT X)--A tunnel connecting Switzerland with Italy through the Saint Gotthard (Gothard) mountain range.

SAN MINIATO--(RWV I)--A church near the Piazzale Michelangelo in Florence begun in the 11th century and completed in the 13th century. Its façade is modern.

SANTA CROCE--(RWV II)--A Franciscan Church in Florence begun in 1295. It contains the tombs of many prominent Italians as well as art by Fra Angelico and others.

SANTA DEODATA--(WAFT I)--Santa Fina (q. v.) served as the original for the fictional Santa Deodata in the novel. The life Forster ascribes to his fictional saint is that of Santa Fina without, of course, the cynicism.

SANTA MARIA NOVELLA--(AH-Gem)--A church in Venice built in 1278 and containing many important works of art by Ghirlandaio, Bronzino, Nardo di Cione, della Robbia, and others.

SANTA MARIA DELLA SALUTE--(PI XXX)--See: Salute.

SANTA SOPHIA--(Two Cheers-Does)--The great cathedral built by the emperor Justinian from 532 to 537. It is dedicated to the Holy Spirit, the second Person of the Holy Trinity. It is now a museum.

SANTAL--(AH-Ron)--A novel (1921) by Ronald Firbank.

SARAI--(LJ VII)--Or Sarah, the wife of Abraham and mother of Isaac in the Old Testament ("Genesis").

SARASTRO--(Aspects VI)--A character in Der Zauberflöte (1791) (The Magic Flute, q. v.) by Wolfgang Amadeus Mozart (q. v.).

He is a wicked magician who kidnaps Pamina, the daughter of the Queen of the Night.

SARGENT--(AH-Me)--John Singer Sargent, 1856-1925. An American artist known chiefly for his portraits.

SARGON II--(AH-For the Muse)--King of Assyria, 722-705 B. C. During his reign, he consolidated the empire and carried the Israelites into slavery (2 "Kings"). He was succeeded by Sennacherib.

SARTOR RESARTUS--(Aspects V)--Subtitled: The Life and Opinions of Herr Teufelsdröckh (1833-34) by Thomas Carlyle (q. v.). The volume consists of two parts: the first on the philosophy of clothes; the second, a biography of Teufelsdröckh.

SASSOON, SIR PHILIP--(AH-Me)--Philip Albert Gustave David Sassoon, 1888-1939. A connoisseur of art, member of parliament, and first Commissioner of Works from 1937.

SASSOON, SIEGFRIED--(AH-Note; Reading; Two Cheers-English)--1886-1967. An English poet noted especially for his vivid, satirical war poetry. It expresses his bitterness toward the romanticism and hypocrisy which often surrounds war. His Collected Poems appeared in 1947.

SATURNALIA--(HE XXVIII)--The Roman festival of the god Saturn celebrated on the 17, 18, 19 December during which all business came to a halt and feasting and wild living were the order of the day.

SATYRS--(Collect Ta-Other)--In Greek and Roman myth a race of immortal goat-men who live in the woods, the most famous of whom is Silenus.

SAVONAROLA--(AH-Gem; AH-Notes; GLD VII; RWV V)-- Fra Girolamo Savonarola, 1452-1498. A preacher and reformer of Florence.

SAWSTON--(SJ XVI; RWV VIII; WAFT V)--The fictional scene, in part, of Forster's novels: The Longest Journey, A Room With a View, and Where Angels Fear to Tread. Its original is Tonbridge, a town 25 miles from London, where Forster went to school (1893-1897).

SAWSTON SCHOOL--(LJ IX)--The school at which Rickie
teaches Latin. The original is at Tonbridge, the school
Forster attended from 1893 to 1897.

SCALIGER, JULIUS CAESAR--(AH-Car)--1484-1558.   An
Italian doctor, philosopher, and writer.

SCALLIES, THE--(AH-Our Div)--Performers who played,
sang, and told jokes during a respite in the war (World War
I) in Alexandria.

SCARBOROUGH--(GLD X)--A municipal borough in North
Riding, Yorkshire, England.

"SCENT OF THE CONIFERS, SOUND OF THE BATH, THE"
--(Two Cheers-Outsider)--Line 17 from "A Subaltern's Love-
Song" by John Betjeman as it appears in Poetry of the Pres-
ent, edited by Geoffrey Grigson (q.v.), p. 78-79.

SCHEHERAZADE--(Aspects II)--The narrator of The Thousand
and One Nights Entertainment (The Arabian Nights).   She is
the daughter of the Grand Vizier and wife of the Sultan. She
tells the stories in order to prevent her lord killing her.

SCHEISS, DR.--(Alex II, 4)--A director of the Egyptian
Government Hospital of Alexandria.   His tomb, an early
Christian sarcophagus, is in its courtyard.

SCHILLER--(AH-Word; GLD IX; Two Cheers-Tol)--Ferdinand
Canning Scott Schiller, 1864-1937.   An English writer and
philosopher, tutor at Oxford (1903-1926); and professor at
the University of Southern California.

SCHIRACH, BALDUR VON--(Nordic; Two Cheers-What)--
b. 1907.   German Nazi politician and leader of the Nazi
youth movement.   He served a 20-year sentence as a war
criminal.

SCHOENBERG, ARNOLD--(Nordic)--1874-1951.   An Austrian
composer of the ultramodern school of music. He came to
the U.S. in 1933 as a refugee from Nazi Germany.   Some of
his works are Verklärte Nacht (1899) and Surrelieder (1913).

SCHOPENHAUER--(RWV XII)--Arthur Schopenhauer, 1788-
1860.   A German philosopher and chief exponent of philosophical pessimism.   His ideas are explained in his major work,
The World As Will and Idea (1819).

SCHUBERT--(GLD IX)--Franz Schubert, 1797-1828. Austrian composer and one of the greatest composers of lieder. He has also composed symphonies, notably his "Unfinished" in B Minor.

SCHUMANN--(AH-Word; RWV XI; Two Cheers-Not Listening) --Robert Alexander Schumann, 1810-1856. A German composer and pianist of the Romantic school. He also composed lieder based on poems by Heine (q.v.).

SCHUMANN PIANO QUARTET--(Two Cheers-Not Listening)-- There are two: the quartet for violin, viola, cello, and pianoforte in C minor, Opus 1 (1829); and the quartet for violin, viola, cello, and pianoforte in E flat major (1842), Opus 47. It is not clear from the text to which one Forster is referring. It would appear that perhaps he was not aware that two quartets existed.

SCHUMANN'S PIANO QUINTET--(AH-Word)--The quintet for two violins, viola, cello, and pianoforte in E flat major (1842), Opus 44.

SCORPIO--(Collect Ta-Machine)--The eighth sign of the zodiac which the sun enters October 24 or thereabouts.

SCOTT, CAPTAIN--(Two Cheers-Ascent)--Robert Falcon Scott, 1868-1912. An English explorer of the South Pole. He surveyed South Victoria Land, the interior of the Antarctic continent, and discovered Edward VII Land (1901-1904).

SCOTT, LADY--(Two Cheers-George)--The wife of Sir Walter Scott (q.v.) née Charlotte Margaret Charpentier. The daughter of a French émigré, she married Scott in 1797.

SCOTT, THOMAS HAMILTON--(Alex II, 1)--d. 1807. His tombstone is in the courtyard of the convent of St. Saba in Alexandria.

SCOTT, SIR WALTER--(AH-JA; Aspects II; GLD I; Two Cheers-George; WAFT VI)--1771-1832. A Scottish novelist, poet, historian, etc. He wrote extensively, producing numerous works which have become household words including the novels The Antiquary (q.v., 1815), Ivanhoe (1820), Kenilworth (1821), and Quentin Durwood (1823).

SEA OF SERENITY--(HE XLI)--An area on the moon.

SEA OF TRANQUILITY--(HE XLI)--An area on the moon.

SEBASTIAN, ST. --(Two Cheers-Whiff)--A Christian martyr
of the 3rd century. He was a soldier who served under the
emperors Maximian and Diocletian. He converted many and,
when he refused to cease from proselyting, he was executed
by archers.

SEBEK--(Alex II, 3)--[Greek: Petesuches,] "he who belongs
to Suchos." In Egyptian myth, the sacred crocodile, the
incarnated soul of the god Sebek, the greatest god of the
Fayyum. His chief sanctuary was at Crocodilopolis.

SEKHET--(Alex II, 1)--In Egyptian myth, the goddess of the
heat of the sun.

SENECA--(Two Cheers-Bishop)--Lucius Annaeus Seneca, 48
B. C. -A. D. 65. A stoic philosopher, tutor of Nero, and
dramatist. He is noted for the type of tragedy which has
come to be called "Senecan. " These plays are generally
marked by extreme violence and bombast. There is little
individuality among the characters. Some of his more important plays are Phaedra, Agamemnon, and Oedipus.

SENSE AND SENSIBILITY--(AH-JA; AH-Notes)--A novel
(1811) by Jane Austen (q. v.). Elinor (Sense) and Marianne
(Sensibility) are two sisters each deserted by a young man
from whom a marriage proposal was expected.

SEPTUAGINT TRANSLATION--(PP-Ph)--A Greek version of
the Old Testament called so because 72 Jewish scholars
translated it from the Hebrew in 72 days on orders of Ptolemy Philadelphus (q. v.).

SERAPIS--(Alex I, 1; PP-Clement)--The Ptolemaic form of
Apis (the bull-god), an Egyptian deity who, when dead, was
honored under the attributes of Osiris and thus became
"Osirified Apis. " He was lord of the underworld and was
identified by the Greeks with Hades, and by the Romans with
Pluto (q. v.).

SET--(Alex I, 3)--The Egyptian original of the Greek Ty-
phon, the god of evil, the brother or son of Osiris and also
his deadly enemy. He has the body of a man and the head

of some mythological beast with a pointed muzzle and high,
square ears.

SEURAT--(Two Cheers-Art)--Georges Seurat, 1859-1891. A
French painter who developed the technique called "pointil-
lism, " a series of different colored dabs of paint juxtaposed
which collectively form the picture. His most famous work
in this technique is his "L'Île de la Grande Jatte. "

"SEVEN-BRANCHED CACTUS, THE"--(Two Cheers-Outside)
--Line 7 from the poem "The Wilderness" by Sidney Keyes
as it appears in Poetry of the Present edited by Geoffrey
Grigson (q. v.), p. 130.

SEVEN PILLARS OF WISDOM--(AH-TE; Two Cheers-Clouds;
Two Cheers-English)--A book (1921) by T. E. Lawrence
(q. v.) which details the trials and tribulations of its author
in his attempts to rouse the Arabs to revolt against their
Turkish masters during World War I. A shorter version,
Revolt in the Desert (q. v.), was published in 1927.

SEVENTY YEARS AMONG THE SAVAGES--(GLD VIII)--A
volume by Henry Salt.

SÉVIGNÉ, MME. DE--(Two Cheers-Bishop; Two Cheers-
English; Two Cheers-Mrs.)--Née Marie de Rabutin-Chantal
(Marquise de Sévigné), 1626-1696. A French writer famous
for her letters to her daughter which record her day-to-day
life in flawless French.

SEWARD, ANNA--(MT)--1742-1809. The "Swan of Litchfield. " An English poetess. She was one of the sources
Boswell (q. v.) used in his life of Samuel Johnson (q. v.).
Sir Walter Scott (q. v.) published her works in three volumes
with a memoir (1810).

SEYMOUR, ADMIRAL--(Alex I, 5; PP-Ph)--Frederick Beauchamp Paget (1st Baron Alcestor), 1821-1895. He saw action in the Crimean War and commanded a naval brigade in
New Zealand during the Maori War (1860-61). He was commander-in-chief in the Mediterranean from 1880-83 during
which time he commanded the bombardment of Alexandria.

SHAKESPEARE--(AH-Consol; AH-Early; AH-My W; Aspects
I; Collect Ta-Celest; GLD I; HE V; MT; Nordic; Two Cheers-
Anon; Two Cheers-Art; Two Cheers-Bishop; Two Cheers-
Does; Two Cheers-English; Two Cheers-In; Two Cheers-John;

Two Cheers-Jul; Two Cheers-Virginia; Two Cheers-Volt; Two
Cheers-What Would)--William Shakespeare, 1564-1616. By
far the greatest of all English poets and dramatists. Little
is known of his life, but he left behind a series of plays
which will live as long as the language exists. Among these
the most memorable is <u>Hamlet</u> (q. v.).

SHANDY, TRISTRAM--(Aspects VI)--The central figure and
narrator of <u>Tristram Shandy</u> (1759-1767) by Laurence Sterne
(q. v.). He suffers various misfortunes in his life not the
least of which limits the amatory phase of that life.

SHARP, BECKY--(Aspects IV)--One of the principals in
<u>Vanity Fair</u> (1847-48) by William Makepeace Thackeray (q. v.).
She is beautiful, intelligent, selfish, and grasping, but thoroughly enchanting. She has a number of affairs and conquests not the least of whom must be every male reader.

SHAW, GEORGE BERNARD--(AH-Ibsen; AH-Mrs. G; AH-Wil;
GLD VIII; HE XXXVIII; Two Cheers-Clouds; Two Cheers-
Raison)--1856-1950. The first of the "angry [or cranky depending upon how one views him] young men. " An Irish-
born dramatist, journalist, critic, amateur philosopher, etc.,
and an early member of the Fabian Society for which he
wrote a number of tracts. The petulance he displayed in
his life colored his plays, the prefaces of which more often
than not overwhelmed the works. He believed in the "Life
Force" a power which he conceived works to raise mankind
to a better level of existence. Some of his works are <u>Back
to Methuselah</u> (1921), <u>St. Joan</u> (1924), and <u>Caesar and
Cleopatra</u> (1924).

SHELBOURNE, LORD--(Two Cheers-George)--Sir William
Petty (2nd Earl of Shelbourne, 1st Marquis of Lansdowne),
1737-1805. An English statesman. He opposed the Stamp
Act (1763) and generally the policy of his government against
the American Colonies. He became First Lord of the Treasurey
and Prime Minister 1782-83.

SHELLEY--(AH-Liberty; GLD VI; LJ IX; New Disorder; Two
Cheers-Anon; Two Cheers-Art; Two Cheers-Edward; Two
Cheers-En)--Percy Bysshe Shelley, 1792-1822. One of the
foremost of the English Romantic poets. He was educated
at Oxford and, while there, published his first poetry. Some
of his finest work is to be found in his lyrics "Ode to the
West Wind, " "To a Skylark, " and "O, World! O, Life! O,
Time!"

SHEMS-UD-DIN--(AH-Salute)--A character in the novel,
House of Islam by Marmaduke Picthall (q. v.).

SHERATON--(GLD II)--Thomas Sheraton, 1751-1806.   An
English designer of furniture which featured slim, tapering
legs.   He produced books of furniture designs which proved
popular as well as influential in directing the tastes of the
public.

SHIRLEY--(Aspects I)--A novel (1849) by Charlotte Brontë
(q. v.).   A mill owner in Yorkshire attempts to introduce
labor-saving devices in his mill despite the objections of
his workers.   To overcome the financial difficulties he encounters, he proposes to Shirley Keeldar, a wealthy young
lady, despite the fact that he really loves Caroline.

SHIRTA, CLEMENT--(GLD I)--Clement King Shirta, 1857-
1926.   English literary critic, journalist, biographer.   He
edited the London Illustrated News (1891-1900) and produced
a biography of George Barrow (1913) as well as Charlotte
Brontë and Her Circle (1896).

SHIVA--(Hill)--Siva.   The third person of the Hindu trinity
representing the destructive principle as well as the repro-
ductive or renovating power.   He is a favorite deity, surprisingly, with ascetics.   He is also the god of dancing and
the fine arts.

SHOOTING AN ELEPHANT--(Two Cheers-George)--A posthumous volume of essays (1950) by George Orwell (q. v.).

SHOSTAKOVITCH--(Two Cheers-Raison)--Dimitry Shostako-
vitch, 1906-   .   A Russian composer of music and a pupil
of Glazunov.   He wrote his very successful symphony No. 1
at 19.   In 1936, he was denounced by Soviet officialdom for
his "unmelodiousness" and in 1948 for his "formalism."   In
each instance, he admitted his "errors."   In addition to orchestral works, he has also written operas: Lady Macbeth
of Minsk and Katerina Ismailova, etc.

SHRAPNEL, DR. --(Aspects V)--A character in Beauchamp's
Career (1874-75) by George Meredith (q. v.).   He is a wild
political radical who is supposed to be helping Beauchamp
with his campaign for a seat in Parliament.   Actually, he is
ruining the latter's career.

SHRI KRISHNA--(PI VII)--See: Krishna.

SHRINE OF THE BODY, THE; and SHRINE OF THE HEAD, THE--(PI XXXV)--Two parts of the legend of the Hindu god Krishna. For a good explanation see A Passage to India, Chapter XXXV.

SHROPSHIRE--(HE XV)--A county in W England on the Welsh border. Its largest town is Shrewsbury.

SHROPSHIRE LAD, A--(RWV XII)--A collection of poetry (1896) by A. E. Housman (q.v.). It contains some of his best known poems.

SHYLOCK--(Reading)--The Jewish money-lender in The Merchant of Venice by Shakespeare (q.v.).

SIBYL, THE--(Aspects II; Collect Ta-Eternal; LJ VI)--In classical legend, a prophetess who was supposed to prophesy under the inspiration of a deity. There were a number of Sibyls in scattered parts of the ancient world: Egypt, Italy, Babylonia, and the most famous, the Delphic Oracle in Greece.

SIDGWICK, HENRY--(Aspects I)--1838-1900. An English philosopher and one of the founders of the Society for Psychical Research (q.v.). He was a disciple of John Stuart Mill (q.v.). A Utilitarian, he believed in prudence and benevolence.

SIDI EL METWALI--(Alex II, 1)--A Mohammedan saint whose wayside tomb is near the Catholic archbishop's palace in Alexandria.

SIDI GABER--(Alex II, 5)--A local Mohammedan saint of Alexandria who is said to fly about at night and who looks after children.

SIDNEY, SIR PHILIP--(AH-Our Div)--1554-1586. An English poet of the Elizabethan period. He produced, among other works, a sonnet sequence, Astrophel and Stella (1580-84), addressed to Penelope, daughter of the 1st earl of Essex. He exercised a strong influence on his own generation of poets as well as on succeeding generations.

SIEGFRIED--(Nordic)--The son of Siegmund (q.v.) and Sieglinde in the Wagnerian opera of the same name. He was raised by the Nibelung smith. With a sword forged from the fragments of his father's, he slays the giant snake which

guards the Rhine gold and obtains the magic ring. With it
he passes through the fires that surround Brünnhilde (q.v.
under Brünnhilde).

SIEGFRIED--(GLD XIV)--An opera by Wagner (q.v.). See:
Siegfried.

SIEGMUND--(Nordic; Two Cheers-Post)--The father of Siegfried (q.v.). He appears in the opera Die Walküre by Wagner (q.v.).

SIENA--(WAFT VI)--A province in Italy and a city in that
province 33 miles S of Florence. It contains many Medieval
and Romanesque buildings as well as Renaissance art. It
was founded by the Etruscans.

SIGNORELLI, LUCCA--(WAFT VII; RWX X)--?1445-1523.
An Italian painter, the pupil of Piero della Francesco. He
attempted a monumental treatment of the human body. He
is known for his frescoes in the cathedral of Orvieto depicting the end of the world.

SIKHS--(PI XX)--In India, the followers of the religious
theories of Guru Nanak (1469-1538). They are non-sectarian
believing in the fundamental truths which underlie all religions; their scriptures are called the Adi Granth.

SILENUS--(GLD VI)--In Greek myth, he is the drunken companion of the god Dionysus (q.v.). He is lazy, wanton, fond
of music and a prophet, and is described as an old, fat,
bald-headed, pug-nosed man.

SIMLA--(PI XIV)--A hill station in the Punjab, India, and
the summer capital for the British when they ruled India.

SIMON STYLITES, SAINT--(PP-Clement)--Stylites [Greek
for "pillar"] d. A.D. 596. He was the most important of a
group of ascetics who lived atop pillars. He lived for 68
years atop various pillars, fasting and praying. He died
atop one that was 66 feet tall.

SIMPSON'S IN THE STRAND--(HE XVII)--An old restaurant
in London famous for its roast beef and Yorkshire pudding,
located in the Strand near the Savoy Theatre.

SIRENS--(Collect Ta-Other; HE XI)--In Greek myth, crea-
tures half-woman and half-bird said to be able to entice sea-

men to their deaths by their songs.

SIRIUS--(AH-My W)--The dog star [from Greek series, "hot, scorching"].

SISTINE CHAPEL--(RWV II)--A chapel in the Vatican built by Pope Sixtus IV (1473-1484), hence its name. The election of a new pope and religious ceremonies are held there. The frescoes are by Michelangelo and other well-known painters such as Boticelli, and Signorelli.

SIVA--(PI VII)--See: Shiva.

SKELTON--(Two Cheers-John)--John Skelton, 1460?-1529. An English poet and tutor to Henry VIII. Despite his outspokenness, he was in favor at the court. He took holy orders in 1498 and became parson at Diss in Norfolk. In his poetry, he used a meter some describe as doggeral which has come to be called "Skeltonic." He wrote many poems the more famous of which are "Colyn Cloute" and "Phylyp Sparowe."

SLATER, MONTAGU--(Two Cheers-George)--1902- . The librettist of the opera, Peter Grimes (q. v.), by Sir Benjamin Britten (q. v.). He is also the author of plays (e. g. , Century for George, 1946; Easter: 1916, 1936 and novels (e. g. , Haunting Europe, 1934; and Man with a Background of Flames, 1954).

SLIPSLOP, MRS. --(Aspects VI; MT)--A character in Joseph Andrews (1742) by Henry Fielding (q. v.). She is the housekeeper of Lady Booby (q. v.). Misshapen and aggressive she almost succeeds in seducing Joseph.

SLOANE STREET--(HE XV)--A street in London, long and straight, which connects Knightsbridge Station with Sloane Square.

SLOP, DR. --(Aspects VI)--A character in Tristram Shandy (1759-1767) by Laurence Sterne (q. v.). He is a bungling country doctor. It is his forceps which flatten Tristram's nose during his birth thus resulting in the first of the many misfortunes the boy is to suffer.

SMERDYAKOV--(Aspects VII)--The half-witted steward and perhaps the natural son of Karamazov in The Brothers Karamazov (q. v.) by Dostoevsky (q. v.). He murders Karamazov and then hangs himself.

SMETANA--(Nordic; Two Cheers-What Would)--Bedřich [Frederick] Smetana, 1824-1884.   Czech national composer, conductor, and pianist.   He was encouraged by Franz Liszt. Though totally deaf by 1874, he continued to compose. Among his many works is the cycle of symphonic poems, "My Country"; the operas The Bartered Bride and Dalibor, and many pieces for the piano.

SMITH, LOGAN PERSALL--(GLD XI)--1865-1946.   An essayist, poet, critic, and writer.   He is the author of Songs and Sonnets (1909), On Reading Shakespeare (1933), Milton and His Modern Critics (1938), and other works.

SMITH, SYDNEY--(Two Cheers-Tol)--1771-1845.   English essayist, editor, clergyman and co-founder of the Edinburgh Review (1802).   He was also a lecturer on moral philosophy, and noted for his wit.   He was canon of St. Paul's (London) 1831-1845.

SMUTS--(AH-Liberty)--Jan Christiaan Smuts, 1870-1950. South African soldier and statesman.   A leader in the Boer War (q.v.), he was one of the principals in effecting the Union of South Africa and was its Prime Minister (1919-24; 1939-1948).

SNOWE, LUCY--(Aspects IV)--The principal character in Villette (1857) by Charlotte Brontë (q.v.).   She is a quiet, hard-working, intelligent girl whose surface calm belies her passionate nature.   She falls in love with Paul Emanuel, a teacher of English in the boarding school at Villette where she also works.

SOCIETY FOR PSYCHICAL RESEARCH--(GLD X)--Founded (1882) in London to study all para-normal manifestations, e.g., appearances of ghosts, messages from the dead received through mediums, etc.   Similar societies now exist in many countries.

SOCRATES--(GLD VI; Hill; PP-Clement)--469-399 B.C.   The greatest of all Greek philosophers.   He was married to Xanthippe, a shrew, and condemned to death by the Athenians for teaching impiety.   Socrates wrote nothing.   What we know of his philosophy comes to us from the writings of Plato (q.v.), one of his pupils.   He held, essentially, that philosophy should investigate ethical questions and that wickedness is the result of ignorance.

SOHO--(LJ XV)--The "Greenwich Village" (q.v.) of London. A district which is mainly inhabited by foreigners especially Italians and Frenchmen.

SOIGNÉ--(Two Cheers-Raison)--French: neat, smart, first rate, carefully done.

SOLNESSES, THE--(AH-Ibsen)--Halvard and Aline Solness. See: The Master Builder.

SOLOMON--(Alex I, 3; Two Cheers-Volt)--Son and successor of David as king of Israel, c. 961-922 B.C. He was the son of David's favorite wife, Bathsheba. He was noted for his wisdom and the building of the Temple at Jerusalem.

SOLVEIG--(AH-Ibsen; Two Cheers-Ascent)--A character in Peer Gynt (q.v.) by Ibsen (q.v.). She is Peer's ideal love and, although she grows old and almost blind waiting for his return, she has power to defy the Button Moulder (q.v.). Her power comes from her faith that her love can reveal the real Peer.

SOMEHOW GOOD--(AH-Word)--A novel (1908) by William Frend de Morgan (q.v.).

SONGS OF INNOCENCE--(AH-Notes)--A collection (1789) of poetry of William Blake (q.v.).

SONS AND LOVERS--(Two Cheers-English)--A novel (1913) by D. H. Lawrence (q.v.). It treats of the relationship between a son (Paul Morel) and his mother characterized by a strong Oedipus complex. Because of his attachment for his mother, Paul finds it difficult to experience love.

SOPHIA--(Aspects II; Two Cheers-Virginia)--Sophia Baines, a character in the Old Wives's Tale (1908) by Arnold Bennett (q.v.). She is a high-spirited young girl and the only member of her family strong enough to oppose her father. She becomes a school teacher and marries, but not happily. She goes to Paris where she is successful in business.

SOPHOCLES--(AH-Note; AH-Troop; Collect Ta-Other; LJ XVI; Two Cheers-Bishop; Two Cheers-Bk; Two Cheers-Does; Two Cheers-What; Reading)--496-406 B.C. One of the great writers of Greek tragedies. He was the first to increase the

number of actors to three.   His dramas are generally involved with human character.   He presented men as they
ought to be.   Some of his plays are Oedipus Rex (q. v. under
Oedipus), Oedipus Coloneus (q. v.), and Antigone (q. v.).

SOPHRONISKA--(Aspects V)--A character in The Counterfeiters (q. v.) by André Gide (q. v.).

SOSIBUS--(Alex I, 1)--A Greek sculptor of the time of Augustus known especially for his reliefs.   He is identified with
the Neo-Attic school of sculpture.

SOSTRATUS OF CNIDUS--(Alex I, 1; PP-Ph)--A Greek architect of the 3rd century B. C.   He built the Pharos (q. v.)
at Alexandria for Ptolemy Philadelphus (q. v.).

SOTER, SOSIGENES, BION--(Alex I, 1)--Scholars at the
Alexandrian Mouseion under the reign of Ptolemy Philadelphus (q. v.).

SOUTHCOURT, JOHANNA--(AH-Mrs.)--1750-1814.   An English religious fanatic who declared herself the woman of the
Book of Revelation.   She died of a brain disease leaving
some 100, 000 followers.

SOUTH KENSINGTON--(LJ XV)--A working class district of
London filled with huge blocks of flats.

SOUTHEY--(Two Cheers-Anon)--Robert Southey, 1774-1843.
An English poet and friend of S. T. Coleridge (q. v.).   He
was appointed poet laureate in 1813.   He wrote an immense
amount of prose and verse much of which, happily, is forgotten.   Some of his better known works are "The Battle of
Blenheim, " "Thalbala, " and "Medoc. "

SPARTA--(AH-Gem)--An ancient Greek city.   It became the
chief state in, and the founder of, the Peloponnesian League.
Its power was broken by Thebes.

"SPEKE PARROT"--(Two Cheers-John)--An anti-Wolsey (q. v.)
poem by John Skelton (q. v.).   It speaks of the goodness of
Henry VII whom Wolsey abuses.

SPENCER, HERBERT--(AH-Wil; GLD X; LJ IV; Two Cheers-
Webb)--1820-1903.   An English philosopher and founder of
evolutionary philosophy which postulates that all knowledge is
based on the single principle of evolution.   Some of his works

are First Principles (1862) and Principles of Ethics (1879-
93).

SPENDER, J. A.--(Egypt)--John Alfred Spender, 1862-1942.
An English journalist and editor of the Westminster Gazette.
He was a member of the Milner Mission to Egypt (1919-20)
and the author of The Comments of Bagshot (1914), The
Changing East (1926), and other works.

SPENSER, EDMUND--(Two Cheers-Bishop)--1522?-1599.   An
English poet.   His greatest work is The Faerie Queene
(1596) dedicated to Elizabeth I.   Some other works are his
Astrophel, an elegy on the death of Sir Philip Sidney (q. v.),
and "The Shepheardes Calender" (1579).   He was one of the
most influential of all English poets.

SPHINX--(Two Cheers-Raison)--A mythological beast with
the head of a human (in Greek myth, a woman; Egyptian, a
man).

SPINOZA--(GLD XIV)--Benedict de Spinoza, 1632-1677.   A
Portuguese-Jewish philosopher who lived in The Hague.   He
was expelled from the Jewish community for his criticism
of Scripture.   He held that there is one infinite substance
and that finite existences are merely modes or limitations
of that substance.

SPOHR--(MT)--Ludwig (Louis) Spohr, 1784-1859.   A German
conductor, violinist, composer of some 17 violin concertos,
oratorios, symphonies, and other works all in a romantic
style.   He was one of the first to use a baton in conducting.

SPRING SONG--(AH-Fo)--A novel (1936) by Forrest Reid
(q. v.).

SQUARE OF THE ANNUNZIATA--(RWV II)--Piazza della SS.
Annunziata.   A square in Florence, Italy, which contains
L'Ospedale degli Innocenti (1421-1424) designed by Brunelle-
schi with terra-cotta decorations by Andrea della Robbia,
and the church of SS. Annunziata (c. 1250).

STACKPOLE, HENRIETTA--(Aspects VIII)--An American
journalist in The Portrait of A Lady (1881) by Henry James
(q. v.).   She is the friend of Isabel Archer.

STAËL, MME. DE--(MT)--Anne Louise Germaine de Staël,
née Necke (Baronne de Staël-Holstein), 1766-1817.   A French

writer, she fled France during its revolution and returned
only to be exiled by Napoleon (q.v.). She returned once
again in 1815. She wrote of her experiences in Dix Années
d'Exil (1821).

STALIN--(Two Cheers-George)--Josef Stalin [Iosif Vissar-
ionovich Dzhugasvili,] 1879-1953. Russian dictator who
seized power after the death of Lenin. After his own death,
his crimes were revealed.

STANLEY--(AH-Our Div)--Henry Morton Stanley [John Row-
lands], 1841-1904. Journalist and explorer. He was sent
by J. G. Bennett of the New York Herald to find David
Livingstone (q.v.) in Africa. Stanley reached him, November 10, 1871, greeting him with the famous "Dr. Livingstone, I presume?"

STANLEY, COL. OLIVER--(Two Cheers-Eng)--Oliver Frederick George Stanley, 1896-1950. A British politician, son
of the 17th Earl of Derby. He was educated at Oxford and
served in World War I; was a member of Parliament (1924);
Minister of Transport (1933-34); and Colonial Secretary (1942-
45).

STANNARD, PAMELA--(England's)--An actress who created
the part of Miss George in the original production of England's Pleasant Land.

STATUE OF LIBERTY--(PP-Ph; Two Cheers-United)--A
statue of a pregnant woman holding a torch aloft in her right
hand and symbolizing liberty. She is a present from the
French people on the occasion of the 100th anniversary of
the United States; it stands on an island in New York's harbor.

STEED, WICKHAM--(GLD XII)--Henry Wickham Steed, 1871-
1956. An English journalist and writer. He was the foreign
correspondent for the London Times in various countries,
also its foreign editor, and its editor-in-chief. He is the
author of Hitler: Whence and Whither (1937), The Bad Man
(1942), and other works.

STEIN, GERTRUDE--(Aspects II; Two Cheers-English)--1874-
1946. An American writer of eccentric prose, an art collector, and a cultivator of writers and artists. She lived
abroad for most of her life, chiefly in Paris. There she
maintained a salon to which came most of the important ar-

tists and writers of her time.   Amid much initial controversy, she produced several works; one, an opera, Four Saints in Three Acts, was a big hit in New York and Chicago.   She wrote Tender Buttons (1915), The Making of Americans (1925) --her magnum opus, and The Autobiography of Alice B. Toklas (1933) among other works.

STEPHEN, JAMES--(AH-Ba)--1882-1950.   Irish novelist and poet.   He is the author of the novels The Charwoman's Daughter (1912) and The Crock of Gold (1912), among others, and the poetry volume Strict Joy (1931) among others.

STEPHEN, LESLIE--(Aspects I; Two Cheers-Edward; Two Cheers-Virginia)--1832-1904.   English critic, biographer, philosopher and father of Vanessa (Mrs. Clive Bell) and the remarkable Virginia (Virginia Woolf, q. v.).   He gave up his holy orders (1875) and called himself an agnostic in Essays on Free Thinking and Plain Speaking (1873).   For the English Men of Letters Series he wrote biographies of Samuel Johnson (1878), Alexander Pope (1880), Swift, (1882) George Eliot (1902), and Thomas Hobbes (1904).   He was also the first editor of the Dictionary of National Biography.

STERNE--(Aspects I)--Laurence Sterne, 1713-1768.   An English novelist.   He was a clergyman, and is known especially for his masterpiece, Tristram Shandy (1760, 1761, 1765, 1767) and for A Sentimental Journey (1768).

STEVENSON, ROBERT LOUIS--(HE XIV; Two Cheers-Anon)-- 1850-1894.   An English novelist and poet.   Educated at Edinburgh University, he was an extremely popular writer producing such novels as Treasure Island (1883) and The Strange Case of Dr. Jekyll and Mr. Hyde (1886).   His poetry appears in A Child's Garden of Verses (1885) and Underwoods (1887).

STOIC PHILOSOPHY--(Alex I, 3)--That Greek philosophy founded by Zeno c. 308 B. C. which held that virtue is the highest good and that passions and appetites should be rightly subdued.

STONEHENGE--(HE XIV; LJ IX)--A prehistoric circle of large stones located on Salisbury Plain.

STONES OF VENICE--(HE VI; Two Cheers-Anon)--By John Ruskin (q. v.) in three volumes (1851, 1852; 1874).   Volume I treats of the history of the city and description of the drive

from Padua to Mestra and the gondola trip through the city.
Volume II describes the Byzantine and Gothic periods.   Vol-
ume III encompasses the Renaissance and the decline of
Venice.

STRABO--(AH-Capt)--1st century B. C.   Author of a history
of Rome in 17 books most of which are extant.

STRACHEY, LYTTON--(GLD X; Tribute; Two Cheers-English)--Giles Lytton Strachey, 1880-1932.   Critic and biographer, educated at Cambridge.   Eminent Victorians (1918) made
him famous.   He also produced a biography of Queen Victoria (1921) and Elizabeth and Essex (1928).

STRACHEY, PIPPA--(GLD XIV)--Author of Memorandum on
the Position of English Women in Relation to that of English
Men.   London, 1935.

"STRANGE IRONY OF FATE, ALAS" etc. --(Two Cheers-
William)--From the poem, "A Summer Night," $\ell\ell$. 57-58,
by Matthew Arnold (q. v.).

STRAUSS--(LJ XVI)--Richard Strauss, 1870-1938.   German
composer.   His most important work was done in the field
of opera: Salome (1905), Electra (1909) and his most popular opera, Der Rosenkavalier (1911).

STRAVINSKY--(Two Cheers-Does)--Igor Fydorovich Stravinsky, 1882-1971.   A Russian composer.   He studied with
Rimsky-Korsakov and lived in France for a time, then in
the U. S.   He was one of the chief exponents of modern
music.   His work changed the course of serious music in
the first third of this century.   This work includes the
symphonic fantasy, "L'Oiseau de Feu" ("Firebird"), and the
ballets: Petrouchka and Le Sacre de Printemps.

STREICHER--(Nordic)--Julius Streicher, 1885-1946.   Anti-
Semitic journalist during the Nazi regime in Germany.   He
was hanged as a war criminal.

STRESSMAN--(Nordic)--Gustav Stressman, 1878-1929.   Ger-
man statesman.   He was Chancellor (1923) and Minister of
Foreign Affairs (1923-1929).   He received the Nobel Peace
Prize in 1926.

STRETHER--(Aspects VIII)--Lambert Strether, a character
in The Ambassadors (q. v.) by Henry James (q. v.).   He is

Mrs. Newsome's chief ambassador sent to Paris to summon Chad back to the family business.

STRUTHER, JAN--(Two Cheers-Mrs.)--Pseudonym of Joyce Maxtone Graham, 1901-1953. An English poet and novelist, she is most noted for her novel, Mrs. Miniver (1939); some of her poetry can be found in Bethsinda Dances and Other Poems (1931) and Other Poems (1940).

STUBBS--(GLD VIII)--William Stubbs, 1825-1901. English clergyman and historian. His chief work is The Constitutional History of England in three volumes (1874-78). He was bishop of Chester (1884), and of Oxford (1889).

STUDY OF HISTORY, A--(Two Cheers-Eng)--By Arnold Toynbee (q.v.). Published in 10 volumes (1934-1954), the work surveys the chief civilizations of the world.

STURGIS--(AH-HOS)--Howard Overing Sturgis, 1855-1920. Forster gives a good biography of the writer in his essay "Howard Overing Sturgis" in Abinger Harvest.

STURGIS, JULIAN--(AH-HOS)--Brother of Howard Overing Sturgis (q.v.) and a prolific novelist.

STURGIS, RUSSEL--(AH-HOS)--Father of Howard Overing Sturgis (q.v.). He was head of a great banking house in England.

SULLA--(AH-Mac)--Lucius Cornelius Sulla, 138-78 B.C. A Roman general and statesman, he was leader of the conservative (aristocratic) party at Rome. He was consul in 88 B.C. There is a biography by Plutarch (q.v.).

SUMMERSON, ESTHER--(Aspects IV)--A character in Bleak House (q.v.) by Charles Dickens (q.v.). She is the orphan niece of Miss Barbary and brought up by her godmother. She narrates portions of the story. She is, in reality, the illegitimate daughter of Lady Dedlock.

SUN YAT SEN--(GLD XI)--Sun Wen, Chung Shan, 1866-1925. Chinese revolutionary hero who helped to overthrow the Manchu dynasty.

SURBITON--(HE XIII)--A municipal borough in Surrey about 10 miles WSW of London.

SURCINGLE--(AH-Troop)--A belt or band passing over a
saddle or pack on a horse's back to hold it fast.

SURREY--(HE X)--A county in S England of about 722 square
miles.

SUSAN--(Two Cheers-Virginia)--A character in The Waves
(1931) by Virginia Woolf (q.v.). She is a lover of nature
and a born mother.

SWAN OF LITCHFIELD--(MT)--See: Anna Seward.

SWANAGE--(HE II)--The home of Mrs. Munt (Aunt Juley) in
Forster's Howards End.

SWANN--(AH-Proust; Aspects VIII; Two Cheers-Our)--A
character in Remembrance of Things Past (q.v.) by Marcel
Proust (q.v.). He is an aesthete, a wealthy broker, and
friend of Marcel's parents. He manipulates social situations.

SWEERTZ, [sic] MICHAEL--(Two Cheers-Not)--Michiel Sweerts,
1624-?1664. A painter, born in Brussels, who worked in
Rome. He painted scenes of Roman street life, portraits,
Christian virtues, etc. He has been called the "Dutch Le
Nain."

"SWEET BE'MI'STER, THAT BIST A BOUND"--(Two Cheers-
William B)--Line 1 from a poem in the Dorset dialect, "Be
'Mi'ster" by William Barnes (q.v.) in Poems Grave and Gay
by William Barnes and edited by Giles Dugdale.

"SWEET SMILING VILLAGE" etc.--(England's)--Lines 35-62
from "The Deserted Village," a poem by Oliver Goldsmith
(q.v.).

"SWEET WAR-MAN IS DEAD AND ROTTEN: SWEET
CHUCKS" etc.--(AH-Consol)--From Love's Labours Lost, by
William Shakespeare (q.v.), Act V, Sc. ii, ℓ. 666.

SWIFT--(AH-Liberty; Aspects VI; GLD XI; Two Cheers-Bk;
Two Cheers-They)--Jonathan Swift, 1667-1745. The great
Anglo-Irish satirist and pamphleteer best known as the au-
thor of Gulliver's Travels (q.v.).

SWINBURNE--(HE V; LJ XXIX)--Algernon Charles Swinburne,
1837-1909. An English poet and playwright. He is the author of Atalanta in Calydon (1865), a drama in classical form

which brought him celebrity. Other works include: Songs
Before Sunrise (1871) and books of criticism (e.g., Shakespeare, 1880; Hugo, 1886; and Ben Jonson, 1889).

SWINNERTON, FRANK--(Two Cheers-English)--Frank Arthur
Swinnerton, 1884- . An English novelist and critic. His
works include: A Brood of Ducklings (1928), Swinnerton:
An Autobiography, and a critical study of Robert Louis
Stevenson (q.v., 1914).

SWISS FAMILY ROBINSON, THE--(Aspects II, MT)--A novel
(1813) by J. R. Wyss. A minister, his wife, and their four
sons are shipwrecked on a deserted island. They build,
gradually, a new life for themselves and, when a ship comes
to their rescue, they refuse to leave.

"SYLLABA LONGA BREVI SUBJECTA VOCATUR IAMBUS"--
(GLD III)--Latin: A long syllable subordinated to a short
[one] is called an iamb.

SYLLABUB--(MT)--A dessert made with sweetened cream
flavored with wine and beaten to a froth.

SYMONS, ARTHUR--(AH-TS)--1865-1945. A British literary
critic and poet born in Wales. Among his most important
works of criticism are The Symbolist Movement in Literature
(1899), and Studies in Elizabethan Drama (1920). His poetry
is to be found in such volumes as The Fool of the World
and Other Poems (1906) and Jezebel Mori and Other Poems
(1931).

SYMPOSIUM--(GLD VII)--A dialogue on love by Plato (q.v.).
Apollodorus reports an after-dinner discussion (symposium)
that he had heard conducted by Socrates (q.v.), Aristophanes,
Alcibiades and others at Agathon's house. Each discussed
his understanding of love. Socrates reports a discourse he
had heard on the subject from the prophetess Diotima which
has come to be called "Platonic love."

T

TABRIZ--(AH-Me)--A city in the Azerbaijan province of Iran.
It is an important commercial city noted especially for the
rugs it exports.

TACITUS--(Two Cheers-In)--Cornelius Tacitus, A.D. 55?-
?117. A Roman historian whose masterpiece is a history of
the reigns of Galba, Otho, Vitelius, Vespasian, Titus, and
Domitian.

TADEMA, SIR LAWRENCE ALMA--(AH-Roger)--See: Alma-
Tadema, Sir Lawrence.

TAGORE, RABINDRANATH--(AH-Adrift; GLD XI; Two Cheers-
India; Two Cheers-Muhammed)--1861-1941. A Hindu poet,
novelist, philosopher, playwright, and painter. He received
the Nobel Prize for literature in 1913. Some of his better
known works are The Gardener, The Crescent Moon, Chitra
(1913), The Fugitive (1921), and Fireflies (1928).

TAJ--(Hill)--See: Taj Mahal.

TAJ MAHAL--(PI XIV; Hill)--The famous and exquisitely
beautiful mausoleum built by Shah Jehan (q.v.) in Agra, India, for his favorite wife, Muntaz Mahal.

TAMERLANE--(AH-Emp)--Timur Leny (Turkish for Timur
[iron] the Lame), 1336?-1405. A descendant of Genghis
Khan (q.v.) and conqueror of Central Asia, Asia Minor,
much of India. He died while preparing to invade China.

TAMINO--(Aspects VI; GLD XII)--A character in the opera,
The Magic Flute (q.v.), by Mozart (q.v.). He is a young
man who falls in love with the daughter of the Queen of the
Night and must rescue her when she is abducted by Sarastro
(q.v.).

TANNHÄUSER--(HE V)--Tannhäuser und der Sängerkrieg auf
der Wartburg (1845), an opera by Richard Wagner (q.v.).
It is the story of a medieval minstrel torn between sacred
and profane love.

TANSLEY, CHARLES--(Two Cheers-Virginia)--A character
in To the Lighthouse (q.v., 1927) by Virginia Woolf (q.v.).
He is the protégé of Mr. Ramsey (q.v.). He is rather
boorish and has a firm belief that women cannot be creative
in the arts.

TAORMINA--(GLD XIV)--A city in the province of Messina
on the E coast of Sicily. It has a church which is built into
a 3rd-century temple, a Greek theatre, Roman ruins, and a
medieval castle. It was founded in 397 B.C. by Carthaginians.

TARBELL, I. M.--(GLD XI)--Ida Minerva Tarbell, 1857-
1944. An American author. She was on the staff of Mclure's
Magazine and The American Magazine and is the author of a
life of Napoleon (q.v.), 1895. Her most important work is
the two-volume History of the Standard Oil Company (1904).

TASSO--(Two Cheers-Raison)--Torquato Tasso, 1544-1595.
An Italian poet and the protégé of Scipio Gonzaga. He was
a lecturer in astronomy and mathematics at the University
of Ferrara. In later life he was committed to an insane
asylum. His most famous work is the heroic-epic poem,
Gerusaleme Liberata (1575), (q.v.).

TATIUS, ACHILLES--(Alex II, 1)--See: Achilles Tatius.

TAYGETUS--(AH-Gem)--The name of a mountain range in
the S Peloponneses, Greece.

TAYLOR, MR.--(PP-Eliza)--One of the group who accompanied Mrs. Fay on her caravan to the Suez.

TCHAIKOVSKY--(Two Cheers-Not Listening; Two Cheers-
Raison)--Piotr Ilyich Tchaikovsky, 1840-1893. A Russian
composer who wrote in a distinctly Russian style. He is
noted for his symphonies ("Pathétique," etc.) which are force-
ful and often tinged with melancholy. He also wrote three
piano concertos, a violin concerto, many orchestral pieces
("Romeo and Juliet," "Francesca da Rimini," etc.), operas
(Eugene Onegin, Queen of Spades, etc.), and ballets (Swan
Lake, Sleeping Beauty, etc.).

TEDDINGTON--(HE XV)--A town in Middlesex, England, on
the Thames.

TELEMACHUS--(Aspects VI)--The son of Odysseus (q.v.)
and Penelope in The Odyssey (q.v.). In his father's absence,
he grows to manhood and is favored by Athene (q.v.). On
his father's return, he helps him in his fight against Penelope's suitors.

TEMPEST--(Collect Ta-Curate)--See: Prospero.

"TEMPESTA, LA"--(RWV IV)--"The Storm," a painting by
Giorgione (q.v.) in Venice's Accademia museum.

TEMPLE OF THE EPHESIAN ARTEMIS--(LJ XX)--The Artemis (Diana) of Ephesus was one of the more famous sta-

tues of the goddess, the daughter of Zeus and Leto, and twin sister of Apollo. She was the goddess of the moon and of hunting, protectoress of women. In Ephesus, she was depicted as the great mother-goddess. Her statue was a great cone surmounted by many breasts. The temple was one of the seven wonders of the world.

TENNYSON--(Aspects V; Collect Ta-Celest; GLD IV; Two Cheers-Enchanted; Two Cheers-Virginia)--Alfred (1st Baron) Tennyson, 1809-1892. English poet and poet laureate. In 1830, he published his first collection of poetry, Poems, which contained "The Lotus-Eaters." In 1842, two more volumes of poems appeared containing some of his finest work: "Morte d'Arthur," "Locksley Hall," and "Ulysses." An elegy on the death of his friend, Arthur Hallam, "In Memorium," was published in 1850. He continued to write copiously, but not better, until his death.

TERRY, SIR RICHARD--(Two Cheers-Does)--Sir Richard Runaman Terry, 1865-1938. British organist and choirmaster; he was organist at Westminster Cathedral (1901-1924).

TERTULLIAN--(Alex I, 3)--Quintus Septimius Tertullianus, A.D. 160?-?230. A Latin ecclesiastical writer of Carthage, he is one of the Fathers of the Roman Catholic Church. Educated for the law, he was converted to Christianity and devoted himself to mastering the Scriptures. Among his many works are Apologeticus (a defense of Christianity) and Ad Martyres.

TESS--(Aspects V)--Tess Durbeyfield, a young, naive country girl in Tess of the D'Urbervilles (1891) by Thomas Hardy (q.v.). Tess meets Alec d'Urberville when she comes to work for the Stoke-d'Urbervilles. He seduces her and she gives birth to their child. She later agrees to marry Angel Clare. He deserts her, however, when he hears of her past, but she does not cease loving him. Alec, meanwhile, still pursues her until she agrees to live with him, whereupon Angel returns and Tess kills Alec.

TESSMANS, THE--(AH-Ibsen)--George Tessman and his wife, Hedda Gabler Tessman, characters in the play, Hedda Gabler (1890), by H. Ibsen (q.v.). See: Hedda Gabler.

TEWFIK, KHEDIVE--(Alex I, 1)--Tewfik Pasha, Mohammed (1852-1892) khedive of Egypt, 1879-1892. He found his nation financially bankrupt and yielded to joint financial control

by the British and the French.   This brought about the revolt of the Nationalists (1881) under Ahmad Arabi (q.v.).
Alexandria was bombarded by the British fleet and Arabi
was defeated by the British forces.   His defeat resulted in
the British establishing a virtual protectorate over Egypt.

THACKERAY--(AH-HOS; Aspects I; MT; RWV X)--William
Makepeace Thackeray, 1811-1863.   An English novelist born
in India, he was educated at Cambridge but left before taking
a degree.   He studied drawing in Paris and published eight
caricatures.   Though proficient as a caricaturist, he is best
known for his prose; his greatest work is Vanity Fair (q.v.).

THAÏS--(Aspects VIII)--A novel (q.v.) by Anatole France (q.
v.) see under Paphnuce.

THALES--(AH-Vo)--c.624-546 B.C.   A Greek philosopher
and political leader, engineer, mathematician and astronomer.   He postulated the theory that water is the primary
substance of the universe.

"THEE, THEREFORE"--(MT)--A poem by William Cowper
(q.v.) written on the death of John Thornton.

THELYPHTHORA, A TREATISE ON FEMALE RUIN--(Two
Cheers-Madan)--By Martin Madan (1780).   A treatise on the
evils of female prostitution which advocated polygamy as a
cure.

THEOCRITUS--(Alex I, 1; LJ I)--A greek poet of the 3rd
century B.C. noted for his pastoral poetry.   He is regarded
as the originator of that type of poetry.   There are some 30
poems, called Idyls, and several epigrams extant.

THEONAS, PATRIARCH--(Alex I, 2)--Patriarch of Alexandria.
In A.D. 285 he dedicated the cathedral of Alexandria to the
Virgin Mary.

THEONAS, SAINT--(Alex I, 2; PP-St A)--Forster identifies
the saint with the patriarch (q.v.).   There are, however,
four saints of that name: A bishop of Alexandria, d. 300,
bishop 281-300; a solitary who lived in Thebaid, d.c.395;
one of a group of martyrs, d. 303; a magician converted by
St. Theopemptus, d. 303.

THEOPHILUS--(Alex I, 2)--A.D. 100's.   One of the Fathers
of the Church.   He was bishop of Antioch and wrote a de-

fense of Christianity.

THEOSOPHY--(Alex II, 1; HE XXXI)--(Greek: "the wisdom of God"]. The name adopted by the Theosophical Society, founded in 1875 by Mme. Blavatsky, Mrs. Beant, and others, to define its religious and philosophical system which aims at the knowledge of God through intuition and contemplation or by direct communion.

THERMOPPLE [sic]--(AH-Troop; Collect Ta-Road)--Thermopylae. The pass in Greece defended by Leonidas and 300 Spartans (480 B.C.) against the army of Xerxes. Leonidas and all of his men were killed.

THIBET [sic]--(PI XIV)--Tibet. A country of central Asia and nominally a dependency of China, now completely occupied by China.

"THIS FORTRESS BUILT BY NATURE FOR HERSELF" etc. --(LJ XVI)--From Richard II by Shakespeare (q.v.), Act II, Sc. i, ℓℓ. 43-46.

THOMPSON, FRANCIS--(AH-Wil)--1859-1907. An English poet. He studied medicine without much success and lived a life filled with poverty and ill-health. His poetry was discovered by Alice Meynell and her husband who helped him to publish his first and most successful volume, Poems (1893), which contained "The Hound of Heaven," his most popular poem. He also wrote some prose including an Essay on Shelley (1909).

THOREAU--(HE XIV)--Henry David Thoreau, 1817-1862. An American essayist and philosopher. He was Transcendentalist and disciple of Emerson, who spoke out against the values of a materialistic society. He was also a lover of nature. His most famous work is Walden, or Life in the Woods (1854). It is the story of his life in a hut which he had constructed on the shores of Walden Pond.

THORNTON, HENRY--(AH-Ba; MT)--Forster's great-grandfather. Forster records his life in the essay "Battersea Rise" in Abinger Harvest.

THORNTON, HENRY JR.--(AH-Ba; MT)--Son of Henry Thornton (q.v.). Forster discusses him at length in Marianne Thornton.

THORNTON, MARIANNE--(AH-Ba; MT)--Daughter of Henry
Thornton (q. v.).   Forster records her life in Marianne
Thornton: A Domestic Biography.

THORNTON, PERCY--(AH-Ba)--A nephew and son-in-law of
Henry Thornton, Jr. (q. v.).

THORPE, ISABELLA--(AH-JA)--A character in Northanger
Abbey (q. v.) by Jane Austen (q. v.).   Catherine Morland (q.
v.) meets her at Bath.   Isabella jilts James Morland for
Capt. Tilney.

THOTH--(Alex II, 3)--In Egyptian myth the symbol of immortality.

THOTMESS III--(Alex II, 4)--Thutmose III, joint ruler of
Egypt with his queen and half-sister Hatshepsut, c. 1501-
1496, 1493-1481 B. C.   He ruled alone c. 1481-1447.   He was
one of the greatest of Egypt's kings.   Through war, he extended his kingdom.   He was also a great builder, enlarging
the temple complex at Karnak and constructing many other
religious structures.

THREE GUINEAS--(Two Cheers-Virginia)--A volume (1938)
of criticism and sketches by Virginia Woolf (q. v.).

THREE HERMITS, THE--(Two Cheers-Three)--"The Three
Hermits." See the essay by Forster, "Three Stories by
Tolstoy," in Two Cheers for Democracy (1951) for a sum-
mary of the story and a description of the characters.

"THREE HERMITS, THE"--(Two Cheers-Three; Two Cheers-
Tolstoy)--See preceding entry.

THUMB, TOM--(MT)--Originally the name of a pygmy in an
old nursery tale of the 16th century.   The name was given
to a character in the History of Tom Thumb (1621) by R.
Johnson.   It was also the name given to Charles Sherwood
Stratton (1838-1883), a midget exhibited by P. T. Barnum.

"THUCYDIDES"--(Two Cheers-In)--A poem by Matthew Arnold (q. v.).

TIBET--(PI XIV)--See: Thibet.

TICINO--(WAFT I)--The name of a Swiss canton crossed by
the St. Gotthard railroad and a river of the same name.

TILNEY, HENRY--(AH-JA; Aspects IV)--A character in
Northanger Abbey (q. v.) by Jane Austen (q. v.).   He is about
24 or 25, tall, very intelligent and very near handsome.   He
is the son of General Tilney and brother of Eleanor and
Capt. Frederick.

TIM--(AH-HOS)--A novel (1891) by Howard Overing Sturgis
(q. v.).

TIMES, THE--(LJ VII)--The London Times founded January
1, 1785 as The Daily Universal Record.   The newspaper's
name was changed to The Times in 1788.

TIMON--(Alex I, 1)--A citizen of Athens of about the time
of the Peloponnesian War.   He was a misanthrope and the
subject of one of Lucian's finest Dialogues.

TIMON OF ATHENS--(Two Cheers-Jul)--A play (c. 1607) by
William Shakespeare.   Timon (q. v.), a rich nobleman of
Athens, ruins himself financially and turns for aid to friends
he had once helped, only to be rebuffed.   He withdraws to a
cave and becomes a misanthrope.

TIMOTHY THE CAT--(PP-Tim)--Monophysite (q. v.) patriarch of Alexandria.   He was supposedly consecrated after a
supernatural vision called for that consecration.

TIMOTHY WHITEBONNET--(PP-Tim)--He succeeded Timothy
the Cat (q. v.) as patriarch of Alexandria.

TINDAL--(AH-Capt)--William Tyndale, d. 1536.   He translated the Bible into English.

TIROL--(WAFT V)--Tyrol.   A province in Austria the
southern part of which was ceded to Italy after World War I.
It is a very mountainous region.

TITANIC--(AH-Jo)--The name of the largest passenger ship
of its day sunk by an iceberg, April 15, 1912, on its maiden
voyage from Southampton to New York.   Over 1500 lives
were lost.

TITIAN--(Collect Ta-Eternal; Two Cheers-Not)--Tiziano
Vecellio, c. 1490-1576.   A Venetian painter who developed a
sumptuous technique suffused with color.   He did, among
other works, a cycle of mythological paintings, one of which,
"The Rape of Europa, " is typical of his work in general.

TO THE LIGHTHOUSE--(Aspects I; Two Cheers-Virginia)--
A novel (1927) by Virginia Woolf (q. v.). The novel has no
conventional plot. It depends rather upon the unfolding of
character notably that of Mr. and Mrs. Ramsey (q. v.),
their children and their friends.

TOBY, UNCLE--(Aspects VI)--The uncle of Tristram Shandy
(q. v.) in the novel of the same name by Laurence Sterne
(q. v.).

TOLSTOY--(AH-Mrs; AH-Proust; Aspects I; Reading; Two
Cheers-Bk; Two Cheers-In; Two Cheers-Jul; Two Cheers-
Not Listening; Two Cheers-Our; Two Cheers-Romain; Two
Cheers-Syed; Two Cheers-Three)--Count Leo Nikolaevich
Tolstoy, 1828-1910. A Russian writer and aristocrat who
believed in non-resistence to evil, abolition of governments
and nationalities and of dogmas and churches. He also believed deeply in God and love of man. He is most famous
for his novels War and Peace (1865-72) and Anna Karenina
(1875-76).

TOM JONES--(Aspects I; Two Cheers-Anon)--A History of
Tom Jones, A Foundling, a novel (1749) by Henry Fielding
(q. v.). It is the story of the infant Tom who is discovered
under mysterious circumstances in the bed of the benevolent
Mr. Allworthy and adopted by that gentleman. The story
describes his early life and subsequent adventures when he
is turned out by Allworthy and is forced to seek his fortune
in the world.

TOMMY--(AH-HOS)--A character in the novel Belchamber by
Howard Overing Sturgis (q. v.).

TONO BUNGAY--(Aspects IV)--A novel (1909) by H. G. Wells
(q. v.) which attacks unethical advertising. It tells the life
of George Ponderevo whose uncle discovers a substance
which he calls "Tono Bungay." He peddles it as a cure-all.
It brings George and his uncle a fortune but no lasting happiness.

TORCELLO--(HE VI)--An island in a lagoon of Venice about
six miles NW of the city.

TORQUAY--(HE XIII)--A popular seaside resort about 30
miles ENE of Plymouth.

TOSCA--(HE V)--An opera (1900) by Giacommo Puccini with
a libretto by Luigi Illica and Giuseppe Giacosa. It is based
on a flamboyant play by Sardou. Tosca, an opera singer, attempting to save the life of her lover, kills his evil jailer
only to discover that the safe conduct he had given her was
false and that her lover is dead. She commits suicide.

TOSCANINI--(Nordic)--Arturo Toscanini, 1867-1957. An
Italian conductor of opera and symphonies. He organized and
conducted the National Broadcasting Company Symphonic Orchestra from 1937.

TOULOUN, IBN--(AH-Mosque)--Ahmad Ibn Tulun. A Turkish slave (A. D. 800's) who became a powerful and influential figure in the Egyptian court of Mamur. Eventually, he
came to rule Egypt.

TOURAINE--(AH-Vo)--Historic region of NW central France.

TOVEY, SIR DONALD--(Two Cheers-Not Listening; Two
Cheers-Raison)--Sir Donald Francis Tovey, 1875-1940. An
English composer and writer. He was professor of music
at Edinburgh University from 1914 and composed an opera,
Bride of Dionysus, among other pieces.

TOWARDS DEMOCRACY--(Two Cheers-Edward)--A volume
of essays (1883) by Edward Carpenter (q. v.) in the style and
spirit of Walt Whitman (q. v.). They express his love for
and faith in the individual. The first essay, "Towards
Democracy," gives the book its title. The collection very
much resembles that of Forster's Two Cheers for Democracy
(1951).

TOWER BRIDGE--(Two Cheers-Lon)--Built in 1886-94 over
the Thames in London, it was designed in the Victorian
Gothic style by Sir Horace Jones and Sir John Wolfe Bary.

TOYNBEE, ARNOLD--(Two Cheers-English; Two Cheers-
Tol)--Arnold Joseph Toynbee, 1889- . Most famous for a
monumental ten-volume History of the World (1934-1954). He
was professor of Byzantine and modern Greek literature and
history at the University of London, 1919-24 and was professor of international history at the same university from
1925.

TRACTARIAN MOVEMENT--(MT; Two Cheers-William)--Also
known as the Oxford Movement. It was formed in 1833 at

Oxford by Keble, Newman, Proude, and Pusey. Basically, it was a reaction to the Low Church and what it stood for. It led many, including Newman, into the Roman Catholic Church.

TRAJAN--(Alex I, 1)--Marcus Ulpius Trajanus (A.D. 52/53-117), Roman emperor, 98-117. He was born near Seville in Spain. He began his career as a soldier and served as Consul (91) and was adopted as his successor by Nerva (97). He extended the territory of Rome in several campaigns in Dacia. He is also noted as a builder constructing many buildings including the forum in Rome which bears his name.

TRAMP ABROAD--(WAFT I)--A humorous description of a walking trip through the Black Forest and the Alps (1880) by Mark Twain (q.v.).

TREASURE OF PRAENESTRE--(AH-Mac)--In the Kirchner Museum, Rome. A group of artifacts discovered at Praeneste dating mainly from the Roman period.

TREVELYAN, R. C.--(AH-Mrs; GLD X; Hill; Two Cheers-Virginia)--Robert Calverley Trevelyan, 1872-1951. A poet noted as a translator of Greek drama. His original work is to be found in his collections of poetry Sisyphus (1908), The Pearl Tree (1917), and others.

TRIANON--(MT)--The name of two chateaux (Grand and Petit) in the park of Versailles (q.v.).

TRINCULO--(Two Cheers-Stratford)--A jester in the play The Tempest (q.v.) by William Shakespeare (q.v.).

TRIREME--(AH-Cn)--A Greek and Roman sailing vessel having three banks of oars, hence its name.

TRISTAN--(AH-Word)--A hero of medieval myth and one of the central characters in the opera Tristan und Isolde (q.v.) by Wagner (q.v.).

TRISTAN UND ISOLDE--(GLD IX; Two Cheers-C)--An opera (1865) by Richard Wagner (q.v.) based on a medieval legend. Tristan is charged with conducting the unwilling Isolde to King Mark of Cornwall whom she is to marry. Unwittingly the two drink a love potion which leads to their deaths.

TRISTRAM SHANDY--(Aspects I)--See: Shandy, Tristram.

TRITON--(Alex II, 1; Collect Ta-Other; PP-Ph)--The son of
Poseidon (q.v.) and Amphitrite in Greek myth. He is usually represented as a man with the lower parts of a fish. He
is the sea-god who makes the roaring of the ocean by blow-
ing through his shell.

TROLLOPE--(Aspects I; MT; Two Cheers-In)--Anthony Trollope, 1815-1882. An English novelist noted for his stories
of Victorian life. He wrote prolifically, but is best known
for his six-volume series Chronicle of Barchester. They
deal with life in, and the affairs of, a cathedral town not
unlike that of Salisbury (q.v.).

TROY--(Collect Ta-Point)--The site of the Trojan War recorded in The Iliad (q.v.), The Odyssey (q.v.), and The
Aeneid (q.v.).

TUCK, FRIAR--(AH-Our Div)--A main character in the legend of Robin Hood. He is the fat, jovial father confessor
of the outlaw.

TULKINGHORN, MR.--(Aspects IV)--The family lawyer of
the Dedlocks in Bleak House (q.v.) by Charles Dickens (q.v.).

TULLOCH, MR. AND MRS.--(PP-Eliz)--Sailed with the Fays
on the Red Sea.

TUNBRIDGE WELLS--(HE XIII; PI XXIX; RWV I)--A municipal borough in Kent SE England about 29 miles from London.

"TUNNING OF ELINOR RUMMING"--(Two Cheers-John)--A
poem by John Skelton (q.v.). For an excellent summary
see: Forster's "John Skelton," in Two Cheers for Democracy.

TURGENEV--(GLD IX)--Ivan Sergeyevich Turgenev, 1818-
1883. A Russian novelist and writer of short stories. His
novels are in the main examinations of social and political
problems of 19th century Russia. Three of them are On the
Eve (1860), Fathers and Sons (1862), and Virgin Soil (1877).

TURKESTAN--(PI IX)--A region in central Asia.

TURNER--(LJ VII)--Joseph Mallard William Turner, 1775-
1851. An English painter noted for his experiments with
color and light.

TURN OF THE SCREW--(AH-Reid)--A tale (1898) by Henry
James told from the viewpoint of a governess who apparently
sees or believes she sees the ghosts of evil servants trying
to take possession of the children whom she has been hired
to teach.

TUSCANY--(HE XXXIII)--A compartimento of central Italy.

TUTANKHAMEN--(Aspects VIII)--fl. 1355 B.C.   A minor
King of ancient Egypt. He is famous for having died young
and for the discovery of his nearly intact tomb in the 1920's.

TWAIN, MARK--(AH-Sin; WAFT I)--The pseudonym of Samuel Langhorne Clemens, 1835-1910.   An American journalist,
novelist, writer of short stories, humorist, and unsuccessful businessman.   He is best known for his humorous stories
of the American mid-west, the best of which is The Adventures of Huckleberry Finn (1884).

TWICKENHAM--(GLD I)--A municipal borough in Middlesex,
SE England, 11 miles from London.

"TWO KNAVES SOMETIMES FROM DIS"--(Two Cheers-John)
--A poem by John Skelton (q.v.).   For a good summary see:
Forster's "John Skelton," in Two Cheers for Democracy.

TYROL--(HE XXXI; WAFT V)--See: Tirol.

U

UFFIZI--(RWV IV)--The Uffizi Palace in Florence begun in
1560 by Giorgio Vasari on the orders of Cosimo I de' Medici
(q.v.) to be used as governmental offices.   It was later
turned to the use of the present museum.

UGANDA--(HE XVII)--A country in E Africa north of Lake
Victoria.   It was a British protectorate from 1894 until
October 9, 1962, when it became a sovereign dominion of the
British Commonwealth.

UJJAIN--(AH-Adrift; AH-Consol; PI IX)--A city of W central
India and one of the oldest on the sub-continent.   It is ranked
as one of the seven holy cities and was once the capital of
the Avanti kingdom (6th-4th centuries B.C.).

ULYSSES--(Aspects V; HE XI)--[Odysseus]. In Greek legend the king of Ithaca, he was the son of Laertes and Anticla and one of the suitors of Helen (q. v.), but despaired of winning her and married Penelope instead. He played an active role in the Trojan War and is the central figure in The Odyssey (q. v.) of Homer (q. v.).

ULYSSES--(AH-Liberty; Aspects I; Two Cheers-English)--A novel (1922) by James Joyce (q. v.). It treats of one day in the life of Stephan Dedalus and his relationship with Leopold Bloom (q. v.) and Molly Bloom (q. v.). The chapters roughly correspond to the events in The Odyssey (q. v.). Stephen is Joyce's Telemachus (q. v.); Bloom, his Ulysses (q. v.); and Molly, Penelope.

"UNCLE AND AUNT"--(Two Cheers-William)--A poem by William Barnes (q. v.).

UNCLE SAM--(AH-For the Muse)--The symbol of the United States. He is depicted as a dignified and strong old man with white hair and beard and dressed in the colors of the American flag. The name came about (1812) in a jocular mis-identification of initials "US" (for United States) on barrels of meat prepared by the Troy, N. Y., merchant Samuel Wilson.

UNCLE STEPHEN--(Two Cheers-For)--A novel (1931) by Forrest Reid (q. v.).

"UNDER THE HILL"--(AH-Ron)--A prose fragment by Aubrey Beardsley (q. v.) published in his magazine, The Savoy, 1895.

UNITARIANISM--(AH-Troop; Alex I, 3; PP-St A)--A system of religious belief which affirms a single personality for God as opposed to belief in the Trinity. It dates from 1773 when Theophilus Lindsay, who held the belief, left the Anglican Church.

UNITED NATIONS--(Two Cheers-George)--The international organization established after World War II to replace the League of Nations (q. v.) with roughly the same purpose (i. e., to establish world peace) and with about the same results.

UN PEU DE FAISAN, S'IL VOUS PLAÎT--(LJ XV)--French: A bit of pheasant, please.

UPPERCROSS--(AH-JA)--Uppercross Great House or Mansion House. The estate and home of the senior Musgroves in Persuasion by Jane Austen (q. v.). It has great gates, high walls and old, substantial, and unmolested trees.

V

VAINGLORY--(AH-Ron)--A novel (1915) by Ronald Firbank (q. v.). For a summary, see Forster's essay "Ronald Firbank, " in Abinger Harvest.

VALBORG, ERIK--(AH-Sin)--A character in Main Street (q. v.) by Sinclair Lewis. He is a tailor in Gopher Prairie. Carol Kennicott (q. v.) is attracted by his good looks and interesting mind. Their slight flirtation is brought to an end when gossip forces him to leave the town.

VALENS--(Alex I, 2)--A. D. 328?-378. Roman emperor of the East, 364-378. He was made emperor by his brother Valentinian I of the West. He waged, successfully, a war against the Goths and made peace with Persia. He was slain by the Goths after his armies were defeated.

VALENTINIAN--(Alex II, 1)--The name of three Roman emperors: the first (A. D. 321-375) emperor, 364-375; the second (372-392) emperor, 375-392; and the third (419-455) emperor, 425-455. All were emperors in the West.

VALENTINUS--(Alex I, 3)--A Gnostic (q. v.) philosopher and teacher probably born in Egypt and educated in Alexandria. He went to Rome (c. A. C. 135-160) where he taught. His disciples included Origen (q. v.) and Clement of Alexandria (q. v.). He was excommunicated because of his teachings which have come to be known as Valentinian Gnosticism or Valentinianism.

VALKYRIES--(Two Cheers-What)--In Old Norse: choosers of the slain. They were nymphs of Valhalla (Walhalla, q. v.) who, mounted on horses, rush into the thick of battle to choose those who are to die. These they take to Valhalla.

VALLEY, THE--(Collect Ta-Story)--The Vallone Fontana Caroso, near Ravello.

VAN GOGH--(Two Cheers-Last P; Two Cheers-Not; Two Cheers-What)--Vincent Willem Van Gogh, 1853-1890. A Dutch post-impressionist painter. In 1886, his painting came under the influence of impressionism and the Japanese prints he so admired. He became obsessed by the symbolic and expressive values of color. His canvasses are alive with color which he applied thickly.

VANITY FAIR--(Two Cheers-Anon)--In Pilgrim's Progress (q.v.) by John Bunyan (q.v.) it is the fair established by Beelzebub, Apollyon, and Legion in the town of Vanity where all manner of lusts and pleasures are sold the year around.

VAUXHALL--(AH-Capt)--Vauxhall Gardens. An 18th-century place of entertainment in London.

VEILED WOMAN--(AH-Salute)--A novel (1913) by Marmaduke Pickthall (q.v.); for a summary see Forster's essay "Salute to the Orient!" Part 3, in Abinger Harvest.

VELAZQUEZ--(Two Cheers-Does; Two Cheers-Not)--Diego Rodríguez de Silva y Velázquez, 1599-1660. A Spanish painter who developed a naturalistic approach to religious painting in which the figures are not ideal types but rather realistic portraits. He became a court painter to Philip IV. He set his court models in more natural poses than had ever before been used. As court painter, he produced his masterpiece, "Las Menias" (q.v.).

VENUS--(AH-Vo; Alex II, 1; Collect Ta-Other)--The Roman Aphrodite (q.v.) the goddess of beauty and sensual love.

VERDI--(Nordic; Two Cheers-C; Two Cheers-George)-- Giuseppe Verdi, 1813-1901. The greatest composer of Italian opera. He is especially known for Rigoletto (1851), Il Trovatore (1853), La Traviata (1853), La Forza del Destino (1867), Aïda (1871), Otello (1887), and Falstaff (1893).

VERDURIN, MME.--(AH-Proust; Two Cheers-English)--With her husband, characters in Remembrance of Things Past (q.v.) by Marcel Proust (q.v.). They are nouveau riche, of unimportant social background and, as a consequence, are scorned by the Guermantes.

VERONA--(WAFT VI)--A city in NE Italy on the Adige River about 90 miles from Milan. It has, among other tourist-attractions, a Roman theatre.

VERONESE--(AH-Vo)--Paolo Veronese, 1528-1588.   An
Italian painter noted for his large-group paintings.

VERSAILLES--(MT)--The name of a town near Paris and a
palace from which it derives its name.   The palace was
built by Louis XIV (q. v.).

VESPERS--(Two Cheers-Raison)--The evening service of the
Roman Catholic Church consisting chiefly of singing.

VICAR OF WAKEFIELD, THE--(Aspects V)--A novel (1766)
by Oliver Goldsmith.   Dr. Primrose, the vicar of the title,
is a good man who goes through a series of trials, not of
his making, but, like Job, is eventually restored to his former prosperity.

VICHY--(Two Cheers-G&G)--A health resort in the south of
France at which was established the emergency government
of France after its defeat by Germany in World War II.

VICTORIA--(PI XXV)--A type of horse-drawn carriage.

VICTORIA, QUEEN--(AH-Ab; AH-Wil; Aspects I; Englands;
HE V; PI II; Two Cheers-Jew)--1819-1901.   Queen of Great
Britain, 1837-1901.

VICTORY--(AH-Mac)--A Roman goddess.

VIJAYANAGAR--(AH-Conso)--The name of a city and of a
Hindu kingdom in the Deccan founded c. 1336.   It was destroyed in the 16th century.

VIKRAMADITYA--(AH-Adrift)--Vikrama, i. e. , "Sun of
Power."   The title assumed by Chandragupta II (A. D. 375?-
413) and Skanagupta (A. D. 455-480), kings of the Gupta dynasty of India.   The title was associated with an earlier,
legendary raja of Ujjain (q. v.).

VILLETTE--(Aspects IV)--A novel (1857) by Charlotte Brontë
(q. v.).   See: Lucy Snowe.

VINCENT--(Aspects V)--A character in The Counterfeiters
(q. v.) by André Gide (q. v.).   He is the brother of George
and Oliver.

VINDYAS--(PI XXIII)--The Vindhya Mountains.   A mountain
range extending ENE across India to the Ganges Valley near
Benares.

VINTEUIL--(AH-Proust; Aspects VIII; Two Cheers-Our; Two Cheers-Proust)--A character in Remembrance of Things Past (q.v.) by Marcel Proust (q.v.). He is a composer. Marcel is fascinated by a phrase in one of his sonatas which he recalls, at various moments, throughout the book.

VIONNET, MME. DE--(Aspects VIII)--A character in The Ambassadors (q.v.) by Henry James (q.v.), she is the French woman to whom Chad (q.v.) is devoted.

VIRGIL--(AH-Proust; AH-Salute; Collect Ta-Other; LJ XVII; Two Cheers-Fer; Two Cheers-Raison; Two Cheers-They)-- Publius Vergilius Maro, 70-80 B.C. The greatest poet of ancient Rome. He was a master of various forms of poetry, especially the epic, and his masterpiece is The Aeneid (q.v.).

VIRGIL'S BIRTHPLACE--(WAFT VI)--Mantua, Italy.

VISHNU--(Collect Ta-Mr; Hill; PI XII)--The second member of the Hindu trinity. He is the preserver.

VISIT TO A GNANI--(Two Cheers-Edward)--A gñáni is, in the East, a wise man. The volume was written by Edward Carpenter (q.v.). It is taken from a larger work of his: From Adam's Peak to Elephanta (1892), a book of travels in Ceylon and India.

VITA NUOVA--(AH-Marco)--A work (c.1291) by Dante (q.v.) in prose and poetry recording his spiritual love for Beatrice (q.v.).

VITTORIO EMANUELE, RE D'ITALIA--(Nordic)--Victor Emmanuel III (1869-1947), King of Italy, 1900-1946. Son of Humbert I, he abdicated in favor of his son, Humbert II, in 1946.

VOLTAIRE--(AH-Liberty; AH-Roger; AH-Vo; GLD VII; Hill; New Disorder; Two Cheers-Bk; Two Cheers-En; Two Cheers-Fer; Two Cheers-Menace; Two Cheers-Two Bks; Two Cheers-Volt)--Pseudonym of François Marie Arouet, 1694-1778. French poet, dramatist, historian, satirist, philosopher, amateur scientist, etc. He was a skeptic and sworn enemy of intolerance. He is most famous for his Candide (q.v., 1759).

VOLTERRA--(WAFT VI)--A city in central Italy about 19 miles SE of Pisa. It has extensive Etruscan remains.

VOYAGE OUT, THE--(AH-Early; Two Cheers-Virginia)--A
novel (1915) by Virginia Woolf (q.v.) in relatively conventional form. See: Rachel.

VYE, EUSTACIA--(Aspects V)--A sensuous woman, in Return of the Native (q.v.) by Thomas Hardy (q.v.), who marries Clym Yeobright to escape the boredom of her life, and,
when the marriage fails and she is about to run away with
her lover, she commits suicide.

W

WAGNER--(Collect Ta-Celest; Collect Ta-Story; GLD XIV;
HE V; Nordic; Two Cheers-C; Two Cheers-Not Listening;
Two Cheers-Post; Two Cheers-Raison)--Richard Wagner,
1813-1883. German composer of operas. His masterpiece
is Der Ring des Nibelungen (q.v.), a series of four operas based
on Northern myths. They are Das Rheingold (1869), Die
Walküre (1870), Siegfried (1876), and Gotterdämmerung
(1876).

WAGS, THE--(AH-Our D)--See: The Scallies.

"WALDSTEIN, THE"--(AH-Word)--The familiar name for the
piano sonata in C, Opus 53 (1804) by Beethoven (q.v.). It
takes its name from Count Waldstein, one of Beethoven's
patrons, to whom it is dedicated.

WALES, THE PRINCE OF--(Hill)--See: Edward VII.

WALEY, ARTHUR--(AH-Ron)--[Orig. surname: Schless],
1889-1966. Assistant curator of the department of prints
and drawings at the British Museum (q.v.). He was also a
translator of Chinese and Japanese literary works including
170 Chinese Poems (1919). He was also an editor of the
works of Ronald Firbank (q.v.).

WALHALLA--(PI XX; Two Cheers-C; Two Cheers-What)--
Valhalla. In Norse myth, literally the hall of the slain. It
was built for Wotan (Odin) by the giants. It has 540 gates
and is the feasting hall for all slain honorably in battle.
They are served by the Valkyries (q.v.).

WALLENSTEIN--(GLD X)--An historic drama (1799-1800) by
Schiller in three parts: Wallenstein's Camp, The Piccolo-
mini, and Wallenstein's Death. Wallenstein (1583-1634) was
commander of the German forces during the Thirty Years War.

WALPOLE, HORACE--(AH-Capt; MT; Two Cheers-Stratford)
--1717-1797. 4th Earl of Oxford. An English author and
politician best known for his Gothic novels, chiefly The
Castle of Otranto (1764).

WALPOLE, HUGH--(Two Cheers-Virginia)--Sir Hugh Seymour
Walpole, 1884-1941. An extremely prolific and popular
novelist who wrote almost exclusively of middle and upper-
middle class English life.

WANGEL, HILDA--(AH-Ibsen)--A character in The Master
Builder (q.v.) by Henrik Ibsen (q.v.). She is a young woman who, as a girl, fell in love with Solness who remains
her hero. She calls him her "Master Builder."

WANGELS, THE--(AH-Ibsen)--See: The Master Builder.

WAPPING--(HE V)--A parish in the Tower Ward, Stepney,
London.

WAR AND PEACE--(AH-Proust; Aspects I; Collect Ta-Co-
ord; Reading; Two Cheers-Bk; Two Cheers-Our; Two Cheers-
Three)--A novel (1865-1872) by Leo Tolstoy (q.v.). It treats
of Russia and France at the time of Napoleon (q.v.) and the
Napoleonic invasion of Russia.

WARD, MRS. HUMPHREY--(AH-Consol; AH-Early; Aspects
VI; Two Cheers-Anon)--Mary Augusta Ward, 1851-1920. An
English novelist, her most important work is Robert Elsmere
(1888). It embodies her view that Christianity can be revi-
talized through its social mission.

WARDOUR--(Aspects II)--Sir Arthur Wardour. A character
in Scott's The Antiquary (q.v.), he is the companion of Mr.
Oldbuck and an aristocratic antiquary.

"WARE THE HAWK"--(Two Cheers-John)--A poem by John
Skelton. For a summary and commentary, see Forster's
essay "John Skelton" in Two Cheers for Democracy.

WARING, PETER--(AH-Reid)--A character in the novel
Following Darkness, by Forrest Reid (q.v.). He fails to
reach maturity unscathed and so loses the love and friendship of Katherine Dale.

WASHINGTON, GEORGE--(AH-Consol)--1732-1799. The first
President of the United States (1789-1797).

"WASTE LAND, THE"--(AH-TS)--A poem (1922) by T. S.
Eliot (q.v.). It sets forth, within the symbolic framework
of the Medieval Grail legend and older fertility rites, the
sterility and sordidness of modern life.

WATERBABIES, THE--(AH-Ron)--Subtitled: A Fairy Tale
for a Land-Baby (1863), by Charles Kingsley (q.v.). It is a
fantasy full of moral didacticism concerning a small chimney-
sweep named Tom who falls into the river.

WATERLOO, THE BATTLE OF--(AH-Notes)--The battle in
Belgium which inflicted the decisive defeat on Napoleon (q.
v.) by Wellington (q.v.) in 1815.

WATERLOO STATION--(HE II)--The principal terminus of
the Southern Region in London and the largest railroad station in Britain. It is located in York Road.

WATKINS, VERNON--(Two Cheers-Outsider)--Vernon Phillip
Watkins, 1906- . Born in Wales, he draws upon Welsh
material and legend for his poetry. His critics, however,
point out that he is an essentially English poet in the "great
tradition." His poetry is to be found in such volumes as Selected Poems (1948) and The Death Bell and Other Poems
(1954).

WATSONS, THE--(AH-JA)--An unfinished fragment of a novel
(c. 1805) by Jane Austen (q.v.). Emma Watson returns to
her home after being brought up by a well-to-do aunt. She
finds herself surrounded by her sisters whose chief interest
is in marriage.

WATTEAU--(AH-Vo)--Jean Antoine Watteau, 1684-1721. A
French rococo painter who is best known for his paintings of
fêtes champêtres (outdoor festivals, or garden parties).

WATTS--(HE VI; LJ I)--George Frederick Watts, 1817-1904.
An English painter and sculptor elected to the Royal Academy
(q.v.) in 1867 but whose popularity dates from about 1880.
He was not interested in contemporary techniques. For him
art was a vehicle of moral purpose.

WAUGH, EVELYN--(Two Cheers-Eng)--Evelyn Arthur St.
John Waugh, 1903-1966. An English novelist and brilliant
satirist. His novels are filled with wit and sophistication.
His best are Decline and Fall (1928), Vile Bodies (1930), and
A Handful of Dust (1934).

WAVERLY--(AH-JA)--The first novel of Sir Walter Scott
(q. v.) not published until 1814.   It treats of Captain Edward
Waverly and his service as a rebel with the Pretender.   After the defeat of the Pretender, Waverly receives a pardon
obtained for him from Colonel Talbot whose life he had
saved.

WAVES, THE--(GLD XIV; Two Cheers-Virginia)--A novel
(1913) by Virginia Woolf (q. v.).   It tells of the psychological
development and relationships of several English children:
Bernard (q. v.), Susan, Neville (q. v.), Jimmy, and Rhoda.

WAY OF ALL FLESH, THE--(RWV XII; Two Cheers-Anon;
Two Cheers-English)--A semi-autobiographical novel (1903)
by Samuel Butler (q. v.).   It is the story of Ernest Pontifex
and essentially a satire of middle-class English family life
of the Victorian era.

"WEAVE A CIRCLE" etc. --(Two Cheers-Raison)--The closing
lines of the fragmentary poem, "Kubla Khan: or, A Vision
in a Dream, " by Samuel Taylor Coleridge (q. v.), ℓℓ. 51-54.

WEBB, MR. AND MRS. SIDNEY--(AH-Mrs; Two Cheers-
Webb)--Beatrice (née Porter) 1858-1943; and Sidney James
Webb (first Baron Bassfield), 1859-1947.   Both were writers
on economics and sociology.   Sidney Webb was one of the
founders of Fabianism (q. v.), and both helped found the New
Statesman (1913) and helped to promote the London School of
Economics and Political Science.

WEBB, MRS. --(GLD IX; Two Cheers-Mrs; Two Cheers-
Webb)--See: Mr. and Mrs. Webb.

WEBB, SIDNEY--(GLD X; Two Cheers-Webb)--See: Mr. and
Mrs. Webb.

WEDGWOOD, HENSLEIGH--(MT)--1803-1891.   An English
mathematician and philologist.   He compiled A Dictionary of
English Etymology (1857) in which he postulated the theory
that language originated in imitation of natural sounds.   He
was the grandson of Josiah Wedgwood (q. v.).

WEDGWOOD, JOSIAH--(Two Cheers-Snow)--1730-1795.   A
famous English potter who perfected several types of pottery
(e. g. , salt ware, queen's ware, and jasper ware).   Aided by
the artist John Flaxman, he developed designs for his pottery
copied from Greek and Roman originals.

WEDGWOOD, JULIA--(MT; Two Cheers-Snow)--See: Snow Wedgwood.

WEDGWOOD, SNOW--(MT; Two Cheers-Snow)--Julia Wedgwood (1833-1913) of the Josiah Wedgwood (q. v.) clan. See: Forster's essay, "'Snow' Wedgwood," in Two Cheers for Democracy.

WELLINGTON, DUKE OF--(Englands; LJ I)--Arthur Wellesley (1st Duke of Wellington), the "Iron Duke," 1769-1852. A British general and statesman noted for his greatest victory, achieved over Napoleon (q. v.) at Waterloo (q. v.) in 1815.

WELLS, H. G. --(AH-Sin; Aspects I; Collect Ta-Intro; GLD-Intro; New Disorder; Two Cheers-Eng; Two Cheers-George; Two Cheers-Last; Two Cheers-Lon)--Herbert George Wells, 1866-1946. Son of an insolvent tradesman, he excelled at cricket, studied science, taught a bit, and then during an illness he turned to writing, and achieved overnight success with The Time Machine (1895). He went on to produce over 100 volumes mostly sociological in intent, and then took up active membership in the Limbo into which go all those novelists who were once popular. Currently, there seems some hope for a revival of interest in his work.

WENTWORTH--(AH-JA; Aspects IV)--Captain Frederick Wentworth, R.N., a character in Persuasion (1818) by Jane Austen (q. v.). When young and penniless, he fell in love with Anne Elliot who returned his affection. Her family, however, persuaded her to break with him. After eight years, he meets her again and seems indifferent to her.

WERLE, GEORGE--(AH-Ibsen)--A son of the merchant Werle, in the play The Wild Duck by Henrik Ibsen (q. v.). A thwarted idealist, he is disillusioned by his father. He can never convince people that his theories are valid.

WESLEY--(MT)--John Wesley, 1703-1791. He became leader of the Methodists in 1729 and, during his lifetime, he composed over 23 collections of hymns and preached over 40, 000 sermons.

WESSEX NOVELS--(Aspects V)--The name applied to a group of novels by Thomas Hardy (q. v.). He uses the name Wessex--the name of an Anglo-Saxon kingdom in England--to designate the SW English counties which serve as the scene of the novels.

WEST END--(Two Cheers-Lon)--An area of London containing, among other things, its theatre district.

WESTMINSTER CATHEDRAL--(Two Cheers-Does)--The Roman Catholic Cathedral in London's Westminster, and the principal Roman Catholic church in England. It is the seat of the Cardinal Archbishop of Westminster and is located on the SW end of Victoria Street near Ashley Place.

WESTMINSTER BRIDGE--(HE VI)--In London, it spans the Thames and is reached from Parliament Square via Bridge Street. It was designed by Thomas Page and built in 1854-67 of cast iron.

WESTON, JESSIE--(AH-TS)--Jessie Laidlay Weston, 1850-1928. A great scholar of Medieval romances. In addition to From Ritual to Romance, which Forster cites, she is the author of The Legend of Sir Gawain (1897), The Three Days Tournament; a Study in Romance and Folklore (1902), and other works.

WEYMOUTH--(HE XXII)--With Melcombe Regis it forms a municipal borough in Dorsetshire, S England. It is on the English Channel some 53 miles WSW of Southampton and is a favorite seaside resort.

WHARTON, EDITH--(AH-HOS)--Edith Newbold Wharton, née Jones, 1862-1937. An American novelist and friend of Henry James (q.v.). Her most famous novels are The House of Mirth (1905), Ethan Frome (1911), and The Age of Innocence (1920).

"WHAT ARE THE ROOTS" etc.--(AH-TS)--From Part I, Burial of the Dead, in "The Waste Land" by T. S. Eliot (q.v.), ℓℓ. 19-22. As Forster quotes the passage, he ends the line and the sentence with the word "images." Actually, the sentence continues for two additional lines.

WHAT HITLER DID TO US--(Nordic)--By Eva Lips (q.v.). Subtitled: A Personal Record of the Third Reich (London, 1940). Translated into English by Caroline Newton with an introduction by Dorothy Thompson.

WHAT I THOUGHT AFTERWARDS ABOUT THE SUBJECT-- (AH-Car)--A dissertation by Cardano (q.v.) written after he

cast the horoscope of Edward VI (q.v.).   For a summary
see Forster's essay, "Cardan," in Abinger Harvest.

WHAT MASIE KNEW--(Aspects VIII)--A novel (1897) by
Henry James (q.v.).   Masie's parents are divorced when
she is six.   She lives with each alternately for six months
of each year.   As a result, she witnesses too much and,
as a consequence, has come to know "everything."

"WHAT'S TO BECOME OF THE WORLD IF MONEY SHOULD
SUDDENLY DIE?"--(Two Cheers-Outsider)--Line 20 of the
poem by Bernard Spencer, "Behaviour of Money," as printed
on p. 188-189 of Poets of the Present by Geoffrey Grigson
(q.v.).

"WHEN I WAS BORN ON AMMAN HILL"--(Two Cheers-Outsider)--Line 1 of the poem "The Collier" by Vernon Watkins
as printed on p. 221 of Poetry of the Present edited by
Geoffrey Grigson (q.v.).

WHEN WE DEAD AWAKEN--(AH-Ibsen)--A play (1900) by
Henrik Ibsen (q.v.).   Rubek, a sculptor, though married, is
strangely attracted to a woman dressed in white.   He comes
to realize that she is his former model whom he has loved.
That affection is rekindled and the two choose death together
rather than life apart.

WHITE PEACOCK, THE--(Two Cheers-English)--The first
novel (1911) of D. H. Lawrence (q.v.).

WHITEHEAD, HUGH--(Two Cheers-Virginia)--He is a minor
official at Court and a friend of the Dalloways in the novel
(1925), Mrs. Dalloway (q.v.) by Virginia Woolf (q.v.).

WHITELY'S--(HE XXVI)--Henry Wilcox suggests that Whitely's,
a caterer, be consulted for his forthcoming wedding to Meg.

WHITMAN, WALT--(AH-Mrs; AH-Two; GLD VII; Two Cheers-
Last; Two Cheers-Raison)--Walter Whitman, 1819-1892.   An
American poet of English, Dutch, and Welsh ancestry.   He
worked as a printer's devil, a journeyman printer, and a
schoolteacher.   His greatest contribution to American poetry
is a series of long poems in free verse collected in Leaves
of Grass (1889).

WHO'S WHO--(Nordic)--The title of a series of annual biographies of contemporary English men and women first issued
in 1849.

"WHY COME YE NOT TO THE COURT"--(Two Cheers-John)
--An anti-Wolsey (q. v.) poem by John Skelton (q. v.).

WILBERFORCE, WILLIAM--(MT)--1759-1837.   An English
abolitionist and philanthropist.   He was the leading layman
in the Clapham Sect (q. v.).   He died soon after the bill
abolishing slavery was passed in Parliament.

"WILD WILBUR PACES BY THE CAVES"--(Two Cheers-
Outsider)--Line 1 from the poem "Wild Wilbur: For an
American Sailor, " by James Kirkup as printed on p. 131 in
Poetry of the Present edited by Geoffrey Grigson (q. v.).

WILDE, OSCAR--(AH-Wil)--Oscar Fingal O'Flaherty Wills
Wilde, 1854-1900.   An English playwright and poet educated
at Trinity College, Dublin and at Magdalen College, Oxford.
He is noted especially for sophisticated and witty comedies
chiefly Lady Windermere's Fan (1892) and The Importance
of Being Ernest (1895) and, in some circles, for the scandal
of homosexuality which shadowed the last portion of his life.

WILKINS, WILLIAM--(Two Cheers-Camb)--William Wilkins,
1778-1839.   An English architect of the Regency who favored
Greek revivalism.   He built Downing College, Cambridge
(1804) in that style as well as London University (1828) and
the National Gallery (q. v.), 1832.

WILLIAM THE CONQUEROR--(AH-Ab)--William I (1027-
1087), King of England, 1066-1087, and duke of Normandy
(as William II), 1035-1087.   He invaded England and successfully subdued it after the death of his cousin, Edward
the Confessor, who had promised to name him his heir.

WILLIAM RUFUS--(LJ XXXIII)--William II (c. 1056-1100),
King of England 1087-1100, and Duke of Normandy (as William III), 1087-1100.   He was called Rufus because of his
fiery complexion.   He was the second surviving son of William the Conqueror (q. v.).   He was a ruthless ruler and
was killed by an arrow from an unknown hand.   His body
was refused religious rites by the clergy of Winchester (q. v.)

WILLIAM WATSON AND SON--(Two Cheers-Bishop)--The
booksellers in Dublin from whom John Jebb purchased his
common-place book.

WILLIAMS, MARGARET ELLEN--(GLD I)--The mother of
Goldsworthy Lowes Dickinson (q. v.).

WILLIAMS, VAUGHAN--(Englands; Two Cheers-John)--Ralph
Vaughan Williams, 1877-1958. An English composer of
many musical compositions among which are The London
Symphony, Sea Symphony, and Sir John in Love.

WILLIAMS, WILLIAM SMITH--(GLD I)--d. 1875. The maternal grandfather of Goldsworthy Lowes Dickinson. He was
a literary advisor to Smith Elder and Co., publishers, and
it was he who discovered Charlotte Brontë (q.v.).

WILLINGDON, LORD--(Hill)--Freeman Freeman-Thomas
(1st Marquis of Willingdon), 1866-1941. A British statesman
who held a number of posts including the governorships of
Bombay, of Madras, and the viceroyship and governor gene-
ralship of India (1931-36).

WILLOUGHBY, SIR--(Aspects V)--A character in The Egoist
(q.v.) by George Meredith (q.v.).

WILSON--(GLD XI; Egypt; Two Cheers-Whiff)--Thomas Woodrow Wilson, 1856-1924. The 28th president of the United
States, 1913-1921. He tried vainly to have his country join
the League of Nations (q.v.).

WILTSHIRE--(Collect Ta-Curate; LJ X)--A county in S England.

WIMBLEDON--(HE IV)--A municipal borough in Surrey and
part of Greater London. It is noted for its lawn tennis
facilities.

WINCHESTER--(AH-Ron; LJ XVI)--A cathedral town in Hampshire, S England. It was once the capital of the Anglo-Saxon
kingdom of Wessex and the seat of the governments of King
Alfred and William the Conqueror (q.v.).

WINDSOR--(AH-HOS)--A municipal borough of Berkshire, S
England and the site of a castle of the same name, the
principal home of England's sovereign.

WINGS OF THE DOVE, THE--(Aspects VIII)--A novel (1902)
by Henry James (q.v.). It treats of the love of Kate Croy
for Merton Dansher. They become secretly engaged. Kate
will not marry him, however, until he is wealthy.

"WINTER MOMENT"--(GLD XIV)--A poem by Julian Bell
(q.v.).

WISDOM OF SOLOMON--(PP-Ph)--A book of the Old Testament. It contains exhortations to seek wisdom, passages on
immortality, and a list of God's care for the Jews.

WISEMAN, CARDINAL--(MT)--Nicholas Patrick Stephen Wise
man, 1802-1865. An English Roman Catholic churchman.
He was archbishop of Westminster. He influenced the Oxford Movement (see: Tractarian Movement) and confirmed
Newman.

"WOAK HILL"--(Two Cheers-William)--A poem by William
Barnes (q. v.) appearing in the volume Poems Grave and Gay
(1949) edited by Giles Dugdale.

WOBURN ABBEY--(MT)--Bedfordshire, England. The house,
built in the 18th century on the site of a 12th-century abbey,
is the seat of the dukes of Bedford.

WOLF, HUGO--(Two Cheers-Not Listening; Two Cheers-
Romain)--1860-1903. An Austrian composer and disciple of
Richard Wagner (q. v.). He composed many works including
an Italian Serenade for small orchestra (1894).

WOLSELEY, LORD--(Alex I, V)--Garnet Joseph Wolseley
(1st Viscount Wolseley), 1833-1913. A British army officer,
he took part in many wars including the Sepoy Mutiny (1857-
58). He commanded the Ashanti expedition (1873-74) and
held high command in Natal (1875), Cyprus (1878) and South-
east Africa (1879-80). He suppressed the rebellion in Egypt
and commanded the Nile expedition which arrived too late to
save General Gordon (q. v.) at Khartoum (1884). He was
commander in chief of the British army from 1895 to 1899.

WOLSEY, CARDINAL--(Two Cheers-John)--Thomas Wolsey,
1475?-1530. An English churchman and statesman. He
controlled public and foreign affairs for Henry VIII. The
son of a butcher, he rose to a position of importance in
England second only to the king. When he failed to secure
Henry's divorce from Catherine, his power failed and he
was arrested on charges of treason.

WOODHOUSE, HENRY--(AH-JA; Aspects IV)--Henry Woodhouse the father of Emma and Isabella in Emma by Jane
Austen (q. v.).

WOODSTON--(AH-JA)--The parish of which Henry Tilney is
the incumbent in Northanger Abbey (q. v.) by Jane Austen
(q. v.).

WOOLF, L. S.--(GLD XII)--Leonard Sidney Woolf, 1880-
The husband of Virginia Woolf (q.v.) and the founder with
her of the Hogarth Press (1917).   He was literary editor of
The Nation (1923-30) and the author of many books.

WOOLF, VIRGINIA--(AH-Early; Aspects I; GLD XIV; Tribute;
Two Cheers-Camb; Two Cheers-Does; Two Cheers-English;
Two Cheers-Raison; Two Cheers-Virginia)--Née Adeline Virginia Stephen, 1882-1941.   An English experimental novelist
noted for developing a new method of revealing characters
by their effects upon their surroundings in such novels as
Jacob's Room (1922) and Mrs. Dalloway (q.v.) 1925.   She
also used the stream-of-consciousness method in these novels as well as in To the Lighthouse (1927), Orlando (1928)
and The Waves (1931).

WORDSWORTH--(AH-Ibsen; AH-JA; Collect Ta-Co-ord; Reading; Two Cheers-Enchanted; Two Cheers-George)--William
Wordsworth, 1777-1850.   The greatest of English Romantic
poets who, unlike others of that circle, outlived his genius
and produced in later life nothing to equal his early poems
and sonnets many of which have become widely and commonly known.   With Coleridge (q.v.) he produced a volume,
Lyrical Ballads (1798, 1800, 1802, 1805) which was a collection of poetry revolutionary for its time.   In 1843, long after the furor which that volume produced had died down, he
succeeded Southey (q.v.) as poet laureate.

WORTHING--(AH-Mrs. G)--A seaside resort on the English
Channel 47 miles S of London.

WOTAN--(Two Cheers-What)--Odin, Wodan, Woden.   In
Norse myth, he is the supreme god and creator, god of the
atmosphere, of wisdom, of eloquence, and of the underworld.
He is the husband of Frigg and father of Thor, Balder, and
Hödr [Hoth].

WREN, SIR CHRISTOPHER--(GLD IX; Two Cheers-Camb;
Two Cheers-Lon)--1632-1723.   One of the greatest of Eng-
lish architects.   He is responsible for rebuilding many of
London's churches after the Great Fire (q.v.) including St.
Paul's (q.v.).

WUTHERING HEIGHTS--(Aspects II)--A novel (1847) by Emily
Brontë (q.v.).   It tells the story of Cathy and Heathcliff who,
though separated in life despite their love, are re-united in
death.

WYCH ELM--(HE I; MT)--The tree which stands before
Howards End in the novel of the same name by Forster. He
notes in his biography of his great aunt, Marianne Thornton,
that the original stood in front of his boyhood home, Rookrest, Stevenage, Hertfordshire.

X

XANTHIPPE--(LJ IX)--The wife of the philosopher, Socrates
(q.v.). She was somewhat of a shrew.

Y

YAHOOS--(Two Cheers-Bk)--Beast-men in Gulliver's Travels
(q.v.) by Swift (q.v.). Gulliver meets them in the land of
the Houyhnhnms.

YDGRUN--(Two Cheers-Bk)--An anagram of Grundy. She is
the chief goddess in the land of Erewhon in the novel (1872)
of the same name by Samuel Butler (q.v.). She is worshipped in heart and in deed rather than in word. She demands
rigid conformity.

YEATS, WILLIAM BUTLER--(AH-Note)--1865-1939. Irish
poet and dramatist, leader of the movement of the Irish
Renaissance. He was influenced by the Pre-Raphaelites (q.
v.), William Blake (q.v.), Shelley (q.v.), French symbolism
Maeterlinck (q.v.) and Hindu mysticism. His poetry largely
treats of mystic and celtic legendary themes. His later
poetry contains highly developed symbolism. He has written,
among other poetic works: The Wanderings of Oisin and
Other Poems (1889), The Wild Swan of Coole (1919), The
Winding Stair (1929). His dramatic works include: The
Countess Kathleen (1892), Cathleen ni Houlihan (1902), and
Plays in Prose and Verse (1923).

YEOMAN OF THE GUARD--(PI V)--A comic opera (1888) by
Gilbert and Sullivan. The yeomen are the "Beefeaters," the
guards at the Tower of London.

"YET THERE THE NIGHTINGALE /etc."--(AH-TS)--Lines
100-103 of "The Waste Land" by T. S. Eliot (q.v.), in his
Complete Poems and Plays 1909-1950 (New York, 1952).

YNFANTA--(AH-Wil)--Infanta.   The daughter of Isabella II
(q. v.) of Spain.

YOGA--(PI XXVII)--A practice of Hindu philosophy which attempts to unite the human soul with the Universal Spirit
through a physical system of exercise which aims at with-
drawing the physical senses from objects.

YONGE, CHARLOTTE--(Two Cheers-In)--Charlotte Mary
Yonge, 1823-1901.   An English novelist and religious disciple
of John Keble.   He urged her to present his religious views
in fiction.   The result was The Heir of Redclyffe (1853), the
first of a long series of novels which included historical and
romantic works.   She also wrote a life of Hannah More (q.
v.), 1888.

YORKSHIRE--(HE VIII)--A county in N England which includes
the city of York, a county in and of itself.

YOUNG TOM--(Two Cheers-Fo)--A novel (1944) by Forrest
Reid (q. v.) and the third of a trilogy of novels on boyhood.

YRAM--(Two Cheers-Bk)--An anagram for Mary, the jailer's
daughter in Erewhon (1872) by Samuel Butler (q. v.).   She is
attracted to Strong and teaches him the language and customs
of Erewhon.

YSAYE--(HE VIII)--Eugène Ysäye, 1858-1931.   A Belgian
violinist who toured a great deal playing many new works.
He was also a composer and conductor.   He wrote, among
other works for the violin, six concertos, and an opera in
the Waloon dialect.

Z

ZAGLOUL--(Alex I, 2)--The Mameluke (body-servant) of
Saïd Hassan who built a mosque in Rosetta (1600).

ZAGLOUL--(Egypt)--Sa'd Zaghlul (Zagloul) Pasha, 1857?-
1927.   An Egyptian statesman and lawyer.   He was minister
of instruction, and minister of justice.   After World War I
he became head of the Nationalist Party and became premier
in 1924.

ZENITH--(AH-Sin)--The mid-western American city in Babbitt (q. v.) by Sinclair Lewis (q. v.) and the home of Babbitt.

ZENO--(PP-Tim)--426-491. Emperor of the Eastern Roman
Empire, 474-491, and the son-in-law of Leo I.

ZENODOTUS--(Alex I, 1)--A Greek scholar of the early 3rd
century B.C. in Ephesus. He was made the first superin-
tendant (librarian) of the library in Alexandria. He was the
first critical editor of Homer.

ZEUS--(AH-Mac; Alex I, 1; Collect Ta-Mr; Collect Ta-Point;
HE XVI; PP-Clement)--The "living one," the Greek name for
the Roman god Jupiter, the son of Cronos whom he dethroned
and Rhea. White is sacred to him. He was the chief among
the gods on Olympus (q.v.).

ZHOR, JIRI--(Nordic)--The pseudonym of Karel Pošva, 1903-
Czechoslovakian author.

ZIMBABWE--(Two Cheers-Duty)--In NE Southern Rhodesia,
the site of the ruins of a citadel, a temple and huge walls.
They are probably the work of the Bantu and date not earlier
than the 14th century.

ZODIAC--(AH-Vo)--A division of the heavens into 12 equal
parts proceeding from E to W, each part distinguished by a
special sign.

ZOROASTER--(AH-Gem)--[Zarathustra]--fl. 618-553 B.C.
Credited with founding Zoroastrianism (q.v.) the religion of
ancient Persia (q.v.), this ancient Iranian prophet also
wrote the Gathas, 17 religious poems within his main work,
the Avesta.

ZOROASTRIANISM--(Alex I, 3)--A religion of ancient Persia
(q.v.) founded by Zoroaster (q.v.), the essential feature of
which is a belief in the existence of two spirits: the wise
one (Ahura-Mazda) and the spirit of evil and darkness
(Ahrumin). The two are in conflict in this world chiefly
centered upon mankind.

ZULEIKA DOBSON--(Aspects I)--A novel (1911) by Max
Beerbohm (q.v.). For a summary of the plot see Forster's
Aspects of the Novel, Chapter VI.

ZWEIG, ARNOLD--(Nordic)--1887- . A German-Jewish
novelist, essayist, and playwright. He was exiled in 1933
from Nazi Germany. He wrote, among other works, The
Crowning of a King (1937) and translated Poe and Kipling.

ZWEIG, STEPHAN--(Nordic)--1881-1942.   Austrian-Jewish
novelist who fled his country because of Nazi persecution.
He is the author of Beware Pity (1939) and of the play Jeremiah (1916).

Appendix: Forster Works Used in this Glossary (1st Editions American Editions)

Abinger Harvest.   London, Edward Arnold, 1936; New York, Harcourt Brace, 1936.

Alexandria: A History and a Guide.   Alexandria, Egypt, Whitehead Morris, Ltd., 1922; Garden City, N. Y., Doubleday (Anchor Books), 1961.

"Arctic Summer," in Tribute to Benjamin Britten on His Fiftieth Birthday, edited by Anthony Gishford. London, Faber and Faber, 1963.

Aspects of the Novel.   London, Edward Arnold, 1927; New York, Harcourt Brace, 1927.

Collected Tales.   New York, Knopf, 1947.

England's Pleasant Land.   London, Hogarth Press, 1940.

Goldsworthy Lowes Dickinson.   London, Edward Arnold, 1934; New York, Harcourt Brace, 1934.

The Hill of Devi Being Letters from Dewas Senior.   London, Edward Arnold, 1953; New York, Harcourt Brace, 1953.

Howards End.   London, Edward Arnold, 1910; New York, Putnam, 1911.

The Longest Journey.   Edinburgh, William Blackwood, 1907; New York, Knopf, 1922.

Marianne Thornton 1797-1887: A Domestic Biography.   London, Edward Arnold, 1956; New York, Harcourt Brace, 1956.

Nordic Twilight.   London, Macmillan, 1940 (Macmillan War

334

Pamphlet #3).

A Passage to India. London, Edward Arnold, 1924; New York, Harcourt Brace, 1924.

Pharos and Pharillon. Richmond (Surrey), Eng., Hogarth Press, 1923; New York, Knopf, 1923.

A Room With a View. London, Edward Arnold, 1908; New York, Putnam, 1911.

"Tribute to Desmond MacCarthy." The Listener (26 June 1952), p. 1031.

Two Cheers for Democracy. London, Edward Arnold, 1951; New York, Harcourt Brace, 1951.

Where Angels Fear to Tread. Edinburgh, William Blackwood, 1905; New York, Knopf, 1920.